GIANT SABLE LANDS
A N G O L A

P9-ELR-561

16°E **17°E** **18°E**

Malange

Cuanza

Cangandala

CANGANDALA
NATIONAL
PARK

10°S

River

Luando River

LUANDO

INTEGRAL

Capunda

NATURE

Cuanza River

RESERVE

11°S

Quimbango

Luce River

Sautar

Lussingue R.

Andulo

Nharea

Mulundo

Luando River

Luasso River

12°S

Camacupa

Benguela Railway

Cuito

16°E **17°E** **18°E**

LEGEND

- ▦ Nature Reserve
- ◉ Provincial Capital
- • Town/Village
- —— Road
- ⋯⋯ Picada
- ┼┼┼ Railway

PRINCIPAL EXPEDITIONS

Livingstone 1854	Statham 1920	Keynes 1954
Cameron 1875	Powell-Cotton 1922	Lee 1960-61
Serpa Pinto 1878	Curtis 1923	Estes & Estes 1969-70
Varian 1913-19	Vernay 1925	Estes 1982
Blaine 1919	Gray 1929	Malange Expedition 2001
	Yebes 1949	

A Certain Curve of Horn

Published simultaneously in Canada
Printed in the United States of America

FIRST EDITION

Library of Congress Cataloging-in-Publication Data

Walker, John Frederick.
    A certan curve of horn : the hundred-year quest for the giant sable antelope of Angola / John Frederick Walker.
        p. cm.
    Includes bibliographical references (p.).
    ISBN 0-87113-858-1
    1. Sable antelope—Angola.   2. Antelope hunting—Africa—History.   3. Angola—Description and travel.   I. Title.
QL 737.U53 W26 2002
599.64'5—dc21   2002066576

DESIGN BY LAURA HAMMOND HOUGH

Atlantic Monthly Press
841 Broadway
New York, NY 10003

02 03 04 05   10 9 8 7 6 5 4 3 2 1

A CERTAIN
CURVE OF HORN

THE HUNDRED-YEAR QUEST FOR THE
GIANT SABLE ANTELOPE OF ANGOLA

JOHN FREDERICK WALKER

ATLANTIC MONTHLY PRESS
NEW YORK

FOR ELIN AND GAVIN

WE CARRY WITH US THE WONDERS WE SEEK WITHOUT US:

THERE IS ALL AFRICA AND HER PRODIGIES IN US.

—Sir Thomas Browne

CONTENTS

PROLOGUE

October 18, 1999, south of Luanda, Angola

I should step back from the crumbling edge of this sea-clawed cliff—a sheared-off face of red sand that could give way and send me and my brief regrets to the rock-slapping waves below. But I'm hoping to see something from this height. The afternoon sun, half-lidded by leaden cloud banks, is surprisingly strong and the broken light glinting on the gray ocean makes me squint. Then I see it, the sand-barred mouth of the Cuanza River gaping out from the eroded African coastline to the north, and follow its curving course inland until it disappears into the interior war zone.

Why am I standing today on this half-eaten hill? Because of a mysterious animal I first came across in a book. I was a small boy then, but that chance moment made me wonder what it would be like to go to Africa and search for the beast. That vague and fleeting daydream has grown into a determination to know the animal's fate. The answer lies far down the dark Cuanza, deep in the *miombo* forest, where two rivers join to embrace the no man's land no naturalist has dared visit for almost twenty years, the realm of the antelope the Angolans call the *palanca preta gigante*.

I have yet to see a living one. But in anticipation, I've burnished an image of the animal in my mind and carefully placed it in the same imagined scene over and over again. It is in a dark, leafy forest where blotches of sunlight quiver in torn patterns on the ground, mimicking the sparse canopy of branches and leaves above, hidden by a screen of underbrush at the edge of the woods. Fingers of light jab through the lattice of tree trunks to pick out a ripple of black fur, the gleam of a dark eye.

Then the scene comes to life, and an antelope the size of a small, heavily muscled horse steps out of the shadows into the morning sun. He is a master bull, the very monarch of his tribe. His glossy, grackle-black fur seems even darker in contrast to the bright white underbelly and inner legs and the white stripes that streak his slim, equine face like tribal markings. A shaggy, upright black mane crests his thick neck and powerful shoulders. And crowning all, a pair of colossal knurled horns that rise straight up above the eyes and sweep back in gleaming five-foot-long arcs ending in points as smooth and sharp as awls, thick-shafted curved spears streaked red from the animal's habit of stropping them on trees until the trunks are flayed bare of bark and run with crimson sap.

As the beast struts out, a dry-season panorama of a grassy clearing unfolds before him on which a dozen smaller, chestnut-colored, more modestly horned cows graze near several four-foot-high termite mounds. Several young calves nervously dart in among them, nibble at the soft grass, lie down, and then jump up again. The bull ignores the herd, but scans the edge of the forest for potential rivals prowling for straying females. Forefeet planted on the edge of a termite mound to survey his surroundings, hind feet stretched out behind, he stands stock-still, posing, as if he knows he is a living masterpiece. Arrogant and aggressive, he finds little in his natural world to fear. Few predators—even wild dogs or leopards—will readily risk the sword-swipe of his horns. Satisfied no challenges lurk, he lowers his heavy head to nip some tender shoots. . . .

What is this creature that stalks my imagination? He is a superlative specimen of *Hippotragus niger variani*, the royal, or giant, sable antelope, the last great quadruped of Africa to be brought to the world's notice. That was in 1916, when two pairs of skulls and head-skins, given to the British Natural History Museum by H. F. Varian, the chief engineer supervising construction of a railway across the Portuguese West African colony of Angola, were recognized as evidence of a previously unknown subspecies—and the most majestic antelope in all of Africa.

You can find the known range of the giant sable easily enough on a map of Africa by putting a finger at the point where the equator starts to cut across the continent at Gabon on the Atlantic and then following the coastline down past the mouth of the Congo River into Angola. Just above ten degrees latitude, cupped in the calm waters of the Baía do Bengo, lies the capital, Luanda. Just south of the city, below the swelling coastline, the wide Cuanza reaches the ocean. Trace that meandering river inland, first eastward—across a country larger than France, Spain, and Portugal combined—then southeast through the rugged highlands until you reach the elevated plateau in the very heart of the country. Find the twisted territory between the upper Cuanza and its tributary, the Luando. Keep your finger there, and look for a much smaller area just north and to the east of Cangandala, southeast of the city of Malange. These are the only lands where Africa's greatest antelope exists, in a precarious population that as far as anyone knows has never numbered more than two thousand and has often dipped to just several hundred.

In English, "royal" or "giant" rightly implies that the animal is the supreme example of its kind, far grander than the "common" (if one can call them that) sable antelope found in fair numbers elsewhere across Africa's southern savanna, but says nothing about the sacred status of this creature among the Lwimbi and Songo peoples who have long shared its realm. The fact that both tribes have often denied its existence to outsiders and misled foreign hunters makes it clear that the great dark antelope—*Sumbakaloko* to the Lwimbi, *Kolwah* to the Songo—is more than totem to these peoples: it is taboo. The antelope's wariness surely helped, but only local reverence for it could have kept its existence a secret from Europeans for more than four centuries after the Portuguese first landed on the shores of Angola.

Early on, the creature had the good luck to have been hidden in the heart of the colony, far away from European settlers, who had exterminated its short-horned South African cousin, the *blaaubok*, by the beginning of the nineteenth century. But in recent decades it has had the tragic misfortune of being trapped in the middle of a deadly, unending civil war, surviving in part because of its symbolic significance to both warring sides. During the years of armed clashes and periods of uneasy stalemates, rumors of sightings of the giant sable surfaced every so often, tantalizing scientists anxious to study it and alarming those concerned about its dwindling numbers. The giant sable has never been seen outside its own territory—no zoo has ever had one on display, there are no captive breeding programs, no herds outside Angola, no frozen sperm banks, nothing that could be used to restock its habitat if the natural population has sunk to near extinction.

3

Some have said there are no giant sable left. Others say they must still be there—and I intend to find out if they're right.

When I began this strange and troubling quest, I hadn't realized how many others had felt the pull of this regal antelope. It's been less than a century since the giant sable stepped onto the world's stage, but throughout that period it has been the focus of fierce passions and greeds competing to determine its future—atavistic, scientific, economic, political. Far more than a zoological treasure, the giant sable is at once a touchstone trophy animal, a potent conservation symbol, a magnet for zoos and game breeders, and a living emblem for Angola. As such, it is certain to be a prized pawn in the power politics of African wildlife conservation—if the war dies down.

Already the story has become a far different tale than I thought it would be, less about an animal than about those entangled in its spell, driven to possess this creature either by killing it, unlocking its biological secrets, or controlling its destiny. I realize now that the fate of the giant sable is inextricably bound up with Angola's dark history, and that what the animal means to those who seek it can't be understood apart from humanity's long struggle to come to terms with the natural world. At first I told myself I was simply a witness to events, but like all the others I've become caught up in the intrigues and clashes of wills that swirl around the majestic beast and the bitter ironies that govern its precarious existence.

PART 1

ONE

Tracks in Shadow

I came across the book that started it all on a boyhood bibilographic expedition in the old municipal library in Fort Lauderdale, Florida. Treading carefully on its creaking wooden floors, I followed the Dewey decimal system around the dim and sagging stacks to 799.27 and the Dark Continent. All that warm summer I had been absorbing tales of true adventure by Carl Akeley, W. D. M. Bell, Jim Corbett, Colonel Patterson, Frank ("Bring 'em Back Alive") Buck, and scores of other authors, and when I spotted the promising title, *Hunting in Africa East and West*, written in 1925 by the Curtis brothers, I took it off the shelf.

The black-and-white photographs in the book were the first pictures of the giant sable I had seen, and they shocked me. In one, the head of a just shot bull lies at the feet of Richard Curtis's young wife, Anita. Dressed in a long skirt and loose blouse and shyly—perhaps unhappily; the expression is hard to read—looking out from under the brim of her pith helmet, she holds the horn tips timidly in her hands. The fresh, wet cape of skin trailing from the animal's neck is draped on the ground like a bloody *muleta*. Several curious Africans peer over her shoulders like a silent native chorus. Later I learned that safari photographs are often contrived, staged, or faked. But even as a boy I knew instinctively that the camera had caught an exact, candid moment in the unsettled mix of emotions on her face. The same raw rub of reality was apparent in the photograph captioned "My giant sable head and Thomas, my gunbearer." It was Richard Curtis's trophy again, this time turned in splendid profile by the smiling African's firm grasp of the horns, the bowed head of the animal with its unseeing long-lashed eyes an expressionless mask. I stared at the pictures for a very long time. The layers of fused meanings—the comingling of

7

conquest and defeat, beauty and blood—compacted into those two photographs took me years to even begin to understand. As I boy I could not take in the conflicting messages of the hunt, only the sublimity of the animal slain.

I felt something strangely confirmed by its profile. The sensation was the kind you have when you turn around a piece of a puzzle and feel it click into the mental space of a half-recognized shape—in this case, the archetype of nobility in the bestiary of my imagination. What I understood as a boy staring at those black-and-white overly contrasted photographs in Curtis's hunting memoir was that the animal looked exactly the way it ought to look. It was perfect—a creature almost heraldic in its stateliness, more like a proud beast from legend than one of this earth.

I know now that the magnetism of this antelope—the almost gravitational pull—emanates largely from the incomparable geometry of the bull's horns, which are as mathematically proportioned as the interior of a chambered nautilus. To follow their perfect sweep is to treat the eye to a visual Doppler effect of ring after closely set ring rising from the skull, expanding in precise increments along the great arched shaft before they fade smoothly into conical, rapier points in perfect diminuendo. Animal to animal, there are subtle variations among these crescent curves that open out to straightened tips. But the shape always has a tension, an aching flex like a drawn bow at the precise moment of release.

The impression these photographs made awakened in me the inchoate desire to seek out the animal. So did the text, and one passage in particular left me wanting to know more:

> It was only just before the last great war that its origin was discovered by H. F. Varian, an English engineer engaged in building the new railroad inland from Lobito Bay in Angola to the Katanga copper mines. Between the Cuanza and Loando Rivers in Angola, Varian found a new species of antelope with immensely finer horns than the common sable and a somewhat different face-marking. This was the giant sable antelope . . .

Who was Varian? And what did a railroad have to do with the discovery of the giant sable? These and other questions that occurred to me competed with all the others that had crowded into my young mind. I had to wait until much later for the answers.

By then I realized how strange it was that this great beast had remained so long undiscovered by Europeans. The explanation of that puzzle, like all the others, had to be prized out from the story of how Angola was colonized.

AS AFRICAN COLONIZERS, the Portuguese have often been described as the first to come and the last to go; it's not precisely true, but true enough. By the mid-1400s, the Portuguese had begun to venture down the Atlantic coast to seriously explore and exploit sub-Saharan Africa. Although Arab traders had established trading posts as far south as Zanzibar on the East African coast by the tenth century, and in the 1420s Chinese vessels had established contacts there as well, neither the Arabs nor the Ming Court followed up their early forays. As a result, fifteenth-century maps of southern Africa were hardly more complete than they had been a millennium before: the coastal outline became vague south of the Canary Islands on the Atlantic coast, and the Comoro Islands on the east.

But the cartography of Africa began to change in 1434, when Prince Henry ("the Navigator") of Portugal, fired by dreams of tapping directly the sources of the West African gold long coveted by Europe, commissioned a caravel and its crew to sail past Cape Bojador, some one hundred miles south of the Canary Islands, at that time the farthest point south European ships had reached on the Atlantic coast of Africa. Soon after that tentative trip, other Portuguese explorers, sustained by an amalgam of iron faith and sheer greed, were traveling farther down the coast in their armed, maneuverable little ships, braving the stormy Atlantic and the terrors said to lurk in its depths. In doublet and hose, round-helmeted and armed with sword and spike and arquebus, silhouetted against their billowing, red-crossed sails, they played their part daringly, landing in (and claiming) the small coastal enclave of Guinea-Bissau in 1446 and thereafter returning from Africa with handsome profits in the form of gold and ivory and captive heathens that could be ransomed.

9

By Prince Henry's death in 1460 the Portuguese had reached Sierra Leone, and the goal of greater riches lured them farther south. In 1482 the Crown gave Diogo Cão the command of two ships to explore beyond Cape Santa Caterina—today's Gabon. Each of Cão's vessels carried a massive six-foot-high *padrão,* a stone cross to be planted at each expedition's most important landfalls. Their inscriptions read:

> In the year 6681 of the world, and in that of 1482 since the birth of our Lord Jesus Christ, the most serene, most excellent and potent prince, King John II of Portugal did order this land to be discovered and these to be set up by Diogo Cão, an esquire of his household.

The next year, 1483, was half over before Cão, sailing down a humid equatorial coast of endless green swamps and steaming curtain walls of mangrove trees, and later past high red cliffs glowing in the setting sun, reached something worthy of marking with a *padrão*—the yawning mouth of a river so vast that its foaming waters freshened the sea a hundred miles from the coast. We know it now as the Congo River, in the upper northwest corner of modern-day Angola. Cão sailed on another six hundred miles down the continent, past the mouth of the Cuanza, to plant a second cross south of today's Benguela in Angola, in the mistaken belief he had reached the southernmost tip of Africa.

That error would be corrected in 1488, when Bartholomeu Dias rounded the Cape of Good Hope. This potential new route to the Indian Ocean was successfully tested by Vasco da Gama's voyage to India a decade later. These expeditions gave Portugal a toehold in East Africa that later led to control over a significant swath of the coastline. Eventually they secured a colony there, Mozambique, to match, at more southerly latitudes, their western enclave in Angola, as if hoping to cinch in the lower continent from opposite coasts. The Spanish, French, Dutch, and British followed, in different degrees, with their own explorations. The landmass of Africa drawn on maps began to approximate the geographical form we now find familiar. But it would take another four centuries to fill in the outline.

Angola is thought to have had four million inhabitants when the Portuguese arrived. The original inhabitants of the country were the San, or "Bushmen," and the Khoi. They were hunters and gatherers, but there is evidence of large, sedentary fishing communities along the Congo River as far back as the Late Stone Age (6000 B.C.E.). Starting in the first century C.E., an influx of Bantu-speaking peoples from the north and east brought the use of iron, agriculture, and animal husbandry with them; these migrations reached their peak in the 1400s, just prior to the arrival of the Portuguese. By that time the patchwork of ethnolinguistic regions that remains today was largely in place. It included the Kongo-speaking inhabitants of the lower Congo, the Mbundu of the middle Cuanza, and the Ovimbundu of the central plateau (still the largest ethnic group in Angola today), as well as numerous other peoples. Although the village was by far the most important social and economic unit, larger political structures—chiefdoms and kingdoms—had developed in the precolonial era.

The first Portuguese landings and initial contacts were no more than shallow, coastal penetrations; tiny slivers in the side of a sleeping giant, sufficient for small-scale bartering for spices and gold and the occasional raiding party. But soon enough these intrusions began to fester: the Portuguese started slaving, acting as ferrymen for Africans in the trade, taking captives from point of sale to point of purchase along what came to be known as the Slave Coast. They quickly discovered their own uses for them. The Portuguese needed labor to work their sugar, cotton, and cocoa plantations on Madeira, the Cape Verde Islands, São Tomé and Príncipe, and not long after, Brazil. Other European countries also required a huge labor force for their growing New World plantings of cotton and sugar, and all found sufficient reasons to justify the trade in human lives.

This is the dark heart of the historical matter, the beginning of a crushing oppression of the native populace that continued, in one grisly form or another, until Angolan independence in 1975, after which this disregard for human life would be revisited on the divided nation like a curse, in the form of unending civil war. As contemporary accounts make clear, it wasn't that the Portuguese colonizers failed to notice the cries and lamentations and agonies of their captives. The chronicler Gomes Eannes de Azurara said of the human cargo he saw at Lagos in 1444, "What heart could be so hard as not to be pierced with piteous feeling to see that company?" A modern sensibility might conclude that the sufferings of the natives simply didn't matter enough to stop the lucrative practice. Azurara saw it differently; he felt reassured these same souls would receive knowledge of the faith, as well as bread, wine, and clothes, instead of living their lives in "bestial sloth." Whether cloaked in such a rationale or not, over the next three centuries the slave trade became not merely an element of world trade, but a key component of it. Grafted on to indigenous slaving practices—various forms of slave-keeping were commonplace in tribal cultures and the Arabs had maintained a flourishing slave trade across Africa for centuries—the scale of the European commerce in human lives grew enormously. Historians reckon some ten to twelve million people were exported from Africa to the Americas.

Luanda became Africa's greatest slave port. A great marble throne, the Bishop's Chair, stood on its wharves for the use of the prelate officiating at the wholesale baptisms given the wretched souls as they were being led aboard the slave ships. Captives departing from minor ports undoubtedly missed this parting sacrament, but all alike would be introduced to Christianity through the dignity of labor on overseas plantations. Because four million slaves passed through the ports of Angola before Portugal formally ended the trade there at the close of the nineteenth century, and roughly the same amount are thought to have died on forced marches from the interior to the coast, Angola must have lost eight million people.

Colonization was grindingly slow, but inexorable, as the fate of the Kongo kingdom demonstrates. By the time the Portuguese arrived, the realm covered one-eighth of present-day northern Angola, large enough to be divided into six provinces, each ruled by a subchief. The inhabitants worked iron and copper, wove palm cloth, and raised chickens, pigs, sheep, and cattle. At first, contacts with the Portuguese seemed mutually beneficial; by the 1490s, they had brought priests, artisans, even printers to the Kongolese court, and had taken a number of young Kongolese nobles to Lisbon for education. They were happy to provide technology, religious instruction, and military assistance in exchange for ivory, copper, and, most profitable of all, slaves.

But the Portuguese traders, officials, and missionaries soon sided with various factions in the Kongo kingdom to promote their own ends, which revolved primarily around increasing the slave trade. The Kongolese had traditionally used war hostages as slaves, but in many cases integrated them—as subclasses—into society. The Portuguese, however, simply shipped off their captives en masse to foreign lands and were always hungry for more.

The Kongolese king, Mbemba Nzinga, who had become a devout Christian convert and ruled as Dom Afonso I after gaining the throne in 1506, became alarmed. He began to write two successive kings of Portugal a total of twenty-four letters, the first known African commentary on the effects of European contact. In 1512 King Manuel I of Portugal responded with some instructions to the Portuguese community, but what might have been the beginning of a policy of enlightened alliance was flatly ignored by the local traders. By 1526 Afonso was petitioning the monarch:

> So great, Sir, is the corruption and licentiousness that our country is being completely depopulated . . . That is why we beg of Your Highness to help and assist us in this matter, commanding your factors that they should not send here either merchants or wares, because it is *our will that in these Kingdoms there should not be any trade of slaves nor outlet for them.*

Afonso's pleas had no practical effect whatsoever. Even the priests Afonso had invited took up buying and selling slaves. As historian James Duffy put it, Afonso's "greatest flaw was a naive refusal to believe that some Portuguese were able to betray the virtuous principles he had been taught to hold." By 1568 the kingdom had split into warring factions, helped along by scheming Portuguese and invading tribes.

The collapse of the Kongo kingdom marks a turning point for the inhabitants of Angola. It would all be downhill from then on, with brief pauses marking the odd successful resistance against the colonizers. But Portuguese domination, slow as it was, proved inevitable. Luanda, Angola's capital, was founded in 1576, and by 1617, when Benguela was established, Portugal had control of the coast of Angola. The Cuanza River offered easy access from the Atlantic, and fertile valleys inland held the promise of riches, particularly new sources of slaves. At first, slave-trading with the Portuguese enhanced the power of the kingdoms of the interior, because slaves could be exchanged for firearms that could be used to subjugate their neighbors. Later, tribal power waned as the tribes' religious and cultural bases were steadily undermined. This pattern of collaboration followed by native resistance and European conquest seesawed throughout the history of the colonial period. Although open to the contacts which eventually proved their undoing, few of the peoples that the Portuguese encountered were easily subjugated. Some tribes, in fact, weren't brought under "control" until the early twentieth century.

Portuguese expansion was resisted by other Europeans as well as indigenous peoples. In 1641, the Dutch, who had been also active in the coastal slave trade, took over Luanda and formed alliances among the African kingdoms, until the port was retaken in 1648. This episode made it obvious that Portugal's grip on her colony was tenuous, and it would remain so for centuries. By the end of the eighteenth century neither the settlers nor the administrators had effective control of the territory, and even had to compete with the British and French for the slave trade. Only sixteen churches existed in the country, hardly enough to provide evidence of one of the main justifications for colonization, that of a religious mission.

There were distinct reasons for this state of affairs. Portugal made a practice of colonizing with convicts, often recruiting ships' crews from their own dungeons. In fact, right up to 1925, most of the Portuguese in Angola were exiled convicts—*degredados*. Tropical diseases such as malaria took such a toll that almost no Portuguese would willingly emigrate there, forcing the Crown to use assorted murderers, rapists, and thieves to fill posts in the military or commercial arenas. Not surprisingly, most of these types found the slave trade more congenial than farming or practicing an honest skill. Contemporary observers found that even Luanda's elite "were all slave dealers, who would not shrink from the commission of any crime, if it tended to promote their interests." According to an 1846 survey, there were 1,830 Europeans (whites) in the entire colony—Luanda had 1,466 men and 135 women; Benguela had 38 men and one woman. Two years later the population in Benguela was halved by disease. Lopes de Lima, who supplied the grim statistics, explained that

> Living in that country is a continual battle with disease and death: white men have contracted the incessant habit of always walking on the street with their hand on their wrist to observe their pulse, and when they see each other the usual question is—*has the fever gone* . . .

14

By the mid-nineteenth century only the ports of Luanda, Benguela, some settlements along the Cuanza, and less than a dozen forts in the interior were under direct Portuguese control. But the reach of the slave trade extended Portuguese influence much farther, although it would take until the end of the 1800s to penetrate the more populated areas of the central plateau.

Portugal occasionally alleviated the paucity of European women by sending out quotas of orphaned girls to wed the settlers, but impatient *colonos* simply engaged in interracial cohabitation. This gave rise to a *mestiço* class that eventually constituted an important, though never large segment of the colony's population, largely accepted by white settlers and sharing their outlook. Some Portuguese historians point to such liaisons with African women as proof of Portuguese racial tolerance in their colonies. But as another historian, Gerald Bender, put it, "To assume that the readiness of Portuguese and other European men to mate with non-white women was indicative of European egalitarian attitudes, rather than lust, is a gross distortion of reality." But the broader ideology of "Lusotropicalism"—the doctrine that the absence of Portuguese racism resulted in "racially egalitarian legislation and human interaction" in their tropical colonies—was regularly trotted out in justification of Portugal's policies in Angola until it abandoned the colony in 1975.

Because the Portuguese Crown looked to Angola for quick profits and slaves for Brazil, which was seen as a more promising colony, it was never motivated to develop the more systematic rule found in British or French colonies. Early efforts on the part of reform-minded colonial governors to diversify the one-crop economy faltered until the late 1800s; Angolans themselves were a more valuable harvest than anything that could be raised there—even after slave traffic formally ended. Although the conscience-stricken British had abolished the slave trade in 1807 and slavery in their empire in 1834, and the Portuguese, under the leadership of the reform-minded Prime Minister Sá da Bandeira, had followed suit with the decree of 1836 banning slave traffic, this was easily circumvented and had little practical effect on the lives of Angola's inhabitants. Later, by 1856, when the global importance of the slave trade began to wane, Portuguese settlers introduced a novel way to extract additional worth from the natives: a hut tax, which simply encouraged them to move outside areas under direct Portuguese control. Even the compromise decree of 1858, which provided that all Africans then held in slavery would be freed in twenty years, had been violently resisted by Portuguese traders and settlers, who feared that their very way of life would disappear.

H. F. VARIAN DIDN'T "discover" the giant sable. It had been known and apparently revered by the Songo and Lwimbi peoples who shared its territory. But why hadn't the existence of this magnificent quadruped been noted previously by Europeans? There are several reasons. One was that the giant sable covered its own tracks, as it were, by leaving prints that would have certainly been mistaken for the more familiar sable's (for the only thing more "giant" about the giant sable is its horns) or confused with the similar spoor of its stocky, short-horned cousin, the roan. Europeans who first came across its trail in the highland plateau might simply have assumed that the familiar sable, whose range extends into southeastern Angola, in fact occurred farther north as well, never suspecting there might be a shadow beast that left a common sable's impress.

But there is nothing "common" about *any* sable antelope. Never numerous, these splendid animals are found scattered throughout the southern savanna from East Africa and Mozambique across to the southern Congo Basin. Seeing sable antelopes for the first time is always a special experience; for William Cornwallis Harris, the first European to do so, it was extraordinary. Many explorers had encountered Africa's unmatched array of wildlife before, but Harris was one of the first to come to the continent expressly for that purpose. Early explorers largely regarded Africa as a treasure chest to be cracked open and plundered. But it wasn't just the gold and slaves and ivory, or even the diamonds, rubber, oil, coffee, and copper to come that glittered; Africa also held out the possibility of making a great discovery, perhaps solving some vexed geographical puzzle (the source of rivers, the location of lost cities, the mystery of snowcapped mountains on the equator) or single-handedly extending the tree of taxonomy (who knew what startling specimens, unknown to science, remained uncollected?). Harris's determination to collect representative specimens from the African bush netted him the supreme prize, the discovery of a new species—the sable antelope.

Born in 1807, Harris left England at the age of sixteen to serve as a second lieutenant in the military engineers of the East India Company. As a boy he harbored the ambition to become the greatest hunter in the world, and he was able to hone his field skills in the Indian subcontinent. A keen amateur artist, he did as much sketching as shooting of wildlife. Sent to the Cape Colony in 1836 to recover from an Indian fever, young Captain Harris was able to fulfill his long-held dream of hunting in Africa by turning his convalescence into a five-month expedition, accompanied by William Richardson, a fellow ship passenger and sportsman he persuaded to join him. Harris arrived with his teapot, tent, artist's materials, and a barrel of gunpowder. Determined to "bring back correct delineations" of the wildlife of southern Africa as well as trophies, he boasted, "I never moved without drawing materials in my hunting-cap, and during brief cessations from hostilities, found ample employment for the pencil instead of the rifle." His hair-raising adventures into the interior, encounters with Hottentots and renegade Zulus, pursuits of giraffe, elephant, and scores of other species and the like are recounted in his 1838 *The Wild Sports of Southern Africa*, illustrated with his handsomely detailed, stylized drawings.

Months into their expedition, the two adventurers had bagged and catalogued over four hundred animals between them, and were passing through the "picturesque" Cashan Mountains (not far west of modern-day Pretoria) when Harris, in pursuit of a wounded elephant, "spotted a herd of unusually dark-looking antelopes" in an adjacent valley. Checking with his pocket telescope, he saw "that they were perfectly new to science; and having announced my determination of pursuing them, if requisite, to the world's end, I dashed down the slope." Dismounting to observe them at fifty yards, he counted nine chestnut-colored "does" and "two magnificent coal-black bucks—all with scimeter[sic]-shaped horns." They stared back at him. His rifle failed to fire, forcing him to return to camp for another weapon, cursing his misfortune. Three days of tracking followed before he was able to shoot the larger male, which although wounded led Harris "more than a mile over the sharp stones ere he was brought to bay, when twice charging gallantly, he was at length overthrown and slain."

Harris was overjoyed. He wrote, "It were vain to attempt a description of the sensations I experienced, when thus, after three days of toilsome tracking, and feverish activity, unalleviated by any incident that could inspire the smallest hope of ultimate success, I at length found myself in actual possession of so brilliant an addition to the riches of natural history." Entranced by the graceful curve of the yard-long crescent horns, the contrast of the glossy jet black coat and the snow white belly and face markings, he made dozens of measurements and a careful drawing. "We thought we could never have looked at, or admired it sufficiently; my companion observing, after a long pause, 'that the sable antelope would doubtless become the admiration of the world.'" Determined to preserve his prize, he carefully skinned it and returned to camp. It was December 15, 1836.

The next day, Harris turned his safari homeward. Despite attacks by Bushmen, and the loss of over seventy oxen, he was able to arrive with his specimens intact—two perfect heads of every major quadruped in southern Africa, including that of the sable, which he had slept with in his cot for safekeeping on the journey back. He had it preserved in Cape Town by a French naturalist, and eventually sent it to the British Museum. Harris called his discovery "the Sable Antelope," sable being the heraldic color black, but for generations after, the animal would be known as the "Harris buck."

That an even grander race of sable antelopes existed elsewhere in Africa remained a secret. Of course, there were Portuguese who ventured into Angola's interior highlands. Beyond the line of Portuguese forts, "traders and freebooters and priests and campaigners had gone to dwell or preach or fight in distant African communities, sometimes to return and sometimes not." But they never got wind of the beast. Among the tales they might have returned with, there was nothing concerning the animal that they would later call the *palanca preta gigante*.

EXPLORERS CAME TO Africa for a raft of reasons: to do God's work and bring his word to benighted savages; to promote commerce and amass a personal fortune; to make a fresh start by settling new lands, whether they were already occupied or not; to have adventures and experiences that would test one's character, resolve, and strength of purpose; to fight the inner "softness" that was considered the pernicious side effect of ninteenth-century progress; to give in to dark impulses and "go native"; and hundreds more. Many explorers, perhaps most, are more important for what they set in motion—the opening of trade, the jockeying for geopolitical advantage, the colonizing of wildlife itself—than what they accomplished. Yet what they did was amazing enough.

Their chronicles, once the great adventure reading of their day, now stand on little-visited shelves of older libraries. But the maps bound within these volumes of exploration confirm just how tantalizingly close some of these early travelers came to the lands of the giant sable. Put tracings of the routes of Angola's great explorers over each other, and the effect is like looking through layers of wavy glass; proportions and distances vary, names change, villages disappear and settlements shift, mountains move, rivers slither about. Only much later will the geographic features become as fixed as they are on modern maps. Wagon routes eventually became roads, fords turned into bridges, provincial limits were drawn, airports appeared. But the 1850s maps of Angola are poorly drawn, except for the Atlantic coastline; even the extent of the country is indistinct, because spheres of influence had not yet solidified into colonial boundaries. Over the next few years a trio of famed explorers, Dr. Livingstone, Lieutenant Cameron, and Serpa Pinto, would traverse Angola. What they would see—and didn't see—in that land, what they learned there and what they set in motion, would all shape the fate of the colony and the giant sable that lives at its heart.

The missionary impulse brought one famed explorer surprisingly close to the great antelope. In late 1853 Dr. David Livingstone, the Scottish medical missionary, left Linyanti (in the Caprivi Strip of today's Namibia) to ascend the Zambezi with twenty-seven African bearers, food supplies, articles of trade, navigational instruments, weapons, and a magic lantern to show biblical scenes. Livingstone traveled over a thousand miles by boat and ox-back to cross Angola, battling malaria and a host of other ills, but never failing to record detailed observations on the surrounding flora and fauna, down to the variety of grasses and minutiae of insect behavior, and of course, people and their customs. He made a special study of the physiognomy of various tribes and "became so familiar with the dark color as to forget it in viewing the countenance." One might say that Livingstone looked at matters of race through a spiritual lens; he did not view what he saw as the superiority of the white race as something innate, but the result of Christian education—a gift he hoped European powers would confer on black Africans as well.

Upon reaching the settlement of Cassagne to the west of the Kwango River in Angola, Livingstone's men were told by the inhabitants that white men were cannibals and he was taking them to the coast to sell them for food. They were reassured only when he told them he would continue alone if they doubted his good intentions. The party pushed on. "We spend Sunday, the 30th of April, at Nigo, close to the ford of Quize as it crosses our path to fall into the Coanza," Livingstone wrote. "The country becomes more open, but is still abundantly fertile, with a thick crop of grass between two and three feet high. It is also well wooded and watered." He was approaching Malange, skirting the top of today's Cangandala Park, the northern haunt of giant sable, but the great observer was barely conscious of his surroundings, much less primed to make a new discovery. "It would have afforded me pleasure to have cultivated a more intimate acquaintance with the inhabitants of this part of the country," he wrote, "but the vertigo produced by frequent fevers made it as much as I could do to stick on the ox and crawl along in misery."

Clinging to swaying Sinbad, his independent-minded mount, he finally reached the Atlantic a month later, on May 31, 1854. Livingstone spent three months recuperating in Luanda, which he noted "is now in a state of decay." He was fed, clothed, and even fêted by the Portuguese he encountered, and commented favorably on their lack of color consciousness. He had mixed feelings about Portuguese rule, but found cause for hope in progress. Reluctant to abandon his men so far from their homeland, he spurned the offer of passage home on an English cruiser and instead undertook the arduous return trip, largely retracing his route, but coming no closer to the giant sable.

Livingstone would go on to fame as the European discoverer of *Mosi Oa Tunya* ("the smoke that thunders"), cataracts on the Zambezi he would name Victoria Falls, and, in 1856, would reach Quelimane on the coast of Mozambique, becoming the first European to cross the African continent—although by the end of that journey he was so exhausted he had to be carried in a litter. Fifteen years later he was "found" in a weakened state on the shores of Lake Tanganyika by the self-promoting soldier of fortune, Henry Morgan Stanley ("Dr. Livingstone, I presume?" was his famously fatuous greeting). Livingstone refused to give up his search for the source of the Nile, even when he hardly had the strength to wind his watch, and finally succumbed in Zambia in 1873 after nearly thirty years of arduous exploration. His faithful men found him dead, kneeling at the foot of his bed. He may have lost his health, family, and hopes for the rapid salvation of the continent, but his feats of exploration, and more importantly, his crusading efforts to bring the benefits of civilization to Africa, would have far-reaching effects. Livingstone's chilling descriptions of encounters with long, shuffling caravans of slaves in chains or yoked to sticks and whipped when they fell behind deeply affected the readers of his books. His conviction that only a European presence in Africa could bring about the final suppression of the shameful practice of slaving meant, of course, the opening of free trade. As he put it, "No permanent elevation of a people can be effected without commerce." Civilization, he was certain, would come with the Christianity that would follow that commerce.

The impact and influence of Livingstone's *Missionary Travels* (1857) and *Narrative of an Expedition to the Zambezi and Its Tributaries* (1866) was enormous. These works were among the first in a series of texts written by explorers and adventurers who took their inspiration directly from their predecessors' writings. The contemporary Portuguese reaction to Livingstone's works was less admiring than that of the British. Livingstone, they argued, had not been the first to travel extensively in their lands, nor was he the first to cross the continent—not if you included an earlier expedition of two *pombeiros* (native traders), Pedro João Baptista and Amaro José. More importantly, if, despite Lisbon's strict decrees, slavery was still widespread in its territories, as Livingstone reported, well, that was the reality of life in Africa. It would not be the last time Portugal would have to defend its colonial policies.

There were other explorers of note who came close to the lands of the giant sable—but by southerly routes. The first to do so was twenty-eight-year-old Lt. Verney Lovett Cameron, the leader of a search party sent out by the Royal Geographical Society to look for Livingstone, who had not been heard from for over a year. In September of 1873, having marched in from the Indian Ocean to Tabora on the way to Lake Tanganyika, he learned the crushing news that Livingstone had already died. His devoted African followers had refused to abandon his body, and after burying his heart, bore his corpse along with his papers and instruments across the whole of modern-day Tanzania, to Zanzibar. Meeting up with the sad cortege, Cameron gave them supplies, and borrowed several of the doctor's navigational instruments. He then set off to finish the great man's goal of exploring the Lualaba, whose headwaters Livingstone thought might be near the greatest geographical unknown of Africa, the source of the Nile. Cameron failed: the Lualaba turned out to be the mighty Congo, not the Nile.

But in so doing Cameron became the first European to cross the southern continent from east to west. By 1874 he had gone directly west into the Congo Basin, and reached Nyangwe on the Lualaba. Slave traders there suspected that he wanted to open the river as a route for his own slaving, and refused to let him buy or hire canoes to explore farther downriver, forcing him to take an overland detour to the southwest—and Angola.

By September of 1875, Cameron and his porters were approaching the Cuanza River, skirting the southern border of the giant sable territory. Although Cameron was in close contact with the local inhabitants and made careful notes on all he observed, there is not a hint of the giant sable's existence in his writings. Several days later, after trading sufficient cloth to the local ferrymen, Cameron's party crossed the wide Cuanza on rickety native canoes and his rubber boat on October 2, 1875. Heading west, he met up with several caravans, but had little luck in trading. "I had to sell my shirts in order to keep us from actual starvation," he admitted. He soon learned that the inhabitants of every village he would pass from then on were "overwhelmed" with cloth and were interested solely in gunpowder or *aguardente* (spirits)—of which he had neither. Rain, hunger, and sickness took their toll on the expedition and brought it to a halt. Cameron decided to jettison everything but instruments, journals, books, and a half-eaten chicken to risk a forced march to the coast, 126 miles away.

Trying to keep up appearances for his men, Cameron clambered over boulders and hacked through tangled woods, stumbling past bleached human skeletons, some still linked in the clogs and neck forks that told the story of their deaths on some forgotten slave march to the coast. Reaching the top of a steep and rocky ridge, he saw a distant line on the sky, and recognized the ocean. He endured a day of "crawling over rocks and staggering through pools, waist-deep, dammed up in hollows since the last rains and now slimy and stagnant" before staggering down the final slope toward the seacoast town of Catumbela next to Benguela, exhausted but joyfully swinging his rifle round his head.

Cameron found his way back to England to write *Across Africa* (1877). Toward the conclusion of his narrative, he reflects on the great task of civilizing the Dark Continent, and wonders why British steamers can't be "carrying the overglut of our manufactured goods to the naked African, and receiving from him in exchange those choicest gifts of nature by which he is surrounded, and of the value of which he is at present ignorant? The Portuguese hold the keys of the land route from Loanda and Benguela and keep out foreign capital and enterprise, and are morally accomplices of slave traders and kidnappers." His opinions joined others in influencing British policy in the following decades, when the European powers began to divide the spoils of Africa with gusto, and much of the track of his trans-Africa crossing would become an established trade route.

Two years later, in 1877, another explorer brushed up against the giant sable's domain, again by the southern route, but from the opposite direction. Major Alexandre Serpa Pinto, a Portuguese army officer, sailed to Luanda with two navy officers, Hermenigildo Capello and Roberto Ivens, on an expedition sponsored by the Geographical Society of Lisbon. After falling out with his companions, Serpa Pinto set out on his own, traversing southern Africa from Benguela to the Indian Ocean, "for the sole purpose of labouring," he explains, "in the great task of survey of the unknown continent." Like every serious explorer, Serpa Pinto tried to think of everything in the way of supplies needed to cross the continent, including a "mackintosh boat purchased in London," a barrel of *aguardente*, fifty pounds of gunpowder, and various scientific instruments, including a French sextant, German compasses, and English chronometers. For company and comfort, he took a goat, a chattering parrot, and two bottles of 1815 port, one of which, to his intense dismay, was broken when the young African porter entrusted with carrying them stumbled and fell.

Serpa Pinto confesses in his *How I Crossed Africa* (1881) that he alternated between "boundless faith" in the work of his expedition and "shudders of pain and alarm" at his probable fate. He warns his readers that they can only imagine how circumstances in these savage lands conspire to test the moral code of civilized travelers. When he writes, "I would beg my censors to ponder for a moment on my position, accompanied as I was by a mere handful of men, in a country where everything was hostile, climate and inhabitants included," we are primed for his admission a few pages later that he insisted a ne'er-do-well Portuguese be given fifty lashes for unexplained villainies.

Serpa Pinto supplemented the record of his own experiences with what he heard in his travels, passing on much useful advice for anyone who might follow in his steps, including details on the culinary preferences of the people of the Bié Plateau. "They are not positively cannibals," he cautions, "but they do from time to time indulge in a mouthful or two of a roasted neighbor." Although what the major discovered often confirmed his prejudices, he was determined to document his journey properly. Crossing the highlands of Angola, he analyzed the shapes of anthills, and identified every hoofed creature he encountered by its Latin name. He diagrammed the manner in which the Ganguella, Lwimbe, and Loena people shaped their incisors, and commented on their hairstyles, headdress, and clothing, or more precisely, lack of it.

In early June, 1878, seven months after leaving Benguela, Serpa Pinto reached the left bank of the wide but shallow Cuanza as it curved through a vast, marshy, grass- and reed-choked plain nearly two miles across, "enclosed on either side by gentle green slopes clothed with trees." Over fifty yards from bank to bank, but no more than six feet deep, its remarkably clear water ran gently over a bed of fine white sand. He took a sighting: at twelve degrees, thirty-five minutes of latitude; he was roughly forty miles south of the prime habitat of the giant sable antelope. Five days later he crossed the river in his mackintosh boat and four borrowed canoes, and pushed on to the "picturesque" landscapes of the country east of the Cuanza—lofty, wooded hills, splendid trees, impassable underbrush. He found the climate "magnificent"; in fact, the nights were very cold. Despite his antislavery views, he openly advocated conquest of natives not yet under direct rule—a foretaste of Portuguese policy to come. He pointed out that because the land was "inhabited by a people easily subjected, it is in the very best condition for rapid development."

Later that month, Serpa Pinto left camp early one morning "to seek for game northward, where the country was covered with dense forest." After a walk of eight miles, he came to the Cuime River, a tributary of the Cuanza, just below its cataract. It had been a fatiguing day afield, but he'd had "good sport" and seen for himself the river that the natives said was navigable from the cataract west to the Cuanza. He turned back, and did not reach camp until night. It was the closest he would come to the southernmost range of the giant sable. Serpa Pinto's journey across Africa eventually ended at the Indian Ocean at Durban, an extraordinary achievement which made him famous in Europe and a hero in Portugal.

There were other explorers who passed close to the haunts of the unknown sable. Serpa Pinto's erstwhile companions, Capello and Ivens, made a more painstaking but less spectacular expedition across Angola, from Benguela through the northeastern lands of the colony back to Luanda. Their route actually cut across the lower end of the giant sable country in 1878. The two were aware of the impressively horned "harrisbuck," the common sable antelope that the Portuguese called the *palanca preta vulgar*. But even though they made the obligatory crossing of the Cuanza on native dugouts and went on to travel through the lands of the Lwimbe and Songo, noting their appearance and customs—right down to the design of the fish traps the natives set in the rivers—they reported nothing of the existence of a greater *palanca*.

The tribes had kept their silence.

Exactly what lay behind this reluctance on the part of the local inhabitants to speak of the creature they knew well has never been adequately explained. When the existence of the giant sable finally became known to the outside world, hunters would find that it had long been hunted and trapped by local tribespeople—which hardly seemed how a sacred animal would be treated. Guides could be readily recruited to pursue the beast, and yet there would emerge a strange pattern of many of these trackers leading hunters astray in the accounts of those who come next—evidence of a traditional reverence that still lingers.

PERHAPS ALL THESE famed explorers were destined to fail to find the great dark antelope, because none of them were actually looking for such an animal. In addition, without native assistance its discovery would have been a fortuitous accident. But there was one nineteenth-century adventurer who did go in search of it: Frederick Courteney Selous. "A celebrated antelope-hunter," Serpa Pinto called him. He was far more than that. Adventurer, explorer, author, he had become, by the end of his life, the very pattern of an English hero, embodying all that the Victorian age admired in its men. H. Rider Haggard modeled Allan Quartermain, the prototypical great white hunter in his *King Solomon's Mines*, after Selous. In Selous's own life we can see the scope of African adventure beginning to narrow to a singular focus on hunting its wildlife, a process that would culminate in the orchestrated encounters between client and licensed species in the contemporary hunting safari. In fact, the growing institutionalization of big-game hunting in the twentieth century ensured that the giant sable, once discovered, would become the ultimate antelope trophy. But it all began with Selous.

Seduced by the tales of African adventure he read at Rugby, young Frederick announced to his housemaster that he wished "to be like Livingstone," although it is safe to say that whatever he took away from reading the good doctor's works, it was not the missionary impulse. At the age of nineteen he landed in South Africa with £400 in his pockets, determined to make his way into the interior to live the free life of the hunter. It was September of 1871; across the map of Africa the scattered indigenous kingdoms, caliphates, empires, and sultanates appeared to counterbalance the modest coastal enclaves scooped out so far by colonial powers. To Europeans, Africa looked wide open.

Months later, he had already hunted lions (unsuccessfully), and survived being lost for days in the veld. The day before reaching the frontier of Matabeland, just over the border of modern-day South Africa, he saw his first sable, which he described as "one of the handsomest animals in the world." He marched on with his porters to the settlement of Bulawayo in today's Zimbabwe, founded in 1870 by Lobengula, who had succeeded Mzilikazi as king of the Matabele that year. Decades before, when they pushed north from Zululand, the proud Matabele had been driven from the Transvaal by the Boer trekkers, but not without "washing

26

their spears" in their white enemies' blood; ever after, they remained suspicious of white intruders. The imperious king, whose imposing height and bulk could only be approached by visitors on their hands and knees, was curious about his visitor's intentions. "I said I had come to hunt elephants," Selous wrote of the royal interview, "upon which he burst out laughing, and said, 'Was it not steinbucks [a diminutive species of antelope] that you came to hunt?'" Selous persisted, and begged for permission. Lobengula waved him away: "Oh, you may go wherever you like, you are only a boy."

Shortly thereafter Selous met Cigar, an experienced "Hottentot" hunter who'd been a former jockey in the Cape Colony. The two of them, accompanied by a few "Kafir boys," went after elephant on foot. Selous carried his own ponderous four-bore muzzle-loader, a bag of powder, and a pouch of bullets, each of which weighed a quarter-pound. This fearsome cannon left its mark on Selous when a servant inadvertently gave it a double charge—the bone-crushing recoil gave him a permanent facial scar. For the next decade he hunted and traded across southern Africa, returning to Bulawayo from one trip alone with 5,000 pounds of ivory. To finance his safaris, he shot scores of elephants, up to five a day, often on foot, an exhausting and decidedly dangerous activity. As result, he had innumerable close calls, but commented that, "There is nothing, I should fancy, like elephant hunting on foot to keep the blood in good order."

But back then, there was always more game; at least that's the way it seemed. Selous wrote of seeing an entire river valley in South Africa "alive with game" in 1873—giraffes, vast herds of buffalo and zebra spilling forth to the horizon, even kudu and both black and white rhinoceroses scattered among the rest. If he found the animals had been shot out in one territory, there were always other lands to be explored. Selous regretted the disappearance of game, but like many in that era, took it for granted that wildlife was a dwindling resource: certain species would decline or even become extinct as a side effect of the progress of human settlement. The notion that public land might be set aside to safeguard the environment had only just taken hold: Yellowstone, the world's first national park, had been created the year before, in 1872.

Still, the "bag" Selous admitted to in his books was so formidable that he was accused of engaging in wholesale slaughter. His answer was that he rarely fired a shot except to supply meat for himself, his followers, and hungry locals. Given that he sometimes shot as many as four or five elephants or giraffes in a single day, however, it might be more accurate to say, as his his friend and biographer, J. G. Millais, put it, that he "never shot an animal except for a definite purpose."

One of those purposes was to collect specimens of African animals. Unlike most early European hunters in Africa, Selous had a naturalist's mentality overlaid on an adventurer's wanderlust. Back then, African animals were for the taking, to be shot for the sake of shooting them, but also to be collected and wondered at, and usefully studied. By 1874, Selous had determined to collect the very best specimens of big game he shot. Eventually, as his fame spread through his books, he would be hired to procure specimens for the British (Natural History) Museum and other institutions. Interestingly enough, it was a visit to an Italian museum that would lead Selous to undertake a safari in search of the animal that could explain the existence of a certain curve of horn he discovered there.

On one of his return trips from Africa, Selous visited what is now the zoological collection of the Natural History Museum of Florence. That particular collection, "La Specola," housed south of the Arno, was first opened to the public in 1775. By the time of his visit it held a vast collection of animal specimens. Selous could probably have identified virtually any large mammal found in southern Africa from the most minimal of clues—a claw, a hoof, a scrap of skin. But he was taken aback by a single five-foot-long horn, a huge half-loop of ringed thickness trailing off into a perfect point. What animal grew that great arc of ridged keratin? It looked like an immense sable horn, but it hardly seemed possible. The best sable he'd ever shot was from Mashonaland (in today's Zimbabwe) and carried horns of forty-four and a half inches. "I measured this phenomenal horn," he wrote, "and I am sure that there is no mistake about its length of 61 inches, though where it came from nobody knows."

The horn is still there; in the old catalog its provenance is given as "Africa australe"—southern Africa. It was added to the museum's collection in 1873. Unfortunately, nothing else is known about it. One can make guesses about where it came from, and how it got there, but all that is certain now is that it is a giant sable horn. Selous could not know that, but he knew what it had to be—evidence of a grander, more impressive animal, one not yet seen for what it was. The hunter never forgot it. "For years he tried to find out where it came from," Millais wrote, "without success." That the great horn in Florence must have come from a race of extraordinary sables made the enigma all the more worth solving. Selous had a special regard for sable; like many, he regarded them as the most "high-couraged" of all the antelope tribe, and was impressed by their tenacity when pursued. "They use their horns with marvelous quickness and dexterity," he wrote, "and if, as they stand or lie at bay, an assegai is thrown at them, they often break the shaft with a sweep of their long curved horns on the instant the head of the weapon strikes them; while if a dog seizes them anywhere about the flank or hind-quarters, he will almost certainly have a horn driven right through him before many seconds." But it was more than fierceness that drew Selous to the sable. "Where they have not been much persecuted, sable antelope are amongst the least shy of wild animals; and the bold and noble bearing of a herd of these antelopes, standing on the slope of a wooded hill, gazing with curious though fearless eyes at the first mounted man to invade their haunts, could not fail to strike the least impressionable of hunters."

According to Millais, Selous "always thought that somewhere in Africa there were greater sable antelopes," and what he found in Florence only convinced him that he was right. He believed that the sable antelopes along the banks of the Chobe River in northern Botswana carried finer horns than South African sables, and the desire to settle that nagging question may have been one of the reasons he had long wanted to return to the "Promised Land beyond the Zambezi" he had first visited for elephant hunting. He finally had the opportunity in 1888 and planned a year-long safari—in effect, the first quest for the giant sable—to penetrate farther west.

Selous left Bamangwato in eastern Bechuanaland (later Botswana) in April of that year for the Zambezi River to the north with two wagons, five horses, sixteen donkeys, a number of porters, and a few trusted African assistants to drive the wagons, shoot, skin, and interpret. After he left his wagons and crossed the four-hundred-yard-wide Zambezi with his donkeys and men, the troubles began: one man died of fever, most of the porters deserted, and a series of extortionate chiefs made increasingly extravagant demands before he could proceed farther. To avoid having to pass through the territory of Mwemba, "the biggest scoundrel" of the Batongas, he struck north. After five days of traveling, the rough, sharply conical hills challenged even the sure-footed donkeys. On the third day the hills became more rounded, and Selous, in pursuit of tinier trophies, "spent a couple of hours during the middle of the day in catching butter-flies, and took several good ones, amongst them some of the handsome *Achræa acrita*," noting that they were identical with those found between three and four thousand feet on the northern and eastern slopes of the Mashuna country south of the Zambezi.

At the village of chief Monzi, the Batonga headman told Selous that he was the first white man to pass through his country since Dr. Livingstone thirty-five years before. "I found it impossible to get any precise informa-tion about the country on ahead," Selous wrote. If he had, he might have altered his plans. At the second village he passed after leaving Monzi's the people were all Mashukulumbwe. The men of the tribe were completely naked, and plastered their hair into a fantastic point, a perfect yard-high conic section that shot straight up off their heads, slightly curving forward, sometimes at an angle, like an elongated dunce cap. The effect sounds comical, but in appearance it was chillingly menacing, as early photos of these warriors illustrate.

The horns of a particular antelope had definite importance for the Mashukulumbwe: Selous noted "in the apex of these conical head-dresses a long thin strip of sable antelope horn, looking like a piece of whalebone, which though strong enough to stand upright, yet waved with every move-ment of the head." When feeling bellicose, each warrior carried "a large bundle of finely-tapered throwing spears, about seven feet long, all villain-ously barbed."

Anxious to avoid the Mashukulumbwe, Selous conferred with his men, but out of ignorance, headed directly into their territory. At every village the Mashukulumbwe stared at him and his men; at one, the head-man persuaded Selous to stay on and shoot some game for them. The villagers seemed friendly enough and crowded around their campfire the first night, but the next night no one showed. "I must confess that I felt uneasy," Selous recalled, and lying under his blanket, he could not sleep. One villager came to warn his men that all the women had left the vil-lage—something was very wrong. Selous had pulled on his shoes and put on his cartridge belt, and was just reaching across his blankets to get a few more cartridges, when three guns were fired at him and his companions. Miraculously, none of them were hit, and they dashed for the surrounding long grass under "a perfect shower of barbed javelins." A detachment of Mashukulumbwe rushed out of the grass and two of the warriors fell over the stumbling Selous, who jumped up and plunged deep into the safety of the bush.

"I now thought no more of firing at them," he recounted. "I had had time to realize the full horror of my position. A solitary Englishman, alone in central Africa, in the middle of a hostile country, without blankets or anything else but what he stood in, and a rifle with four cartridges." To say that Selous was tough hardly sums up his powers of endurance. He was a man who routinely shrugged off malaria, ignored broken collar-bones, and once crawled out from underneath a wounded elephant that had gored his horse. Still, his survival skills would be put to the test. He had no choice but to try to make his way back to the village of chief Monzi, several days' march away, the last settlement where he had received any-thing like a friendly welcome, and where there was at least the slim possi-bility some of his men might turn up as well. Using the Southern Cross as his guide, he began his lonely trek, swimming crocodile-infested rivers, hiding in the grass from searching patrols of Mashukulumbwe tracking him—he heard their voices and saw their conical, sable horn–tipped head-dresses waving—keeping an eye out for lions, and looking for something he could shoot for food, yet afraid to waste any of his handful of cartridges or draw attention to himself by the noise. After another two weeks of near-fatal encounters with treacherous chieftains and fortunate escapes made possible by natives who remembered his earlier friendly dealings, he managed to reunite with his African assistants, who had also miraculously escaped, but learned that twelve of his party had been killed. Selous had lost so much vital equipment that he was forced to return to the Transvaal, instead of "spending the summer beyond the Zambezi," as he had intended to do.

The great hunter never reached Angola, never solved the mystery of that certain curve of horn he saw in Florence. Instead, he went on to guide a gold-prospecting expedition in Mashonaland in 1899; then claimed by Portugal, the region was considered by the British to be in their sphere of influence. Selous had a low opinion of the Portuguese; he regarded them as rapacious colonialists and poor hunters to boot. Anxious to forestall Portuguese imperial designs on the region, he approached Cecil Rhodes on the matter and ended up in his employ. A year later, in the service of Rhodes's British South Africa Company, Selous led a column of two hundred pioneers into Mashonaland, securing it for the British Crown by acting as an intermediary between Rhodes and Lobengula, the mighty chief who had laughed at his ambitions as an ivory hunter twenty years before. Rhodes's company had already duped Lobengula into granting mineral concessions in his kingdom, Matabeleland, as well as Mashonaland, over which the chief claimed sway, a move that proved the thin edge of the colonizing wedge. It was a common colonial stratagem: native chiefs would be shown treaties, letters of intent, and proclamations—pulled out at the opportune moment from the explorer's boot—and urged to "sign," or mark them with a daub. These legal fictions gave a toehold to commercial interests, offered a variety of pretexts to meddle in native affairs, and were helpful in fending off competing colonial powers. Such ill-gotten papers were also useful back home in various European capitals; they could be waved at anticolonialists and provided the necessary fig leaf for greed-driven policies.

The pioneers quickly gained control over what was to become Rhodesia, putting down a bloody revolt in 1893, and toppling the once powerful potentate. "You have said that it is me that is killing you," Lobengula told his defeated people in a final, bitter speech. "Now here are your masters coming. . . . You will have to pull and shove wagons; but under me you never did this kind of thing." He fled north, and was reduced to taking poison when he heard that the last of his warriors had surrendered.

Another revolt in 1896—actually a war for independence—was equally unsuccessful. Selous, who at that time was newly married and farming in the colony with his young English wife, certainly shared Rhodes's imperialist attitudes. Yet he could not help sympathizing with the Matabele, wondering at one point "why they shouldn't try" to recover their lands. But the reports of the killings of pioneer families—some two hundred Europeans, including women and children, hacked to death—enraged him and the other settlers who fought back. The rebellion was savagely crushed; the Matabele short stabbing *assegais* were no match for the British Maxim guns. That year Rhodes spoke of Selous as "the man above all others to whom we owe Rhodesia to the British Crown."

Selous returned to England at the end of 1896. But Africa stayed with him, like the siren vision of the only woman he ever admitted to admiring there—a Portuguese quadroon he once saw gliding past on a boat on the Zambezi, reclining languorously on mats under the shade of a grass-thatched canopy. His writings had made him world-famous, and Theodore Roosevelt, an ardent admirer, invited him to the White House a year later. When Roosevelt began planning his African safari after leaving office, he naturally turned to Selous, who spent months helping to organize the ambitious collecting expedition for the Smithsonian and the American Museum of Natural History. Selous accompanied Roosevelt for the first part of the trip—one photograph shows them both sitting on the cowcatcher of a Kenyan train, the stout T. R. wearing a pith helmet, the still trim Selous his wide-brimmed hat.

At the outbreak of World War I, the sixty-three-year-old Selous was living in Surrey with his wife, writing and cataloguing his collections. He promptly volunteered for the army, knowing that his immense knowledge of the bush would be invaluable in Britain's African colonies. Selous would embrace Africa one last time. He was made captain of the 25th Royal Fusiliers, the official name of the Legion of Frontiersmen, a ragtag group soon whipped into shape by the rigors of bush warfare. At sixty-four, Selous led his troops through thick swamps and tight skirmishes, but sometimes wandered off alone with his butterfly net to collect specimens after an exhausting march. After a year of continuous service, he was awarded a D.S.O. for his gallantry and endurance. He died in action from a German sniper's bullet January 4, 1917 between Kisaki and the Rufiji River in today's Tanzania, in the northern part of the vast game reserve that now bears his name.

"He led a singularly adventurous and fascinating life," Roosevelt wrote after Selous's death, "with just the right alternations between the wilderness and civilization." One sepia-toned photograph of him, taken shortly before his death, conveys the image perfectly: humoring the photographer, he has paused in the field with a rifle across his shoulder. Shirtsleeves rolled up his muscular arms, his double Terai slouch hat set at a rakish angle, a white, squared-off Van Dyck beard contrasting with his deep tan, he looks calm, confident, commanding, his eyes pale and piercing even in a black-and-white photograph.

It is no longer possible to have the kind of adventures Selous did—much less to be universally admired and honored for it. His time in Africa coincided with the final phase of the colonization of that continent, an era when the European settlers still thought in terms of inexhaustible wildlife and the white man's burden. Selous was not just the greatest of the hunter-naturalists; he was quite possibly the last one who could have done what he did before a certain element of self-consciousness and artificiality would become an inevitable part of the enterprise, turning the unapologetic stance of the early explorer into the defensive posture of the modern trophy hunter.

The giant sable antelope was recognized as a subspecies in February of 1916. Did word of Varian's discovery reach Selous before he died? Apparently not. But the great hunter would undoubtedly have liked to have known of it.

Two

Varian's Giant

The sable antelope specimens that H. Frank Varian brought from Angola before World War I are now buried in the immense morgue of mammalian remains and surplus taxidermy that fill the storerooms of the Natural History Museum in London. It was there, off a dim corridor of dark-paneled offices and cluttered laboratories behind the first-floor exhibition halls, on the back of a wall covered with Indian water buffalo, across from several Marco Polo sheep, below a wildebeest and above Lord Derby's Eland, hanging chest high, that I found the skull and horns of Varian's "Giant."

I wasn't disappointed. In fact, I had to take a deep breath.

The skull, minus the lower jaw, had been mounted long ago on an inverted wedge of wood to permit the huge hoops of backward-sweeping horns to clear the wall. The slim, pony-sized skull seemed preposterously small to carry the horns, which sprouted up behind the empty eye sockets, close to each other, like twin saplings. Each one was far too thick at the base for my fingers to encircle, and their curves opened out in perfect parabolic arcs to their dark polished tips, high above my head. The rings on the horns were flattened on the sides, as if worn down. I traced this curious Braille but failed to follow the ridges from back to front, my fingertips slipping off each one as it sank into the surface of the horn before emerging again. Each ring formed a step in a series of discontinuities that started prominently and closely spaced at the skull and mounted upwards, becoming softer and farther apart, to merge, forty-seven transverse ridges later, with the point.

Lifting the cream-colored tag wired to one horn, I read the information written on it in sepia ink in a careful copperplate hand: *Hippotragus niger variani*, No. 16.2.21.1. *Luando River, Angola*. Also listed was Varian's name, the curator's (Thomas), the circle-and-arrow male symbol, and the telling, capitalized, underlined word "TYPE." A type specimen is nothing less than the ur-example, the one first recognized as constituting a new species or subspecies, and used to describe it—the Platonic form of the animal, as far as taxonomy is concerned. The scientific name on the tag linked a beast and a man. *Hippotragus* places the animal with the tribe of "horse antelopes"—a group that includes roan, oryx, and addax—in the family *bovidae*, to which all antelopes, sheep, goats, and cattle belong. *Niger* ("black") further distinguishes it as a sable antelope. *Variani* identifies it as the subspecies honoring Varian's unexpected contribution to science.

FRANK VARIAN'S IRISH father had been forest officer for the Northern District of Ceylon, but was better known as a big-game hunter, accompanying the Prince of Wales (later Edward VII) on his first elephant hunt there. He died at thirty-four in 1882, "principally from the effects of various too-close encounters with elephant and buffalo," as Varian put it, and the family, including six-year-old Frank, returned to England. In Ceylon, the boy had lived in an atmosphere of "big-game and elephant-hunting talk"; in England he was surrounded by silent trophies of the chase, including the skull and feet of the record elephant for Ceylon, "Malampe Rogue," shot by his father in 1882. Young Frank eventually studied engineering but had to give it up when money ran short. He thought of going to Burma to work for a teak company, but close friends in Hampshire, one of whom had just returned to recover from wounds he'd received in the recent Mashonaland rebellion (the same one Selous had fought in), stirred Varian with tales of African adventure. His friends were heading out to the fledgling colony of southern Rhodesia, and he was quick to join them.

Varian and his companions arrived in the mosquito-bitten port of Beira in Mozambique (Portuguese East Africa) on May 24, 1898, Queen Victoria's seventy-ninth birthday. After a two-day rail journey to Umtali (today's Mutare in Zimbabwe), he set off in an ox-wagon convoy for his first night on the veld, prefaced by "a glorious sunset over the mountains of Manicaland, the fabled country of *King Solomon's Mines*." By the time the wagons reached Salisbury, Varian had gotten lost in the bush, learned to make campfires from dried dung and to keep up the cook-pot, and suffered brutally from the cold (he'd imagined that all of Africa was hot, and hadn't brought any warm clothing). But he reveled in the experience, and later thought of this crash course in bushcraft as a perfect *Jock of the Bushveld* introduction to Africa.

After a year of frontier life in Salisbury, Varian was no closer than before to a career in engineering. A friend and medical officer for the Mashonaland Railways contractors came to his aid. At a dinner party with the firm's chief, the doctor inveigled a commission for him, informally scribbled on the flap of an Egyptian cigarette box: "Varian all right, starts tomorrow morning." His thirty-year career working on the pioneer railroads of Africa had begun.

Before the great scramble for colonies that commenced in the last quarter of the nineteenth century, the map of interior Africa was still largely composed of sketchily bordered territories and vaguely outlined spheres of influence. By 1912, it was a continent carved up as precisely as a butcher's diagram of a side of beef. The major European powers jockeyed for their share; minor powers were left with lesser scraps. Among many that were parceled out, the coastal Cabinda enclave, created when the Belgian Congo acquired a corridor to the sea along the Congo River, was given to Portugal as compensation for withdrawing from Nyasaland (today's Malawi) at the 1884–85 Berlin conference. Later it would prove to be a choice tidbit for the colony of Angola—although geographically separate, it was oil-rich.

By the end of the nineteenth century railways had become important levers in the struggle to pry open Africa and then stitch together the emerging colonies. No one recognized that better than Cecil Rhodes. He dreamed of British dominion over Africa, crowned by a railway (an "All-Red" route) that would stretch from the Cape to Cairo. Backed by his political power in the Cape Colony (he became prime minister in 1890), his immense diamond mining interests (which led to the formation of De Beers Consolidated Mines in 1888), and his expansionist British South Africa Company (which would stake out huge claims in southern Africa), Rhodes had the drive and the means to make his imperialist visions reality. His successful efforts to bring Bechuanaland (now Botswana), Matabeleland and Mashonaland (now Zimbabwe), and Barotseland (now Zambia) under British sway helped put an end to the ambitions of other powers to cinch and girdle Africa from coast to coast. Portugal's hopes of expanding into the territory between Mozambique and Angola and linking these colonies came to nothing, as did the French fantasy of joining the French Congo on the Atlantic with the outpost of French Somaliland on the Red Sea, or for that matter, King Leopold's Nile dream of extending the Congo Free State all the way to Khartoum. A year after the Mashonaland rebellion was put down, Rhodes had pushed through the construction of a 600-mile railroad south from Bulawayo to Mafeking in the Transvaal. Although his ambitious rail schemes were never fully realized, and he lived to see only a portion of them built, these pioneer railways managed to span most of southern Africa by the 1930s, linking Cape Town north to the Congo, from Beira on the Indian Ocean across to Lobito on the Atlantic.

Rhodes himself had given Varian the nod. The young engineer had met him once in Beira, on what was to be the empire builder's last trip to the colony that would be named after him. Varian had been discussing a technical problem with the consulting engineer in the construction office of the railway, when Rhodes walked in. Varian could feel Rhodes's keen gray eyes upon him and, after Rhodes stepped out, heard him ask in his high, thin voice, "Who is that young man? I like his face." Varian worked on the construction of the Victoria Falls Bridge, the one that fulfilled Rhodes's wish that when passengers crossed this spectacular span in the coming Cape-to-Cairo route they would feel the spray from the falls from the open windows of the cars. Later, he extended the line northeast from the falls across the Batoka Plateau and the Kafue River to Broken Hill (modern-day Kabwe north of Lusaka).

He had more than engineering problems to face on that particular job. Following a survey party through the region in 1905 to take up work on the bridge, Varian found himself in the country of the Mashukulumbwe. The very same cone-headed warriors who nearly killed Selous were soon to make good on their promise to slay whomever they could on the forthcoming construction by murdering several workers. It was late one afternoon when his wagons crossed the Magoy River some thirty miles south of the bridge crossing. Varian settled for the night outside the kraal of Meninge, one of the outlying chiefs of the Mashukulumbwe, but none of the villagers came near with the usual presents or offers to trade. He admitted to feeling "a little nervous" when he finally realized that this was the very same village in which Selous had been attacked some years before. It was a long night, but it passed without incident. Eventually Varian overcame his misgivings and even hired some Mashukulumbwe to work for him, although he always made them camp some fifty yards from his tent, and was careful to keep them in view "as they sat around their fires at night, feasting and talking, with their naked bodies and three-feet headdresses gleaming in the firelight."

In 1906 Varian returned to Broken Hill after a six-week reconnaissance safari of the Zambezi-Congo watershed to the north and was struck at how desolate the deserted railhead looked. Past a few wattle-and-daub mine buildings and a grass hut trading outpost, Rhodes's Cape-to-Cairo Railway trailed off like an unfinished thought in the brush-burned open plain, without even a buffer stop at the rail terminus. A solitary telegraph post stood at attention. But Varian had completed his assignment here; the next railway he would extend would be on the other side of Africa.

On his return to England a year later, he was offered the chance to work on a new railway and promptly sailed on the Union Castle cargo ship *Alnwick Castle*, bound for the port of Lobito in Portugal's West African colony, Angola. Varian mentions nothing of the 5,000-mile London-to-Lobito sea voyage. But he must have given some thought to the railway material and stores filling the hold of the ship. He was to take up the position of chief assistant engineer supervising construction of the Benguela railway across Angola from the Atlantic coast to the copper mines of Katanga in the Belgian Congo. It would form a vital line in a growing network of rail lines that would enlarge and redraw Africa's trade routes, but it was already seriously behind schedule and facing a host of difficulties—no water on the route, steep gradients, gorges to be spanned, and a mixed African labor force beset by constant disease, including beriberi, sleeping sickness, and malaria.

What made a railway across Angola attractive was the gleam of copper in the Katanga district of the Congo, just over the yet to be demarcated frontier with Angola. Both Livingstone and Cameron had reported tales of great mines in that region, huge ingots of copper being smelted, and copper crosses used as money. Rhodes commissioned expeditions to investigate the mineral wealth of his new colony as well as the "no-man's land" of Katanga, hoping to extend the British South Africa Company's reach. He asked Robert Williams, head of Tanganyika Concessions and a Scots entrepreneur who shared Rhodes's views, to investigate. Williams found mineral deposits in the colony, but warned their exploitation would require a shorter rail line than the one to Bulawayo from the south. Rhodes commissioned him again in 1899, and this time Williams sent out an expedition that found significant copper deposits near the Belgian Congo. Because King Leopold of the Belgians was convinced there was no mineral wealth to be exploited in the country he ran as a personal fiefdom, Williams was able to obtain sole prospecting rights over 60,000 square miles of Katanga.

When Rhodes died in 1902, Robert Williams took up the effort to extend the pioneer railroads—not to Cairo, but at least to the north—by developing economic objectives that would justify their construction. Primary among these was a plan to tap the El Dorado of Katanga with its great buried reefs of copper. Looking at the map of Africa made it clear: the shortest possible rail line from Katanga to the nearest port would cross Angola's varied and mountainous terrain to Lobito on the Atlantic coast. Such a line would bring those riches thousands of miles closer to England than by any other route. What made the railroad at all possible was that the Portuguese military was in the last stages of a war of "pacification" to bring the central highlands under control.

The Ovimbundu of the closely populated Bailundo region of Angola's Bié Plateau were traders, not warriors. But resentment against the Portuguese had been building for years over the price collapse of the low-quality rubber they traded, the demoralizing rum trade, continuing expropriation of their lands by *degredado* settlers and Boer farmers, and forced conscriptions which took thousands of Ovimbundu annually to labor on faraway plantations, never to return. When the Bailundo chieftain was imprisoned for allegedly not paying for rum for native celebrations, his advisor, Mutu ya Kevela, launched an uprising in conjunction with several nearby kingdoms in a forlorn effort to expel the Portuguese, telling his war council: "Before the traders came we had our own home-brewed beer, we lived long lives and were strong."

It took two years for the Portuguese, with their African mercenary troops and superior artillery, to subdue the natives, who had only muzzle-loading muskets for weapons and the rocky outcroppings of their rugged land for cover. The Bailundo Uprising of 1902, as it was called, came to a predictable conclusion with Mutu ya Kevela's death and fields of ashes where villages had been. "For the Portuguese," James Duffy wrote, "this was a classic native war: the punitive expeditions were organized quickly; the Africans fought bravely but foolishly; every Portuguese soldier was a hero; and, finally, thousands of Africans were killed while Portuguese losses were minimal." (Warfare with indigenous tribes had flared up sporadically since the Portuguese had arrived in Angola, and it would take until 1919 to crush the last holdouts—the Dembos, who were no more than a hundred miles from Luanda.)

Before 1902 was over, Williams obtained a concession from the Portuguese government to construct a 1,300-mile-long railway to cross Angola, and hired George Pauling & Co. as contractors—the builders of the Beira and Mashonaland Railways. British investments would pay for almost all of the expenditure. But it was an extraordinary gamble; any payoff would be far in the future. Later, Varian would reflect that "probably no line ever built in the history of the world has stretched so far to such a distant goal, and passed through country with so little prospect of remunerative revenue on its way." Financial problems plagued the undertaking from the beginning, and the terms of the concession dictated a route from the seacoast that was unnecessarily long. The Germans, hoping to gain a fingerhold in Angola as part of their African strategy, schemed in Lisbon to get the concession canceled if the line could not be laid on schedule.

The *Alnwick Castle* steamed around the Atlantic coast of the continent and cut across the Gulf of Guinea, past the Ivory, Gold, and Slave Coasts tucked under the great bulge of West Africa, bringing Frank Varian to the middle of the Angolan coast and another pioneer railroad. It was August 12, 1907, and given the time of year, the weather should have been pleasant, though Lobito was anything but. Having seen a good deal of Africa, however, Varian doubtless took it in stride. From the sea no one would suspect a harbor. All that was visible was a line of palms and a few squalid fishing huts and bungalows on stilts built trustingly near the surf; beyond, barren limestone cliffs. But the beach turned out to be a three-mile-long spit of sand a few hundred yards across and parallel to the shore, a breakwater enclosing a natural harbor some sixty fathoms deep. The settlement was only three years old, built to service the new port—currently consisting of a wooden pier jutting out from the sand spit—some fifteen miles of mangrove north of the much older, larger coastal town of Benguela.

Lobito's hidden harbor had previously been used by slave ships to evade the British Royal Navy in the second half of the nineteenth century, decades after the dedicated commerce in black humanity had supposedly ceased. After the formal abolition of slavery in 1878, a system of forced labor had been substituted to ensure there would be no lack of labor for Portugal's cocoa plantations on São Tomé and Príncipe, as well as the colony's new coffee and rubber plantations. The old slave trade in the interior went on much as before, but instead of buying slaves outright, traders "contracted" for them. Several thousand such *contratados* a year would be brought in chains from the interior to Benguela and packed off to the ocean cocoa islands in what were, for them, death ships. The contracts (largely oral) ran five years, but at the end of the working period no one ever returned; the exhausting work, the harsh climate, the poor diet, and the cruel conditions saw to that. The year before the engineer arrived, one observer wrote of watching a young African mother trying to climb a swaying ship's ladder from a boat crammed with *contratados*:

> At last she reached the top, soaked with water, her blanket gone, her gaudy clothing torn off or hanging in strips, while the baby on her back, still crumpled and pink from the womb, squeaked feebly like a blind kitten. Swinging it round to her breast, she walked modestly and without complaint to her place in the row that waited the doctor's inspection. In all my life I have never heard anything so hellish as the outburst of laughter with which the ladies and gentlemen of the first class watched the slave-woman's struggle up to the deck. It was one of those things which made one doubt whether mankind has been worth the travail of our evolution.

This was the Angola that Varian entered when he disembarked.

THE YOUNG ENGINEER would not have struck those expecting him as a physically imposing man. Varian was short and wiry, with a stiff posture and a nervous energy. In the field, he wore a pith helmet—it was widely believed that Europeans should avoid exposure to the equatorial sun, and more rakish headgear would not have been his style—along with a khaki shirt buttoned to the neck. He may have been small and slight, but he was bush tough. After first battling a shaking fever with quinine in Mozambique, he'd developed the habit of sleeping with mosquito netting to ward off bites long before the connection between the insect and malaria was understood. As a result, he never succumbed to the disease again, which only added to his reputation for tirelessness. He'd survived jumping off a mountainside to escape a speeding train. He'd been in charge of unruly railway crews of Greeks, Italians, Chinese, Irish, and various Africans, and dealt with drunkenness, gambling, shootings, knife fights, and mamba bites. His discipline and drive made him a magnet for nicknames. In Beira, the workers had called him *M'pondera*—the man who did not sit still.

Varian had his work cut out for him. Because the railway concession was committed to the route originally surveyed by the Portuguese, the beginning of the line was a given, even though it meant that the direction was twisted and that several mountain ranges had to be climbed and a waterless region traversed. The concession also required that the rails had to reach Catengue, some seventy-five miles into the mountainous interior, in ten months. The Bié Plateau arises so abruptly from the coastal lowland that at fifty-two miles from Lobito Varian could still see the ocean in the west from the tracks, and the route would have to skirt peaks that reached 8,500 feet after that. There was no local labor available for this grueling construction; it had to be imported. Some seven thousand West Africans from various British territories and French Equatorial Africa, and two thousand Indians from Natal, were employed on this section. Advancing in a cloud of dust and smoke, the plate-laying train with its cars of iron rails, pins, telegraph wire, nuts, bolts, and tools lurched forward a few yards at a time, attended by hundreds of laborers shouldering the steel sleepers and sixty-pound rails and hammering them in place, followed by gangs of pick-and-shovel workers heaping and packing earth around the rail bed. But there was no water to be found in the hot, dry, mountainous region behind the coast. It was the land that Cameron had struggled through in his desperate march to the sea, a yellow-and-gray landscape of sparse scrub and dust-covered baobabs known as the "Thirsty Country." Wagons, camels, and lines of porters were pressed into service to bring water rations up the tracks, and crews of rock drillers, special barges, tracks, and engines had to be sent out from England. To keep on schedule, work in the precipitous gorges continued throughout the day and all night by the wavering glow of electric lights suspended on cables to illuminate the rock faces swarming with human labor.

The railway would have to cross the "Hungry Country" as well. A 200-mile-wide uninhabited barrier of sandy ridges and thick scrub where nothing edible grew, it had been a dreaded crossing since the days of the first native caravans. Skeletons still marked the paths of those who under-estimated their food supplies. It was a prospect that gave Varian some concern. For one thing, there was a complete absence of stone for build-ing or ballasting in those barren wastes. But as the months went by, and the rail line pushed its way slowly across the mountains, the more confi-dent he became. By the time the initial objectives of the concession had been met, the young engineer had been put in complete charge of con-struction and maintenance of the track already laid. "Matters became easier," as Varian laconically put it, and, save for some trouble with the Senegalese laborers (they were "prone to riot"), work on the railway settled into steady progress. Varian found he finally had some days at leisure. He began hunting again.

Varian had first hunted big game in Mozambique to supply his crew with meat. He would later consider himself lucky in not being able to afford an expensive high-velocity rifle. Instead, he used a well-worn, not very accurate single-shot Martini-Henry rifle discarded by a local professional hunter. The rainbow trajectory of the breech-loading weapon taught him to stalk carefully and get as close as possible to game to ensure a clean kill. "I always like to think that I never let a wounded beast get away," he wrote, "nor did I leave meat lying around unused, as sometimes happens when trophies are the chief consideration." It was a "gospel" he was to carry with him throughout his subsequent years of hunting in Africa, and it stood in marked contrast to the buck fever of big-game hunting he witnessed in those days. All too often, he wrote, "the success of a shooting trip was judged by the number of animals destroyed, irrespective of age or sex, with the consequence that there was a good deal of unnecessary and undesirable slaughter." He attributed this bloodlust to those new to the sport; experienced hunters "were more interested in the collection of particular specimens," although he himself thought trophies a nuisance to collect and transport in the bush.

There could be a number of reasons to pick up a big-game rifle in Africa. Years before, when Varian was in the Pungwe River district of Mozambique, railway work had been interrupted on occasion by lions that carried off sleeping laborers and made a meal of them. Fortunately, the Shangaans that made up most of the African labor force would form a band the next day and, armed with their *assegais*, hunt down and slay the offending felines, saving Varian the trouble. But he had to shoot hippos and crocodiles when they held up native river traffic and disrupted the railway supply route. And then there were those species that in those days everyone, including Varian, considered pests: leopards (which he permitted his long-time gun-bearer, Alexander, to shoot on sight) and wild dogs. "Personally," he admitted, "I never had any compunction in shooting up a pack of wild dogs, even if it meant fouling a clean rifle and having to clean it again oneself." Varian's attitude toward them was colored by his view that they were "the cruelest of all hunting animals, as they do not kill cleanly, but with the utmost savagery, tearing at the flanks and tender parts of the hunted animal before it falls, and devouring it before it is completely dead"—as if these predators could be held to the highest standards of British sporting ethics.

Varian felt differently about Sheila, his faithful Irish deerhound. When she died from a lion mauling in Rhodesia, he was determined to make her grave hyena-proof, and had his Mashukulumbwe laborers build a huge rock cairn over it. And he was grieved by the accidental death of Jock, his camp monkey in Angola, a "game little hero" who used to snitch his shaving gear and ride like a jockey on his hunting dogs round and round the encampment. Varian saw no contradiction between his tender regard for pets and his hatred of "vermin," or his disdain for indiscriminate shooting yet satisfaction in skillful stalking and clean kills—it was all part of his personal ethos and his complex stance toward the natural world he loved.

Frank Varian was also an enthusiastic amateur naturalist, and like many, wanted to be taken seriously for his efforts. Today, save for the lucky comet watcher or assistant on a fossil dig, amateurs rarely add to the advancement of science, but in the nineteenth and early twentieth century, hunters who were also sharp observers, like Frederick Selous and Theodore Roosevelt, were, on occasion, able to make direct contributions to zoology. Several of the railway lines that Varian worked on passed through untouched game country, territories where there was little authoritative information on the fauna to be found. Varian began sending reports to *The Field* in England, detailing the different species of wildlife he had encountered while working on the pioneer railways. In those days *The Field* ("The Country Gentleman's Newspaper") covered the full range of field sports, including shooting, stalking, and big-game hunts, as well as natural history—everything from snippets on tropical rat fleas, notes on the flying frogs of Java, articles on dogs nursing otter cubs, and more serious pieces on the role of scent glands in the classification of deer—contributed from all over the British Empire in letter-to-the-editor style.

By the end of 1908 the Benguela Railway had only reached Cubal, 123 miles inland; it would take until the end of 1912 to reach Huambo in the central highlands, still only halfway to the giant sable territory in the heart of the country. But the shimmering steel rails cut a permanent swath across the landscape, far more enduring than the faint foot trails of the early explorers, the well-worn paths of the slave caravans, even the rutted ox-wagon tracks that preceded it—all of which the bush could easily reclaim, overgrow, and sink without a trace. The railway was relentless; it laid open the land as it had never been exposed before, forcing it to yield up its secrets.

One puzzling object unearthed east of the source of the Cuanza by a Belgian prospector-geologist now rests in the Royal Museum in Tervuren. A modest-sized carved wooden piece, it has turned out, years later, to be the oldest known wooden sculpture from central Africa. Created over a thousand years ago, the artifact eludes analysis; it appears to be a ritual bowl, but it could be interpreted as a stylized quadruped; turned over, it might be a ceremonial mask. The center of Angola would soon disclose another unsuspected treasure with its own multiple meanings: the giant sable antelope.

Whenever he could, Frank Varian led the survey parties that preceded the laying of the rails. Often, he rode on horseback, but frequently marched on foot, preceded by a handful of porters. On these forays into the interior Varian usually found that the best rail route would roughly retrace the *via dolorosa* taken by the shuffling feet of the old slave caravans that linked Benguela to the sources of the Zambezi, the same path taken in part by Cameron, Serpa Pinto, and Capello and Ivens. The anticipated passage through the "Hungry Country" had also been pioneered by wagon. Major Boyd Cuninghame, a highly regarded sportsman, cricketer, and polo player with a taste for adventure, had been commissioned by Robert Williams to lead an ox-wagon expedition to bring out the first copper from Katanga to the coast. In 1904 Captain Cuninghame cut 600 miles of road through the bush from the outpost of Moxico, itself 600 miles inland, into the Congo, returning with twenty tons of copper to Benguela. On his second expedition several years later he met up with Varian in the highlands to arrange to transport another twenty tons of copper the rest of the way to the coast by train. Varian was eager to hear more about the country he would encounter in the interior—the geography, the natives, and the game. At that time, the frontier between Angola and the Belgian Congo had not been defined, nor had the inhabitants near the border been "pacified"; in fact, they were cannibals. The animals that might be encountered to the east were more pleasant to think about than the people.

Intrigued by what he had learned of them, Frank Varian sent a short piece from Lobito to *The Field* in early 1909 reporting on various Angolan mammals. It ran in the March 20 issue under the title "The West Coast Duiker." After discussing the proper classification of a living specimen of a little antelope (a black-rumped duiker) he'd managed to ship to the Regent's Park Zoo, he gave a brief rundown on the species he'd seen or heard of in Angola, from an unfamiliar dik-dik (an even smaller antelope than the duiker) to elephant, eland, roan, and kudu, and then added the following: "Sable antelope have been shot on the Quanza River, 300 miles inland. A 54½-inch head was obtained there about three years ago by Mr. Essington Brown."

This passing remark—only later recognized as the first mention of the giant sable—did not go unnoticed. Up to that date, the very longest sable horns listed in Rowland Ward's authoritative *Records of Big Game* were two inches shorter. A month later *The Field* published an acid reply from an experienced African hunter attacking Varian's claim. "This measurement is so remarkable that it would be interesting to know if the head was measured in the proper way, i.e., the tape being drawn quite tightly round the arch of the horn, and not depressed into the rings, a very usual way of measuring by the inexperienced, but one that adds some 4 inches to the true measurement." The piece was signed with a pen name perhaps taken from the correspondent's weapon of choice: "Mannlicher."

Varian never forgot this stinging attack on his credibility. Forty years later, he still smarted from the insinuation that he must have pressed the tape down with his "fingers in the corrugations" of the horns to obtain the length alleged. But he had made the mistake of making a claim he could not really substantiate. In the October 9 issue, Varian tried to offer a convincing explanation. "Personally I only saw a photograph of them, that was given to a man to take home to Mr. Rowland Ward. I know Mr. Brown well, and I heard a lot about the horns from various shooting men who saw and measured them . . . in the usual way, i.e., stretching the tape tight along the curve from base to tip." Unfortunately, "the head itself was lost, together with other trophies, at a river crossing" in one of Captain Cuninghame's wagon expeditions across Angola to the Congo. Eight months later he was able to supply *The Field* with the photograph, which showed an African framed as if in giant parentheses by the impressive separate horns he held.

Mannlicher was still lying in wait. A week later, he attacked Varian again, reiterating his "loose tape" charges. He found the photograph unconvincing and the fact that the horns had been cut or broken off the skull suspicious. "Fifty-inch sables are few and far between," he reminded the readers of *The Field*, taking the opportunity to mention that his own best sable trophy measured an impressive fifty and one-quarter inches. He dismissed the evidence with the observation that "Mr. Varian does not refute my suggestion as to the method of measuring this head."

There was no reply to this. Varian had never actually seen the horns and in any case they were lost and their length could not be confirmed. He would have to live with his wounded pride. It wasn't until 1911 that Varian found any factual support for his assertion that Angola harbored the largest race of sables yet known. By then he had been engaged on some reconnaissance work south of the Cuanza, following an exhausting daily routine that began at 5:00 A.M. with a whistle in the dark, a light breakfast as the tent was struck and loads made up, a nonstop walk until eleven o'clock, an hour break, and then another march until midafternoon. Varian would have been at the tail of the chattering procession, marking his maps, when he met up with the Reverend Fred Lane, a missionary trekking to the coast from the interior with some native porters. Varian gives no details in his memoirs, but in those days encountering another European in the remote bush was hardly an everyday affair. Eager for any news of the interior, he would certainly have invited the missionary to join his camp for a meal and to spend the evening in conversation by the fire.

At some point—when setting up camp, most likely—Varian spotted the head and horns of an "outsized sable" on one of the porter's loads. He promptly questioned Lane, who told him that he'd obtained the head from a native who lived in the same district on the Cuanza where the large head Varian had written about two years before originated. Varian realized he was finally looking at proof of his claim that greater sables could be found near the river. Then it struck him with even more force: it might even be an answer to the question that had long intrigued naturalists—where had the great anomalous curve of horn that so puzzled Selous in Florence come from? He questioned the natives closely and was told "that the *Sumbakaloko*, as they called it, was two days' journey to the north." Varian knew nothing of that little-explored region. It would take a few horses and porters only a few weeks' time to investigate, but Varian had to supervise the laying of track toward Huambo, and he would not allow himself to neglect his work. But neither would he miss the chance to make careful measurements of the splendid horns. Soon after he wrote to *The Field* to give the details— fifty-four and three-quarter inches on the outer curve—and report with satisfaction that the head ("probably the largest ever obtained") was on its way to England, adding Rev. Lane's address in Greenwich so that doubters could ask to verify the measurements. A week later, an eager reader wrote in to state he had visited Rev. Lane and confirmed the claim.

Varian's reputation for hard work and fair treatment out in the bush continued to gain him honorifics. His colleagues called him "the inexhaustible"; his Angolan workers dubbed him *Kwangoni*, which meant "he will not let you down," shouting it out whenever he approached a strange village. The bush telegraph carried his reputation far and wide—even deep in the Congo, where ferrymen would take *Kwangoni* across rivers without payment. But of all the names he had ever been given, the one he'd found puzzling at the time he'd acquired it in northern Rhodesia now seemed strangely prophetic: *M'pala-pala*—the sable antelope. In truth, he had only begun to be involved with this creature.

Some months later, in 1912, Varian returned to England on leave. In London, he visited the Natural History Museum on Cromwell Road in South Kensington. In those days, it was better known as the "British Museum (Natural History)," having split off from the British Museum only in 1883. Behind its imposing Romanesque facade, then as today, was one of the world's greatest libraries of taxonomy. The possibility, however slim, of being credited by the museum with the discovery of a new species fired Varian's enthusiasm. In his mind, the British Museum had no equal as a scientific authority, and he hoped for some acknowledgment of his efforts as a naturalist. As evidence, he was presenting the skin and skull of a black-rumped duiker, the same small antelope he'd sent to the Regent's Park Zoo. He was eager to share what he had learned of Angola's fauna, including a dik-dik whose range was not known to extend so far north. Perhaps he might even mention the large, tawny-colored hunting dog the natives spoke of that had not been described anywhere else. But the reception he got at South Kensington from Oldfield Thomas, F.R.S., F.Z.S., the preeminent zoological curator, was polite but cool.

A photograph of Thomas at work in those days shows him seated behind a paper- and book-strewn desk in a dark-paneled room cluttered with tables of skins and skull-topped cabinets shelved with jars of organs, softly lit by the yellow glow of tall, begrimed windows. Thomas is leaning forward, studying a large volume, his suit rumpled, his white hair neatly parted. If Varian was received in that setting, he would have certainly understood that Mr. Thomas was a busy man. And doubtless he would have been kindly reminded that he was not the only amateur naturalist in colonial Africa offering specimens to the museum. And yes, Thomas would have concurred that the larger fauna are important, but Mr. Varian would have to agree that it was very likely every large species of mammal from that part of the world had been accounted for. The okapi, that strange, striped, forest-dwelling relative of the giraffe, had surely been the last that would be discovered. It had come to light a dozen years before, despite a range confined to the deepest, least-explored jungles of the Belgian Congo. But what was still of interest were the smaller mammals. Could he send on skins of any that seemed unusual? Yes, Varian would be happy to supply the "bats, rats and moles" that were wanted. He left the building with a limited, informal, but valid mission as a bona fide museum collector.

For years afterwards, Varian regularly shipped his little finds from his beach house in Lobito to South Kensington. These were filed away, and in due course he would receive an official receipt and perfunctory thanks. Later, when he was asked to collect further specimens, he discovered, much to his chagrin, that he had sent the identical animals years before. Even more galling, other collectors eventually had species named after them for which Varian suspected he "might have received the credit had not my earlier finds been so successfully pigeon-holed in some limbo of the Natural History Museum." Adding one of the few direct complaints in his memoirs, he found the whole business "a little unfair."

But that would be in the future. On his return to Angola in 1913, Varian received alarming news. The year before, a small party of Boer hunters had managed to cross with their wagons over the swamps that guarded the southern boundary of the yet to be explored giant sable lands east of the Cuanza and found it full of game. It had been too late in the season to hunt effectively; the rains and the long grass made it difficult to travel or spot animals. But they left this unspoiled corner of Angola with a quantity of meat and skins and a number of sable heads with astoundingly long horns, some five feet in length. Varian was dismayed that the Boer "raiding party" had sold some of the large sable heads they'd obtained for high prices, and worse, planned to return en masse the next dry season to hunt for skins and meat. In his view, the Boers were largely responsible for the relative scarcity of game in the more accessible parts of Angola. After the first Boer War, a number had made the hard trek across from the Transvaal, finally settling in the highlands of Angola, where they subsisted primarily by hunting. Although he had no specific knowledge then of the sables that might be found in the region east of the Cuanza, he already believed that they represented something far out of the ordinary. A meat-hunting expedition into the district would mean nothing less than "the complete extinction of the finest antelope in Africa, bearing the most magnificent horns of all."

Varian immediately appealed to the Portuguese governor at Moxico, Senhor Lami, who had jurisdiction over the upper Cuanza region. After traveling through the district with Varian and Senhor Marianno Machado, the manager of the Benguela Railway, the governor acceded to Varian's request that he intervene. He promptly closed the district for hunting, an act which Varian credited with saving the still mysterious sables. But he knew the decision was only a temporary measure. The district was an outlying one, and covered an area larger than that of Corsica or Crete— too huge to police. Already he'd heard reports of poaching now that news of the sables had spread; the poachers were being paid a shilling for them, but the horns would command far more than that before reaching their final destination.

In early 1914 *The Field* ran a small item from an Englishman who'd obtained a pair of sable horns via South Africa that measured sixty-two and three-quarter inches on the outer curve, causing a flurry of excited letters from naturalists ("Surely there is a mistake," etc.). One offered the tantaliz-ing remark: "Wherever all these long-horned sable antelope came from has not yet been revealed; but it is probable that they were obtained in some district which has but recently become accessible to sportsmen." Even Mannlicher weighed in, pointing at Angola as the obvious source of these impressive specimens, while denigrating them as mere "picked up heads" instead of great trophies that someone had actually shot. With talk like that, it was only a matter of time before trophy hunters would come.

But for the next several years, the sables of the Cuanza would be spared pursuit by foreign nimrods. A ghastly war of trenches and poison gas and shocking carnage that would tear Europe apart forestalled travel to Angola. It also put an end to the work on the railway, which had reached Chinguar, halfway between Huambo and Cuito and some 322 miles into Angola. Varian was anxious to return home and join up, but the threat posed by bordering German South-West Africa meant that every vital bridge and crossing of the line had to be guarded, and he had to stay on until the end of 1915 to help with the security measures. After they were in place, Varian offered to resign to return home, but the company gave him leave at half-pay.

On board the RMS *Kenilworth Castle* in mid-January of 1916, Varian wrote to Oldfield Thomas a note on shipboard stationery in his linked and looping scrawl. "I have a small box of skins for you from Angola," he began, and explained that he'd have it forwarded. "I hope to come and call on you later. I am on my way home to join the service for the war. Royal Engineers, I hope." Back in London, Varian paid a visit to the museum. Thomas was extremely pleased to receive his collection of small mammal specimens, as it included a number of rarities. As Varian was leaving—and doubtless choosing his words carefully—he mentioned that in spite of the museum's lack of interest in the larger Angolan animals, he thought some of them showed distinct differences from the classified varieties, and "would repay a little study." Thomas was intrigued. Exactly what did he have in mind? Varian said he could send him the head-skins and horns of a sable bull and cow he'd brought to England that differed in face markings and horn length from the ordinary sable antelope found in southern Africa. Out of curiosity, or perhaps just to be polite, Thomas said he'd be happy to accept the offer. Varian sent him the specimens, along with a passing mention that there might be a connection between them and the still unexplained five-foot-long horn in the Florence Museum. . . .

A few days later Varian received "an almost excited letter" from Thomas, warmly thanking him for "one of the most important gifts the museum has received for a long time." Thomas had in fact been staggered; the differences were so striking in both horns and marking between the specimens Varian had supplied and ordinary sables, he thought at first he was confronted with evidence of a completely distinct species. But after "considerable hesitation" over how variable the face markings might prove to be compared with typical sables, Thomas decided to adopt a more conservative position: at the very next meeting of the Zoological Society of London he would propose distinguishing this magnificent Angolan animal as a separate subspecies.

Varian promptly replied to Thomas from his club, the Bath on Dover Street. "I was extremely pleased to get your letter with such good news of the sable. I found another piece of face skin of another head in the case I brought the specimens in. I have asked to have it forwarded to you in case it is any use. It will be splendid if there is enough to definitely get a separate species definitely named as you suggest and I am very grateful to you." He closed with a promise to forward a sitatunga skin and the hope that he would be able to see Thomas again soon.

On the day Varian wrote the letter, February 8, 1916, the Society met at half past five o'clock, at its Regent's Park offices. After the usual shuffling of chairs, the knocking and refilling of pipes, and the reading of the previous minutes, members could look forward to presentations on such subjects as Antarctic larval fishes (in drawings exhibited by lantern slides), the successive antler formations of a deer that died of cancer, and a new collection of Somaliland moths. Mr. R. E. Holding led off by exhibiting the skull of a roebuck, showing an unusual deviation in the direction of the suture of the right frontal bone. Then Oldfield Thomas brought out the scalp, frontlet, and horns of the male sable antelope, together with the female mask and horns that Varian had sent him.

"This magnificent animal," Thomas reported, "differed widely from the ordinary sable." The horns of the male measured fifty-seven inches along the front curve, "immensely finer horns" than the forty-five to fifty inches of a good South African or Nyasaland sable, much less the comparatively modest under-forty-inch horns of the East African race. Thomas then drew the members' attention to the unusual face markings, particularly "the complete obliteration of the usual prominent white streaks running from the anteorbital white tufts forwards to the sides of the muzzle, the whole of the upper side of the face being therefore deep black. . . ." After further detailed description, he made the telling observation that the well-known horn in the Florence Museum, "which had long been a wonder to all sportsmen," could therefore be presumed to belong to this new subspecies. In conclusion, Thomas announced that considering "Mr. Varian had taken great pains to secure specimens of this animal, and to obtain information about its range," and had taken steps "to induce the local authorities to give it protection," it was with much pleasure that he proposed to distinguish it as a new subspecies under the name *Hippotragus niger variani,* and to register the new type specimen as B.M. No. 16.2.21.1.

How living creatures are classified and given their scientific names is a complex subject, and has its own history. Since the 1960s taxonomists have abided by the International Code of Zoological Nomenclature, which superseded many previous conventions and agreements governing how organisms can be named (and disputes settled). Even in Thomas's day it was no simple matter to do what he did; there were any number of "knotty points," as he referred to them. Numerous scientific names given to mammals before World War I have since fallen into disuse as a result of continual revisions made to the classificatory schemes of zoological taxonomy. But Thomas's recognition of the subspecies *Hippotragus niger variani* would remain unquestioned for the next eighty years.

On February 19, *The Field* published a notice by R. I. Pocock, one of the members in attendance at the Zoological Society's meeting, of Oldfield Thomas's proposal "to regard the Angolan black-faced, long-horned sable as a distinct race . . . named after Mr. H. F. Varian," who had "most generously presented" heads and horns "of each sex to the national collection in the British Museum." A photo of the bull sable's skull and horns accompanied the text. This public recognition could hardly have been more gratifying for Varian, particularly as he was about to go off to war—or at least, so he thought. At the War Office, where he'd already sent an application in advance, the engineer was told he was too old: almost forty. After all his efforts, and the distance he had traveled, Varian was bitterly disappointed to be turned down. Every man was needed; the situation looked dark for the Allies at the beginning of 1916, and the longest and one of the bloodiest engagements of the war, a conflict that would suck in two million combatants, had just begun—the Battle of Verdun.

But once again the intervention of an old friend got him what he wanted. That afternoon, by chance, he met a fellow hunter, now a general on forty-eight hours' leave, who offered to take up his case at a dinner party with someone who could help. At nine o'clock the next morning Varian received a message at the Bath Club. Inside was the news he hoped for: report to the War Office as soon as possible. In the very same office where he'd been refused the day before, he was asked if he could appear in three days' time at the Royal Engineers' Depot.

Varian quickly wrote a response to Pocock's notice in *The Field*, posted it, and then sent a note to Oldfield Thomas on February 25. "I would have liked to have come to see you again but will not be able to do so for some time as the War Office has called me up and I have to report in uniform 2d Lt. on Monday morning and proceed to Longmore for training." Ever the naturalist, he reminds Thomas that he has sent him a sitatunga body skin, and that the head is available if he wants to examine it. Varian's letter of acknowledgment to *The Field* appeared a day later.

It starts with a small correction: Mr. Pocock, Varian points out, should not have credited him with shooting the sable specimens; he only "collected them for identification." Varian would have considered it vulgar to boast, much less gloat, but his clear satisfaction at the outcome emerges between the next few lines. "It is about seven years since I first mentioned, in a letter to *The Field* on the game in Angola, the existence of this large species of sable east of the Quanza river. I mentioned Mr. Essington Brown's horns of 54½ in., a length which was somewhat strongly disputed by your correspondent 'Mannlicher,' who doubted the correctness of the measurement. Some years later I measured a pair out there of 56¼ in. belonging to Mr. Lane, a missionary, and I wrote to you accordingly to support my previous statement. Since then these heads have become comparatively dwarfed, and at present I know of four which measure over 60 in." Varian cautions that "these animals only exist in a restricted district, so far as is known at present, and they are not plentiful." He adds a final touch: "Before I left for England I had the satisfaction of seeing the governor's proclamation of that district as a special game reserve."

Mannlicher's letter in the same issue, also written in response to Pocock, lacked even a hint of apology, much less humility. He never mentioned Varian: "Much as I deprecate the constant nomination of new sub-species, I am glad to see Mr. Pocock's letter in which he separates the sable antelope of Angola from those of other districts . . . I shot one in Barotseland eleven years ago which measured 50¼ in., then about high-water mark for sable; but the extraordinary heads that have since been traded from Angola opened up a new type. I think there is small doubt that if a few really experienced shikaris hunted in that country, the limit might reach 65 in. or over." Mannlicher's mean-spirited response did not matter; the controversy was finished and Varian had been vindicated.

The next day Frank Varian reported for service. Ten days later he was in France, attached to the Fourth Army on the Somme. Varian described his reconnaissance work reporting on the possibilities of connecting Allied railways with those behind the German lines as "a most interesting job." The winter of 1917–18 ("a very cold one at that") was spent on railway work in the Ypres Salient behind Passchendaele. Robert Williams had applied to the army to have Varian released so he could return to Angola; shipping losses from submarine attacks made plans to ship nitrates from South America across the Atlantic to Lobito and then to England look attractive to the war effort. But by then Varian was the only one of six officers in his company that had escaped being killed or wounded. He would not abandon his men, and asked to be allowed to remain where he was. He must have been injured shortly after that, however, because a second application for his release came through when Varian—now Captain Varian—was hospitalized in Rouen, just before the Armistice. This time he accepted, and returned to Africa.

THE GIANT SABLE had stepped out of the shadows of the *miombo* forest onto the pages of sporting journals and scientific proceedings and into the imaginations of all those who would desire to embrace it, possess it, and know it. The first of many to seek the newly recognized antelope was Capt. Gilbert Blaine, a sportsman and a respected naturalist. Oldfield Thomas had expressed hope in his 1916 paper that "a complete specimen of this splendid addition to the list of African Antelopes would soon be obtained for the National Museum," and Blaine arranged with the museum to do just that, in the company of Capt. P. Van der Byl, who also hoped to collect giant sable specimens. They traveled out together, arriving in August of 1919. After proceeding upcountry to Huambo, they set out for the giant sable country, then 150 miles from the railhead.

Varian, who was engaged in reconnaissance work for the railway to reassess the route after the war, decided to pay them a visit before the rains started in September. It wasn't entirely a social call. By now he had a proprietary interest in the animal; he was, in a way, the beast's godfather. From this point forward, Varian would often be critical of other collectors and their motives, and highly protective of the animal he had struggled to bring to the world's notice. Of course, his idea of honoring the antelope was to mount guard on the species, not protect each individual creature. He was perfectly aware that "his" antelope would be a magnet for museum collectors and "specialist sportsmen engaged in the collection of rarer species." He had to see for himself what they were up to.

Varian put out inquiries along the way, and long before reaching their camp, the "bush telegraph" had told him that the two hunters had had no luck, even though they had been there for weeks. When he reached their camp, Varian discovered that Van der Byl had contracted malaria and would have to be evacuated to a nearby mission station, and eventually the coast to return to England empty-handed. But that evening Blaine staggered into camp late, and triumphant: he had shot his first giant sable for the museum.

Varian did not record his reaction. But it would have been difficult for the engineer to dislike Blaine. He was a distinguished collector who had traveled throughout Africa, a man of science who wrote detailed papers on the taxonomy of herbivores with the kind of eloquence that gave his expeditions the air of an aesthetic enterprise. In his later articles, Varian often resorted to quoting large chunks from Blaine. Blaine wrote lovingly of the majestic giant sable bulls and the subtly variable arcs of their immense horns. Every exquisite detail was described with a connoisseur's discernment—the hair inside the ears, the tan patches on the backs of the hocks, the glossy black forehead and foreface, even the buff color of the "lacrymal tufts with extension upwards in the form of a frontally converging whorl of hair to the level of the eyebrows." He described the prototypical giant sable bull, "black among black shadows," in the forest, resting in beds of pink flowers, disclosing his presence only by a great pair of curving horns rising above the undergrowth, and how the surrounding herd at rest would "all rise together as by a preconcerted signal, and wander off slowly grazing." The bulls, he noted, have a "peculiar pungent smell, which pervades the whole animal and clings to the skin for weeks after death, in spite of daily exposure to the sun and wind."

By the end of the autumn of 1919, Capt. Blaine had collected a half-dozen giant sable specimens, bulls, cows, and juveniles, for the Natural History Museum. Although Varian never said so, he may well have chafed at this, thinking how much more fitting it would be if *he* could be the one to supply the museum with a complete and splendid specimen of the "new sable." In any event, he regarded Oldfield Thomas's wish as a promise he had to redeem personally, and shortly after the visit Varian decided to hunt for a giant sable bull himself. Ever the conscientious engineer, he felt he could spare only a few days from his reconnaissance work. After spending a day with Blaine, Varian moved off with his men twelve miles to the south, where he had seen signs of sable on the way up.

The next day, he and his men located a herd with eight cows and a mature bull but, as he had not seen any others for comparison, refrained from shooting. If he was going to collect a single specimen for the museum, then it had to be more than a good example; it had to be an exemplar of the race. The following day he hunted hard with no luck. Varian was no amateur in the African bush, but he was getting nowhere, even with his own men. He turned to the region's inhabitants, the Lwimbi— "the people of the two rivers." In Varian's opinion, they were a "poor lot"— mere beekeepers. They had no cattle, only a few sheep and goats, scarcely cultivated, and apparently subsisted mainly on wild fruits and honey. But they would have an intimate knowledge of the terrain and the game in this sparsely populated district. He engaged "a likely-looking local native" who offered to show him where the sable were. Varian followed him for hours through the bush. They wandered aimlessly until it dawned on the hapless hunter that his guide was taking an inspection tour of his beehives instead of tracking sable. He quickly dismissed him. Anxious to make up for lost time, Varian hunted from dawn to dusk for two days, but without luck. He was becoming despondent; there was only one day left for the chase.

The next morning he and his men found fresh spoor of what seemed to be a sable bull, but the indistinct track in the dry ground might have been that of a large roan. He followed it until it joined the tracks of a sable herd, confirming his hopes. Pushing through the thick bush was maddening; the flush foliage made it impossible to see ahead, and the unending torment of the mopani bees, tiny insects that clustered in one's nose, ears, and eyes, made stalking the herd a penance. By ten o'clock they found the bush too thick, and the wind all wrong. Circling around in more open country to where they thought the herd was, they finally peered through the brush to find no sign of the animals. "They have flown up into the air," one of the men commented, and Varian could only concur. The wind had shifted and the herd, which had been close by after all, had taken off at the hunting party's scent.

Three hours later Varian had tracked them to where they were resting in more open bush. Through a screen of trees he saw the black form

59

of the bull on the far side of the herd, but one alert young male stood sentry on the side of a prominent ant heap, "the only cover for an approach, with the wind as it was." The big bull looked especially fine, and Varian knew this would be his last opportunity for some time. He would have to crawl on bare knees, alone, in a slow circle through the burnt stubble to reach the ant heap without alarming the younger male. The heat was building in advance of an approaching storm, and the mopani bees would not let up. The insects had forced Varian to crawl with his eyes closed, and he could only stop and slowly swipe the sweat-stuck bugs away with a careful finger when he dared to lift his head to check his painful progress, blinking in the bright sun. After another long, blind crawl with the unrelenting bees clustering maddeningly around every orifice in his head, Varian paused to squint and saw "a nasty-looking brown mass immediately in the path ahead"—a deadly puff adder uncoiling at the intrusion. Fighting the almost irresistible impulse to leap back, Varian slid to the side as smoothly as he could, and then continued the crawl, "accompanied with deep prayer." Reaching the tall ant heap, he gave himself a few minutes to let his heart stop pounding, hoping all the while that the young male hadn't been alerted.

Finally he climbed up the side of the ant mound, took off his hat, and peeked over the top. He had a clear view of the young male's rump, and beyond, "the herd bull, as black as jet, and a magnificent sight, was standing up, side on, rubbing his huge horns against a tree trunk, about one hundred yards away." After digging out the bees that had squirmed into his eyes, Varian brought up his rifle ever so slowly into position without disturbing the apparently dozing sentry. But there was a problem: he had to rest his double-barreled .400/.360 directly on the ant heap instead of cradling it in his hand, something which was sure to throw off the shot. He aimed carefully and as the sights lined up tellingly on the center of the herd bull's shoulder, he decided to take the chance. He squeezed the trigger; the rifle recoiled sharply upwards from the too solid rest, causing the bullet to strike high in the giant sable's shoulder, but knocking him down with his legs spread out from under him. The young male reared up at the ear-splitting report—Varian had fired over his back—and galloped off with the cows. The herd bull staggered back to his feet and cantered off before Varian could get off another shot. After a long, hard chase tracking the wounded sable's blood spoor, coming close several times but unable to get a clear shot through the bush, Varian was finally able to approach the wounded bull, now lying down as darkness was falling, and finish it off.

The storm that had been threatening all day then rumbled and broke, drenching the hunter and his fallen prey, but Varian was determined to save the complete skin and bring it back to camp to be carefully prepared and preserved; it was, after all, the reason for the grave exercise of that hunt. "The head, with its flesh and horns, is itself a heavy burden, but, with a wet skin attached, it made a very awkward load, more especially at night going through bush. There were only two natives and myself to carry it, but camp was reached late in the evening. We had been away from it for fifteen hours of hard going," he recounted, but adding "the results were worth it." Yes, it was a splendid trophy of a hard hunt, yet it was far more than that. Varian himself—the animal's discoverer and guardian—would be able to give this superb specimen, a symbol of all that he had achieved for this animal, to the Natural History Museum.

THREE

"THE FINEST HORNS IN THE WORLD"

The giant sable antelope had all the attributes that triggered pursuit by passionate hunters: it was magnificent and rare and so hidden in its distant forest haunts it would be unattainable to all but the most determined. The measures that were taken to protect it only made it more prized, and from the 1920s through the 1960s the dark antelope would be hunted relentlessly—but it was never easy to seize that great trophy.

IT WAS CHRISTMAS of 1917 when Colonel J. C. B. Statham first met Frank Varian in No. 2 Red Cross Hospital in Rouen. They were both patients there that brutal winter, and the wards full of the sick and maimed kept the scenes of war they'd witnessed uncomfortably vivid. When they discovered that they had golden Africa in common, they spent hours in conversation reliving earlier days in better lands. They shared impressions, experiences, opinions, and of course ended up talking of game. Varian described an animal Statham had never heard of: the giant sable of Angola. Varian would remember that "I told him that I was returning to my job in Angola as soon as I was released from the Army, and that if he cared to come out there I would do what I could for him."

Statham heard something far more seductive than a simple invitation. His first trip to Africa had been a pilgrimage to where Livingstone's heart was buried, and the chance to follow in the footsteps of his boyhood hero through Angola—and to obtain photographs and specimens of this rare animal—was irresistible. He would go "in quest of the giant sable."

In April of 1920, Col. Statham sailed to Madeira to await a Portuguese ship to Angola. Statham's 1922 narrative of his adventure, *Through Angola, A Coming Colony,* is a mix of hunting diary, travelogue, political tract, retold history, and smug racism—in other words, a useful compendium of typical colonial attitudes of the period. He bemoaned the fact that the Portuguese had done such a poor job of colonizing Angola, but saw definite progress in the Benguela Railway, the iron road that was "a sign to all men that the peace of civilization has come at last and to stay." But his aspirations for native Angolans stopped somewhat short: "I like the savage black," he said, "but it is difficult to feel the same degree of friendship for the partly educated Negro."

Arriving in Luanda, the colonel found the capital "full of American oil engineers. A very fine lot of young fellows were these Americans, full of go, or 'pep,' as they themselves call it," he wrote, prophetically noting that they were "very optimistic about the oil future of the country." In fact, so many prospectors, entrepreneurs, and company promoters were competing for oil, timber, mineral, and further rail concessions that he had to reassure the governor-general that his purpose for heading into the interior was only to hunt and photograph animals. Statham spent several days obtaining the now necessary permits for firearms and a general license to shoot, hiring a cook and a houseboy, and buying provisions for his trek; he had decided to enter the giant sable country from the north by taking the Portuguese train directly to Malange before heading south on foot.

At Malange, Statham hired twenty carriers from the workforce that had been commandeered by the local governor. Including food, each porter cost a single escudo (about a shilling) per day, and as Statham was unsure how long his trek would take, the Portuguese kindly allowed him to pay the men on completion of service—provided that their pay was sent to the authorities. The carriers, seven of whom were "undersized" and four of whom were mere boys, protested that they would see little of the wages, but Statham found it "impossible to believe" the majority of officials would practice "such petty larceny." His eighteen loads of equipment, each weighing up to fifty-five pounds, included everything necessary to function in the bush, from a tent and chairs to books of poetry to cooking gear to cameras, cartridges, flour, chutney, and sardines. One load consisted of a giant sable skull borrowed from a local trader, who told Statham it

had been shot "at a place called 'Cangandalla,' some 15 miles to the south."
As soon as he saw the skull, he "realized how much better it would be to
have the real thing than a picture" to query any natives.

Nineteen miles southeast of Malange city, Statham's briskly marching caravan reached the military post of Cangandala, where the district officer had him to dinner. Afterwards he sent for the *sovas*, the headmen of
the neighboring villages, to question them about the giant sable. Statham
knew that the animal was called *Sumbakaloko* by the Lwimbi tribes in the
area. But the name meant nothing to these Songo. "The moment, however,
the natives saw our giant sable skull, they all said '*Kolwah, Kolwah . . .*'"

The *sovas* told the white men that the *Kolwah* was only found south
of the Luando, between that river and its parent stream, the Cuanza—
omitting mention (for they must have known otherwise) of another population centered just a day's march to the east. Statham failed to notice the
contradiction between these claims and the fact that the head he'd brought
came from Cangandala; his plan was to march south to determine the
northern boundary of the giant sable lands. In fact, after he published his
account, both Varian and Blaine credited him with doing so—the giant
sables east of Cangandala, a small population of several hundred, would
not be "discovered" until the 1960s.

After leaving Cangandala, Statham pushed south toward the reedy
banks of the Cuanza, where, hoping to bag a sitatunga in the failing light,
he fired at "a glimpse of a brown shaggy body and a big pair of long twisted
horns moving in the swamp," but only wounded it. Three days later, one
of his men discovered the decomposing carcass and recovered the horns.
It is the beginning of a series of overeager, trigger-happy hunts that seem
all the starker for being followed later in his book by a solemn recitation
of hunting ethics ("Stalk with infinite care, and when you have come up
with the animal, shoot to kill, for it is, at the very least, the beast's due that
he should suffer as little as possible for your sport"). Several days later he
and his line of porters crossed the Luando River, some fifteen miles from
its junction with the Cuanza. Statham had now entered the long, tilted
watershed between the two rivers flowing to the northwest. It was open,
high plateau country, some 3,000 feet in altitude at the conjunction of
the rivers, slowly rising to over 4,000 feet in the hilly and forested southern end. As the region was narrow, varying from twenty to thirty miles in

width, Statham decided to make a series of traverses across it, working his way down. After a three-hour march he reached a settlement on the small stream of the Rumelia. There the natives told him "that all the country between the Luando and Cuanza rivers is the 'house' of the giant sable." But the great beast, they explained, would not be found beyond the deep, wide, crocodile-guarded rivers, nor beyond the inhospitable swamps some 150 miles to the south.

The next day, hunting in the forest, Statham and his men stumbled upon a bull sable a hundred yards off, its forequarters hidden by a tree. The sight of its huge curved horns, clearly visible on both sides of the tree trunk, so astonished the hunter that he simply stared at the animal in wonder. By the time he recovered and began to approach, the bull ran off and eluded their dogged pursuit. But Statham's luck changed on August 16, his "red-letter day." He found a herd of twenty or thirty sable grazing in open grassland, "the sun glinting on the bright chestnut coats of the cows and the deep black skin of the one big sable bull." Its horns looked immense, even though it was the farthest away. Statham stalked the bull, but the herd grew alarmed. Opening fire at 250 yards and missing several times, he finally hit the bull with his fourth shot. The rifle jammed, but one of his "boys" arrived with a back-up weapon. He approached the badly wounded, slowly walking sable, and knocked it down with another shot. "He lay so still that I thought he must be dead, and walked up to him somewhat carelessly. When within some 10 yards, the bull jumped up and charged me, and I had some difficulty in avoiding the sweep of his horns just before he was killed at very close range."

Statham examined his prize: the body seemed much larger than an ordinary sable's, a shoulder height roughly four feet, nine inches, "and the horns, which were very massive and had little curve, 54 inches." Although he was happy to be in possession of a "splendid trophy," he was far from satiated, and killed two more in the next three days. Statham then struck camp and headed southeast, where the fields around the local villages were full of tantalizing sable tracks but no animals that could be found. The only sable he encountered was in the form of a cracked and weather-worn skull, the empty sockets staring out from a village grave. As they passed through the area, the natives shyly pointed out a small bush near the chief's house, covered with the skulls of hares, duiker, genet, ratels, and several other animals which he could not identify. The meaning of that mysterious array of bones in a bush—that it represented a hunter's shrine honoring the ancestral shades who govern success in hunting— escaped Statham. He could only think of the threatening skies and that tracking, which had been difficult on the dry, dusty ground, would be easier after the first rain softened the earth.

STATHAM WAS TOO swept up in his own immoderate passion to be curious about that hunter's shrine, but something half-hidden partly emerges from his narrative: the special regard for the great antelope that the Songo and the Lwimbi held in his day, and which would persist for decades afterwards. Songo and Lwimbi beliefs about the giant sable have never been adequately studied, and the wars that have engulfed Angola in modern times and scattered its peoples may have eliminated the chance of ever doing it. But among closely related peoples of the region, antelope horn is widely used in divination, as well as a repository of supernatural substances. The larger the horns, the more majestic the antelope, the more power resides in them. Such potent horns, added to a deceased hunter's shrine, become a threshold of communication with the shades. The tip of a horn, touched with powdered white clay, is the point of contact with the hunting ancestor, the horn and rings the passageway to the spirit world.

The Songo were known as fisherfolk, the Lwimbi beekeepers; both cultivated crops and kept chickens and goats. Their hunting may have been limited, but their beliefs about it were similar to those of the traditional hunting cults common to tribes found throughout the larger region. The Ndembu of northwestern Zambia on the Angolan border say that *Wubinda*, the bow-hunters' cult, is the oldest. Its offshoot, *Wuyang'a*, the gun-hunter's cult, grew from the introduction of muzzle-loading weapons by Ovimbundu traders from the Angolan highlands who traveled to the east through the lands of the Songo and Lwimbi in the latter half of the nineteenth century, exchanging firearms for slaves they could sell to the Portuguese.

66

In both cults, a hunter, whether equipped with a bow (*wuta*) or, more rarely, a precious ancient flintlock (*wutawakesi*, or "bow of fire"), learned that he faced not only the visible dangers of the bush but the invisible afflictions of "witches, sorcerers, ghosts, were-lions, and persecuting ancestors," as anthropologist Victor Turner, who studied the Ndembu in the early 1950s, had described it. Each cult had similar but different rites, or grades of initiation; attainment of huntsmanship at each level required not only proficiency in killing animals but knowledge of the cult mysteries, which revolved around the understanding of how failure in the field pointed to a "malignant manifestation of a deceased hunter ancestor," who might cause game to disappear, make the hunter mysteriously miss his aim, and so on. In the stage of *Mukaala*, Turner was told, the afflicting ancestor-shade wears skins and leaves, whistles in the bush to warn game of the hunter's approach, glows like marsh light to lure the hunter into a swamp, and rides the lead animal of a herd of antelope, causing them to bolt before the hunter can get within range. Each stage of advancement in a hunter's prowess is marked by a period of misfortune brought about by the failure to propitiate the shades of ancestors with proper offerings at their shrines, the failure to share meat from the hunt with the village, or some other grave failure to observe what is required of a true hunter.

What was disturbing to the Songo and Lwimbi was not so much that others came from far away to hunt the giant sable, but that they did it without the help of the shades—and without incurring their wrath. That Africans feared the colonials goes without saying; their apprehension is evident in the rite of *Mundeli* in the bow-hunter's cult. Turner was told by Ndembu hunters that *Mundeli* was an affliction brought by the Ovimbundu from Angola, who thought that the Europeans they first saw must have come out of the sea—they were as pale as drowned people with bleached skins. The Ovimbundu called them *ondele*, the word for "ancestral shade," because they were as white as spirits. Turner quoted one Ndembu's explanation of how the stage of *Mundeli* manifests itself: "The hunter has been unlucky and killed no animals for a long time. He then dreams he sees a European near the water," or in a *katala*, a little ritual hut that serves as a halfway house for the dead. "The European tells him, 'From now on I am not going to give you an animal because you have erred with regard to me.'"

Perhaps the Songo and the Lwimbi were torn between wanting to assist and ingratiate themselves with these all-powerful European hunters, and fearing that helping these slaughterous men would be dangerous. The meat the whites could share with those who helped them hunt was alluring for many, but for others it might well have seemed ill-gotten, tainted. What foreign hunter ever impaled bits of choice flesh from the hunt on the sharpened tips of a bush shrine's forked branches, the ones that stood for the tines of antelope horns, to honor the hunters who came before? Was it disturbing that the white man did not understand or care about the cult of hunting and the role of the shades? Did the tribes fear that their ancestors would look with displeasure on those who aided such impious slayers of animals? All that is known is that those who tried to deflect foreign hunters from their pursuit of the great antelope only succeeded in delaying them for a time—nothing more.

AFTER THREE WEEKS of hunting, Statham had given completely in to his bloodlust, and could not stop. The beasts fell, more or less predictably, to his bullets. He recited, as if to remind himself, all the reasons photography was superior to shooting, but he was largely deaf to his own arguments, and let the seductive power of the antelope excuse his excesses. Exhausted from the heat and effort and plagued by malarial mosquitoes at night, Statham succumbed to fever and was reduced to choking down the foul water from the local salty springs to check his raging thirst. Although so weak from the attack he had to be carried in a hammock, he went out hunting the next day and wounded a sable bull, who staggered off into the forest.

Statham and his men moved south to the right bank of the Cuanza, past villages that had been abandoned years before, after epidemics of smallpox swept through the area. He found the Songo people there much reduced in number, and their villages "small and wretchedly built." Statham cut back across the watershed toward the Luando and to the Portuguese post of Quimbango, and then south again, where most of his films were destroyed in a fire set by a falling candle. "Within a minute I had lost the work of weeks," he noted bitterly. "There are not even ashes left." The handful he would bring back and publish would have to suffice, stark black-and-white images of distant herds silhouetted against the horizon and of fallen bulls on the forest floor.

After the disastrous fire, Statham headed east, to the rolling country tucked between the smaller Luce and Lussingue Rivers that Blaine and Varian had penetrated the year before. Statham saw sable tracks everywhere in this land of glade and open forest, full of what the Lwimbi called the "sable bush"—a slender stemmed plant that wound its tendrils around bush and trees, its dark green oval leaves accented by a small fragrant pink flower—a favorite of the animals when the grass they normally fed on was rank or dry. In this *palanca* paradise, temptation came again to Statham, this time in the form of a herd of thirty sables grazing in the shadows of an open forest near the Luce River. It was an hour before sunset, and Statham was quick to notice the five bulls, including one huge, grand specimen. "My one desire," he insisted, "was to get a photograph, and replace some of those that had been lost." Crawling toward the sable in the failing light with his bulky, long-lens camera, his grumbling local guide behind him with his gun, the stalker saw the herd falling back quietly from them as fast as they could creep forward on hands and knees, "and all this time the sun was sinking lower, the shadows were lengthening, and all hope of taking photographs was slowly dying out." The penitent shooter's resolve began to waver when the guide began pleading in a hoarse, insistent whisper in the white man's ear that he wanted meat for his village.

Statham exchanged the cumbersome camera for the familiar heft of his rifle and let the question be decided "by the big bull of the herd." Suspicious, watchful, the bull broke away from the cows and walked slowly back to challenge the intruders, neck arched, mane erect, shaking his great horns. At a hundred yards, the bull stopped and pawed the ground. "A splendid sight," Statham recalled, declaring that he "bitterly regretted the hopeless light and his useless camera." Suddenly, the bull—perhaps warned by a glint of dying sun on the rifle barrel—turned and gave Statham a glorious view of his great bowed horns in profile, leaving the hunter weak with desire. "I was after all but the villain of the story, where the sable was the hero; and by these immense horns I was tempted, and fired." The bull walked shakily forward with a dignified step, and then fell over dead.

Statham was thrilled that the bull was as impressive under the tape as he looked in life—he was a fifty-nine incher. "I hope the reader will not judge me a butcher," he confessed, offering a weak defense centering on the "discontent of the meatless Negro." But he swore off shooting for the next week to concentrate on photography.

Did Statham finally realize that his quest had been fulfilled several times over, and that piling up yet more pairs of horns in camp would only further darken his dubious accomplishment? Perhaps his passion had simply been exhausted. In any case, his journey through the giant sable country was over. By September 23 he had forded the Cuanza near the village of Chouso in the marshy south. There his men found the final memento of the expedition into the watershed, a small chameleon clinging to a tree that Statham tamed, named, and kept leashed to his shirt as a lizardly boutonniere. On the rattling rail ride down from Chinguar to the port of Lobito, "Jimmy" entertained Statham's fellow passengers in the carriage with his own little nature dramas, unexpectedly lashing out his eight-inch tongue to snap up unsuspecting flies. When Statham wasn't watching, however, he tried to slip his tiny arms out of his little harness and make his escape.

Statham returned to the subject of the animal with "the wondrous massive horns" at the very end of his book. There he made a plea for the Portuguese to form game reserves and restrict hunting in their colony before the once plentiful wildlife disappeared. "There is one animal that I hope will be saved by new game laws: the wonderful giant sable of Angola," he concluded. "Easy to shoot, a prize to the needy hunter, and largely if not entirely confined to a narrow watershed between two deep rivers, a few herds of the giant sable await certain extermination unless shielded. Only such protection as is afforded to royal game can, and should, save a beast which is so truly royal."

Frank Varian thought these remarks hypocritical. The ghastly photograph Statham included in his book showing a row of seven giant sable bull horns and one set of cow horns, their huge hoops fencing off his tent, disgusted the engineer. Thirty years after seeing it, he still resented that Statham had killed so many bulls: "After he had committed this slaughter, like Satan reproving sin, he announced that no one else should be allowed to kill any more giant sable!" Even so, Varian remembered him with characteristic generosity, as "a keen and clever naturalist" who "came to a sad end in India, stung to death by bees."

But it was clear to Varian that more serious steps had to be taken to protect the giant sable. The poaching of the Boers and the pit traps of the natives were bad enough, but uncontrolled trophy hunting would surely doom the animal, and Statham's book, whatever its shortcomings, had virtually transformed the giant sable into a Grail beast; it was sure to fire the passions of numerous trophy hunters. Once again, the animal's discoverer came to its rescue, and again, luck was on his side. He had been called back to England to report on the information he had gathered on his recent 1919–20 survey expedition, and shortly after his arrival in London, had a morning meeting with Robert Williams and Gen. Norton de Matos to discuss the last 500 miles of the Benguela Railroad across Angola.

Norton de Matos had been Angola's governor-general from 1912 to 1915, and had recently become Portuguese high commissioner for the colony. A vigorous administrator, he used his sweeping powers to encourage foreign investment, open thousands of miles of roads across the colony, and check some of the excesses of the forced labor system. Later, at a grand luncheon party given in his honor, attended by members of the Portuguese embassy, Norton de Matos suggested a walk in the park to follow the banquet. Varian used the opportunity to "explain to him about the rare animal in his territory about which so many people were inquiring." The high commissioner was intrigued. "I asked," Varian recalled, "if it would not be possible to make the Giant Sable Antelope royal game, and to afford the area in which they lived the closest protection." De Matos was sympathetic, and as they were both returning to Angola, he asked Varian to write to him, giving a full description of the species and its habitat. In 1922 the high commissioner issued a decree closing the district to shooting and entry—except by "special license." How effectively this first effort at conservation of the giant sable would be enforced remained to be seen, but the action taken, wrote Varian, "no doubt saved one of Africa's rarest animals from the fate which has overtaken so many others."

SLAVERY IN ANGOLA never really came to an end under colonial rule; it had endured there for four hundred years and was to last, under other names, for nearly a century more. It had provided 80 percent of Angola's commerce before 1832 and the colony's settlers could not conceive of life in Angola without it; for decades they successfully resisted all attempts to end it. When Portuguese prime minister Sá da Bandeira decreed in 1836 that all traffic in slaves from Portuguese possessions should cease, it took until 1845 before an Angolan governor could enforce its suppression. The 1858 compromise decree, promulgated by Sá da Bandeira, provided that all Africans then held in slavery would be set free in twenty years. The humanitarian statesman wanted to bring an end to the practice of "whites continuing to exploit the services of the Negroes, as they have done for centuries." The legislation was met with violent protests. In 1869 the government in Lisbon made all slaves *libertos*, which meant that they were to be paid as workers until freed in 1878. This effort may have only served to give the *colonos* the idea that they could keep their slaves as long as they called them something else. Subsequent legislation on the issue attempted to do two contradictory things: grant Africans their independence on paper while guaranteeing Europeans an unending supply of labor in practice.

A new set of regulations came into effect in 1878 which sought to replace free labor with forced labor; unfortunately for Angola's native population, it contained a clause on vagrancy, which was easily exploited: Africans not already under contract were routinely declared vagrants, and forced into servitude. By 1899, all pretense was dropped in the revised native labor code. A committee of the Overseas Ministry put it baldly:

> The state, not only as a sovereign of semi-barbaric populations, but also as a depository of social authority, should have no scruples in *obliging* and, if necessary, *forcing* these rude Negroes in Africa . . . to work, that is, to better themselves by work, to acquire through work the happiest means of existence, to civilize themselves through work . . .

Africans who had capital or a paying profession, who farmed a suitable plot, or who produced goods for export in suitable quantities were considered to have fulfilled this obligation; all others—except, supposedly, women, children, and the sick and aged—could be forced to fulfill it by the public authorities. To ensure there be would be enough work to go around for these indolent blacks, the services of Africans could be requisitioned from the provincial authorities by various governmental agencies, private companies, and individuals. The minimal obligations of employers toward their workers—how they were to be transported, fed, housed, paid, and the like—lacked enforcement guarantees, which meant they could be, and would be, ignored with impunity. It was commonplace to give these laborers the most difficult work in the fields and factories; after all, their complaints could be answered by floggings with a hippopotamus-hide whip, which cut the skin horribly. "Very frequently," as one contemporary account put it, "one heard in the late hour of a warm mysterious African night piercing shrieks of pain from the poor wretches who were being beaten by the company officers or head men, generally hard-hearted mulattoes."

The colonial authorities largely shrugged off muckraking investigations into its labor practices. But it was not as if there hadn't been any internal efforts to change the system. Over the centuries, a series of reform-minded Portuguese in Angola sought to mitigate the unceasing exploitation of the land's indigenous peoples. Historians credit the eighteenth-century governor-general of Angola Francisco de Sousa Coutinho with decrees that threatened punishment for enslaving free Africans. By the early 1900s a few Portuguese were boldly accusing their countrymen of treating Africans as little more than beasts of burden. "Our anti-social policy does not know how to civilize the black, it only knows how to punish him, and punishes as treason that which is merely ignorance," wrote one observer. By 1917, however, the international outcry over contract laborers on São Tomé resulted in the repatriation of almost all workers from the islands after their terms were up, although the pittance that they earned for their years of grinding toil was paid in cloth and a handful of trade goods.

Statham, who stopped at São Tomé briefly on his way to and from Angola in 1920, scoffed at the talk of "Portuguese slave traffic"; he thought it as groundless as the stories of Belgian "rubber atrocities" in the Congo, hysterical propaganda put out by "a certain press, controlled and supported by faddists and Little Englanders."

COLONEL STATHAM'S PASSION for the giant sable was soon shared by others, including a family from Boston. Hoping for the usual lion and buffalo, among other game, but also hoping to photograph trees and collect flowers and lizards, Richard C. Curtis and his brother Charles Jr., their father, Charles Sr., and Richard's wife, Anita, arrived in Nairobi in May 1923 for a three-month safari. No less a guide than Philip Percival, who accompanied Theodore Roosevelt on his East African expedition and was later to become Ernest Hemingway's "white hunter," was their outfitter. Charles Sr. had been to Africa before but it was all fresh to his sons and Anita — the personalities of the porters and idiosyncrasies of the horses, the bright hopes of morning hunts, the stalks and reassuring boom of the .450 double, the misery of missed or wounded and lost quarry, the midday meal followed by an hour of reading (Jane Austen was a favorite), the "commissary work" of shooting guinea fowl.

At night the chairs were pulled close to the campfire, pipes lit, the day's events recalled and the next day's excitement planned. The family swapped hunting yarns with Percival and dreamed aloud of trophies to come. That is how Part II of *Hunting in Africa East and West* opens, one evening on the Loita Plains when the talk had turned to the newly discovered giant sable. "A better setting to dream of further adventures could not be imagined," Richard Curtis wrote, "well out in the lion country and well removed from such limitations as maps and time-tables." They had read Colonel Statham's book, and took it as gospel "that the giant sable antelope was worth having at any price," for no other head in Africa would "bear comparison." The Curtises were determined to take up the quest and seek the beast themselves. Unfortunately, they knew next to nothing of Angola, but they thought they could "land somewhere on the coast and take a railroad inland."

Two weeks later, their safari in the Kenya Colony was over. It was the end of July, and Charles had to catch the first steamer north through the Suez Canal to return home, but Anita, Richard, and his father took a steamer from Mombasa to Cape Town and then another up the coast to Portuguese West Africa. "Such little details as distances, hotels, porters, food, and guides were all unknown," Curtis recalled, but they were optimistic it would somehow work out. Landing in Lobito on September 3, the Curtises discovered that Frank Varian, although called away on business, had put his house on the beach and his servants at their disposal. "We used to shudder as we passed the only local hotel; one look was enough to show how much we owed to Mr. Varian."

Their luck continued to hold; they had arrived not only at the right month but the right week to hunt giant sable. Realizing there was no time to lose, they split up: Charles Sr. took the train to Chinguar to make arrangements at the railhead, while Richard and Anita stayed to push their supplies through customs and take out the shooting licenses then required. "I believe that in theory the law requires a further special license for sable that can be obtained only at Loanda," Curtis noted, but this last requirement was waived, although they were limited to one sable apiece. They even took out a license for Anita, thinking to try for a third sable to offer to a museum. Clearly, it was not difficult to obtain a "special license" in the Angola of 1923.

Curtis and his wife boarded the Benguela Railway for Chinguar, some three hundred miles inland. Varian was waiting for them on the station platform at Huambo. As he had with Statham, he felt that he might as well be of assistance to any legitimate expedition for the giant sable if he expected to have any influence. He recommended that they head for the few square miles of land between the Luce and Lussingue Rivers, some seventy miles upstream from the junction of the Cuanza and the Luando, where most of the best heads had so far been shot.

Back on the train they spotted Charles Sr. on the platform at Bela Vista, just short of Chinguar. The efficient elder Curtis had already made contact with a missionary whose headquarters happened to be on the same street in Boston where they lived, and arranged to have tents, provisions, and the men already hired sent 130 miles ahead in a Ford truck, with a young resident Englishman, Alan Chapman, in charge. On September 10, the family headed northeast by automobile, delighted to be moving along at a twenty-five-mile-an-hour clip on dirt roads "almost as broad, as smooth, and as straight as any turnpike at home." These impressive motor tracks in the interior had all been built in the past several years by conscripted native labor—thus, as Curtis observed, "practically free of cost." In fact, the Portuguese authorities were so proud of them that oxcarts were prohibited for fear of causing ruts, although a wavy footpath weaving from side to side in the middle of the road showed that local Africans were allowed to use them, as long as they walked. The entire village of Capango turned out to witness their arrival at the English mission; theirs was only the seventh automobile the locals had ever seen.

The next day they sorted their loads and assembled their porters—mission boys, farm hands, and outlying natives. Eager to be off, they caved in to demands for wages far in excess of the going rate, settling on sixteen cents a day on the march, eight cents per diem in camp. ("I'd hate to carry fifty pounds on top of my head for fifteen miles a day at that price," Curtis conceded, noting that their food, three pounds of meal and beans a day, only added six cents more.) The three Curtises, Chapman, two trackers, a cook, seventy-one porters, and a couple of children, including a five year old who "marched along with an empty water gourd on top of his head," struck off that afternoon for the giant sable land. There were no horses, mules, or donkeys available for them—just hammocks slung on a twelve-foot pole carried by two men. Only Anita Curtis used hers regularly. Father and son spurned theirs, although it was difficult to walk in boots in the narrowing, winding ruts of the native paths without tripping, and the porters set a surprisingly brisk pace. It was the end of the dry season, the rains were overdue, and as they approached the Cuanza, the open scrub grew into seamless bush and the atmosphere grew close and warm.

Entering one settlement, Curtis was startled to see the villagers running out the back gate, something Statham and Varian had both experienced when they too had been mistaken for colonial authorities. "That was all, but it was enough to illustrate Portuguese rule," he commented. "Only a couple of the elders remained behind—I suppose they felt old enough to be safe—and bowed respectfully, one hand raised in salute and with heads up."

Curtis found the bush hot, thick, and confusing, crisscrossed with numerous branching paths, but the first man in line, who knew the way, blocked off each misleading side track as it came up with a warning branch. Two days after starting, they suddenly came upon the Cuanza, "a real river a hundred and twenty-five yards across and far too deep to ford." Curtis, his wife, and Chapman crossed to the settlement on the opposite bank in a dugout canoe. When they landed, "the whole village burst into roars of laughter" at the sight of Anita Curtis—possibly the first white woman to cross the upper Cuanza—wearing pants.

Several hours later the Curtis men, father and son, Chapman, and the two trackers they'd brought, Augusto and sharp-eyed Thomas, went hunting for camp meat and returned with three fat reedbuck. Later that night, by the light of the campfire, they were treated to the mission porters singing Christian hymns in Umbundu, including "God Save the King" and "Onward, Christian Soldiers." In gratitude, Anita brought out her hymnal the following Sunday and sang a few hymns herself for the mission boys, who recognized each one from the tune. But it was the "pagan porters" from Chapman's farm who insisted on carrying Anita in her hammock over streams, not trusting her to the mission boys, all the while "maintaining a continuous chatter of encouragement, warning, and advice to one another, with a grunt each time the pole was shifted from one shoulder to another or settled with a bump on top of their heads."

They paid a courtesy visit to the village of Mulundo, the residence of the absent chief of the Lwimbi, and were struck by the contrast of its serene hilltop setting and grove of great green trees and the surrounding sameness of bush. They found the settlement "surprisingly neat and clean," with square, mud-matted thatched-roof huts and the odd chicken pecking in the dirt. Curtis was not impressed with the inhabitants, however, finding them a "hungry, scattered tribe. They own no cattle and cultivate hardly at all. A little manioc and a little honey is all they live on." Curtis and his father persuaded some villagers to pose for photographs with Anita. In one, a man holds a long brass pipe and the women wear necklaces, beaded headbands, and aprons of skins. Anita smiles; the others frown.

The next day the expedition marched for some sixteen miles and pitched camp just south of the Lucé River. The next morning the hunters split up; Curtis took Thomas and one porter north, slowly and quietly through a continuous forest of stunted trees just coming into leaf, a "basket-work of branches" of limited visibility and in the grassy openings, numerous anthills, some spikelike and several feet tall, others "shaped like Japanese lanterns," and some towering fifteen to twenty feet high and supporting trees. They found tracks at about 7:30 A.M., and an hour later, after crawling behind Thomas on hands and knees to peer around the corner of a huge anthill, Curtis spotted his first giant sables: "I caught a glimpse of a dozen golden-chestnut cows, and then I saw a black beast, a coal, pitchy black, that seemed to belong to another race—the herd bull."

They followed their tracks until three in the afternoon. "Six times we came up with them, and twice I caught a flash of the bull's horns, great enormous horns out of proportion with the rest of his body, that made me catch my breath." Several times Curtis came close enough to fire but hesitated; he could shoot only one sable on his license and desperately wanted to be sure of a "big head." He attempted a shot with his .30-06 Springfield on one stalk, but only succeeded in wounding a cow that stepped in front of the bull. Curtis lost his temper and "used most improper language. All Thomas said was 'no,' and I still wonder what he meant."

All that week Curtis hunted hard with Thomas from sunrise to sunset, walking very slowly through the thick woods, knowing that "the next step might show a flash of chestnut or jet-black shadow. But as the sun climbed up and the day grew hot, the morning excitement began to die." By noon the temperature was over ninety and he was too tired and thirsty to take much interest in a lunch of hard-boiled eggs, nuts, and dates. The poor visibility made it all seem hopeless. Not that he didn't find tracking seductive. "To find a heart-shaped print stamped clean in the burnt, powdery soil and to follow its wanderings among the trees, to know that the herd must be just ahead . . ." But he couldn't tell fresh spoor from days-old tracks. Thomas, however, knew if it was from the night before or that very morning from the subtle layering of dew and dust, and Curtis left it to him to find sables. They spotted little other game and Curtis decided that "the giant sable insists upon reigning alone and drives everything else out of the country."

Half their hunting days were over if they were to catch the next steamer north, and neither Curtis nor his father, guided by Chapman, had had any luck. A day later, at their camp, thunderclouds towered, blackening the sky, and by sunset thunder rumbled in the distance, punctuated by lightning; at seven the first downpour of the season dampened the parched earth. With the ground likely to be perfect for tracking in the morning, the unlucky hunters decided to join forces. Leaving the camp at 5:30 A.M. the next morning, they found the large herd within an hour. Charles Sr. took careful aim at the herd bull with his .450 Holland & Holland from a sitting position, and toppled the beast with his first shot, although it managed to fade back into the woods as the copper-colored cows raced off. With Thomas slowly reading the tracks, the hunting party followed the trail for three hours, dreading the thick, cylindrically curled dried leaves that cracked loudly underfoot and betrayed their approach.

At long last, Thomas spotted the bull; Curtis, in the lead, managed to shoot him again, but it took three additional shots to put him down. Curtis was overwhelmed. "Unquestionably a giant sable has the finest horns in the world and my father was the first American to shoot one. We were thrilled; our trip is a complete triumph, and to kill a big sable on such a short safari was really wonderful luck." The black beast was massive and muscular and carried fine horns with a curve of fifty-three and one-half inches. Curtis marveled at how hard the animal was to kill; it had traveled for five hours with a .450 bullet that had missed the heart by inches and had absorbed several more solid hits before succumbing.

While his father rested in camp the next day, Curtis, Chapman, Thomas, and a porter went out. For two hours they saw nothing but an old track of a big bull. But soon after passing a small tree where the bull had stropped his horns on the bark, Thomas saw the animal and crouched down. It took a 300-yard crawl on hands and knees across the burnt stubble before he and Thomas reached the cover of an anthill. The jet black bull was 160 yards away, and suspicious, his head held high, his horns thrown back. Curtis tried to shove his Springfield through the dry heavy grass on the anthill, but it snagged in the vegetation. He sat up and leaned his rifle against a pencil-thin sapling, breathing so heavily that the sights were wobbling crazily around their target. He fired twice and the mortally wounded giant sable ran off and then stopped among the trees. Curtis fired wildly and missed; then, kneeling for steadiness, he shot him again. The bull moved forward and then, as if it had forgotten something, stopped again. Curtis shot the last cartridge in his magazine. The antelope was still standing as Curtis reloaded but it sank to the ground as he ran toward it.

Chapman, Thomas, and the porter, all smiles and hand claps, joined Curtis at the fallen bull. "I never was so pleased. No beast could be more wonderful than the giant sable. I measured my horns off on my belt where I had marked off fifty inches," he wrote. "They were half an inch shorter than my father's, with a half an inch more spread. Everything was as it should be." Jubilant, they tramped back in the thick heat, the bloody head perched on Thomas's shoulders. It must have been shortly after arriving in camp that those two vivid pictures included in his book were taken.

The weary smile on Thomas's face is clearly one of satisfaction at the outcome of a hard hunt, but Anita Curtis's hesitant expression, a combination of troubled gaze and questioning look, seems to ask if the severed head at her feet was all that their quest had been about. But what they hoped to accomplish had been achieved—so it must have been. "Our two heads were big enough for ourselves," wrote Curtis, "and we didn't want and couldn't hope to beat them. But our luck had been so good that it didn't seem proper to trespass on it, and we were all tired out." Their passion spent, they had no interest left in using the third license, even for a museum specimen. They broke camp the next morning, and retraced their steps to the coast without incident.

Anita Curtis had her own trophies to bring home: her flower collection. Having determined long before leaving Boston that she did not want to shoot, she decided instead to make a serious collection of the flowering plants she found in the African bush. The procedure was simple: she picked a flower (roots and all), put it between a folded sheet of manila paper, placed the sheet between blotting paper, and squeezed it dry in a light wooden press. A change or two of blotters and a day or so of additional pressing, and the specimen was ready to be packed away. She returned to the United States with over a thousand specimens collected in Kenya and Angola, and gave her collection to the Arnold Arboretum in Brookline and the Gray Herbarium of Harvard. Sixteen of her specimens turned out to be species unknown to science, and almost all of those were found in the sable country across the Cuanza. Included among these finds were great purple orchidlike flowers, a small plant with two distinctly different colored blossoms on the same stem, and a pleasantly scented leguminous one with little jasminelike flowers on which the giant sable browsed. This sable flower was named *Lactuca variani*, in Varian's honor—a final bouquet to the chief engineer in gratitude for the hospitality and assistance he gave to the family from Boston.

AS THE RARITY and magnificence of the giant sable became better known, it became a natural history prize, giving rise to far grander expeditions, ones that still sprang from hunters' urges but found justification in collecting the scientific specimens required for museum study and display. That is why in New York a female and a juvenile giant sable now rest motionless in an understory of golden grasses and shrub, their legs tucked beneath them, next to a young male standing still against sparse *brachystegia* branches as an alert, dark brown bull keeps watch. They will keep their poses, as they have for decades, because they are mounted and on display in the giant sable diorama in the Akeley Hall of African Mammals in the American Museum of Natural History. They are, in the words of the accompanying bronze plaque, the "gift of Arthur S. Vernay."

Arthur Stannard Vernay was no ordinary hunter. A British-born antiques dealer with offices in New York and London, he was equally at home in the drawing rooms of Park Avenue or the backcountry of Tibet or Burma, able to discuss period furniture and elephant hunting with the same aplomb. Vernay's taste for far-flung adventure was largely channeled into the fifteen major expeditions he made for the American Museum of Natural History from 1923 to 1946. He brought his passion, social connections, money, and a sense of noblesse oblige to bear on each of these elaborate undertakings, ensuring their success, and he was made a trustee of the museum in 1935. The period of Vernay's involvement with the institution coincided with what might be called the golden age of museum collecting and the display of megafauna, when advances in taxidermy pioneered by Carl Akeley and the development of the diorama permitted mounted animals to be shown in scenes that depicted their natural settings with growing accuracy. The American Museum of Natural History, founded in 1869, wasn't the oldest of such museums in the country—Philadelphia, Boston, Washington, and Chicago had established important natural history collections before it. But it was well funded, ambitious, and competitive. It sponsored over two hundred field expeditions in the 1930s, thirty-five in the peak year of 1930. These efforts amounted to far more than a race against other institutions to see who could put on the most impressive exhibits of the world's rarest and most spectacular animals. They were also fueled by the belief that animals in many parts of the world were disappearing as their habitats were being destroyed, and that natural history museums had an obligation to preserve and record what they could of the mammals that remained before it was too late.

Carl Akeley, the sculptor and legendary preparator who made a number of African expeditions, devoted the latter third of his life to the creation of an exhibit hall in the American Museum of Natural History to "preserve and portray Africa for posterity." By the time of his death in Africa in 1926, Akeley's goal had become one of the creeds of the museum. A year later, its president, Henry Fairfield Osborn, wrote that "only a paleontologist like myself can measure the full extent of the coming calamity to science and to art when the entire wildlife of Africa shall have vanished," leaving only a "few remaining remnants" to linger on in a handful of preserves. At the time, this bleak prediction was largely unquestioned by naturalists, which was why securing representative specimens of the continent's animal life for the stupendous two-story hall Akeley envisioned was an urgent and important undertaking. Osborn was particularly gratified by the generosity of the men who, like Theodore Roosevelt, led the necessary expeditions, and reflected on Akeley's prescience in taking artists to Africa to add accurate color and supplement the elaborate photographic record made there: "Thus through the union of generosity and artistic genius, the African Hall becomes the Valhalla of the vanishing wildlife."

Vernay was one of those who advanced this colossal scheme. He was already a prominent donor, having led a six-month expedition to India in 1923 with Lt. Col. J. C. Faunthorpe, "the authority on tiger shooting from elephants," to form a collection of animals of the Indian plains for the museum. Vernay had recently seen a mounted specimen of the giant sable, possibly Varian's, at the Natural History Museum in South Kensington. His interest in the species wasn't just sparked, it was "aroused." Here was the greatest antelope of Africa, a prize of prizes that could be wrested from the bush before it disappeared and put on display in permanent form, not as a personal trophy but to honor this masterwork of nature. Vernay would do it while it could still be done. Osborn shared his excitement; as news of the giant sable spread, every important natural history institution wanted to have one or more on exhibit. The museum's president urged "the immediate acquisition of a complete group of giant sable" for the African Hall.

VERNAY KNEW THAT the museum would put his newfound passion for the giant sable to use, and for him that made all the difference. He liked his hunting wrapped in a mantle of scientific respectability. "It has been my experience in shooting," he explained, "that one is filled with enthusiasm during the chase until the moment the aim is taken; the trigger is pulled, the quarry is killed, and then there is always a moment of intense regret that one has taken the life of one of these animals. When shooting for a museum that feeling was somewhat relieved by the knowledge that the animal obtained would not only be of scientific interest, but of general interest to the public for many years; I hope generations to come."

The 1925 Vernay-Angola Expedition, as it came to be called, was no hunting trip with some scientific collecting tacked on, in the manner of the Curtis safari. There was hardly any zoological material from Angola in any American museum, and the opportunity to broaden the collecting was eagerly seized upon. Herbert Lang, assistant curator of mammalogy, and a veteran of six years in the Belgian Congo, joined the expedition and became its principal organizer; Rudyerd Boulton, from the department of birds, was appointed ornithologist, and the scope of the trip became a virtual biological survey. Lang drew up a wish list of Angolan mammals, from the aardwolf to the zorilla—some sixty-one species in all—but that was just the start. "Many months were required to perfect our arrangements," Vernay wrote later. The well-stuffed files in the museum's archives detail the effort required, from attempts to wheedle discounts for passages on the Cunard Line to obtaining snakebite serum to putting pressure on the State Department in Washington to ensure the necessary cooperation of the Portuguese authorities.

Vernay wrote to Lang at the end of December 1924 from his office on Forty-fifth Street to explain that he would virtually underwrite the entire expedition and directed him and Boulton to arrive in Angola two months in advance to make the necessary arrangements. Vernay reminded him that "the principal objective of this expedition, apart from forming a general collection which we will make as representative as possible, is to obtain a complete group of the Sable Antelope . . . I look forward with much pleasure to our journeys, etc." Vernay signed the letter with loops and flourishes.

Lang calculated the field expenses, including a caravan of 150 porters, added travel costs, shotguns and cartridges, photographic and camping equipment, and food (including whiskey and Worcestershire sauce), and estimated the grand total at $14,635.32. Vernay thought Lang was cutting things too fine. He dashed off a letter to him on board the RMS *Aquitania* in early January 1925: "Your food list seems to be rather on the short side," he noted, and reminded him, "The health of the party is of paramount importance." On the other hand he didn't want to overspend on a movie camera.

Vernay did what he could in London by meeting with Portuguese officials (including General Norton de Matos, the former high commissioner), obtaining letters from the president of Portugal, and dining with a principal in the Benguela Railway, "so we shall get special facilities there. Also, Mr. Varian, after whom the giant sable is named, will be instructed to give us all the help possible. I hope from your end the [Portuguese] Government situation is being put in order." On his return to New York, Vernay had a meeting with Lang on March 5, just days before Lang and Boulton's scheduled departure. Astonished to learn that no credentials had been obtained from the Portuguese government, he made it clear, as Lang put it, that "it would be impossible to send an expedition to Angola without having such matters properly arranged." Lang also had to arrange for shipping two tons of camp equipment and three thousand rounds of ammunition.

A day later, Lang obtained a letter from the State Department which apparently reassured Vernay and put the expedition back on track. Vernay wrote Lang that he was relying on him to determine the most advantageous route for the expedition to take once he arrived in Angola, and asked Lang if he had remembered to number the boxes of equipment, prepare a list of expenditures to date, and arrange a way for Vernay to get cablegrams from his office to the nearest telegraph office in Angola "to where we are at the time, [so] a runner can bring it out to camp." He planned to join the scientists in Lobito about the middle of June to proceed by rail into the interior. Lang, staggering under the pressure, scrambled to pull everything together.

On March 14 Herbert Lang and Rudyerd Boulton sailed out of New York harbor on the RMS *Aquitania*. The next weeks at sea would be all the break Lang would get before plunging into the next phase of the expedition, but in fact he had to board ship with several matters unsettled. Fortunately, he could count on the redoubtable Miss Evans of the mammalogy department to straighten out the rat's nest of confusion over requisitions for the expedition (his field socks were supposed to be charged to the museum, not Mr. Vernay, for example), and chase down copies of his recent piece on the frozen mammoth, as well as send out reprints of his article "How Squirrels and Other Rodents Carry Their Young." Unfortunately, he had forgotten to tell her what to do about the uncatalogued bottle of four bats from the natural history museum in Genoa.

But Lang had more pressing matters on his mind: the necessary round of appointments with Portuguese colonial officialdom in Luanda. After days of various delays in the capital, Lang left for Lobito, where he hired Alan Chapman, the guide who had accompanied the Curtises, and his brother Harry, and let the museum know that after purchasing a Ford truck, he and Boulton had collected "several hundred mammals, nearly as many birds, over 550 fish, both sea and fresh water forms, about 750 reptiles and batrachians, several thousand crustaceans and molluscs and many other invertebrates," as well as two boxes of Cretaceous fossils. Lang added that "Mr. Vernay will now soon arrive and then we will do even better."

Lang had contacted Frank Varian and apprised him of Vernay's expected arrival in early June. It had been eighteen months since the Curtises left. These new sable seekers were no mere family of hunters following their fancy. They were the leaders of a full-scale museum expedition, with its small army of porters and four trucks full of equipment. The expedition's arrival had already caused ripples throughout government and commercial circles in the colony. It was clear that Varian's assistance would be expected rather than hoped for—a command performance, as it were, for the chief engineer. Varian did what he could, and offered a special railcar to take Vernay and his entourage to Huambo, where Lang had established the main base camp. And he must have also explained to Lang that it was too early to proceed directly to the sable country; the natives would not have burned the underbrush yet. The ideal season was September and October, when the rains would have just started and the grass had come up in the burnt stubble.

Vernay arrived June 9, and stayed with Varian, who passed on some hunting tips. After a couple of days of further preparations, Vernay set off with Lang in an inspection car on the Benguela Railway to Huambo. That car broke down, as well as its replacement, and they finally arrived in Huambo "enthroned in a mealies wagon, eighteen hours behind schedule." They then turned the expedition southward to Moçâmedes "for a series of springbuck." Lang wrote the museum at the end of July from Huambo that "Mr. Vernay thoroughly enjoys the success of his expedition. Just a few days ago a fine bull Eland and a capital Lion fell to his rifle . . . Far from Mr. Vernay's interest waning, he is pushing on with surprising energy and keenness. His prospects for Sable Antelope are excellent, and tomorrow morning we move eastward into their range." Boulton headed for the hills for special birds, Lang went off to collect small mammals and reptiles, and Vernay took Alan Chapman to seek the giant sable.

Vernay and Chapman traveled eastward to the Cuanza, making a river crossing in long native dugouts. They were three days' march from the animal's prime habitat. Vernay found it "an inhospitable country, sparsely inhabited by a tribe known as the Lwimbis, an inferior race physically and mentally." The Lwimbi they hired as porters, he noted, could only carry a fifty-pound load, as compared with the sixty-pound loads common in East Africa. Three days' tramping in the bush brought them to "a cluster of half a dozen native huts, and miserable hovels they were. The *sova*, or headman, told us their hunter—who is a mighty man among the natives—was away but would return soon." They decided to rest and wait.

Soon, Vernay wrote, "we saw a fine-looking savage approaching. He was almost seven feet tall and, with his big bow and one large, carefully constructed and well balanced arrow, his native axe, and a sparse drapery of skins, he made a picturesque figure. Alan and I were duly impressed and decided to engage this mighty-looking savage whose name, we found, was Tarti." The hunter told them that he had found giant sable a few days ago, and that "their size exceeded one's dreams." Vernay and Chapman both knew he was exaggerating, "but nevertheless the next day we started on our quest." They hunted for three days with Tarti but saw no sign of sable.

They began to wonder about Tarti's methods. He seemed unaccustomed to crawling through burnt stubble to stalk and preferred to spend hours in a tree or some hidden spot to wait for game. Apparently, it was the way he managed to kill antelopes small and large—duiker, reedbuck, roan, and giant sable. But they began to lose faith because of Tarti's "perni-cious habit, when stalking, of taking pungent snuff, so that we never knew when he might be seized by a fit of loud sneezing at the most inopportune time, frightening any game within earshot." He seemed an incompetent hunter, yet oddly, he was famous among all the natives. "On entering a village," Vernay recalled, "Tarti always received a vociferous welcome. Natives sprang up from around their fires and cried, 'Ohosie! Ohosie! Ohosie!' To which he replied with gravity, 'Ondombo.' Alan told me that the native greeting meant, 'The lion,' a tribute to Tarti's ability as a hunter, while his salutation was simply a recognition of their compliment. He said 'Great,' much as one would say, 'Yes, I *am* the great lion.'"

Clearly, Tarti was trying to deter the foreign hunters. But they could only be thrown off the trail temporarily. Disappointed by the mighty savage, Vernay and Chapman moved out of his territory to the Tetie, a small stream that fed into the Lussingue, near the area Varian had recommended. Within four days they had obtained two cow giant sables, a small bull, and a calf, but there were only mixed satisfactions in that. Vernay always found shooting females "disagreeable," even if it was required. A big male was another matter. So far, he had only a quick glimpse of his principal quarry, a giant sable bull, in the dim light of daybreak, but it was too distant for an accurate shot. Vernay grew anxious; only four days remained before they had to break camp. He decided to send Chapman northward to hunt while he went south. If either man succeeded, they would send a runner to the other so that they could leave as soon as possible. Vernay took an Umbundu tracker with him, but saw no bulls the next two days. He stumbled wearily into camp that evening. No word had come from Chapman, and Vernay told the camp boys that they would pack up and leave tomorrow. But after a hot bath in a canvas sling tub, a good meal, "and the wonderful quiet of the African evening, with time to think things over, aspects changed." He told the camp staff that the trackers had to be ready at 4:30 A.M. for a final attempt.

Dawn was breaking as they set out the next morning. By seven, the sun was bright, and Vernay was moving noiselessly through waist-high grass, followed by the trackers, who were looking to the right, "when I saw on my left a black object moving in the grass. A motion of the hand and the men slid silently into the grass and disappeared. Cautiously turning about, I saw a splendid bull giant sable antelope, with superb scimitar horns, boldly carried, walking parallel to us within a hundred and fifty yards, wholly unconscious of our presence. I shall never forget that sight."

The bull stepped behind a fallen tree, putting Vernay into an agony of apprehension. If the animal walked deeper into the bush with the tree blocking the hunter's view, Vernay could try to follow, but he knew the beast "would have disappeared at the slightest sound." Then he saw its dimly visible form passing like a dark ghost behind the dead leafy branches of a screen of bush, and reappearing in the clear. Vernay did not hesitate. The rifle cracked, the sable stumbled; "and the next shot gave us the prize which completed the habitat group of the giant sable." It was a "fine, old bull with horns measuring 54½ inches almost perfect in symmetry and with large base measurement. He was just what we wanted—a representative example of the bull sable in perfect condition." Four hours later, skinners from camp had meticulously removed the skin and preserved the skeleton; by eleven that night, the skin had been salted and packed. Chapman showed up empty-handed the next morning and they started toward the Cuanza. It was August 15, 1925.

Herbert Lang wrote his final report of the Vernay-Angola Expedition on board the SS *Winfried* at the end of August, in the form of a letter to the museum's acting director. Vernay and Boulton had left for Southampton on an earlier ship, he explained, while he stayed on to arrange the shipping of some eight thousand specimens, from ants to elephants, which the museum would receive over the next few months. Included in this grand total were fourteen giant sables—nine males and five females, two of which were given to Vernay by Varian. Even without that pair, the sum is considerably more than Statham's grim octet—but of course the killing had more to do with the gathering of information than with personal gratification. Giant sable would never be shot for scientific purposes on that scale again. Lang closed by adding that Mr. Vernay "would be pleased if you would manage to have reporters meet him on board the steamer by which he arrives in New York."

Vernay may have been vain, even imperious at times, but he could also be magnanimous. Lang had long planned to visit South Africa to do some modest collecting before returning home, but was short of funds. Before leaving, Vernay presented Lang with a thousand dollars to support his South African trip. The assistance Frank Varian gave the expedition was remembered as well: he was made an honorary life member of the American Museum of Natural History in 1927, and doubtless Vernay also had something to do with that. Many years and many expeditions later, he came to think of his role as expedition leader as a relatively modest one. In writing to the museum's curator of mammals, Harold Anthony, about the upcoming 1946 Nyasaland (Malawi) Expedition, Vernay brushed off the idea of his group's being all that important. "We are not—just some madmen who love to add something to the joy of living for ourselves and the millions that visit the museum."

ONE OF THE finest mounted specimens of the giant sable on display in any museum is the bull shot by Prentiss Gray in 1929 and featured in the giant sable diorama in the African Hall of the Academy of Natural Sciences of Philadelphia. It's bigger and blacker than Vernay's specimen, with beautifully thick-hooped horns over five feet long. It could be argued that an exceptional specimen is, ipso facto, not a very representative one, but it is a masterpiece of natural history, if only in taxidermic form.

Though mounted specimens may have lost all the obvious attributes of animate creatures, they gain unsuspected evocative power when reborn as furred sculpture. A first-rate diorama can take this transformation to another level. With its display of preserved flora blending almost indetectably into the trompe l'oeil backdrop, and the judicious inclusion of additional species, a diorama surrounds the mounted specimen with a nimbus of naturalism. But the result is an idealized version of the animal in its environment, not so much captured in a particular moment as literally suspended in it, like a dragonfly in amber, held in perfect and permanent stillness and lending itself to extended contemplation. In this sense, museum dioramas can fix at least part of the animal's meaning for us, and hold it in perpetuity.

Thirty years ago mammalian diorama displays were often derided as "dead zoos." But the voluminous cabinets of study specimens behind the lighted scenes, collected in the days when taxonomic science involved little more than direct comparison, calipers, and careful drawings, have turned out to be invaluable repositories of biological material for the kind of advanced genetic research undreamed of before DNA analysis became a common laboratory tool. But I had not come to Philadelphia to examine the study specimens from the 1929–30 Gray African Expeditions for any other reason than to see them, sketch them, touch them. Pondering #14322, the loose-toothed skull of the female giant sable in the diorama, #14321, the sawn-off horn cores of the male (which are almost thirty inches long), and the unsorted bones of the juvenile specimen in a black cardboard box, made me wonder if the hunting required for these dioramas wasn't, in its own way, ecologically sensitive as well as scientifically justifiable. A single animal shot for display can be on exhibit, educating the public for decades, perhaps even a century or more, and its skeleton provides study material for research almost indefinitely. Certainly that was the unquestioned rationale that underpinned the Gray African Expeditions.

PRENTISS N. GRAY was appointed by Herbert Hoover to organize Belgian relief efforts during World War I. He became president of the J. Henry Schroder Banking Corporation in New York in 1923, and soon after brought the firm such success that he was given unlimited vacation time. By 1928, Gray, who had hunted extensively in Canada and the western United States, had the means and the opportunity to hunt in Africa. It's not clear when he fell under the great antelope's spell, but by the late 1920s the animal's reputation had been much enhanced in print. Alexander Barnes, a travel writer who journeyed to Angola (and visited Varian), echoed a then common sentiment when he wrote in 1928 that "every sportsman who has hunted these animals proclaims them to be the most splendid-looking beasts imaginable." Gray began planning an ambitious five-month-long trip that would start in Kenya, retrace Livingstone's travels across the continent, and end in Angola, where he hoped to pursue the giant sable. But Portuguese officials had also taken note of the great Angolan antelope by this time, and, increasingly conscious of their responsibility, had thrown an additional mantle of protection over the prized creature. The new game laws that were promulgated in 1929 strictly prohibited taking the *palanca preta gigante*—although shooting them for museum purposes was still possible. In mid-1928, Gray discovered to his intense dismay that the colonial authorities in Angola had already banned the pursuit of giant sable, doubtless in anticipation of the new game laws coming into effect. If he wanted to hunt the beast, he would have to do it the way Vernay did: as a museum collector.

The bank president knew where to turn. A life member of the Academy of Natural Sciences, Gray wrote to one of its curators, Dr. Henry Tucker. "This was the particular antelope I was most anxious to get in Africa and it is a great disappointment to me," he explained, adding, however, that "the authorities intimate to me that if I could produce a request from an American museum for specimens to be used for museum purposes, it might be possible to give me a special license. If the Academy of Natural Sciences could see its way clear to give me a letter stating that they desire to obtain a group if possible, or a single animal if a group is not possible, I am convinced that we can open this business up." Gray wrapped this request in an attractive offer: "To recompense the Academy I would be glad to collect for them a group, if such is possible, or if it is not possible, to bring back a single specimen for their study, and to collect a group of such other animals as they might desire."

Tucker immediately wrote to Dr. Witmer Stone, the academy's director, who was quick to respond. His letter to Gray a week later came right to the point: "The Academy of Natural Sciences of Philadelphia is particularly anxious to obtain a group of the Giant Sable Antelope for the Museum. Will you secure for us a group of these animals?" Gray got the necessary permission. Like Vernay, he became a hunter who put his passion to scientific use, while using science to fulfill his passion. He too became an enthusiastic supporter of the less glamorous but no less important collecting efforts on the expedition he funded, which came to be called the 1929 Gray African Expedition. With the addition of Wilfred Wedgwood Bowen as ornithologist, the objectives soon went beyond a group of *Hippotragus niger variani*; they expanded to include a representative collection of Angolan birds, motion pictures of a total eclipse of the sun, and East African game: groups of gazelles from Kenya and some six hundred bird specimens from Kenya and Tanganyika (Tanzania).

In fact, by the time Gray and his wife Laura departed from New York on March 13, 1929, the expedition had become only a segment of a trip around the world, which is why they first took a train to San Francisco and then ships to Hawaii, Japan, Hong Kong, and the Philippines. But Africa beckoned, and the Grays skipped India to head for Ceylon, where they could take a ship directly to Mombasa in Kenya. After the train ride inland—on the same line Roosevelt and Selous had ridden together twenty years before—they arrived in Nairobi to find Wilfred Bowen and Philip Percival waiting for them. Gray, not surprisingly, had lined up Percival, who had been in demand as a "white hunter" since the days of the Roosevelt safari. With fifteen "boys," they set off in three Ford trucks for a two-and-a-half-month safari.

Percival took them into the Serengeti, where Gray was thrilled to witness the wildebeest migration but was sure the game would all disappear once the country was settled and fenced. A keen photographer, he did his best to capture what he could of Africa's vanishing wildlife on film. Within a month, he'd shot over seven thousand feet of film, including a sequence showing lions devouring the carcass of a wildebeest he'd shot to lure them out in the open. "After the first nervous few minutes when you are moving in on them and don't know how they are going to take your visit," Gray wrote, filming could become rather routine. "Laura actually sat in the back of the car and embroidered and Percival sat in the front with his gun out the window and read the *Saturday Evening Post.*"

Laura returned to the United States, while Gray and Bowen pushed on with Percival north of Nairobi. Gray was after the usual bag (elephant, rhino, cape buffalo) as well as the group of Hunter's antelope (hirola) he'd promised to collect for the academy. Bowen found the birds at Meru in the Mount Kenya region of great interest—among them, he discovered four new subspecies, one of which, a kingfisher, he named in honor of Gray: *Halcyon albiventris prentissgrayi.* But Gray was thinking of the great antelope on the other side of the continent. "I still have my mind set on the Giant Sable," he wrote the academy in July of 1929, "and will do everything possible to get to Angola."

Like the Curtises' before him, Gray's safari in the Kenya Colony was only a warm-up for the adventure to come in Portuguese West Africa. Unlike them, however, he wanted to cross overland, roughly following

Livingstone and Cameron's trans-Africa route via the pioneer railways that had been recently built. Gray saw it as a chance to follow this historic trail before it became a mere tourist track. From Mombasa, Gray and Bowen took a steamer south to Dar es Salaam and then the railway inland. The line followed the old Arab trade route from the great lakes of central Africa, and ended at Ujiji on Lake Tanganyika, not far from the mango tree under which Stanley met Livingstone in 1871. After the usual customs delays and an eighty-mile steamer trip across the lake they anchored at Albertville (now Kalemie) in the Belgian Congo. There the two Americans encountered the not-so-romantic old Africa. The district commissioner met them at the docks with a gang of convicts, chained together by the neck, to carry their thirty-three pieces of luggage to the hotel.

After pushing on into the interior by rail to Kabalo, Gray and Bowen took the little three-decked Lualaba steamer south on the jungle river (actually the Upper Congo) that Cameron had been forced off by slavers. When they got to Bukama, the local administrator met them in a drunken state, although he'd managed to round up another gang of prisoners to help with their luggage. Catching up with the infrequent trains on the Benguela rail line took several hectic days and a combination of private railcar and auto, but Gray and Bowen and their luggage made it to Dililo on the Angolan border, only to find that the all-important permit to shoot giant sable had failed to arrive. When it was finally tracked down it turned out to be a permit for only two giant sable—not enough to make a museum group. Portuguese reluctance to grant museum permits to foreign hunters was beginning to have an effect.

They decided to make the best of it. When their train arrived at Camacupa, Gray persuaded the local administrator to drive him and Bowen twenty-one miles to the Lwimbi village of Chouzo so they could stand on the high riverbank and look out across the Cuanza to the low range of hills beyond, "the promised land where we hoped to find the giant sable." Gray was as unimpressed by the Lwimbi as the previous visitors to the giant sable lands had been, but conceded that they were serviceable porters and passable trackers. Leaving Bowen in Chouzo to continue bird-collecting, Gray, joined by J. R. Evans, an American resident in Angola, ferried across the Cuanza with fifty-nine porters and struck back into the interior despite a torrential thundershower.

It was late September and the dampened ground showed tracks easily. After a march of two hours the next day they saw their first herd of giant sable, appearing as little more than vague, shape-shifting shadows in the thick bush. Gradually they could begin to make out cows and calves and young bulls as they moved slowly across the forest openings. Then Gray spotted a mature male striding into view eighty yards away. "The bull looked coal black to me and its horns assumed tremendous proportions at first," Gray recalled; "through the glasses, however, they did not seem so long and while I was trying to decide whether they would measure fifty inches or more, the herd caught our scent and was off."

The next few days made it clear that the country was deceptive in its beauty. "The early morning hunt is a great joy," Gray recalled. "Everything is a gorgeous vivid green. The grass is freshly sprouted and just long enough to hide the charred stumps of last year's growth that was burned off. Every tree is in full leaf . . . Everywhere in the shade of the woods grow a profusion of flowers . . . ," he marveled. "It is a joy to be alive." But the fresh hopes of each new day always seemed to wither in the heat. "We approach the hour when the insects are noisiest, noon till two p.m. We have been walking fast for six hours for the natives never seem to stroll. We are getting footsore and hungry. The sun beats down relentlessly through the thin trees whose height, seldom exceeding thirty feet, affords no density of shade. The open *chanas* [large treeless areas] through which we pass are a nightmare, for here the sun strikes us squarely. Everywhere an impenetrable wall of green hems us in," he confessed. "Myriad swarms of tiny green insects surge off some of the bushes and beat against our helmets and faces like pellets of hail. It is impossible to breathe . . ." A confusing maze of monotonous bush and forest seemed to surround the hunters with a great green curtain that moved eerily before them. But the land between the two rivers was about to yield a pair of prizes.

Days later he was studying some sable tracks when his gun-bearer touched his arm and whispered, "*Sumbakaloko*." At first he could not make out the animal, so perfectly did it merge with the tree trunk alongside it. Then a face splashed with white coalesced out of the shadows, and then a whole bull with a great sweep of horns wheeling to escape. Gray fired.

Only a spot of blood on the forest leaves betrayed the beast's wound. Tracking with infinite care over stony ground for several hundred yards, the hunter finally got close enough to give it a finishing shot. Gray was astonished to discover he had shot no ordinary bull. "Imagine my joy when we came up to view a horn that measured 61¼ inches in length and 12 inches in circumference at the base. It was well worth traveling half around the world and crossing a continent to have found such a trophy." He measured and photographed it, and skinned it with care: this one was destined for the academy.

But the day was not over. A half an hour after heading back to camp, Gray and his men came on a herd of giant sable—"eight cows, a calf, and a grand black old bull"—grazing in an open clearing. He studied the horns through the field glasses and became convinced they were nearly as large as the ones he'd just collected. There was a stalk, a wait for it to step clear of the other animals, two shots, then a hard run to catch up with the bull as it lay dying in a clump of trees. But the beast looked up and Gray decided to give it the coup de grâce. It clung to life more tenaciously than seemed possible, bursting to its feet at the crack of the rifle and plunging into the forest as Gray got off two more shots—mortal ones this time. "When we came up we found the sable dead and to our great joy it carried a 59 inch head with 10¼ inch bases."

By one o'clock they were back in camp to tackle the time-consuming task of skinning out two full hides, scraping them clean, and rubbing them down with salt. For a museum mount, each skin had to be removed in its entirety from the carcass with utmost care, using a minimum of incisions—starting at the sternum and tracing the median line down the chest and belly to the tail, from that line out down each leg to the hoof, from between the horns down the back of the neck, then separating with surgical precision the skin from the horn bases, the eye sockets, the gums, peeling and rolling the skin forward, severing the ears and finally the nose where it attached to the skull. Every bit of flesh and fat had to be scraped off the skins, which meant the ears had to be inverted like the fingers of a glove and the scrotum scooped out like a change purse, and then liberally rubbed with salt to draw out the remaining moisture in the hide to prevent putrefaction. The rotting of the secretions in which the hairs were rooted could cause "hair-slip" and bald patches, completely ruining the specimen. The entire skeleton of each, every single bone, had to be scraped clean and preserved as well.

It took until eight o'clock that evening, and used up the last bit of salt. The camp had been in an uproar since the arrival of the giant sable carcasses—the porters were squabbling endlessly over meat. "The boys who hunted with me hid all the tidbits of the two sable I had killed in the bush," Gray noted. "This caused a fearful row when the animals were carried into camp without liver, heart or tongue." But there may have been more to it than that. Those Lwimbi trackers had either kept a few choice viands for themselves, or else those all-important parts of the *Sumbakaloko* were now drying in the wind, impaled on the sharpened branches of a hunter's shrine to appease the ancestors.

Gray had other concerns than tribal beliefs on his mind. Ominously, the hair on his two bull sable hides had begun to slip, making him frantic. By paring down the skins where they were particularly thick, and rubbing in finer salt, he was able to stop the deterioration. Restless, he moved his camp down to Chouzo to join Bowen, and visited Camacupa to obtain more *fuba* or *posho* (corn flour) for the porters. While he was there he was offered two giant sable heads by the local carpenter. Gray was disgusted. "The protection of the giant sable is a myth. They are forbidden to the foreign sportsmen while the natives and the local Portuguese residents kill all they want and sell the heads," he wrote in his journal. "They will soon all be killed."

A week after collecting the two bulls Gray received word that he'd been granted a special license to shoot five sable for the museum and two more for the Angola government. He'd secured the permission, but his luck had fled. Days more of hunting for the cows, young bulls, and calf that were needed produced nothing. As if to test his resolve, one herd bull let him come within forty yards, an easy shot. He was "a splendid big old fellow," Gray wrote, "but, as I had all the bulls I wanted, I could not kill it." He would not stretch the limits of his license. But he was desperate to fulfill the academy's request, the one that had made this great adventure possible. The Lwimbi chief sent Gray ten guides, but each, interestingly enough, had divergent ideas as to where the *Sumbakaloko* was to be found. Gray spent days watching the wall of endless bush "opening a little in front as we advanced and closing behind—never a chance through the foliage to see what lay in its depth—always that impenetrable wall of green leaves hiding the thing we were searching." Gray had been given one extraordinary day afield and would not get another; he would have to return home without the additional animals needed for the habitat group. It was only a mild consolation that Bowen had discovered three new Angolan subspecies of birds and, among the 550 fish specimens collected, one new genus and eleven new species.

In Chouzo, Gray did a parting favor for the Lwimbi, who, in the middle of putting in their maize crop, had been commandeered by the local government and forced to plant coffee trees—the current colonial scheme—right through their village, irrespective of the location of huts or their centuries-old council meeting place. He traded a shotgun to the regional Portuguese administrator in exchange for sparing the village.

Gray and Bowen boarded the train at Camacupa on October 19, 1929, and pulled into Benguela the next morning. "We had crossed Africa and we began to feel we were almost home," Gray wrote, as if to cheer himself up. At Lobito they were put up briefly in Frank Varian's house. But the chief engineer had gone. His thirty-year career with Africa's pioneer railways had come to a close with the opening ceremony of the completed Benguela Railway some months before. Once the line had crossed the Cuanza, no more obstacles delayed the progress of construction, and by August of 1928, the final point had been reached, 835 miles from the coast to the renegotiated border with the Belgian Congo. A year later assorted British and Portuguese dignitaries gathered at the unveiling of the huge boulder brought from the coast to mark the terminus. A brass plate on the granite gave the dates of inception and completion, from the concession granted to Robert Williams in 1902 to the opening ceremony twenty-seven years later. Varian moved on to East Africa, partly to fulfill a desire to see that part of Africa, and partly to investigate possible railway connections to potential mining districts. He traveled much the same route Gray would use months later on the way to Angola, but west to east, by steamer from Bukama down the Lualaba, and across Lake Tanganyika to Ujiji. Varian was deep in Uganda by the time Gray returned to New York.

PRENTISS GRAY WAS not about to let the academy down, despite the 1929 market crash and the Depression that followed. He had expected to pay for the privilege of pursuing the giant sable, and ended up sponsoring (but did not join) another expedition the following year, led by Harold T. Green, curator of museum exhibits, which returned with the cow and calf specimens required to mount the desired habitat group. The academy now had something special in the works, and other American museums had heard about it—the natural history museum world was a small one. Some of them had sent out their own rival expeditions to Angola. In 1930 Arthur Vernay would sponsor the Vernay-Lang Expedition for the Field Museum in Chicago, on which Alan Chapman collected a single bull with sixty-one-and-a-half-inch horns. Ralph Pulitzer led the Pulitzer–Carnegie Museum Expedition in 1930 and obtained several specimens for display in the Carnegie Museum in Pittsburgh, but that museum's plans for a habitat group caught Gray and the academy by surprise. Gray wrote to Charles Cadwalader, the academy's managing director, to suggest dispatching someone to Pittsburgh to see if there were any "bright ideas" that might be incorporated into their own nearly finished diorama—which had been scheduled to be unveiled in May of 1933, mere days after the Carnegie habitat group would go on view.

Those institutions that hadn't procured a habitat group coveted Gray's second, superb, and still unmounted giant sable bull. The California Academy of Sciences offered a bongo specimen to the Academy in exchange. Cadwalader told Gray the academy wouldn't really benefit from the swap, but it did owe a favor to the Museum of Comparative Zoology at Harvard, which had been pressing Gray to donate the specimen to them. Gray, on behalf of the academy, was willing to do so, on the condition that they would mount it. The offer of the "king of the antelope world" was accepted with alacrity. As the succeeding decades have made clear, all these exhibits, which are still on display, showcase an animal even rarer than it was thought to be at the time.

The academy's own giant sable diorama in the African Hall that Gray made possible still retains its power to impress, although Gray himself may have thought the wildlife films he took would turn out to be his longest-lived contribution to natural history. The academy certainly took pride in them. "With many species of these mammals becoming rarer yearly, the Academy is the fortunate possessor of a record of what has been called the closing scenes of the 'Age of Mammals,'" its report on the Gray African Expeditions noted. Sadly, the films all disintegrated with age.

In 1935 Prentiss Gray was killed in a speedboat accident on his way to join a friend for a hunting trip in the Florida Everglades. He was fifty years old.

THE POLICIES OF António de Oliviera Salazar, who ruled Portugal and its empire for decades, shaped the events that would impact the giant sable. Dr. Salazar was an economics professor at Coimbra University when officers from the Portuguese army who had led the country's 1926 military coup approached him for his help. Portugal's economy was in shambles, the legacy of the republic that had been formed in 1910 to address, among other things, the country's chronic financial woes. But the economy had only worsened with the political instability marked by there being nine presidents in the succeeding sixteen years. Salazar later recalled that the army officers had "the quite false idea that to professors such as me all things are known," and at first he refused their offer to become minister of finance. They redoubled their pleas. Persuaded at last, Salazar traveled to Lisbon. A bachelor of austere tastes who drew his social philosophy from the papal encyclicals of Pope Leo XIII, he detested politics. He left after only five days in office.

The situation in Portugal grew worse, and two years later the professor of economics was asked to reconsider. Salazar decided to accept, but only if he were given complete financial control of the government. His extraordinary conditions were met, and from then on Portugal was in his hands. By 1932 he had become prime minister and ruled as a dictator for the next four decades. Salazar put the country's finances on a stable footing for the first time in the twentieth century, but it came at a steep price: political opposition was suppressed, the parliamentary system was emasculated, the hegemony of the Catholic Church was reestablished, and a repressive police apparatus was formed, which included the International Police for the Defense of the State (PIDE). The authoritarian *Estado Novo* (the new state) had been born.

Salazar never set foot in any of Portugal's African territories, but he knew what his country had in Angola. Nearly fourteen times the size of Portugal itself, it was his nation's most valuable possession in Africa, rich in diamonds, oil, and agricultural potential. As minister of colonies before becoming prime minister, Salazar had imposed policies in the early 1930s designed to exploit Portugal's colonies for its own benefit by erecting protective trade tariffs and curbing the foreign investment previously encouraged. After nearly five hundred years of misrule, Portugal under Salazar made its first attempts at integration and development. Better economic opportunities in Angola attracted more Portuguese settlers; by 1940, there were forty thousand of them — 2 percent of the colony's population. The new settlers, most of whom were illiterate peasants, began expropriating choice lands in the interior, resulting in both expulsion of indigenous farmers and the forced cultivation of cash crops such as coffee, maize, and beans.

The vagrancy clause had been dropped from the native labor regulations in the late 1920s, but Africans were still required to work for paid wages for a certain period each year, and could be conscripted by the state if they failed to volunteer. In 1942, the labor system guaranteed a payment of less than $1.50 a month. During the sixty years the forced labor laws were on the books, a half-million Africans fled to neighboring countries, which of course exacerbated labor shortages, making contract labor all the more important to the colonial authorities. This vicious circle could not escape everyone's notice. Salazar's minister of colonies, Marcello Caetano, investigated labor conditions in Angola in the late 1940s, and blamed the mass exodus on the forced labor system, which used Africans "like pieces of equipment without any concern for their yearning, interests, or desires." A former colonial high inspector, Henrique Galvão, became Angolan deputy to the National Assembly and delivered a "Report on Native Problems in the Portuguese Colonies" to a closed session of Parliament in 1947. The scarcity of labor, he noted, had become so extreme that "to cover the deficit the most shameful outrages are committed, including forced labor of independent self-employed workers, of women, of children, of the sick, of decrepit old men, etc. *Only the dead are really exempt from forced labor."* Many laborers met this grim exemption without having anything to say about it: Galvão reported that up to a third of the *contratados* perished under some employers, who had even less incentive to provide for them than outright slave owners would. If a slave became incapacitated or died, he would have to be replaced at the owner's expense. But under the forced labor system, an employer would simply ask the government to provide another worker. Galvão's observations were not appreciated by Salazar's government, which excused the system on the grounds that it was indispensable to the development of the country. He would be arrested in 1952.

Employers that used contract labor included Diamang, the private diamond mining company. According to Gerald Bender, some 5,500 of its 17,500 African workers in 1947 were provided "by intervention of the authorities." They received an average of $25 a year in combined wages, rations, and "various goods." By 1954 their total earnings had risen to $29.50 annually. The Benguela Railway was another large employer. In 1954 it had 12,807 African workers, of whom 1,997 were *contratados.* The company provided food and housing and supported three clinics for its workers, but the bulk of the minuscule wages the *contratados* were paid for their unskilled labor was held back until the end of their contracts—a paternalistic policy insisted upon by the government.

The Portuguese liked to claim their colony was multiracial. But the presence of a few dark-skinned customers in the seaside cafés of Luanda was hardly proof of social equality. The Angolan population was effectively segregated into *indigenas* (indigenous peoples) and *civilizados* (all Europeans, even if they were illiterate, were so categorized, as were the majority of *mestiços*). The latter were considered full Portuguese citizens; the Africans were controlled by laws that required identification cards, six months of labor for the government if head taxes were not paid, and the lack of political and social rights. There was only one way an African in Angola could escape the long reach of the forced labor system, and that was to become an *assimilado* (assimilated nonwhite). This feat was not easy for a black to accomplish: an individual would have to be at least eighteen years old, speak, read, and write Portuguese fluently, have no police record, be able to support a family by means of a trade or salaried position, eat, dress, worship, and behave like a European, have abandoned any traditional way of life and acquired, in essence, a Portuguese outlook. Since there were no primary schools for blacks, save mission schools, few blacks could hope to obtain the special identity card which confirmed *assimilado* status. By 1960 there were only 38,000 black *assimilados* out of a total population of 4.5 million.

One particular African who struggled up through the system was the son of an Ovimbundu chief. He attended mission schools, achieved *assimilado* status, and in 1942 became the first black station manager on the Benguela Railway. The man's achievement would be mere historical detail, were it not for the fact that his own son had been born eight years before in Munhango, a small town on the rail line, not far from the southernmost point of the giant sable reserve. The boy dreamed of driving a steam locomotive, but his father told him he should aspire to be a doctor.

The boy would cast a long shadow over Angola and its giant sable. His name was Jonas Malheiro Savimbi.

ONLY A FEW nonnative hunters—Varian, Blaine, and Statham among them—had preceded the Curtises to Angola, but far more followed the Boston family. By one estimate, over a hundred giant sable were shot in the 1920s and 1930s despite the restrictions imposed. That number, over a twenty-year period, would not have seriously threatened the antelopes, but there were uncounted others in that period that must have been poached by colonials and natives alike. In 1933 the London International Convention committed European powers, including Portugal, to take steps to protect wildlife in their colonies. In response, a number of parks and reserves were proclaimed in Angola by 1938, among them the *Reserva do Luando*, an area of some 3,200 square miles congruent with the outlines of the tableland enclosed between the Cuanza and the Luando Rivers from their junction in the north to the swampy region in the south.

The reserve was created without regard to the Songo and Lwimbi peoples who had always shared this land with the giant sable, and the colonial government never explained to them why it cared more for the antelope than it did for them and their fields. In effect, the Luando Reserve, like the other parks and reserves in Angola, became little more than a private hunting preserve for the privileged few. The prohibition on hunting the giant sable could be waived, and was, time and time again, for those with museum credentials or the right political connections. After the Second World War—which, like the First World War, kept down the numbers of foreign hunters—there were others who found museum collecting provided a unique opportunity to hunt the *palanca negra*.

Varian himself contributed to an ever-widening interest in the giant sable as the ultimate antelope trophy by writing the chapter on Angola in Maj. H. C. Maydon's influential *Big Game Shooting in Africa*, published in London in 1932. Between its covers those planning an African safari (or just dreaming of it) could read the famous authorities of the day on such subjects as stalking mountain nyala in Abyssinia, shooting elephant in the Congo, pursuing lion in Somaliland, and hunting the giant sable antelope of Angola—that is, if one could get a permit. Varian's chapter quoted generous chunks from the seductive prose of Blaine's monograph and included a photograph that showed an ordinary sable's skull and horns in profile set inside a giant sable's with room to spare. Among the many readers who pored over this section, one in particular gave it rapt attention. He was Edward, Count de Yebes, a Spanish grandee and big-game hunter. The year was 1941.

"The giant sable antelope began to fascinate me," the count recalled. "Later it became an obsession, an urge that had to be appeased." What he read in Major Maydon's volume provided him with the first detailed information he could find on the animal. Hunters have their own dark aesthetics by which to judge the appeal of trophies, and what it would mean to bring home a head the likes of the giant sable, to display for all to see the crowning glory of its horns, is nothing that needs to be explained to any of that brotherhood. But what makes a given hunter focus on a particular species is a deeply individual matter. "Big-game hunters have their inexplicable whims," Yebes admitted. "Ernest Hemingway felt the same toward the kudu; Major Maydon's attraction was the addax." For him, the handful of differences that set the giant sable apart from other antelopes, other sables, made it into a magic beast, the rarest of trophies, the very "head of heads."

It would require years of diplomacy and strategy—using every so-cial connection, finding the proper levers of influence, importuning the right people—and, of course, considerable resources to realize his dream, but to Yebes that was all part of the expected struggle. Like a long march, a hard climb, or miserable weather—great difficulties made a successful hunt all the more a triumph. In 1949 Yebes finally obtained the combined cooperation of the Portuguese minister for colonies, the ambassador to Spain, and the governor of Angola. His efforts resulted in a permit to shoot one giant sable for Madrid's natural history museum and one for his own collection. Next to that, the planning and paper-work to import rifles and cartridges and other game licenses were tri-fling impedimenta.

The Count de Yebes was a well-known hunter. His book, *Viente Años de Caza Mayor* (*Twenty Years a Big-Game Hunter*), published in Madrid in 1943, had an extended (and still much discussed) philosophical prologue by José Ortega y Gasset that was later published separately as *Meditations on Hunting*. Yebes was also a crack shot. There was no question about the weapons he would bring: his favorite 9.3mm magnum rifles, of course—the ones he had always used in Spain. Yebes had enlisted the aid of Dr. Abel Pratas, the head of Angola's game department, and so was able to preface his giant sable hunt with a twenty-five-day safari in the Cuene River region of southern Angola, bagging everything from reedbuck to elephant, all by one-shot kills. By the time he arrived in the village of Mulundo near the Cuanza, below the Lussingue River, it was October—perfect timing. Be-fore starting out on his search, he hired a native boy, Caundo, who proved to be the worst tracker he'd ever had in Africa.

On his second outing the count found a herd of giant sables, twenty-eight in all, presided over by an enormous bull. His first sight of giant sables in the wild did not disappoint. "The size of the beasts and especially of their horns made a fantastic sight," he wrote, "giving the impression of prehistoric days." Yebes was even impressed with the animal's *cojones*—to him they looked twice the size of a roan's. He wanted the bull, the one that looked as if it had stepped out of a cave painting, but the clumsy Caundo could not be relied on; he crunched loudly across the burnt stubble in his heavy leather sandals. If this was a conscious attempt to warn off the sables, it wouldn't work on Yebes. He ordered him to stay behind, and well hidden. Yebes may have been a Spanish nobleman, but he was tough and wiry and willing to work for his trophy. For two hours he crouched and crawled on hands and knees, stalking "the most despotic and dictatorial herd-boss that it has been my luck to pursue." The bull would not let himself be taken easily. Finally the herd wandered out into a flat, treeless opening about 175 yards from the thicket where Yebes waited. When the bull finally stepped away from the females, the hunter fired at his shoulder. He dropped in a heap. Through the dust of the stampeding herd, Yebes saw him struggle to get up, and then fall back dead. The tape told the story: sixty inches—"Not too bad!" he thought; the record head was sixty-four and three-eighths inches. The count had fulfilled his dream, but his license gave him another chance to repeat his triumph, and he began thinking about a solitary old bull the locals had told him about.

Caundo pleaded to accompany him again. In spite of his evident shortcomings, Yebes had to concede that the boy had brought him luck, and finally agreed. The next morning they spotted the lone bull together, but Yebes took no chances. He made Caundo wait again while he stalked him. He soon realized that the beast was larger than the first, but "considerably more sly and crafty." Yebes could feel that the creature sensed danger, but the hunter was careful not to let the wind carry his scent to the sable. For three and a half hours, with Yebes crouching through stubble, brush, woods and "belly-wriggling" across an enormous *chana*, the antelope managed to elude the hunter. Using termite heaps as cover, Yebes got within two hundreds yards of the alert bull, now still as a statue. He fired.

"Down he went like a ton of lead," Yebes wrote, "and without a kick!" He ran toward his kill, and was awed by its beautiful form. Caundo rushed up, eager to help with the measuring tape. "I could not believe my eyes and had to check the measurement several times," Yebes remembered, "for it was sixty-five inches."

The count had shot the world-record giant sable.

BY THE 1950S political "winds of change" began to sweep across Africa, carrying the seeds of independence movements that would soon topple colonial rule with the same alarming speed with which it had previously been imposed on the continent. Western attitudes toward Africa's wildlife began to shift as well, growing increasingly divided in the face of contradictory impulses—the urge to hunt, the passion to preserve, the desire to know more—all of which would be played out in the conflicting conservation strategies of future decades. Not surprisingly, the ways in which the giant sable was sought also began to change. The hunters would not be left behind—such atavistic desires never seem to die—but the individual quests undertaken for the creature now broadened to include capturing it on film. Statham, who had proclaimed photography the equal of hunting, may have had a hard time convincing himself of that, but by the mid-1950s, there were those who would be content to take away a different kind of giant sable trophy: its image. Among them was the explorer and filmmaker Quentin Keynes, who made a trip to the interior of Angola in 1954 to make motion pictures of the rare antelope.

Born in London of Anglo-American parents, Keynes is the nephew of John Maynard Keynes and the great-grandson of Charles Darwin. Exploration appealed to him early. As a boy, he had collected stamps and become curious about the countries that issued them. He often describes himself as a "high-school dropout" who educated himself by travel. "My father finally accepted what I was doing when he saw a piece I wrote about one of my expeditions appear in the *National Geographic*," he explained. That article, published in 1951, included a series of elephant photographs Keynes had taken on a months-long Cairo to Cape Town trip. He never looked back, and embarked on a life of exotic travel, to remote islands like St. Helena, Ascension, the Galápagos, and the Falklands, to India and Sumatra and elsewhere, but mostly to Africa, making 16mm films of whatever struck him—animals, people, places.

Keynes was a tall, slightly stooped man with a shock of white hair and an aristocratic beak of a nose by the time I met him in the late 1980s. I found something of the nineteenth-century gentleman amateur about him, and perhaps more than a whiff of the British eccentric. "I have odd passions about all kinds of things," he readily admitted, and has collected "all sorts of books—books about elephants, books about rhinoceroses, books about Charles Darwin, books about explorers, books about Bugattis." One of his greatest collecting passions has been the work of Sir Richard Burton; he has an outstanding collection of the explorer's rare books, letters, manuscripts, and memorabilia. He regards it as a wry twist of fate that he is distantly related to John Speke, Burton's rival claimant to having discovered the source of the Nile. Keynes has a first edition of Livingstone's *Missionary Travels*, inscribed by the doctor to Sir Roderick Murchison, the president of the Royal Geographic Society. When Keynes retraced the Scottish missionary's expedition up the Zambezi, he had the moving experience of coming across what he believes were Livingstone's initials carved in the interior of a hollowed-out baobab tree.

In his own way, Keynes is also a collector of animals; like the books he pursues, the scarcer and more out of the ordinary the creature, the more interest it holds for him. A man who is fascinated by the dodo, the thylacine, the coelacanth, and other extinct or near-extinct species was certain to be entranced by the giant sable of Angola. "I've always loved excessively rare animals," he told me. "And the giant sable is almost number one on my list." He got the urge to seek it after visiting Angola in 1951, a trip on which he filmed Bushmen and explored the coast up to Luanda.

That was the year that Portugal declared its African possessions "overseas provinces" to emphasize their ties to the mother country, but they remained what they had always been: colonies. Only about 1 percent of Angola's African children were attending school in the early 1950s, but fully 10 percent of the black population were classed as *contratados*; their wages had risen to $3 a month. The settlers needed workers, particularly for their labor-intensive coffee plantations, which had boomed after World War II: Angola had become the fourth largest coffee producer in the world, with over a million acres under cultivation. Despite being so far behind, Portugal in the early 1950s was determined to do something about its backward African colonies. In Angola there were now agricultural stations, hydroelectric projects, even the tentative beginnings of tourism—although development plans included nothing for education or social services.

The year that Keynes traveled there he met Newton da Silva, a Portuguese businessman living in the growing coastal fishing city of Moçâmedes (now Namibe) in southwest Angola, who was a keen amateur naturalist and the author of articles on Angolan flora and fauna, including a long pamphlet on the improbability of any quagga (a zebra-related mammal) having survived in Angola. Da Silva had never seen a giant sable, but he was a close friend of Dr. Abel Pratas, whose permission would have to be obtained to even enter the Luando Reserve. Keynes went to work on persuading Senhor da Silva to go with him.

Keynes's trip three years later to find and film the giant sable was largely invented as it went along. Once the permissions, visa problems, missing wire transfers, lost letters, and endless complications over departure dates were out of the way, Keynes and da Silva and two African helpers set off in da Silva's battered truck for Huambo in early August, where an English friend of Keynes's, Patrick Lindsay, would join them. It must have been a dusty trip: in those days there were only fifty-three miles of asphalt roads in the entire country. After passing through Andulo, they crossed the Cuanza near Dando, taking their vehicle on a pontoon raft— actually four dugouts lashed side by side—towed across the rushing water by a half-dozen natives pulling on an overhead cable. Once in the reserve, they drove to a small trader's store at Quimbango, then went south to Kamakalaga in the heart of giant sable country, where they were treated to lions roaring outside their tents at night. Late on the first day afield, their local guide whispered "*Sumbakaloko*," and pointed to a herd of over thirty animals. The wary antelopes would not let them get within 500 yards—too far even for a telephoto lens. A lone bull that appeared in the distance as they made their way back to camp in the failing light was out of camera range as well.

They saw the herd on two occasions over the next two days, but never close enough to photograph. But early the following morning, within a quarter-mile of the camp, they came on the same herd quietly feeding in the open. The animals moved slowly off as they approached, always keeping the same distance between them. But two black bulls stopped following the rest and squared off, lowering their heads to thrust out the full curves of their horns, then lunged at each other and began smashing their horns together. Engrossed in their fight, the giant sables ignored the photographers creeping up on them with their cumbersome equipment. "At one time the only sound I could hear over my pounding heart was the click-clacking of the animals' horns," Keynes recalled. "I was so excited that my hands were shaking while I put up the tripod and screwed the camera into position."

But the bulls were oblivious and fought doggedly for twenty minutes, raking the ground and sending up clouds of dust. Down on their front knees, their heads bowed, they clashed their horns together in a ritualized fashion like dueling kendo swordsmen. Their tails switching and whirling, they pushed each other back and forth, dug into the earth, then backed off to smash into each other again, tangling their horns and trying to throw their opponent off balance. They suddenly looked up from their fight and stopped, stunned to see their human audience. "But it was my turn to be astonished when after a bit they started to come towards us in a slightly menacing way," Keynes recalled. "It flashed through my mind that the sable antelope can be a dangerous animal, but somehow I couldn't help feeling, for a fleeting second only, that it was almost worth getting killed to get a movie at such a moment. They made you feel that they were in control of the whole show, until they veered off in a magnificent sweep and at a terrific lick toward the forest." Keynes caught their thundering exit on film, their powerful bodies stretching out like those of racehorses at full gallop, legs pumping, their heavy heads and horns plunging up and down like hacking scimitars. Afterwards, the shaken but elated witnesses paced off the torn-up earth of the battle scene: it was nineteen yards long.

Keynes had already planned to flesh out the story of his filming of the giant sable by seeking out those individuals still living who had preceded him to Angola on their own expeditions for the antelope. After his return from the reserve, and while still in Africa, he received a reply from Frank Varian, who was then living in retirement with his wife in Cape Town. Varian wrote and congratulated him on his successful filming— "It is a trip that I have always wanted to do with a cine camera, as I did not possess one when I was in Angola"—and added that he looked forward to hearing "all about the country that I used to know so well in the past." Keynes immediately made plans to go to Cape Town, and spent three days with Varian. Varian struck Keynes as rather modest, considering his accomplishments. But then Varian was of the old-fashioned school that thought honor could never be sought; it could only be given. He was proud of his role as a builder in Africa and in bringing the magnificent antelope to the world's attention. He was happy to praise Keynes for the fascinating record he had made of "his" animals. Keynes took several photographs of him at his desk, while he looked up from a letter or reviewed his recently published memoirs, but the most interesting shows the two of them standing together, the tall, lanky thirty-four-year-old Keynes in a suit and tie with a camera slung around his neck, the shorter Varian, snappily dressed in a blazer with a silk scarf in the breast pocket, erect and vigorous-looking at seventy-eight.

Keynes had another invitation that fall, from the Count de Yebes, suggesting he come to Madrid for a visit. The timing was perfect; he'd leave for Spain from Cape Town. Keynes had asked the count if he could film the world-record sable, now in the Madrid Museum, and Yebes agreed. On the much-anticipated day, Keynes brought his equipment and the mounted animal was dutifully removed from its glass case and brought outside for filming. Luckily, Keynes took some additional still photos— he discovered later that he'd forgotten to load his motion picture camera. But the stills are impressive enough; one shows the Madrid taxidermist who'd mounted the antelope on a ladder, framed under the arch of the beast's horns, struggling to hold a tape measure along the curve of one from the base to its tip, his arms outstretched. The horns are so large and deeply curved that had the living animal bent double, he could hardly have brought the points into play for defense.

While visiting the count, Keynes received a letter from Scotland from Gilbert Blaine, then in his eighties, who had just heard from Frank Varian. He hoped Keynes could come visit him, as he felt sure that they "would have much to talk about." When Keynes returned to London and wrote that he couldn't come, Blaine replied that he understood, adding in a wistful note that "the only 'trophy' I now possess of all my collection, is the skull and horns of a giant sable, which is very ornamental and a reminder of one's hunting days."

Keynes had taken seventy-five feet of film and a couple of dozen still color pictures of the giant sables fighting, and da Silva took a number of shots as well. When Keynes finally arrived in London in October of 1954, he already had interest from several newspapers and magazines in his photos. But all he could show them were four photographs da Silva had taken and passed on to him. Keynes's own negatives had yet to arrive; as he later found out, the police had impounded them, giving him fits of anxiety until he could extract them from the colonial bureaucracy. *The Times* (London) ran a story on Keynes's trip using da Silva's photographs in late October. In November, *The Illustrated London News* ran two pages of photographs, including color ones by Keynes, and several months later, *Look* magazine in the United States ran a similar story. Varian was delighted when Keynes sent on the *Times* story. In January of 1955, he wrote again: "Are you going on any safaris this year? I am afraid that my safari days are now past but I cannot complain when I look back on my time in Africa since 1898." It was a theme he would return to over and over in letters to Keynes over the next two years.

By then Varian was eighty-one years old and looking forward to a final tour of the lands he had explored and the pioneer railroads he had helped to build. But he had become increasingly dismayed at the signs of colonial unrest that threatened to undo the work of those who "opened up" Africa. Although he thought self-government possible among "the more advanced peoples," he believed, along with many of his generation, that "the stabilization of the continent generally will, in the future, depend on the Colonial powers retaining their coordinating influence over the variety of people within their borders." It was not to be. In the late fifties, African nations would begin to shake off their colonial overlords. In Angola's struggle for independence a decade later the Benguela Railway would be dynamited, shattering the spine of the iron road on which Varian and so many others had expended such immense effort.

When Keynes wrote Arthur Vernay in 1955 about his film, he received a long reply from Vernay's home in Nassau, where he had retired in 1941 and founded the Society for the Protection of the Flamingo in the Bahamas. "Of course, I remember meeting you two or three years ago, when we had a good 'jungly' talk," Vernay wrote. "I was delighted to hear of your success with the giant sable antelope, and I am sure that your pictures are quite unique." The only other ones he could recall were those he saw in Statham's book—"It was an interesting expedition, but it was not what I would call a 'top-hole' Museum expedition"—and he remembered Prentiss Gray as "a very good hunter." At seventy-eight, Vernay still had the urge to explore the Dark Continent: "I do anticipate a short expedition somewhere in Africa, possibly again to the Kalahari or to Nagamiland as I must have one more sniff of the African bush and the wonderful skies one sees there."

Four

ENTER THE BIOLOGIST

Like others before them, field biologist Richard Estes and his wife Runi had gone to Angola in search of the giant sable. What they wanted was not a trophy—only an understanding of the antelopes' life cycle. In 1929, when Prentiss Gray witnessed a Serengeti lionness chase down a wildebeest he had shot and wounded, Philip Percival told him that he had never seen an actual lion kill in all his twenty-four years in the bush, "and he knew of no white man that had." That admission, coming from the most famous professional hunter of his day, sounds astonishing to anyone who's become overly familiar with today's television wildlife documentaries of African game. It is easy to forget just how difficult it is to observe, much less film, the complex daily routine of animals. Human hunters, like animal predators, have a very narrow focus when they're afield. The hierarchies of groups, territorial advertising, courtship rituals, methods of stalking and browsing and the like were all noted by guides like Percival, but only as an accidental by-product of seeking specific animals worthy to be singled out as quarry. Only the most curious, like Selous in his naturalist mode, would spend significant time in pure observation unrelated to hunting. Estes and his wife were members of a new breed in the bush: those who would track down their chosen animals to watch and record their behavior. Before they began their study there had only been a few brief scientific accounts of the giant sable (of which Estes thought Blaine's the most informative) and a few papers written by Portuguese investigators who had spent a month or two in the Luando Reserve gathering information on the *palanca preta gigante*. But almost nothing was known about what the giant sable did or where it went during the rainy season.

I first talked to Richard Estes by telephone in 1994, but I didn't actually meet him until four years later, when I drove up to Peterborough, New Hampshire, to visit him and his wife and hear more about the year that the two of them spent observing the giant sable. Estes met me at the kitchen door off the garage of his Victorian house, gave me a quick, toothy smile and a firm handshake, and suggested I call him Dick. Then a lean seventy year old of medium height, he had thinning silver hair and a trim white beard framing a weathered face and wore aviator-style bifocals. I followed him into his office, a small, dim, and cluttered room next to the kitchen that overlooks the Contoocook River below. An out-of-date computer sat on a desk strewn with journals, filing cabinets bulged with papers, books teetered precariously in stacks—Estes had been away again on the fieldwork that has made him one of the world's foremost experts on the behavioral ecology of African mammals. He riffled through unsteady piles of papers for articles he wanted to show me, and then brought them out to the living room, where a few African mementos—an ostrich egg, several baskets, a pith helmet that the Portuguese used to hand out to the *sovas*, and a variety of wildlife photographs—shared space on the crowded bookshelves. His Austrian-born wife, Runhild—Runi for short—came into the room. She had a streak of gray in her thick dark hair, retained a trace of a German accent, and possessed an unflappable manner that nicely balanced her husband's barbed humor, intensity, and flashes of impatience.

Estes was born in New York, but grew up in Memphis, Tennessee, where he had relatives who raised chickens on their farm and where he hunted squirrels and game birds. Every summer, his family returned to the East Coast. The year he was ten, they stopped at the American Museum of Natural History in New York on the way to visit relatives in Massachusetts and his interest in animals took a different turn. "We stopped and looked at the Akeley Hall and it had a decisive impact on me," he said. "I don't think I realized it at the time, but I had a mental image of myself sitting on a *kopje* [rock hill] and watching all these species of plains game, antelopes and zebras, around a waterhole scene." His mother died when Estes was eleven, his father a few years later. He went to live with his uncle and aunt and attended a succession of boarding schools until he entered Harvard, class of 1950.

Steered into a premed program, Estes found himself studying chemistry when what he really hoped to do was work with large mammals. Discouraged, he thought he might become a nature writer, and tried majoring in English, then switched to social relations. He still wanted to go to Africa. But by the time he graduated he had developed severe back problems, and took a job as an assistant editor and staff photographer at *Yankee* magazine, just down the road from where he now lives. After four years, he quit with the intention of finally going to Africa, but ended up doing a screen treatment for a Cinerama film on Africa that never got produced and writing a book on the history of the Atlantic coastline that was never published. Still determined to go, he contacted Harold Coolidge, one of the founders of the World Conservation Union (IUCN), who wanted to send him to Burma to join a wildlife survey, with the promise that he'd help get him to Africa afterwards.

In the meantime, Estes had discovered the works of Konrad Lorenz. "I read *King Solomon's Ring*, and I said *that* is the field I'm interested in!" With the support of Coolidge and others, Estes was able to study with Lorenz at the Max Planck Institute on his way to Burma, where he did research on the Sumatran and Javan rhinoceros and collected birds. Now he knew he needed to go to graduate school. "But it was essential that I be able to do my fieldwork in Africa," he said. He was accepted at Cornell in 1961, took a year of coursework, and then, at last, went to Africa. He was in his mid-thirties. In Tanzania's Ngorongoro Crater, Estes undertook the first comparative multispecies study of plains game—wildebeest, zebra, eland, and Thompson's and Grant's gazelles. "I soon discovered it was next to impossible to do all these animals in depth," he told me. Besides, there was competition—a German researcher already working on zebras who didn't want Estes near his animals. Estes decided to concentrate on the wildebeest. He also happened to meet someone else who'd come out to Africa: his future wife.

Runi had grown up in Austria and had spent four years in Germany. She was in Tanzania visiting her parents, who had moved there to farm, and her sister, who was there as well. She was in her early twenties, and had taken a job with a safari company near Arusha. It was Christmas of 1963 when Estes first met the slim, pretty young woman. They were married in a small Tanzanian church in 1964 and came to the United States a year later so he could finish his dissertation. After getting his doctorate, "the smart thing to do would have been to look for a job," he said, "but I wanted to go back to Africa."

Estes was attracted to the idea of investigating an animal that hadn't been studied properly, particularly an endangered species, in order to help conserve it. The giant sable fit the bill perfectly. But to do a thorough study, he first needed to look at sable populations elsewhere in Africa. In the end, the entire project, supported by a variety of grants, required two years (1968–70) and took him and Runi across Africa. Zoologists recognize three other well-defined races of sable besides *variani;* the scarce East African sable (*Hippotragus niger roosevelti*), which has the shortest horns of all and is found only in the coastal hinterland of Tanzania and Kenya; and two races of the "typical" sable, the widespread *Hippotragus niger kirkii,* and the *Hippotragus niger niger* (black, black) found south of the Zambezi, in which females turn nearly as black as the males. (Because *H. n. kirkii* and *H. n. niger* males look similar, trophy hunters usually ignore the distinction.) Sables are found only in Africa's southern savanna, primarily in the *miombo* woodland zone a thousand miles wide that girdles the continent from Tanzania and Mozambique to the southern Congo and Angola — the largest continuous dry deciduous forest in the world. The Esteses would end up studying *Hippotragus niger* populations in East Africa, Zambia, Botswana, Rhodesia (now Zimbabwe), and South Africa before setting out for the giant sable lands.

THE ESTESES BEGAN their sable research in the Shimba Hills near Mombasa, Kenya in the fall of 1968 and stayed in East Africa until April of 1969, when they traveled in their Land Rover to Zambia and Botswana's Chobe region. By June, Estes and his wife had reached Victoria Falls, where Runi suffered violent headaches from a bout of tick-bite fever. Both met and became friends with Jeremy Anderson, a research officer at the park working on a waterbuck cropping project — who, much later, would also become deeply involved with the giant sable. They finally entered Angola in early September. In Luanda the couple conferred with various

Portuguese officials, toured nearby Quiçama Park and saw elephant, roan, eland, and the local red buffalo, and drove on to Malange city.

They glimpsed their first giant sable on September 20 in Cangandala National Park, on a drive organized by the game warden, but spotted a better one—a solitary male in the distance, with long, curved, but not very thick horns—the next day. The morning of the following day they saw a shy herd of a dozen animals that slipped into the forest. After returning to the warden's house they went out alone to explore, walking along a path to a native village. It was spring, and Estes was struck by the luxuriant flowering of trees and plants amid the burned stubble. He noted in their field journal that by five o'clock, "odors are unlocked and a fragrance fills the air that is like ten kinds of night-blooming jasmine." But they were eager to push on to the Luando Reserve, their principal study area, and crossed the Luando River by pontoon ferry on September 27. After a long drive down a rough track, they finally arrived that evening at the central settlement of Quimbango. The *fiscal de caça*, or game warden, Senhor José Alves, was happy to put them up. The next morning he treated them to a breakfast of reedbuck steaks, and gave them a tour by truck of his corner of the reserve, bouncing over the *picadas*, the dirt tracks that passed for roads, at breakneck speed. They spotted giant sable, but the warden's dog leapt out and chased them off.

The Esteses quickly decided it would be best to build their own mud and thatch native-style three-room house on the outskirts of the village so they could have some privacy. The African villagers were insatiably curious to see what they might do next and had already formed the habit of simply standing and staring at them. Estes staked out the measurements for a house on a hillside overlooking the small Quimbango River and Alves recruited five villagers to start work clearing and digging and cutting poles. Meanwhile, they camped nearby in their tent and set up housekeeping. Estes found boards and built a bookcase; Runi cleaned the vehicle, unpacked, and set up their files. The warden's wife sent over cabbage and beans and her husband dropped off a hunk of reedbuck.

They managed to squeeze in an afternoon drive in their vehicle on October 2, taking the warden and two African game scouts to where the scouts had seen a herd of sable the day before. They were able to observe the giant sables closely. "Quite tame," Runi wrote in her diary, and noted the physical characteristics of the subspecies: longer horns, the absence of a cheek stripe, and the retention of brown hocks, even in full-grown bulls. As expected, there was pronounced sexual dimorphism: mature males look very different from the females: they're bigger, blacker, carry massive horns, and have pendant, black-tipped penile sheaths "as an added masculine garnish"—physical traits that enhance their ability to compete for females. Before the antelopes caught their scent and ran off, Estes listed their sex and ages and began recording their individual peculiarities of horn shape and coloring.

The next morning they were out by six o'clock to find the same herd. The landscape was lightly forested with *Brachystegia* and *Julbernardia paniculata*, tall spreading trees with lacy, pinnated leaves; under their open canopy enough sunlight fell to support a variety of grasses and bush. The researchers explored the edges of nearby *dambos* (small meadows) and *anharas* (larger floodplain grasslands) but had no luck and returned home. Shortly after, the two scouts arrived on bicycles to report that they had found the herd close to where the Esteses had been looking. In the late afternoon they tried a different area themselves, driving off the main *picada* to an open spot where they spotted a herd of twenty-one sables. Runi wrote in the field journal: "16:50—new sable herd . . . an open piece of woodland on edge of *vlei* (a dried-up, grassy water pan), many ant-heaps, especially of needle variety. Tsetse murderous. Sable very much bothered by them. So are we!" They had forgotten to bring the screens they routinely used in the Land Rover's open windows. If they weren't careful, hundreds of these bloodsucking carriers of disease—notably sleeping sickness—would fill their vehicle in minutes. "Nothing keeps them off," Estes complained later. "Insect repellent is just salad dressing to them."

They had made a start; now they needed to organize their research. They had already spent a year in Africa becoming familiar with other sable subspecies before coming to Angola. "Everything else," Estes once told me, "had been preparation for studying the giant sable." But it wasn't easy. The language barrier made it difficult to explain to the game scouts, Antonio and Julio, that they should go off on their own to locate giant sable herds and report back, and only expect to accompany the two of them when the Esteses requested it. Eventually, they got their message across, and the *auxiliares* would head out in one direction while they went off in another.

Despite the additional trackers, the giant sable could be difficult to locate. "Vain search in usual area," "fruitless search in A.M.," and the like appeared regularly in their field notes. But they knew they simply had to put in the hours out in the bush to accomplish anything.

The couple drew up a map of the reserve, using the system of the twelve numbered *picadas*, so they could keep track of herd sightings and begin to understand the habitat preferences of the animal. Because sable are particularly active in the morning and late afternoon, most days the Esteses woke early and left before breakfast. Sometimes they took turns observing, but most often they went out together. Runi packed some sandwiches so that they could stay out if the observing went well. They usually drove to where the sable had last been seen, and then got out on foot to look for sign; at other times, if they were lucky enough to glimpse a herd from a *picada*, they might quietly observe them from the car, as the animals had become habituated to vehicles.

On a typical morning they would roll slowly down the faint track of a *picada* until they came to a likely-looking *dambo*, pull over, and turn the engine off. They'd listen intently for several minutes and watch the woodland edge in the distance through the bug-dotted windshield, scanning the bush carefully with binoculars. After a while, there'd be the smell of coffee from the opened thermos, the sound of a slurp from a cup. Peanuts—the tiny, barely feathered Myer's parrot chick Runi had adopted—was usually along for the ride in his little box on the dashboard, and had to be kept quiet with soft clucking noises and bits of chewed-up nuts. Then, just when Estes was thinking of getting out and looking for a sign or starting the engine and pushing on, indistinct forms hidden in the dark shade of the forest edge would begin to transform into giant sables stepping cautiously out into the open and the bright morning light. Estes would open the field journal and check his watch, then note the time, location, weather, vegetation, and number, age, and sex of the animals. *Ym, f, f, f, 2ym, 3c, big ♂*, he'd scribble—yearling male, female, female, female, two-year-old-male, three calves, big male.

Estes carefully recorded what they did and didn't do. All would certainly graze, some might browse on the *quinsolle*, the juveniles would spar or the bull would chase a young male away from the herd and then thrash a bush for good measure, and then all would lie down to rest, including the crèche of calves that had been scrimmaging—playfighting by bunching together. Some minutes later, they would all rise and move on. The smallest calf, perhaps a month old, tan in color, tiny horn buds just visible in the binoculars, would often get up last and lag behind, possibly a leopard's lunch. Afterwards, Runi often collected samples of the grasses the sable fed on; later, at camp, she would press and notate them for later analysis, and plant some in a test plot to verify the vegetation type.

To monitor herd movements, the researchers needed a way to track specific animals. They looked for the odd markings that set one sable apart from another, such as the unusual coloring of a cow or "a faint dark scar in white rump disc, right side" of one young male. As these sable began to be easily recognized, they were given names. There was "Red Top," a big dark bull with a chestnut splash behind the horns; another, for obvious reasons, was "Slit Ear." Females were not always chestnut-colored; "Blondie" was a lighter-colored cow with a yellowish mane. "Lassie" was a flop-eared female; a cow with a twisted horn tip was "Kinky." The huge-horned, dominant old bull with the stately stride, sometimes found off *picada* 9 with his large herd, became "Patriarch," a.k.a. "Big Daddy," commonly shortened to "Pat" or "B. D." in their field notes.

One night the moon was bright enough to allow them to drive behind the main study herd with their lights off, trailing them as they wandered desultorily over a large burned *anhara*. Just before midnight, a black form separated from the enveloping darkness below the distant trees and coalesced into a massive but unidentifiable bull. "The moonlight glanced off his great scimitar-shaped horns," Estes later wrote, "highlighting the ridges and leaving the grooves etched in shadow." The two of them watched the cows give way as he strode into the herd, head held high, neck arched, tail stiffly extended. Subadult males passed carefully behind him, "heads low to the ground, chins drawn in, tails clamped—like cowed dogs." The bull approached the cows aggressively, and each one fled in turn. Then he singled out a one-horned female, "following her every twist and turn as she dodged through the herd," Estes recounted. The never-repeated moonlit scene of the milling herd, the cow's hyenalike scream of fear and the bull's braying roar remained a vivid memory.

Eventually the accumulated miles of driving and the hours of observation began to pay off. The animals fell into the distinct social classes they'd seen in other sable populations: nursery herds of females and their young, bachelor herds of juvenile to adult males, and territorial males. They found the nursery herds, led as always by the oldest cow, variable in size and composition, even from day to day, but apparently occupying the same localities year after year. Estes knew from their previous studies that because female sables normally remain in the area where they grow up, "knowledge of the home range is passed on from generation to generation, and descendents may occupy the same indefinitely, like human clans."

The size of the home range of a particular herd could vary dramatically; some herds would travel miles to find a better range as the seasons changed. Although the rains increasingly restricted their movements to the main study area about five miles from Quimbango, the Esteses would eventually distinguish some eleven nursery herds in the reserve, with an average of two dozen individuals each—a higher number than they saw in the other sable populations studied. Rank order in these herds, as in other races of sable, was enforced by the usual means of intimidation, ranging from stiff-necked postures to outright hooking and stabbing with horns. Juveniles, including males up to three years old, were dominated by all adults.

In many antelope species, yearling males are driven out of the nursery herds by intolerant territorial males and form bachelor herds. Male sables—so long as they act submissively and haven't turned so dark in color that they resemble adult males—are tolerated into their fourth year. "It's not that the breeding males can't tell the difference," Estes told me. "But the lack of obvious differences doesn't trigger an innate response. Hence they tolerate the presence of the younger males." By the time bulls reach their fifth to sixth year, they break off from other bachelors and stake out a territory of their own, patrolling it and marking it by pawing the ground before defecating (the "dunging ceremony") and thrashing saplings with their horns, all as part of a complex strategy to improve their chances of reproducing. Alone in the woods, such solitary bulls leave little evidence of their presence other than droppings and tracks. Eventually, they seek to become "master bulls," like the ones they formerly submitted to when they were part of the nursery herd, and to successfully gather and defend their own herd. Estes found that the half-dozen territorial bulls in their study area kept a buffer zone of a mile or more between their territories and those of neighboring bulls.

Although they knew that a territorial bull dominates all other classes of sable, it took time to determine whose herd was whose. A nursery herd might be unaccompanied for weeks, and the territorial bull, inconspicuous in the forest, might be content to bring up the rear as it followed the lead cow. On the other hand, if the bull was preoccupied with directing the herd, examining the females, or chasing off assertive younger males, he could be observed very closely—as long as they or the scouts weren't spotted and the wind was in their favor. When two young males followed Red Top's herd from behind, they saw the bull defecate in defiance, and then charge the nearest of the two rivals, running him off. He then returned to the herd, always moving between the other male and the cows, stopping only to demonstrate his prowess by slashing a handy sapling vigorously with his horns. Two days later Red Top put on a strenuous effort to control his herd's movements when the herd approached a neighboring bull's territory. He repeatedly cut them off, advancing with his head outstretched or lowered, or held high in combination with a straight tail in a display of dominance. Bulls often chase recalcitrant cows, sweeping their horns and snorting or even resorting to blows with the curve of their horns. But not every territorial male seemed as concerned over their herd's movements as Red Top; in comparison, Patriarch seemed almost casual at times, and could be found lagging well behind his herd. Perhaps he had no fear of rivals; giving the brash three-year-old male in his herd a full view of his proud profile was usually enough to put the youngster in his place.

Estes once observed Patriarch, more than a mile into another bull's territory, strut boldly up to the resident herd and begin displaying himself to the cows. The resident bull, who had been resting with his back turned, came forward diffidently to challenge the intruder. The two bulls posed for each other sideways, then faced off, heads shaking, necks arched in high-horn presentation, and then lunged together, clashing and clacking horns, grunting and thrusting for advantage. Staggered by several solid blows from Patriarch, the resident bull broke off, turned tail, and ran. Surprisingly, the conqueror did not stay to lord it over the cows. Having made his point, Patriarch withdrew at a stately pace to his own territory, which allowed the resident bull to reclaim his territory and herd by default. On another occasion, when Patriarch's herd wandered into Red Top's territory, Patriarch followed them as if he belonged there. An agitated Red Top, anxious to avoid confrontation, kept a respectful distance from Big Daddy, slinking back to the herd only after the great bull's ostentatious departure. Estes wondered about this behavior; perhaps, he speculated, younger bulls continue to be impressed by the dominance of "master bulls" who have successfully defended their territories and resident herds for years.

Over the course of their studies, Richard and Runi Estes would see endless demonstrations of an entire repertoire of threats, submissive displays, and fighting techniques giant sables used on each other. Females asserted themselves by rubbing their horns on one another's necks or rumps, or more dramatically, aiming their horns at an opponent, or as a last resort, charging. Near equals circled each other in "lateral display," standing head to tail in erect and confident posture. Juvenile males — even calves — constantly honed their fighting skills, clashing, thrusting, fencing, and jabbing with their short horns. All these blows and swipes were normally directed at the head and horns, save when two adolescents faced the same direction and fenced shoulder to shoulder, one parrying the hits, Estes noted, like a "fencing master toying with a pupil," the other striking past his guard with a sudden stab over his own shoulder or under his opponent's neck. Such a deadly move would be fatal if delivered by a full-grown male; fortunately, the use of this maneuver fades with age and combat between adult bulls is largely limited to spectacular horn clashing.

A territorial bull often commanded respect simply by standing erect, chin tucked and tail raised, a posture that displayed his potent power perfectly. It brought on obsequious behavior from young males who paid homage by approaching in a cringing posture, head low and tail tucked, but ready to avoid a swat of the bull's great horns, which were held at a ready and threatening angle. Females singled out for attention by such bulls were equally and eagerly submissive; no herd animals wanted to be punished with a charge from an enraged bull.

When it came to reproduction, a giant sable bull would rely on investigation, selection, and aggression. He rode herd on his females, frequently spot-checking their urine, throwing his head back and baring his teeth in the characteristic *flehman* grimace that facilitated drawing urine molecules into the vomeronasal organ. This discriminating sniff, a form of ungulate urinalysis that reveals the reproductive status of the female, is, among sables, also practiced by females and even calves. Like a sultan giving the eye to the least of his harem, a bull encouraged by the results of this sexual litmus test may take a sudden fancy to any of his copper-colored cows. There might be a pas de deux of "courtship circling" followed by an approach from the rear to lift a foreleg high up between the female's hind legs—an antelope grope to check receptiveness that often brings on the female's open-mouthed "fear-gaping" response. Sable bulls do not take a slow response for an answer. Estes summarized one such brutal encounter between Red Top and the cow he'd singled out this way:

> One female giant sable was hotly pursued around and through her herd, which she was reluctant to leave, the chase punctuated by his bellows and her drawn-out cries. Run to exhaustion, she finally lay prone like a calf, but the bull persisted, standing over her and prodding her with a foreleg until she rose. The pursuit was then renewed. This went on intermittently for 2 weeks until the unfortunate cow came into heat. Then she stood with her head low holding out her tail almost horizontally waiting to be mounted, but moved a little when the bull reared, and circled head-to-head with him. Meanwhile, though, she rubbed her head and horns on his rump (*soliciting?*) and once jabbed him lightly. He mounted 5 times in a few minutes, the last 2 complete mounts including ejaculatory thrusts.

Sable are seasonal breeders, and the giant sable was true to form. The sable rut in the reserve took place in August and September before the rains; the birth of calves coincided with the end of the rains, sometime in May. The first giant sable calves the two researchers saw had been born a month or more before they had arrived in the reserves and had been concealed for several weeks in dense grass or in the woodlands at the base of a tree. The calves stayed hidden until their mothers came to suckle them, but the mother/calf bond was rather casual; once they rejoined the herd, calves stuck together and sought out their mothers only to nurse. After a few weeks, cows typically stopped suckling their calves and walked off. Small calves attempted to follow before giving up, uttering plaintive and surprisingly birdlike chirping noises that the Esteses had heard but didn't associate with the animals until they saw them actually making the sound. Mothers with misplaced young (or ones lost to predators) gave the same call in a lower register for several days before abandoning their search for them.

Partly as a result of their restricted mobility, Estes came to regard the results of their year-long study as modest. Still, early on, they were able to correct several misimpressions. It seemed quite likely that Varian was wrong in thinking the giant sable was larger in body than the ordinary sable—a view that Thomas had also held, based on the imposing skull of the type specimen—although Estes now concedes that in the absence of good comparative measurements, the question remains open. But more important, they were able to show that Portuguese claims that the giant sable had to migrate from the reserve or were forced to higher ground during the rainy season, where they became vulnerable to lions, were completely unfounded. As grazers and partial browsers, the animals were restricted in their movements by the seasonal availability of bunch grasses at a tender growth stage. When the rains started, the sable retreated to the woodlands. Estes noted that Blaine had correctly deduced the reason some fifty years before. The open meadows and larger grasslands became waterlogged with the rains and the wiry-stemmed grasses there had poor nutritional value; the natives used them for thatching. During the rainy season, the most palatable grasses were to be found at the edge of the grasslands in the *miombo* woodlands and around termite mounds.

Estes began to mull over other questions. He was not surprised to find sable visiting waterholes on a near-daily basis, even during the rainy season—they are, after all, among the more water-dependent antelopes. But they also frequently visited mineral licks, the bare patches of whitish clay soil at the base of termite mounds, often licking and even eating this calcium-and phosphorous-rich soil. As these two minerals are the main inorganic constituents of bone, he wondered at first if such behavior might possibly influence giant sable horn development. But later Estes would discount this; since *H. n. niger* often frequents mineral-rich habitat and has only average horn length, the size of giant sable horns must be a matter of nature, not nurture. Still, giant sables were clearly attracted to various sources of these minerals and could even be observed chewing on bones. In the predator-thin *miombo* woodand, not all the remains of kills and the carcasses of animals that died of old age or starvation end up in the crushing maws of hyenas. Bleached femurs and vertebrae of warthogs, roan, reedbuck, and yes, even the previous generation of giant sable, all were potential bone-building material to the great antelopes, an osseous recycling that conjurs up the memento mori of a young territorial male champing on a cracked rib of his ancestor, the master bull of his day.

RICHARD AND RUNI Estes's study marked a turning point for the giant sable. The desire to encompass the antelope's meaning by the godlike action of taking its life and then fixing its bodily form in glass-eyed taxidermy now had a new rival: the equally godlike goal of knowing the living beast through and through, from its behavior right down to its genetic code. The hunters had thought they could possess the giant sable by killing it and taking its horns as proof. Biologists would now embrace the animal by determining its precise place in the natural world.

But the animal could not be understood apart from the human world in which it was enmeshed. There had been tribes in the giant sable's habitat long before the Portuguese had come to Angola. And there was evidence that the animals actually benefited from at least one aspect of human impact on the environment: the yearly burning of the *miombo*. The two researchers had seen how the sable followed the cycle of seasons. When the rains tapered off in April, and the upland woodlands begin to dry up, the animals sought the still green grasses along the *mululos*, or drainage lines. In May, when the rains had ended and even the trees had gone dry, the sable haunted the swamps and springs that still had green growth. They then stayed there, searching for increasingly limited grazing, until the burning in June. These annual fires may have been set for thousands of years by the tribes—no one really knows—but the burning has shaped the animals' environment and supplemented their sources of nourishment. The natives first burn the woodland undergrowth and the *anhara* grasslands; within weeks the grasslands flush with new growth, drawing the giant sable into the open. Later, the *mululos* are burned, after which small shrubs flower. "This extended burning regime," the Esteses wrote, "produces a mosaic of pastures at different stages of regrowth and provides green forage for the sable and other grazers at a time when they otherwise would have to subsist on dry hay." Of course, sable could do just that if they had to—the Esteses had seen that in Rhodesia (Zimbabwe), but the condition of those animals had been poor, in marked contrast to the sleek appearance of the giant sable, even at the end of the dry season. Once the woodland pastures in the reserve began to revive with the rains that start with scattered thundershowers in early September, the sables returned once again to the woods.

The giant sable faced no competition for grazing from other herbivores, and had few natural enemies; carnivores were now largely confined to spotted hyenas, leopards, and wild dogs (lions had become rare in the region, although one was seen outside Quimbango at five in the afternoon). That left only human activity as a negative factor in the conservation of the antelope. Although burning, at least on a tribal scale, worked in the giant sable's favor, other human activities clearly did not.

Fifteen years before, in 1955, the Portuguese had raised the status of Luando to a "strict nature reserve," which in theory offered total protection for the resident wildlife. In practice, however, this was selectively enforced. Although the *fiscal* could shoot animals other than sable for his own use, the tribespeople in the reserves were forbidden to do so—they had the rivers to fish in. Nevertheless, the presence of hunting dogs in the villages, not to mention bows and arrows, seemed to point to official indifference so long as the quarry was restricted to minor species. If the Songo were interviewed about hunting practices (always using the pretense, of course, that it was an inquiry that concerned the "old days"), much information could be gleaned about traditional hunting methods—how anteaters were dug out of their burrows, mole rats trapped, civet cats ambushed and clubbed, guinea fowl snared, and the like. The sable was never mentioned.

Estes and his wife once asked two natives fishing in a small pool, surrounded by wet ground crisscrossed with sable tracks, if they had seen any sign of *palanca negra* and were told emphatically *no*. The warden's explanation was that local inhabitants would never say where they had seen sable. He assured the Esteses no native would dare poach a giant sable.

Whether this was due to a residual taboo, the stiff fine of a hundred thousand escudos (over $3,500 then), or simply that the Portuguese had made it clear that killing the animal would bring down the wrath of the colonial government was anyone's guess. But at the time of their study, the sable seemed well protected from poaching in both Cangandala and the Luando Reserve. Of course, for some well-connected hunters, shooting the *palanca negra* was still possible, even after the area was declared a reserve. Such "official hunts" were not restricted to museum collectors; governors and judges participated. Even so, Estes doubted the severity of the impact. "It is unlikely," he later wrote, "that hunting on its own was ever a major threat to the sable population." Certainly, the numbers taken by legal hunting *could* be controlled, and limited as necessary.

Habitat loss, however, was a serious and uncontrolled threat. The human presence in the reserve was no longer what it was when the cultures were tribal, the technology preindustrial, and the population small. There were now over sixteen thousand people in the Luando Reserve — mostly Songos, some Lwimbe, even some Suelas, plus a few dozen Europeans. The human population in the reserve had risen almost 40 percent in the last decade. "Even at present population levels the damage by human activity is severe, especially in woodland habitat," Richard and Runi Estes wrote in one report. "Clearing for cultivation, cutting of trees for fences and as building material for houses, for beehives, etc., are the main causes of damage." There was evidence that humans and animals were competing for the same resources. In fact, sable could be attracted to rice plantings, which were being cultivated within the animal's traditional home ranges. They were not attracted to manioc, but the Esteses noted that "the Songo seek out the best available woodland soils for their manioc plantations, which also represent the best wet-season habitat for sable." Unfortunately, even the best soils of the reserve lacked nutrients. Manioc could only be grown for eighteen months — after which the land had to lie fallow for at least thirty years before it could be replanted. The ridged furrows of these fields remained, scarring the landscape decades after abandonment.

The implications were obvious: population growth and unchecked clearing, cultivation, and burning would gradually destroy the giant sable habitat.

What made the situation worrisome from a conservation viewpoint was that it was extremely difficult to calculate what the population of giant sables might be. Large tracts of the reserve still remained unexplored—not surprisingly in an area that was almost as large as the island of Jamaica. In fact, Estes realized, the long foot safari that Statham had made in 1920 probably meant that the colonel had seen more of the reserve than any European before or since. And there was no way, without first mapping the extent of suitable giant sable habitat, to determine sable densities by random sampling. Nevertheless the Esteses calculated there might be one thousand animals, perhaps two thousand, in the reserve itself, and maybe several hundred more in Cangandala—similar numbers to those presumed by Portuguese investigators. Whatever the actual count, it was clear there were not many giant sables, and perhaps had never been—underscoring the fact that each herd of giant sable required many square miles of *miombo* to survive.

Adding to the sense of mystery were tantalizing reports of giant sable sightings outside the reserve and park. It seemed evident that the Luando Reserve was the center of the animals' habitat, but they may well have once ranged outside the land between the two rivers in some numbers. "Lack of evidence is no proof that the giant sable was not once found in a broader range," the two wrote. Given that the *miombo* woodland covered three-fifths of Angola, there was "no obvious reason why it should not have inhabited a wider area"—and it might still do so. After all, only the Songo had known of the existence of the herds in Cangandala before the 1960s. Estes gathered as much evidence as he could. Although it was all anecdotal, some of the reports were intriguing. Several sightings fell between Cangandala Park and the Luando Reserve, suggesting that the two areas were part of the animal's larger range. Estes concluded that the areas ought to be combined in a larger single unit whose expanded boundaries might better serve the animals, but how that might be accomplished, considering the extensive human settlement in the area, was another matter.

The two researchers mulled over the growing conflict between animals and people for the limited habitat of the reserve. Moving people out of the reserve—much less a larger park combined with Cangandala—was a drastic solution that seemed to put animals before people. Whether this was realistic or workable was not for them to say; they only knew that something radical would have to be done to ensure the giant sable's future. Perhaps the villagers could be helped to develop their river fishing to compensate for any loss of manioc cultivation in the woodlands? In truth, if the colonial authorities concluded that conserving the animal was important enough, they would not hesitate to move tribal peoples around, and wouldn't be concerned about compensating them either.

But in 1970, government officials had more than the welfare of antelopes to worry about: under attack by nationalist rebels, Portugal was fighting to hold on to its African colonies, and saw enemies everywhere. Field research was a perfect cover for clandestine bush contacts. Possibly for that reason, the Portuguese had been suspicious of the two researchers from the start. At the end of October, they had an unexpected visitor in Quimbango, one J. A. Silva. "He is sent by the Ministry," Runi wrote in her diary, "to assist us or something, quite unclear, but he speaks some English." He described himself as a "retired" government official—an *intendente*, or superintendent—who was familiar with the area. He was also quite friendly and helpful. It was only later that the Esteses realized that the government must have suspected them of being spies and had sent him out to check on their activities. If Silva had any doubts about them, he must have reassured himself soon after his arrival. He accompanied them on occasion but quickly grew bored. Eventually he left them alone to pursue their research while he used his time to take a number of striking photographs of the animal. Silva's presence was a sign that the impact of the independence movement was being felt throughout Angola. Another, more obvious, was the infrequent but startling sight of army patrols, soldiers in trucks rumbling down the main *picada* of the reserve.

THE YEAR 1961 had marked the beginning of the end for Portugal in Africa. The Portuguese didn't know that, of course, and reacted with shock and outrage at the anticolonial uprisings in Angola. But it was strange how they professed to be surprised by the events of that year.

In retrospect there had been a number of indications of serious unrest. In 1959 fifty-two Angolan dissidents, mostly Africans and *assimilados* but also a number of Europeans, were put on trial for subversion; another fifty-two were arrested the following year. News of these incidents was carefully suppressed. Then there was the hijacking off the coast of Venezuela of the Portuguese luxury liner the *Santa Maria* on January 22, 1961, which received unavoidable international notice. It was seized by Captain Henrique Galvão, who as a deputy had delivered the incendiary report on forced labor to the Portuguese parliament in 1947 and had been arrested four years later for organizing an opposition group. After spending seven years in jails and hospitals, Galvão had escaped to Latin America. His plans were to take the pirated ship and his small band of two dozen Portuguese and Spanish rebels to Angola, in hopes of taking it over and provoking a coup d'état in Portugal. The *Santa Maria*, with forty-two U.S. citizens on board, was located by the U.S. Navy three days later. Ignoring Portugal, the United States negotiated directly with Galvão to release its citizens in exchange for safe passage. Although he got no farther than the Brazilian port of Recife, where he was given asylum, Galvão managed to focus world attention on Salazar's dictatorship and its oppressed African colonies.

On February 4, the day the *Santa Maria* had been expected to land in Angola, the Luanda jail and two police barracks were attacked by crowds of Africans, each several hundred strong. Seven policeman were killed, and at their funeral the next day, rioting broke out again; this time two dozen rioters were killed, a hundred were wounded, and another hundred were arrested. Reprisals were carried out in the African slums and political prisoners executed. With their ruthless suppression of dissent, the Portuguese were making good on their boast that nothing like the Mau Mau uprisings that had so plagued the Kenya Colony could happen in Angola. But a month later terrorists struck the coffee farms.

Angola was to experience a particularly violent outbreak of the same nationalistic fervor that since 1957 had created as many sovereign states as colonies south of the Sahara. Some nations had been granted independence, others had wrested it from the colonial powers in bloody struggles. It was a long and growing list: Ghana, Guinea, Nigeria, the whole cluster of states that had once been part of French West Africa and French Equatorial Africa, and what had once been the Belgian Congo, right on Angola's border. Not far from that frontier, a rebellion broke out on the coffee plantations of northern Angola on March 15, 1961, and quickly spread across a 250-mile-long stretch of the coffee-growing region. African *contratados* joined the terrorist attacks on the isolated farms of settlers, traders' shops, and police posts and killed, tortured, and mutilated their employers and overseers. Some four hundred Europeans, *mestiços,* and *assimilados* died in the first several days and hundreds more over the next several months, as did uncounted Africans not part of any plot. A week after the outbreak the first Portuguese troops, skirting ambushes from rebels hiding in the tall elephant grass, managed to reach the affected areas, and began evacuating the surviving Europeans, who had barricaded themselves inside small villages and churches.

A closer look at the rebellion and its aftermath is both revealing and repulsive. The photographs the Portuguese took of the carnage were stomach-turning. Did the *catana*-wielding killers fear the *colonos* would come back to life if they weren't dismembered? In the days after the attacks stories filtered out of beheadings, gang rapes, and disembowelments, of finding bodies with stiff dead hands clutching where cut-off breasts had been, people that had been split lengthwise on planks in their own sawmills—the Portuguese had heard enough. Settlers reacted by forming vigilante groups that killed Africans in all parts of Angola, and the military sent in planes to napalm the *indigenatos* in the region indiscriminately. There were some 2,000 white troops in the colony before the uprising; by the end of the summer, airlifts and troopships brought in nearly 25,000 Portuguese soldiers to "pacify" the countryside. Given the ensuing slaughter, whole villages and their inhabitants engulfed in flames and the like, it's safe to conclude photographs of the reprisals would have easily matched the gruesomeness of the ones of the uprising. One notorious photograph from that time showed a smiling Portuguese soldier holding the severed head of an Angolan on a stake. By May of 1961 vigilante violence against Africans had reached such proportions that the government had to step in and curb it. The official death toll soon exceeded 2,000 Europeans and 50,000 Africans. There were more numbing numbers to come: by the end of the year, up to a half-million *indigenatos* had fled across the Congo border, many arriving mutilated, wounded, and burned, a testament to Portuguese brutality.

Salazar had been stunned by the events. Not long before, a typical photograph of the dictator showed him in a crisp, beige double-breasted suit, gray hair slicked back from his somber but confident face, taking a moment away from his many burdens of state to give the camera a look that simultaneously reassured his supporters and quelled his critics. But now, the supreme leader who would admit to occasional errors in judgment, but never to mistakes in principle, had been shaken to the core by the uprising. "The work of centuries," he concluded grimly, "had been destroyed in a month."

The Portuguese government blamed everyone but themselves for the Angolan bloodbath. The claim that it was a resurgence of the savage tribalism that Portugal had been fighting against for hundreds of years struck a sympathetic chord with those who still saw Africa in nineteenth-century terms. (What happened on that single day, March 15, 1961, Robert Ruark wrote, was "worse than the combined atrocities of the Portuguese in 500 years of colonization.") The further claim that the revolts were caused by outsiders served to deflect attention from genuine Angolan grievances. Yes, the attackers were outsiders, but they were Angolans too, part of the roughly one million Africans then living beyond their country's borders. The fact that the uprising occurred on the same day that the United Nations voted on a resolution calling for self-determination in Portugal's colonies made it obvious that it had been a carefully planned and directed rebellion. As a result, Portuguese assertions that the revolt had been communist-inspired and communist-directed seemed more plausible, and won Portugal grudging sympathy in some quarters as a bulwark against revolutionary African nationalism.

Portugal's effective use of censorship, control of education, and ruthless policing kept organized nationalist opposition from developing until relatively late in Angola. But in spite of government repression, a number of underground proindependence groups had sprung up in the 1950s and 1960s. To many across the continent and elsewhere, their leaders were nationalist heroes. To the Portuguese, the rebels were terrorists bent on driving them from the African soil they called their own.

At the beginning of the 1960s, Portugal would face more than Angolan revolt. World opinion had been moving against Lisbon's insistence that its African territories were integral parts of Portugal and thus whatever happened within these vast borders was a domestic affair. The United Nations heard denunciation after denunciation of Portugal in Africa. The Ghanaian delegate summed it up: "The world must realize that the Portuguese territories are slave states and have always been slave states." In December 1960 the General Assembly overwhelmingly passed a resolution calling upon colonial powers to end their dominance over the peoples in their possessions. The United States abstained, but voted for the March 15, 1961 General Assembly Resolution which called on Portugal to comply with the December resolution (Britain and France dissented). A UN subcommittee was appointed to look into the Angolan situation. Its report urged Portugal to undertake drastic reforms and prepare Angola for self-government.

The climate of opinion had changed dramatically in the years since the Second World War, when the Allied powers began seriously considering at what date African and Asian colonies might achieve independence. During the war, one Labour politician in Britain voiced a common view about giving the colonies their independence: it would be "like giving a child of ten a latch-key, a bank account, and a shotgun." At the same time, the U.S. State Department opined that it would take a hundred years for the Belgian Congo to be in a position to govern itself. And Portugal, in its view, had been so morally debauched as a colonial power it would take a thousand years for some of its possessions to achieve self-government. Twenty years later the argument had changed: now, the idea that a people had the right to govern themselves, however poorly they had been prepared to do so, was in the ascendant.

World opinion largely agreed that Portugal ought to give up its possessions as a botched job. The British, perhaps fearing instability in its remaining colonies, stopped well short of that. Then too, Portugal had been a British ally since the treaty of 1373 covenanted them to "be friends to friends and enemies to enemies." And Portugal, although neutral in the Second World War despite Salazar's open admiration for the Fascists, had allowed the British and American flotillas and air forces to use the Azores as a base. The airfield there remained a key facility for NATO forces, of which Portugal was one. As a consequence, the Kennedy administration found it awkward to support UN calls for African independence at the same time that it needed Portugal as a staunch ally. Although concern for NATO unity would overshadow African concerns, the United States put Portugal under considerable pressure to reform its colonial policies.

Salazar refused to give in under the chorus of criticism. For status-starved Portugal—roundly regarded as a second-rate power, kicked around at the Berlin West Africa Conference in 1885, taunted and humiliated—its colonies were of supreme importance, a source of pride that never failed to recall the glorious past endlessly celebrated in monuments and textbooks. Colonialism had always been a "highly visual phenomenon," as historian Paul Johnson observed. "It abounded in flags, exotic uniforms, splendid ceremonies, Durbars, sunset-guns, trade exhibitions at Olympia and the Grand Palais, postage stamps and, above all, colored maps." Indeed, Portuguese teachers would show schoolchildren the map of Angola superimposed on the map of Europe to illustrate the Estado Novo's slogan that "Portugal is not a small country." To retain the fading images of empire, Portugal had to hold on to its colonies in Africa. After the events of 1961, of course, it was too late for any regrets that it hadn't fulfilled the promise of creating a multiracial, African *civilização* in Angola.

The Portuguese had always made much of their historical mission, but they were never in a rush about it. So what did they have to show for half a millennia of colonial rule? A repressive regime which virtually guaranteed that only a handful of Africans could break out of the *regime do indigenato*—the native underworld of poverty and social degradation. The number of *assimilados* remained at less than 1 percent of the population, largely because there were hardly any educational institutions. Illiteracy among the African population was 97 percent. The number of high school graduates in the entire country could be counted in the dozens, and most of those were white. By comparison, the Belgian Congo had nearly one million students enrolled in primary schools in the early 1950s; at that time, Angola had less than 15,000, two-thirds of whom were white. In 1956 about 1 percent of African children in Angola attended school, compared with 11 percent in northern Rhodesia. It was a matter of policy; unlike other colonizing powers, Portugal did not use schoolteachers to impart civilization—it preferred employers. But Angola did have 250 miles of paved roads by 1960.

Salazar saw no choice but to respond militarily to the uprisings. But Lisbon had finally recognized that Africans in Angola might possibly have some reason to be hostile to Portuguese colonial rule, and thus be receptive to the nationalist movements—or even join them. Once the rebels had been driven out, and control regained over much of the territory, a flurry of reforms intended to "win the hearts and minds" of the Africans were enacted. Forced labor was abolished, the distinction between "civilized" and "noncivilized" citizens wiped out, and the expropriation of lands forbidden. More administrative and judicial reforms followed. While other colonial powers were divesting themselves of their African territories, Portugal had begun to take the colonization of Angola seriously. Now that the forces of nationalism had taken hold, it was much too late to develop the land and its resources and marshal its people, who could hardly be expected to regard a few belated reforms as a counterweight to five hundred years of exploitation. But Portugal would try.

Some government officials argued that Africans would be persuaded by genuine and sweeping changes, that their lives would be materially improved if they stayed loyal to the colonial authorities. Others thought that Portugal lacked the time and resources to make any radical alterations in Angola. What was essential was to physically isolate the African population from the nationalist rebels. Concentrating the rural population into fewer villages that could be guarded by the army (and supervised by the secret police) would minimize contacts with the nationalists. Development schemes could not be implemented until "secure" villages had been created. Policy seesawed between efforts to control and develop, and while Portugal did in fact invest significant resources into improving the lives of Africans, the massive resettlement schemes that were finally imposed in Angola simply perpetuated the colonial system which always benefited whites. It also created colossal human upheaval in the countryside. Although Angola had experienced mass disruptions before—from tribal invasions, slaving raids, wars of "pacification," contract labor, and expulsion by settlers—this one would be different. As Gerald Bender wrote, "The radical changes it provoked in traditional societies were so profound that rural Angola will never again be the same."

In the 1960s guerrilla activity had been largely limited to border attacks launched from sanctuaries in neighboring countries. The government made strenuous attempts to secure villages in the north and even constructed new schools to attract the labor required by the coffee industry, which had become the colony's principal export earner. By 1966, however, fighting had shifted to the eastern frontier with Zambia. Peasant support of the nationalists there convinced many Portuguese officials that it was too late for reforms, and that virtually the whole African population had to be regrouped into strategic hamlets. By 1967, forced resettlement would become the focus of Portuguese counterinsurgency efforts.

Over one million Africans would be driven from their homes and fields—often at gunpoint, beaten if they resisted, their huts burned—and trucked to villages organized by the military. The ones near the fighting would be surrounded by barbed wire and set up to provide local defense. In all of them, widely dispersed Africans were crowded into large settlements alongside roads patrolled by the army. Each family had to build its own hut and report any strangers or missing persons; anyone caught in the fields after dark might be shot as a terrorist. Spies and informers were recruited by the secret police (PIDE), and those suspected of cooperating with the rebels were publicly beaten. Outbreaks of contagious diseases in the crowded resettlements were common and deadly. The Africans who were uprooted were thrown together without regard to their cultural differences; a fisherman might be sent to a farming area, a farmer to a military zone where he would be put to work building roads.

The *Sanzala de Paz*, or "village of peace" policy, would be imposed throughout much of the Angolan countryside, and eventually, even in the Luando Reserve. There, some five hundred tiny, scattered settlements were consolidated into sixty-odd villages "strung like beads," as Richard Estes put it, along the main north-south road. Clustering settlements in this way meant that several villages, each with its own headman or *sova*, had to reside in what had formerly been the territory of a single *sova*. The villagers coped by keeping one home to show colonial authorities while quietly maintaining a simple shelter in the bush to work the fields in their former village lands. The Portuguese army declared the forcible removals in the giant sable reserves complete the year before the Esteses arrived.

IN THE FAR-OFF vastness of the Luando Reserve, Angola's growing struggle for independence seemed far away. "We were there in the eye of the storm" was how Runi Estes explained it to me; "there was little obvious unrest." A picture Estes took of her in front of their house after the rain had gone in April shows her holding up a large, broad-leafed uapaca plant, with its central flower. She looks tanned and happy. In June and July the mostly man-made fires that sweep through the *miombo* expose the thin soils of woods and grasslands alike to the relentless sun and wind. Estes remembers well how by four in the afternoon the haze of smoke and dust dimmed the sun to a glowing red ball. By August it was a relief to picnic on the banks of the northern Cuanza, swim in the shallows of the now quiet river, and soak in rock pools formed by rounded gray boulders. A slide taken then shows Estes sitting in one under a small waterfall; he's wearing horn-rimmed glasses, and laughing as the water streams over his head.

By mid-September of 1970 the couple had completed their conservation study. They'd followed the giant sable through their annual cycle, and would spell out their recommendations in their final report. It was time to leave. They'd heard that Brian Huntley, a South African ecologist working with Angola's Serviços de Veterinária, was coming to the reserve and they wanted to leave their house for his use, but knowing the efficiency of African termites, also hoped it would still be standing when he arrived. They left their propane refrigerator and small sofa behind, as well as the little plaque over the door that pointed out that a research grant from the National Geographic Society had helped pay for the modest structure. Runi made the last two entries in the field journals. The day before leaving, she noted, they made a short "foot safari" up the path to the *anhara*. "There are at least three new manioc fields in the woods . . . Saw several scrapes." The last of the heart-shaped sable tracks they would see were tellingly intermingled with the footprints of the tribespeople on the paths to their fields. They knew that the animal was destined to lose in any clash with people over the resources of the reserve, but hoped for the best. They had no idea that horrific human conflict would engulf the entire country in a few years' time, blotting out for the rest of the century any realistic hope that a conservation program for the *palanca preta gigante* would be implemented. The day they drove off, the last sign they saw of the animals was a pile of dung on the edge of the woodland. The giant sables were returning to the forest.

THERE WAS ONE more thing I wanted to see before I left the Esteses' house—the head of the giant sable Richard C. Curtis shot in 1923.

I walked into the hallway and looked up the stairwell at it in the dim winter light. The dark trophy hung on the wall, its head bowed to accommodate the horns. After climbing the stairs, I paused on the landing to reach out and touch the muzzle of the now long-dead inert beast fixing me in the empty stare of his glass eyes. The fur felt coarse, and the head was a lot bigger than I imagined it would be, almost horse-sized. From the front, the polished, knurled, almost ebony dark horns were quite close, spreading little more than a foot apart at the very points. One stiff ear was snapped off at the tip, and the muzzle had the faint trace of a cheek stripe, like a visual echo of the ordinary sable. It seemed strange to be looking at the animal of those compelling photographs in the book I had read as a boy.

"I take it you've read the Curtis book?" Estes asked.

"Several times," I answered. In fact, the book was in my shoulder bag. "How did that head end up here?"

By a strange coincidence, he explained.

After the Esteses returned from Angola, they moved to Manchester-by-the-Sea, a coastal town near Gloucester, Massachusetts. Mrs. Richard C. Curtis, then a widow in her seventies, lived a half-mile away, on the same street. Years before her husband had died after a long and debilitating illness, and she lived alone. Through friends, Anita Curtis had heard of the young couple who had recently returned from a country she had traveled to a half-century before, and she asked them to tea. Runi remembered her lovely old home on Smith's Point with grand ocean views from the windows and the startling sight of a giant sable head hanging in the stairwell. Anita Curtis spoke with happiness of the long-ago expedition to secure that trophy. All that had ever troubled the trip—the difficulties and hardships, doubts and hesitations—had been rubbed away by repeated recollection. She and her husband had shared a great adventure in a far-off land and the final memory of it remained like a perfectly pressed flower, somehow still fragrant and vivid. She regretted that the giant sable mount had faded, however, and Richard Estes endeared himself to her by offering to touch it up with some shoe polish. She gave them a copy of the book her husband and his brother had written. They visited her from time to time over the next few years until they moved to Philadelphia in 1974 and lost touch with her.

Several years later, on a return visit to Manchester-by-the-Sea to see friends, Runi got a call. Anita Curtis had died, and left her house to friends. In cleaning out her effects, they'd found a small scrap of paper with the name "Estes" and the words "giant sable" written on it in a desk drawer. Did Runi and her husband have any interest in the cumbersome head? Otherwise, the old horns would be thrown out. Runi immediately drove over in her station wagon and picked up the giant sable mount, as well as a second pair of sable horns on a plaque—doubtless the elder Curtis's trophy from that expedition—and took them away. Estes ended up giving the second set of horns to Harvard, and hung the Curtis head in the stairwell of their house.

FIVE

CAUGHT IN THE WAR ZONE

The giant sable had always faded into the forest when threatened, but for the rest of the twentieth century the *miombo* would provide little refuge. The dark antelope became trapped in its own habitat, slowly encircled and repeatedly endangered by a ghastly, catastrophic, decades-long war that had been coming for a very long time.

To many Portuguese, the Angolan independence movements of the 1960s and early 1970s—MPLA, FNLA, UNITA—seemed faceless, menacing compounds of tribal savagery, foreign agitation, and communist rhetoric. But there were Angolans behind the acronyms. At first armed with little more than the bitterness of their experiences under colonialism, they soon found the political theories, roles, and backing that allowed them to attack their country's rulers—but their differences would prove irreconcilable.

The Popular Movement for the Liberation of Angola (*Movimento Popular de Libertação de Angola*), or MPLA, which had its roots in earlier anticolonial groups, was formed in 1956. Its later prominent leader, Dr. Agostinho Neto, was Angolan, born in 1922; his father had been a Methodist pastor. A soft-spoken Mbundu, he was one of the few blacks to attend Luanda's top secondary school and he studied medicine in Portugal on a Methodist scholarship. Neto actively participated in opposition politics there and his nationalist views were clearly evident in his striking poetry. "Western Civilization" sums up his view of colonization:

> *Tins fixed to stakes*
> *driven in the earth*
> *make the house*

Rags complete
The intimate landscape

The sun piercing the cracks
awakens the inhabitant

After twelve hours of slave
labour

Breaking stones
carrying stones
breaking stones
carrying stones
in the sun
in the rain
breaking stones
carrying stones

Old age comes fast

A reed mat on dark nights
enough for him to die on
thankfully
and of hunger.

Neto's activities and all too vivid writings brought him to the attention of the PIDE, the Portuguese secret police, and he was in and out of Portuguese jails throughout the 1950s. After receiving his medical degree in 1958, he returned to Luanda and was targeted by the authorities. Dr. Neto was arrested in 1960, flogged in front of his family, and taken to jail. When hundreds of villagers from his birthplace and its neighboring town marched to protest his arrest in 1960, Portuguese troops killed thirty of the protestors, wounded two hundred others, and destroyed their villages to boot. The MPLA went into exile. Neto, deported to Cape Verde and then Lisbon, eventually escaped and was elected president of the MPLA at its first party conference in Leopoldville (later Kinshasa) in the Congo in 1962.

Holden Alvaro Roberto, who later founded the National Front for the Liberation of Angola (*Frente Nacional de Liberatação de Angola*), or FNLA, was the son of a Baptist mission worker. He was born in Angola but was taken to the Belgian Congo at the age of two and educated in a mission school in Leopoldville. He spent most of his life in exile in the Congo, and met various nationalist African leaders there, including Patrice Lumumba. Roberto was president of UPA (the Union of Angolan Peoples, or *União das Populaçõs de Angola*), a forerunner of the FNLA, and the organization behind the March 15, 1961 uprising. "This time the slaves did not cower," Roberto was quoted as saying. "They massacred everything."

Jonas Malheiro Savimbi, who was to found and lead the National Union for the Total Independence of Angola (*União Nacional para a Independência Total de Angola*), or UNITA, also came from a religious background. His father had been an active Evangelical Church pastor as well as a Benguela Railway stationmaster, and the young Savimbi attended a Protestant school in Dondi and a secondary mission school in Cuito run by Catholic Marist Brothers. In 1958 he took the train to Lobito to sail to Portugal and study medicine on a scholarship. On the voyage there, a black American sailor gave him books by Marcus Garvey and others on Marxism, which fired his interest in freedom movements. In Lisbon, Savimbi participated in anticolonial politics while pursuing his medical studies; the PIDE jailed him briefly for these extracurricular activities. He met Agostinho Neto, who was by then the most prestigious black Angolan nationalist, and who had just been released from prison.

Neto was ardently anti-Salazar and took the position (which later proved correct) that without change in Portugal, Angola would never achieve independence. He encouraged Savimbi to continue both his studies and political struggle, but told him that the struggle came first. Savimbi, fearing further persecution from the PIDE, secretly left Portugal in 1959 for Switzerland, crossing the Spanish border in the trunk of a sympathetic communist's car.

Savimbi began studying medicine in Switzerland and became involved in liberation politics there. Soon after, he was approached by Holden Roberto, who traveled to Lausanne to meet him. Roberto warned him the MPLA was communist in outlook, and dominated by *mestiços*. Savimbi, who was having second thoughts about communism and was suspicious of *mestiços'* leading a liberation movement in a mostly black country, kept his options open. He traveled to East Africa, where he met several leading African nationalists, including Tom Mboya, who would become a cabinet minister in Kenya's first postcolonial government. Mboya took Savimbi to meet Jomo Kenyatta, at that time under house arrest, but able to receive visitors. The young student was thrilled to meet Kenyatta, by then an African legend; in 1963 he would become independent Kenya's first prime minister. Savimbi was particularly impressed by one of Kenyatta's sayings: "When the missionaries arrived the Africans had the land and the missionaries had the Bible. They taught us to pray with our eyes closed. When we opened them, they had the land and we had the Bible." Both Mboya and Kenyatta urged Savimbi to join Roberto's movement.

Savimbi flew to Leopoldville (Kinshasa) in the Congo in February of 1961 to be inducted into the ranks of the UPA, just weeks before the bloody March 15 revolt. Politics had taken the place of medicine, but the son of the pastor and stationmaster was still determined to get a degree, and enrolled as an undergraduate in the Department of Law and International Politics at Lausanne University. For the next several years, Savimbi juggled academic work with liberation politics — but the latter took up most of his time.

He was appointed the UPA's secretary general, the first Angolan of Ovimbundu origin to be given a major position in the organization, most of whose members, like Roberto, were drawn from the Bakongo of northern Angola and the Congo. Savimbi effected his group's merger with a smaller nationalist group (the Democratic Party of Angola, or PDA) in March of 1962 to form the FNLA. A week later the new organization announced the formation of the Revolutionary Angolan Government in Exile (GRAE), with Roberto as president and Savimbi as foreign secretary. Within months, nearly every independent African government formally recognized the GRAE. These actions further weakened the MPLA, already badly split by internal disagreements and unable to follow up the February 4 uprisings. By late 1963 the Congolese government ordered the MPLA to cease activities on its territory. Agostinho Neto, who'd been elected president of the fractured organization the year before, led his remaining followers over the Congo River into Congo (Brazzaville), then governed by a sympathetic left-wing regime. The MPLA's fortunes had bottomed, and it would look elsewhere for support.

But the FNLA/GRAE had troubles of its own. Despite backing from the Congolese government and military aid and guerrilla training from Algeria, Ghana, and other countries, it was unable to hold its own against Portuguese counterattacks in Angola. Roberto refused to widen the independence war beyond the north of Angola and took to being driven around Leopoldville in a black Mercedes. Increasingly at odds with Roberto, Savimbi developed his own following among fellow Ovimbundu in the FNLA and cultivated personal relationships with several African leaders, including Egypt's Gamal Abdel Nasser. Distrustful of Roberto and the FNLA's ability to mount an effective campaign of liberation from foreign bases, he announced his withdrawal from the movement at the Organization of African Unity's 1964 summit in Cairo.

Savimbi wanted to form his own freedom movement based inside Angola, and traveled to East Germany, Hungary, Czechoslovakia, Bulgaria, China, North Vietnam, North Korea, and the Soviet Union to look for support. Only China showed interest; it offered money and training for his cause. By 1965 Savimbi had completed his final examinations in Switzerland for his degree—what it was and whether it was ever awarded is in dispute, but from then on he would style himself "Dr. Savimbi"—and joined eleven recruits, chosen from Angolan exiles in Zambia, for a year-long course of guerrilla training in Nanking. In March of 1966, Savimbi's own movement, UNITA, was launched at a local chiefs' meeting at Muangai, a Chokwe village in eastern Angola.

The three nationalist movements—MPLA, FNLA, and UNITA— were never able to form a united front against the Portuguese. For one thing, they were separated by ethnic, regional, and class differences that had been exacerbated by Portuguese rule: when the colonial authorities weren't undermining traditional tribal authority, they were pitting one ethnic group against the other. The MPLA had developed support among the Mbundu and the urban disaffected in cities such as Luanda. Multi-racial, Marxist, and nationalistic, it had also developed the most explicit links to the international ideological Left. The FNLA had a clear Bakongo ethnic orientation—the ancient dream of a separate Kongo nation had never died—but no discernable ideology. UNITA, despite its early Maoist orientation, soon took on Ovimbundu overtones. Rural-based, it also posited itself as the alternative movement to the Marxist MPLA. There were further differences: the MPLA leadership included many *mestiços*, and spoke Portuguese, as did UNITA's Ovimbundu elite. The FNLA's leaders spoke French. Neto, Roberto, and Savimbi ruled their movements autocratically. But the main reason for lack of unity was simply that these leaders had no interest in sharing power.

For Portugal and a string of other nations eager to promote their own ends, the antagonisms and divisions among these movements were useful and easily exploited. Outside powers lined up to back their favorites. The MPLA received military and humanitarian aid from Algeria, Morocco, and Sweden. At one point, thinking that the United States would support the African nationalism it espoused diplomatically, Neto had asked for its assistance; he was turned down. But the MPLA had other friends. Because of its roots in the communist parties of Portugal and Angola—and the fact that Neto made it appear to espouse Soviet ideals—the MPLA received some of the aid that the USSR was giving national liberation movements across southern Africa. It also began to receive military support from Eastern Bloc countries. "That people fighting for their independence will take aid from wherever they can find it is clear," Neto had declared in a broadcast. "To win our independence we should even take aid, as they say, from the Devil himself."

The former Belgian Congo, with its substantial exile community of Angolans, was a natural rear base for guerrilla warfare in the Portuguese colony, and successive leaders there usually supported Holden Roberto. Col. Joseph-Désiré Mobutu had deposed and disposed of Patrice Lumumba in 1961 with CIA assistance and would stage another coup in 1965; an anticommunist despot, he renamed himself "Mobutu Sese Seko" and his country "Zaire" in the early 1970s. A word had to be coined to describe his version of rapacious rule: "kleptocracy."

The United States, which had its doubts about Salazar's ability to resist the rebel movements, had maintained contact with Holden Roberto since the days of the UPA. In fact, the National Security Council put Roberto on the CIA payroll. He received a yearly $6,000 subsidy, upped to $10,000 in 1962, for "intelligence gathering." But Roberto, looking for more substantial assistance, turned to China, which was extending aid as part of its Third World competition with the Soviet Union. At Kenya's independence ceremonies at the end of 1963, China's foreign minister promised Roberto "large-scale military aid."

When Jonas Savimbi and his band of guerrillas entered Angola in 1966, their armament consisted of knives and a Soviet-made pistol given to Savimbi by Sam Nujoma, the leader of SWAPO, the liberation movement in South Africa–controlled South-West Africa (later Namibia). Savimbi used Chinese money to buy ten standard NATO 7.62 rifles in the Congo for his fighters. To gain UNITA credibility as a liberation movement, Savimbi led them on an attack on Cassamba, a Portuguese timber outpost, in early December. It was a failure; they lost several men and were driven off. A second attack, a few weeks later, had the impact Savimbi hoped for. On Christmas Day 1966, his men, backed by untrained, poorly armed Chokwe recruits, launched an attack on the Portuguese barracks, airfield, and jail in Teixeira de Sousa (now Luau), the last stop on the Benguela Railway just before the Congo border. According to one account, a half-dozen Portuguese were killed, including the PIDE chief. Savimbi lost several hundred men, but the Portuguese were forced to close the border and shut down the railway, stopping vital copper shipments and commercial transport from the Congo and Zambia. Kenneth Kaunda, the president of the newly independent Zambia, was furious at the UNITA attack. When the line was derailed twice more in later months, Zambia expelled the UNITA movement and its leader. Savimbi spent a year in exile in Cairo.

By the time Savimbi reentered Angola clandestinely in July of 1968, his new liberation movement was moribund. He established a base west of Luso (now Luena) near the forested headwaters of the Lungu Bungo River, south of the Benguela Railway, a district populated by scattered Chokwe. Savimbi hoped to win over the same region that the MPLA was seeking to extend its military operations into: the "Hungry Country." The Portuguese had another name for the region: *terras do fim do mundo*— the lands at the end of the earth. In those vast desolate spaces, there were no front lines, and rebel and colonial forces alike could claim control. Over the next few years, Savimbi quietly regrouped his forces. His activities during this period are not well documented. Later, he would quote a proverb: "If a non-swimmer falls into a flood, he grabs any stick of wood that gives him a chance to be saved." He struck a secret deal to collaborate militarily with the Portuguese: in exchange for tracking and ambushing MPLA forces in eastern Angola, UNITA would not be attacked. The would-be liberator of Angola had begun a pattern of duplicity that over the next several decades would take him increasingly closer to gaining political power by military means.

Bitter infighting among the independence movements hobbled their effectiveness against the Portuguese army, but nothing would stop the colony's inexorable pace toward independence. The brutal resettlement schemes of the colonial government succeeded only in driving more of the rural population to the nationalist movements they were supposedly being isolated from. Eventually the strain of fighting colonial wars on several fronts began to wear down Portuguese resolve. They had lost their Indian outpost of Goa in 1961; two years later war broke out in Guinea-Bissau, the year after that in Mozambique. Salazar's patriotic appeals and authoritarian measures sent thousands of young soldiers to fight in interminable and unwinnable conflicts. By the mid-1960s staggering military expenditures forced Salazar to relent on his policy of excluding or limiting foreign investment, opening the door to the influx of outside capital. Gulf Oil was among the first to take advantage of this change of policy and found oil outside Cabinda in 1966.

On August 3, 1968, Portugal's dictator toppled from power, felled by a stroke. By autumn, Marcello Caetano had replaced Salazar, although no one told Salazar; he died believing he still ruled. Caetano promptly declared there would be no change to his predecessor's colonial policies. "Portugal cannot gamble away the values that, in the shade of her flag, have turned barbarous lands into promising territories on the high road to civilization," he wrote. But the realities began to sink in: it was too late for reform—that same year a confidential report showed that at that time only 1,205 people of all races in Angola could be considered to be practicing a "liberal profession" (a category that included not just doctors, lawyers, and engineers, but bookkeepers, nurses, private teachers, insurance agents, and masseurs). And there was no way to stamp out the insurgency. A 1969 Benguela Railway report noted that the eastern half of the country was completely lost as an agricultural area. Despite the fact that the inhabitants were reduced to eating worms, insects, and leaves, the military intensified its use of defoliants and herbicides the following year. By the early 1970s, Portugal was forced to keep fifty thousand troops in Angola alone; roughly 40 percent of the country's annual budget was swallowed by military spending.

Portuguese military documents from that period attributed 59 percent of guerrilla attacks in Angola to the MPLA, 37 percent to the FNLA, and only 4 percent to UNITA. Although UNITA communiqués regularly cited attacks on Portuguese troops, its principal military activity seems to have been confined to sabotaging military trains on the Benguela Railway between Luso and Munhango—Savimbi's birthplace—and skirmishing with the MPLA. The few adventurous journalists who managed to trek into UNITA territory in the late 1960s and early 1970s would be shown villages, schools, and clinics in what Savimbi described as the "Freeland of Angola." UNITA gained recruits among the peasants, who had smoldering resentments against the Portuguese, and as his ranks swelled, Savimbi established an army structure, including military police (the "Dragons") and his own personal bodyguard of some four hundred handpicked soldiers; he no longer risked direct combat. But he lived with the people he hoped to liberate.

Dubbed *Molowini*, or "Son of the People," at UNITA's second policy-making congress in 1969, Savimbi cut an impressive figure. He dressed in camouflage fatigues and wore a beret pulled smartly to the right. Powerfully built, very dark-skinned, broad-featured, and bearded, his most striking features were his riveting eyes. He transfixed his listeners—soldiers, tribespeople, and journalists alike—with his eloquence and the force of his convictions. He argued that his was the authentic Angolan liberation movement, based entirely within the country and drawing support from the people, not imposed from outside by leaders who gave orders from the safety of foreign bases. Multilingual (he spoke English, French, Portuguese, Umbundu) and charming, with a ready fund of stories and proverbs, he quickly gained a foreign following through the stories and dispatches written about him. Hiding with reporters in the bushes next to the tracks, he pointed out passing trains that once carried dignitaries in paneled carriages down the route plotted by Varian, now reduced to cautiously pushing a green armored railcar of soldiers or a load of sand in front of a locomotive. Savimbi emphasized that UNITA did not attack freight shipments, only military convoys, although, he assured them, he could dynamite the rail line anytime he wanted. After the railcars passed, the stationmaster's son posed for photos astride the tracks of the Benguela Railway, next to a kilometer marker that showed just how far it was from the terminal in Lobito.

IN THE EARLY 1970s, Portugal was beset by strikes, demonstrations, protests, and acts of sabotage against the authoritarian government. General António de Spínola, a hard-line officer given to wearing a monocle and carrying a swagger stick, had been lauded for directing offensives against the MPLA and FNLA during his tour of duty in Angola from 1961 to 1964. Now, as governor of Guinea-Bissau, he had become disillusioned by the Caetano government's squandering of the opportunity to reach an accommodation with the liberation movement there. Supported by Gen. Francisco da Costa Gomes, the Portuguese army chief of staff, he published a slim volume, *Portugal e o Futuro* (*Portugal and the Future*), arguing for free debate on a variety of issues, and warning that Portugal faced defeat in its colonial wars unless it quickly established peace. The book was banned, and both Spínola and Costa Gomes were dismissed. But the way was now open for the Movement of the Armed Forces (MFA), a clandestine group of officers, to conspire against the regime. On April 25, 1974, the dictatorship was overthrown in a military coup. The Portuguese celebrated in the streets and put carnations in the barrels of patrolling soldiers' rifles.

The mood was rather different in the colonies. There, the Portuguese forces were paralyzed and refused to fight, and the settlers became alarmed and confused. At the beginning of May, General Costa Gomes flew to Luanda and declared that the Angolan nationalist movements would be accepted as political parties as soon as fighting stopped. The army's military operations were suspended to allow the guerrillas to arrange ceasefires. There was one problem: unlike Mozambique or Guinea-Bissau, where there was one effective liberation movement to deal with, Angola had three that were bitterly divided—and each had its own backers who would undermine any steps toward a peaceful transition. A rapid succession of events complicated the picture. In May, China reacted to the developments by sending advisors to train FNLA troops and 450 tons of arms to its base in the Congo. In the meantime, Savimbi, who had been the first nationalist leader to enter into talks, signed a truce with Portuguese officers on June 17 in Cangombe, a stop on the rail line near his base of operations. The FNLA dismissed Savimbi as a "vile creature of colonialism." By July, Spínola, now Portugal's president, had to face the inevitable, and Portugal proclaimed the right of its African colonies to be independent. The same month, the CIA upped its payments to Holden Roberto to $10,000 a month. By August, the Soviet Union reacted to Chinese and American initiatives by declaring its support of the MPLA and by December had made plans to ship arms. Portugal, already in the process of withdrawing from its other African colonies, reached cease-fire agreements with the FNLA and the MPLA in October. UNITA, having already signed a cooperation treaty with the FNLA, signed a peace accord with the MPLA in December.

The new year of 1975 started promisingly enough. Agostinho Neto, Holden Roberto, and Jonas Savimbi met in Alvor with Portuguese representatives to sign the Alvor Accords, which outlined plans for the withdrawal of Portuguese troops and peaceful competition for October elections leading up to independence, scheduled for November 11. But having failed to hold on to Angola, Portugal was now eager to wash its hands of it, and never became fully involved in supervision of the process of decolonization. In January 1975, Neto met with Cuban envoys in Dar es Salaam and handed them a letter urgently requesting that they use their country's influence among "friends and allies, especially from the Socialist camp, so that they may grant useful and timely aid to our movement, which is the only guarantee of a democratic and progressive Angola in the future." The United States would later claim to Congress that it intervened in Angola only after Cuban military advisors began arriving, but in fact, as historian Piero Gleijeses has made clear, it had intervened weeks before the Cubans began arriving in late August.

Days before Neto's appeal, the 40 Committee of the National Security Council had authorized the CIA to send $300,000 to Holden Roberto, tripling the amount his annual stipend had reached. Although aware that it would be encouraging civil war, the United States was unwilling to sit on its hands while the Soviet Union extended its influence in Africa. Despite the fact that the United States and China had long been backing

Holden Roberto, and Soviet moves could be interpreted as attempts to counter these initiatives, Washington took the position that it could not let the Soviet-backed MPLA take power in Luanda unopposed. It wasn't that the MPLA was Marxist; so was the government of newly independent Mozambique. In fact, all the countries that quickly emerged from Portugal's African empire after 1974, including Guinea-Bissau, Cape Verde, São Tomé, and Príncipe, had left-wing governments, and the United States established normal diplomatic relations with every one—except Angola.

What was at stake, as Piero Glijeses has noted, was prestige. Henry Kissinger, by then secretary of state in the Ford administration, put it bluntly: "Playing an active role [in Angola] would demonstrate that events in Southeast Asia have not lessened our determination to protect our interests" even when those stategic interests, as some in the administration admitted, were marginal. Kissinger credited Kenneth Kaunda for galvanizing American national policy on the issue of the growing Soviet military presence in Angola. During the Zambian president's visit to Washington in April 1975, Kissinger recalled Kaunda arguing forcefully that the MPLA was more than Marxist; it was "a tool of Moscow." He feared the prospect of a Soviet-backed government controlling the Benguela Railway, which carried half of his nation's imports and exports. The only other alternative, to ship through Rhodesia and South Africa, was politically unacceptable. He urged support for Savimbi, "a man of humility and good qualities," and, coincidentally, the rebel leader whose troops were in a position to control the rail line. Some months later, Kissinger summed up Kaunda's challenge in blunt terms: "My assessment was if the Soviet Union can interfere eight thousand miles from home in an undisputed way and control Zaire's and Zambia's access to the sea, then the Southern African countries must conclude that the U.S. has abdicated in Southern Africa . . . Therefore, I thought we had a major obligation perhaps not to reverse the situation for which it was too late, but at least to balance the power so that we were not faced at independence with an undisputed claim by the Communists in Luanda."

That the MPLA was, as one State Department official argued, best prepared to lead the Angolan people was deemed irrelevant—there was a cold war on. As Gleijeses wrote, "The United States bore no responsibility for the outbreak of the civil war, but Kissinger did his best to smash the one movement that represented any hope for the future of Angola."

But opposing the Soviet-supported side in Angola was a difficult policy to pursue. The Ford administration was largely preoccupied with the impending collapse of the government of South Vietnam, and the State Department's Bureau of African Affairs took the position that superpower rivalries should be kept out of Africa. Besides, after the recent humiliating withdrawal of U.S. forces from Vietnam, there was no public support left for fighting communism in remote Third World countries. Further, Congress was busy holding hearings in an effort to rein in covert operations. At that point, would an aggressive diplomatic effort to curtail the arms buildup in Angola—perhaps by applying pressure through the UN or the Organization of African Unity, or undertaking some energetic shuttle diplomacy between Washington and Moscow—have led to such a solution? Twenty-five years later, Kissinger maintained that undercover actions had been "the only means" available "to resist a Communist-sponsored takeover of Angola." In his view, announced, formal intervention "would only have forced other governments to react more openly—making a diplomatic solution that much harder to achieve."

As the covert Angola operation was put into play, there were considerable difficulties in letting the CIA run such a massive military undertaking. Congressional committees would have to be apprised—or simply fed lies—in such as way as to elicit tacit approval for actions that would not have been openly adopted in the immediate post-Vietnam era. Although over $31 million was finally spent, funds were doled out slowly to avoid controversy. For cover, and because CIA personnel were not trained to command military units, the agency had to recruit mercenaries in Brazil, Portugal, and Africa. To maintain the fiction of noninvolvement, U.S. planes took the weapons to Kinshasha, and South Africa airlifted them to Angola. But despite delays and difficulties—and by December, congressional restraints—the Angola operation would go forward.

By March, less than a month after the fragile transitional government had taken office in Angola, the FNLA, encouraged by Mobutu, was attacking the MPLA in Luanda and northern Angola. The MPLA received some war material from the Soviet Union, but had gotten the bulk of its aid from Yugoslavia and Algeria. Open warfare broke out between the rival movements in mid-May. After attacks on its supporters, UNITA entered the civil war. African leaders, alarmed that the Alvor Accords had collapsed, arranged for Neto, Roberto, and Savimbi to meet in mid-June in Nakuru, Kenya. The discussions, chaired by Kenya's Jomo Kenyatta, led to an agreement to denounce the use of force. But hostilities, fueled by foreign support, resumed as if there had been no pause. There would be more attempts, but there was little hope that genuine reconciliation was possible now between the warring parties; the wounds went too deep, and the stakes were far too high.

Clashes between the MPLA and FNLA broke out in the streets of Luanda in July. The MPLA managed to seize control of the capital by arming its civilian supporters and drove the FNLA from the city. FNLA guerrillas, buttressed by Zairian troops, crossed the border and pushed south to try and recapture Luanda before the November 11 deadline for independence. The MPLA's hold on Luanda was tenuous, and the Cuban delegation that came in early August to clarify the aid the MPLA had requested was welcomed warmly by Neto. The MPLA leadership complained that Soviet aid had only recently resumed after a three-year hiatus. The amount of arms being sent was "paltry, given the enormity of the need." In a letter to Raúl Castro, minister of the armed forces, the Cubans reported that "at this time the two camps in Angola are well defined, the FNLA and UNITA represent reaction and world imperialism and the Portuguese reactionaries, and the MPLA represents the progressive and nationalist forces . . . We believe that we must help them directly or indirectly to remedy this situation . . ." By the beginning of August Fidel Castro began considering military intervention in Angola, and on August 15 he sent a message to Leonid Brezhnev, urging Moscow to increase support to the MPLA and to assist in transporting the military advisors that were needed to check the threat of foreign assistance to the FNLA and UNITA. But the Soviets were not convinced the situation warranted it, and Cuba did not rush to the MPLA's aid. In fact, it delayed its response for months.

The U.S. covert operation had begun in July. To advance its efforts, John Stockwell, an experienced CIA operative chosen to head the task force that would oversee assistance to the FNLA and UNITA, violated orders and traveled in Angola with Roberto and Savimbi. In August, Stockwell flew to Kinshasa to meet with Roberto. The CIA man was not exactly inconspicuous; in fact, he was dressed entirely in black except for a large silver cross on a chain that hung around his neck. He wore a thick mustache, long sideburns, and dark glasses. Kissinger would later say that "one must not confuse the intelligence business with missionary work." Stockwell's appearance—the sinister minister look—might have suggested a man with that sort of conflict, but back then his loyalties were still undivided. He was there to assess exactly what sort of allies the United States had embraced.

The FNLA leader wore dark glasses too, but he never took them off. He also wore a neatly tailored bush jacket, a golf cap, and never smiled. Stockwell knew that Roberto's aims for Angola sounded like Neto's—independence, democracy, agrarian reform, economic development, pan-African unity, and the like. However, Roberto, in an effort to gain U.S. support, took steps to underscore the differences between his movement and the overtly Marxist MPLA. He had his forces repeatedly kidnap and kill MPLA activists.

Roberto had often been accused of never visiting Angola, much less the war fronts. After the FNLA had been driven out of Luanda, Mobutu and the CIA pressured Roberto into taking personal command of the battlefield. Stockwell spent several days with him north of Luanda, where the MPLA had been retreating. Roberto made a great show of rapid decisions and frenetic activity for the CIA man, even jumping out of the car to thrust clumps of grass under the tires when they got stuck in the sand. The first battle scene they encountered was in Caxito, some twenty-five miles northeast of Luanda. Every building had been hit by mortar fire, and many were razed to the ground. Stockwell and Roberto walked carefully through the ruins. When Roberto kicked some rubble, uncovering a grinning decayed corpse, he retched in reaction. Stockwell cynically observed that "the author of the bloody revolt of 1961, who insisted that revolution without bloodshed was impossible, was himself weak-stomached."

Driving back, Stockwell was lost in calculations. The United States could beat out the Soviets, he thought, but only if it could get the right weaponry and leaders into Angola immediately. He drafted a two-page report on the situation. The MPLA was underequipped and disorganized, he argued, and could be toppled by a coup—if the United States acted quickly and decisively. Later, Stockwell reflected that "since there was no chance of the National Security Council taking bold action in August 1975, I might have served my nation better if I had attempted to discourage them by emphasizing the frailty of the FNLA army to which the United States had affixed its prestige."

So far, the FNLA had received the lion's share of the CIA's largesse. Stockwell needed a look at "the Angolan long shot," Jonas Savimbi, and his UNITA movement. Stockwell was surprised to be flown down to Silva Porto (Cuito) in UNITA's own Lear jet—the gift of a London/Rhodesian investment company betting that Savimbi would prevail, and offer access to Angola's mineral wealth. Stockwell was taken to a small house in the center of town, where he saw a stocky, bearded African in a dark green utility uniform who sized him up with a flashing glance and introduced himself as Jonas Savimbi. The UNITA leader took Stockwell to a nearby party meeting, where he mesmerized a packed auditorium with his oratory: "Savimbi's voice was rich and well modulated. As he spoke his whole body turned to different parts of the audience and he leaned forward and gestured, reaching his hands to the people, then drawing them back to his chest," Stockwell recalled. "When he nodded, the crowd agreed; his displeasure was theirs also; answers to his questions came thundering back in unison, 'UNITA,' 'Angola . . .'"

Stockwell was as impressed with Savimbi's determination and outlook as he was by his popularity. He asked him what he needed. In contrast to Roberto, who had requested uniforms and boots, Savimbi asked for weapons. "My men can fight barefooted," he told Stockwell. "Without guns and ammunition they cannot fight." This "strapping mesomorph" seemed a born leader: organized, capable and willing to delegate responsibility. "The CIA's managers should understudy this man," Stockwell wrote. He would report back to the agency the most significant finding of his trip: Savimbi appeared to have a much larger, better-led army than the FNLA's, an "unexpected asset" in the war with the MPLA. Stockwell and Savimbi flew east to Cangumbe, and then drove toward Luso (Luena), where UNITA forces were besieging the town. Savimbi's strategic objectives, Stockwell noted, were the Ovimbundu highlands and the Benguela Railway.

At Chicala, the rail stop before Luso, the two of them got out to look at the tracks. Stockwell stared at Varian's achievement, the receding rails converging to a perfect perspective point on the western horizon. It was some five hundred miles to Lobito harbor. Turning, he looked east down the line; it was another five hundred miles to the copper mines of the Congo. Standing between these shining rails in the middle of the African bush, he was struck by the brutality and betrayals required of a CIA case officer and the pointlessness of the operations he'd been involved with. Savimbi looked impatient, and Stockwell felt a flash of resentment at what he saw as the guerrilla leader's "clear objectives and clean conscience."

But Stockwell could not fathom Savimbi's political leanings. The UNITA leader told him he would never seek help from the Portuguese, "but otherwise he had no prejudice. And no profound ideology. He was neither Marxist nor capitalist, nor even a black revolutionary. He was an Angolan patriot, fighting for the freedom of the Ovimbundu people. He had accepted North Korean training for his men, and Chinese money and arms. He liked Americans. If South Africa would give him the help he needed, he would accept." Stockwell had seen enough. He flew home.

In fact, South Africa would do more than help Savimbi; it would fight alongside him. It had been monitoring developments in Angola for some time, with increasing alarm. For the apartheid government of Prime Minister John Vorster, the prospect of a Soviet-backed government taking power in a country that shared a border with South Africa–controlled Namibia and sympathetic to the rebel SWAPO movement there was intolerable—a threat to its stability and regional power. Savimbi first made contact with the South Africans in the summer of 1974, and over the next year argued for his vision of an anticommunist Angola that would be friendly to South Africa. As a result, South African officials held discussions with UNITA (and the FNLA) in May, and once they'd received assurances of their hostility to SWAPO, began supplying arms to both movements. By September, South Africa had dispatched special forces to Angola to train UNITA and FNLA troops—all with the covert approval of the United States and the assistance of the CIA.

But Washington and Pretoria had failed to take Fidel Castro into account. The same month, three Cuban ships left for Angola with almost three hundred military instructors and a variety of weaponry on board.

For weeks, the MPLA had been battling FNLA troops north of the capital. Although outgunned by Roberto's army, the MPLA brigade had Soviet-supplied mortars and antiaircraft and light infantry weapons and was much better organized. North of Luanda, the MPLA swept back through Caxito and nearly took Ambriz, the FNLA base. The MPLA held a press conference to show captured U.S. arms, which bore U.S. Air Force shipping labels. To check the MPLA, Mobutu sent in two elite commando battalions, which joined the FNLA and retook Caxito, then advanced toward Luanda itself. They were a very thorough army, not hesitating to burn villages in their path and kill and dismember the inhabitants. In mid-October 1975 the South Africans led an invasion—code-named "Operation Zulu"—coordinated with the CIA and buttressed by a thousand UNITA and FNLA soldiers, north from Namibia's Atlantic coast to march on the capital. The MPLA, assisted by the recently arrived Cuban advisors, marshaled their forces, hoping to slow the advancing army.

THE PORTUGUESE, UNDERSTANDABLY, had been fleeing from Angola since June. At the end of August, it was clear that the Alvor Accords had come to nothing, and Lisbon called off the October elections. But it had had enough of its greatest colony; it would stick with the November 11 deadline for independence. Portugal took a very long time to wake from its fading dreams of empire. But when it did, five centuries of history were swept away in days. How impossible it seemed now that Angola had ever been called a "coming colony," or the "African Cinderella." Luanda, the once indolent, elegant colonial city by the bay, full of parks and flowers and seaside restaurants and nightclubs, was now racked with rumors: the FNLA was already outside the city, or maybe already inside, hidden and waiting; the blacks in the slums were being organized and the *catanas* sharpened in readiness; only one more ship was coming, or the last freighter had left; the airlines were all overbooked; the police were long gone and so were the garbage collectors. The last was certainly true, because the city looked filthy and smelled like a dump and dogs roamed the streets in packs. Settlers who had driven for days still poured in from outlying districts, spreading their own tales of terror and warnings of what was to come. Stripped of their illusions, with armies advancing on the capital from the north and south, the Portuguese frantically packed up all they had into sacks, suitcases, bags, boxes, bundles, drums, and crates, and shoved and screamed and pushed their way onto the last flights and the departing ships.

There was nothing left for them but anger. They tried to take everything of value with them, stripping their apartments bare, hollowing out their houses. In a rage telephones were ripped out, typewriters smashed. Twenty thousand cars were shipped out, but hundreds more were simply driven into walls or crashed into each other in the streets of Luanda—no one wanted to leave them for the Angolans. Hospitals, banks, and schools were trashed and abandoned, the yachts in the harbor blown up. North of the city, three million bags' worth of unharvested coffee rotted on the trees and cracks split the drained swimming pools the rich planters' families had once splashed in on torpid afternoons. Ah, well; hadn't Salazar himself said that there were no eternal or perfect regimes?

To prepare the populace, FNLA planes dropped leaflets over Luanda with pictures of Holden Roberto and the caption "GOD RULES IN HEAVEN HOLDEN RULES ON EARTH." But those who were left wondered if the South Africans might take the city first. By November 7, Operation Zulu forces had captured Benguela and Lobito and were pushing north toward Luanda. A day later the FNLA/Zairian forces north of the city advanced on the capital. The distant pounding of artillery could be heard like an approaching storm as the last remaining Portuguese troops took final snapshots of each other on the ramparts of Luanda's sixteenth-century fort or next to the statue of Prince Henry the Navigator. Three days later, in a brief and guarded ceremony, the Portuguese high commissioner, Adm. Leone Cardoso, proclaimed Angolan independence, but, not wanting to play favorites, declined to hand over power to anyone. The Portuguese left the way they had come: by ship.

Meanwhile, a different crowd gathered in the cathedral square to wait for the clock to strike midnight. On a small speakers' platform, in a breaking voice, Agostinho Neto read a text proclaiming the People's Republic of Angola. Cheers rang out, and then the lights went out. As the crowd dispersed, soldiers began shooting wildly into the air. FNLA gunners shelled the pumping station the next day, leaving Luanda without water for two days.

To counter Neto's announcement, the FNLA and UNITA jointly declared independence as well, the FNLA in Ambriz, UNITA in Huambo.

The Portuguese name for that city, Nova Lisboa, had been one of Norton de Matos's measures, an effort to move Angola's capital inland to encourage settlement in the interior. Now the city had reverted to its old name, and the statue of de Matos, who was remembered only for his 1921 decree banning the use of native languages in schools, had been pulled down by UNITA soldiers. But the midnight independence ceremonies were poorly attended; sporadic violence had already broken out between FNLA and UNITA troops and the two sides would openly battle a month later. In Washington, the CIA gave the 40 Committee an upbeat report: the military balance in Angola had been tipped in favor of the FLNA and UNITA.

Cuban advisors had been in Angola since late August, but in response to the South African invasion, Castro had thrown full military support to the MPLA in November 1975 — catching the Soviet Union by surprise, and making the Soviet leadership spectators to a war they were expected to make winnable. Over six hundred Cuban soldiers were airlifted to Angola, along with the fearsome forty-barreled multiple rocket launcher, the so-called "Stalin organ," capable of raining down 122mm. shells on enemy troops. A single hit was deafening, capable of shattering a house or penetrating a bunker, and exploding into fourteen thousand slivers of steel. Code-named "Operation Carlota," the plan called for deployment of troops to bolster the shaky MPLA as soon as independence was declared. Despite hesitations over the scale of the conflict and its implications for U.S.-Soviet relations, Moscow would not be outdone by Havana. By the end of November, Cuban soldiers, armed with Soviet-supplied tanks and rockets, joined with MPLA troops to push the FNLA north of Luanda, raining artillery fire on the fleeing soldiers, crushing them decisively. Cuban troops managed to check the South African advance from the south with determined fighting and devastating ambushes, halting them a hundred miles outside the capital.

The South Africans had been trying to help Savimbi free up the vital ends of the Benguela Railway and sent another army column on to Teixeira de Sousa, the last railroad post held by the MPLA. UNITA only controlled the center of the line, and Savimbi was under enormous pressure from Kaunda to reopen the entire system before independence. Success would mean continued Zambian support, even, perhaps, recognition; failure would mean Kaunda would have to come to terms with the MPLA. But the Cubans blew up a major rail bridge to the west of Teixeira de Sousa, sinking South Africa's plans and Savimbi's hopes. South Africa had not planned to stay in Angola past November 11. Savimbi flew to Pretoria to try to persuade Prime Minister John Vorster to delay withdrawal. But his political fortunes were about to plummet.

Fred Bridgland, a Reuters correspondent, had already traveled to UNITA-held territories and interviewed Savimbi before stumbling across fair-haired white soldiers, whose English betrayed a South African accent, driving armored cars at Silva Porto's airstrip at the beginning of November. With another correspondent, he managed to get on a UNITA flight to Rundu, just over the border in South African–ruled Namibia, where he saw a military staging post—columns of Panhard armored cars, Hercules C130 transport planes, and more white soldiers. When reporters quizzed Savimbi on November 13 in newly captured Lobito on whether South African troops had assisted his recent victories, he admitted that some white troops—"technicians"—were working for UNITA, just as Cubans were helping the MPLA. But the damage was done. After Bridgland's story that South African troops had entered Angola appeared in *The Washington Post* on November 22, Nigeria switched its backing from UNITA to the MPLA and sent it $20 million. The African leaders who had previously castigated the Soviet arms buildup—a group that included Tanzania's Julius Nyerere and Uganda's Idi Amin—did an about-face at the news that the despised South Africans had entered the fray, and shifted their support to the Soviet effort. In fact, much of the international community saw South Africa's intervention on behalf of the FNLA and UNITA as legitimatizing Soviet and Cuban support for the MPLA. Stockwell would later comment that "the propaganda and political war was lost in that stroke. There was nothing the [CIA] Lusaka station could invent that would be as damaging to the other side as our alliance with the hated South Africans was to our cause."

In Washington the plug was about to be pulled on the CIA covert operation. The cover story devised for congressional consumption—that the United States was merely supplying weaponry to the noncommunist side—came apart after a series of news leaks and press reports on the South African invasion and possible U.S. collusion. Angered at being lied to, concerned about the cost of the war and that the United States might be dragged in deeper, the Senate Foreign Relations Committee endorsed an amendment introduced by Senator Dick Clark to cut off additional spending on Angola operations in mid-December. Kissinger, furious at leaks and congressional efforts to rein in the Angola operation, put his views bluntly in a staff meeting: "The Chinese will say we're a country that was run out of Indochina for 50,000 men and is now being run out of Angola for less than $50 million." The Senate, split between those who feared Angola would turn into another Vietnam and those who felt the United States should stand up to the Soviet Union, went into an unusual closed debate. Senator John Tunney offered an amendment to the Defense Appropriations Bill to cut off all funds directly involving Angola, which eventually passed the Senate and the House over Ford's and Kissinger's strenuous objections. As one congressman put it, "I feel no need to involve the United States in the internal affairs of an African nation simply because the Russians are supporting one side against the other." Shortly thereafter, Senator Clark would reintroduce his amendment to cut off military funds to Angola; it was finally enacted into law in June 1976, the same month the CIA began writing citations and commendations for over a hundred people involved in the Angola program. A disillusioned John Stockwell would resign a year later and write an exposé of the entire operation.

The MPLA's successes in the field in December were due to the deployment of Cuban troops and Soviet firepower. Back in August, Stockwell had argued that if the United States wasn't going to "put the MPLA out of business before the Soviets could react," its national interests would be furthered "by staying out of the conflict"; feeling its way along with "small amounts of aid would only escalate the war and get the United States far out on a fragile limb." Now Congress had sawn it off. The MPLA was also winning politically. Diplomatic recognition had been extended by over a dozen countries starting in mid-November, and by early December, fourteen of the forty-six member states of the OAU had recognized the MPLA as the legitimate government of Angola.

South Africa had counted on U.S. backing for its Angola intervention. The United States had been in close but discreet contact with the Pretoria government, helped coordinate their respective efforts through the CIA, and had talked of supplying military equipment. Now it was quickly dissociating itself. South Africa had also received the blessing of

Zaire and Zambia. It was always hard to know with Mobutu, but Kaunda's anti-Soviet position would soon crumple under the growing tide of recognition for the MPLA. As outside support for its Angolan adventure evaporated, South Africa's resolve weakened; it was not, as its defense minister put it, "prepared to fight on behalf of the free world alone," and began pulling its troops back toward the Angola-Namibia border in early January 1976.

To disguise the fact that UNITA was losing, Savimbi distracted a pack of journalists who had belatedly come in mid-January to confirm the presence of South African troops by sending them on a 250-mile trip on the Benguela Railway. Fred Bridgland, who had been forgiven for his disclosures, went along for the bizarre ride. "A big and beautiful steam locomotive built in Glasgow more than 50 years earlier pulled a column of freight cars filled with UNITA soldiers, and at the back we reclined in an ornate private passenger carriage with a rear viewing platform," Bridgland wrote. At Luso, the correspondents, none of whom had seen—or would see—the war firsthand, persuaded a young railway man to take them up the line in his little electric rail inspection car to view what was left of a rail bridge across the Lumege River that had been blown up by the MPLA.

They should have been alarmed by the speed at which the car was approaching the twisted wreckage of the bridge, but the mostly British party chose to keep a stiff upper lip and ignore the impending disaster. By the time the driver slammed on the brakes, Bridgland wrote, "it was much too late. The railcar skidded at great speed, and we plunged down the remnants of the broken rails on the bridge towards the riverbed. We were halted in middive towards oblivion by a twisted girder. We hung precariously in midair, above the water, before crawling silently out of the debris and clambering back up the hanging line towards safety." The hapless reporters would suffer three more rail and road crashes in the next twenty-four hours, which inspired them to christen UNITA's territory "The Land With No Brakes."

By then, there was no way of stopping UNITA's fall or the MPLA's rise. With Cuba's overwhelming military presence and several hundred million dollars' worth of Soviet armaments, the MPLA routed the FNLA and pushed UNITA back to Huambo and Silva Porto. Savimbi, unsure of U.S. intentions, flew to Kinshasa for urgent consultations with the CIA.

In the summer of 1975, long before the massive Cuban and Soviet buildup, the CIA had called him on the carpet for the overtures he'd been making then to the MPLA for a negotiated settlement. At that time Savimbi had been told that the United States wanted no "soft" allies in its war against the MPLA. Savimbi knew that UNITA was at its weakest, and that the MPLA would now insist on total victory.

No matter; the CIA still had a few tricks left. The agency began recruiting mercenaries—20 Frenchmen, a dozen Portuguese—to assist Savimbi, and funded Roberto to assemble a force of about 150, 100 of whom were already fighting for the FNLA. Many of the recruits were dubious (two of them were London street sweepers recruited right off the pavement), and one turned out to be a psychopath. Costas Georgiou, a Greek Cypriot and a former British paratrooper, a.k.a. Tony Callan, became Roberto's field general. He had a habit of beating his troops. When twenty-five mercenaries attacked some FNLA soldiers, mistaking them for Cubans, Callan tracked them down, executed fourteen of them, and left their bodies to rot in the sun as an example to others. Callan and a dozen other mercenaries (including three Americans) were finally captured by the MPLA and put on trial in Luanda for war crimes. The judges in Luanda, declaring that "packs of dogs of war with blood-stained muzzles are out to cut down peoples' revolutions," found them guilty; a number were executed. It was a public relations disaster for the FNLA and UNITA.

Jonas Savimbi lost six hundred men when MPLA and Cuban troops captured Huambo in early February, the same day that the OAU embraced the People's Republic of Angola as a new member of the pan-African group. France and Portugal quickly extended recognition. But the CIA was not about to give up on Savimbi. Even though the Tunney Amendment was signed into law on February 9, 1976, the CIA still had $9 million left in funds allocated to the Angola Task Force. It made twenty-two air shipments of arms, including antitank missiles, siege mortars, and antitank cannon, from Kinshasa to Gago Coutinho (now Lumbala N'Guimbo) near the Zambian border, Savimbi's last remaining outpost, to ensure his survival.

Savimbi wrote a letter of farewell from there to Kaunda. "The machine of war that Cuba and the Soviet Union have assembled in Angola is beyond the imagination. To prevent the total destruction of our forces we have decided to revert immediately to guerrilla warfare." He thanked

Kaunda for all his support, and added that "whatever stand your government takes on Angola, we will accept with resignation." After MPLA MIGs bombed Gago Coutinho on March 13, Savimbi and his followers abandoned the city the next day and embarked on their own 1,200-mile "Long March" into the interior and the Ovimbundu highlands, pursued by MPLA and Cuban troops. Savimbi had vowed to the CIA that he would never leave the Angolan bush alive.

Several days later an executive jet flew into Lusaka from Luanda. The MPLA's foreign minister, José Eduardo dos Santos, and his seven-member team were met by a delegation of Zambian government officials. On April 15, 1976, Zambia recognized the MPLA as the legitimate government of Angola. Zambian freight would once more be welcome on the Benguela Railway. Agostinho Neto would also have talks with his long-standing enemy, Zaire's President Mobutu, who, like Zambia's Kenneth Kaunda, needed railway access to ship his exports, and had also backed the losing sides. Neto and Mobutu quickly came to an understanding: Mobutu would shut off all aid to the FNLA and UNITA. When Roberto complained, Mobutu sent his police to sack the FNLA's office and burn its records. In exchange, Zairian copper and cobalt would also be shipped by rail again — that is, once the bridges destroyed in the war were rebuilt.

And that is how Angola gained its independence.

THE GIANT SABLE could not escape the conflict. In fact, its survival had already become increasingly imperiled in the final years of colonial rule, just when the Portuguese, as if struck by second thoughts, started to pay serious attention to Angola's wildlife. Conservation efforts had begun promisingly enough with the proclamation of a number of national parks and reserves in the late 1930s and the impressive list of decrees and regulations that followed. But, when the occasion demanded it, the laws would be ignored. In the late 1960s, with the approval (or acquiescence) of the fauna department, over three hundred head of game were killed in a single day in Quiçama Park south of the capital by the ruling elite and its privileged guests, and over a dozen giant sable were shot in a single hunt in the reserve supposedly set aside for their protection. An international outcry over the conservation situation in Angola led to a government inquiry in 1972, and a conference on conservation was held in Sá da Bandeira (now Lubango). But Portugal was slow to implement the recommendations that came out of that meeting; two years later a cattle ranching company was still using Quiçama Park as its private grazing grounds, and oil companies were allowed to prospect throughout the park. In Iona National Park on the Angolan coast bordering Namibia, police and military units hunted oryx with impunity and gangs of poachers shot mountain zebra, black-faced impala, and rhinoceros.

After the overthrow of the Salazar-Caetano regime in 1974 and Lisbon's recognition of Angola's right to independence, the settlers had even less incentive to respect the country's wildlife than before. A *colono* who poached four elephants in Bicuari National Park shrugged off the charge: "If the blacks are going to be given Angola, I'm not leaving them any." Quiçama Park became an abattoir as its herds of red buffalo, eland, reedbuck, and roan were butchered to supply a lucrative bush meat trade in the slums of Luanda, leaving only scattered sun-bleached skeletons and a maze of jeep tracks behind on the park's grasslands. After the transitional government took charge, however, things took a distinct turn for the worse. MPLA soldiers began hunting daily in Quiçama, and forced the remaining rangers at gunpoint to transport the carcasses to MPLA camps. In Iona, the last rhinoceroses were wiped out; in Bicuari and Cameia National Parks, rangers witnessed unheard-of carnage. It was dangerous to object. UNITA troops sentenced two rangers investigating poaching to 150 lashes each with a heavy hide *sjambok*. Outside the parks, poaching turned to pure slaughter; the FNLA machine-gunned herds of elephants, and Cuban troops strafed buffalo from the air. Even the annual burning of the rural grasslands went out of control; from the Congo border to Namibia, the entire country seemed to smolder, as if in recognition of its collapse into civil war.

The remaining park rangers gave up in the summer of 1975 when the warring sides began commandeering their vehicles, radios, and homes, and escaped while they could. José Alves, the game warden in the Luando Reserve, hastily left for Portugal with his family. There was no means of outside communication available for the African game scouts left behind.

All that emerged from the giant sable lands were stories of how the locals were being told that the parks would disappear after independence, and disturbing rumors of *palanca preta gigante* being shot on the northern boundary of the reserve.

ANGOLA HAD FINALLY fought its way to independence, but it had won precious little; its war-shadowed future would continue to be shaped by others for decades to come. Both East and West were still too committed to their struggle for global power to leave the former Portuguese colony alone.

The Kremlin certainly had reason to feel smug. Not only had its side emerged victorious, but in early 1976 Luanda appeared to be taking its cues from Moscow. To solidify its hold on power, the MPLA was following standard Soviet practice in dealing with its opponents, jailing its dissenting founding members along with FLNA and UNITA followers, and carrying out "extra-judicial" executions. Encouraged by their Angolan protégés, the Soviets sent vast amounts of propaganda for the MPLA to absorb—an entire planeload of leaflets of Brezhnev's speech at the 25th CPSU Congress, two planeloads of anti-Maoist literature, countless portraits of Lenin—although there were a few difficulties. Agostinho Neto, despite his expressions of gratitude, did not always show the deference to the Soviet leadership that they expected. The Cubans, however, were careful to reassure Moscow that the Soviet Union was Angola's most important international ally. But Cuba was clearly setting its own international agenda, and its troops were not in Angola simply to support Soviet policy. Their presence gave Castro stature as a Third World leader, certainly, but even the CIA (and Kissinger) conceded he was a committed and genuine revolutionary.

"Things are going well in Angola," Castro told East German communist leader Erich Honecker a year later, shortly after visiting Luanda to confer with Neto and lay wreaths on the graves of Angolan and Cuban soldiers. He could point to improvements in education, health, transportation, coffee, and sugar production. But, he admitted, the poorly organized army was a problem. It was doing almost nothing to fight UNITA, which was particularly active in the country's center. The Soviets were supplying weapons, but "the Cuban units," he lamented, "have been the only ones fighting the bandits." Nonetheless, Castro planned to leave less than half the Cuban troop strength used in the war for liberation stationed there, some fifteen thousand men. By the end of 1978, Castro estimated, there would be seven thousand left.

But other countries were not ready to concede Angola to the communists—even though U.S. recognition of Angola seemed not just possible, but likely when the Carter administration took office in 1977. However, after the Angola-based Congo Liberation Front invaded Zaire in May 1978 in an effort to topple Mobutu, the United States suspected Cuban, Soviet, and Angolan complicity, and quickly reverted to anticommunist form. In May 1978, the CIA told the Senate Foreign Relations Committee that it was planning to supply "covert arms aid to the Angolan rebels"—i.e., UNITA—indirectly, to circumvent the Clark Amendment. In congressional testimony later that month, Gerald Bender repeated what Angolan government officials had told him: "You [the U.S.] stand and scream at us about our relations with the Soviet Union, but you don't do anything positive about it. On the contrary, you drive us further and further to the Soviets." Despite overtures from Luanda, the normalization of relations between Zaire and Angola, and the reopening of the Benguela Railway line to permit shipments from Zaire and Zimbabwe to Lobito, the United States still looked for ways to indirectly support UNITA, including encouraging Morocco and China to supply the movement with arms and assistance.

But it was South Africa that went to war.

The apartheid government—led by P. W. Botha after John Vorster resigned in 1978—saw its regional security threatened by Soviet and Cuban "expansionism" and by Angola's direct support for the African National Congress and the Namibian independence movement, the South-West Africa People's Organization (SWAPO), both of which operated from bases on its territory. The South Africa Defense Force (SADF) began launching raids into Angola from Namibia in April 1976, initiating twelve years of direct military involvement. Roads, bridges, villages, shops, livestock, and the just reopened Benguela Railway were targeted, and hundreds of Angolans died in the raids, inflicting heavy damage on an already crippled economy and infrastructure.

The SADF launched a massive operation on Cassinga in early May 1978, provoking an international outcry. In an airborne assault, several hundred paratroopers attacked a settlement some 150 miles north of the Namibian border. The Angolan government asserted that it was a Namibian refugee camp, and that 612 people, including women and children, had been killed. South Africa did not dispute the casualties, but claimed it was a SWAPO base. The commander who led the attack, Col. Jan Breytenbach, later gave an account of the battle in which he remarked that "they were certainly the best armed refugees I have ever come across. They put quite a number of shots through us, myself included."

It was not the first time, and it would certainly not be the last, that interpretation of events would differ dramatically in the Angolan conflict. What was clear, however, was that South Africa's efforts to destabilize Angola were met by a buildup of Cuban troops in response. It was also clear that without South African support during this period, UNITA would likely not have survived. Although anxious to downplay his continuing connections with Pretoria's apartheid government, Savimbi was frustrated at the lack of press coverage on UNITA's struggle. He attributed this to the MPLA's clampdown on Western journalists. "It is not in their interest to publicize the continuation of a war they thought they had won," he said in a statement released in October 1976.

Starting that month, he would get renewed press attention from Leon Dash, a *Washington Post* reporter who began a seven-month stay with Savimbi and his UNITA forces, and wrote a series for the paper on his extraordinary journey that appeared in August 1977. Dash traveled with the guerrillas on foot, entering Angola through Zambia, surviving bouts of fever and eating grubs to get his story. He found plenty to observe, noting that it was UNITA policy to execute MPLA officers, because there was nothing else to do with "hard-line Marxists." He also saw what the war was like for civilians. Nineteen-year old Celeste Cango Antunes had been married for a month when MPLA soldiers attacked her home town of Mussende, west of the Luando Reserve, and took the couple to Andulo along with three of her brothers, who were forced to join the army. She and her husband were put in a small house and given two plates of rice a day. When UNITA attacked two weeks later, "my husband ran away and left me," she told Dash. "I ran out of the house toward the UNITA men and shouted, 'Brothers, don't shoot me' with my hands up.'" She was clubbed to the ground by a soldier, and taken prisoner. Dash first saw her as she was led into the guerrilla camp, blindfolded and wearing a blood-spotted striped yellow pullover. A boy whipped off the towel over her eyes, and as she stared at her jeering captors, "fear gradually replaced her bewildered look, her legs began to quiver, and urine trickled down to her ankles and into her dirty white sneakers. The guerrillas laughed harder." When she attempted a feeble, left-handed clenched-fist salute and mumbled "*Viva* UNITA," the guerrillas howled, "THE RIGHT ARM, THE RIGHT ARM!" Celeste dropped her left arm, quickly thrust her right into the air, and whispered the slogan again. "No, very bad!" the guerrillas shouted at her. "Very weak!" She gave up and stood silent, her fingers touching the scab on her cheek where the soldier had smashed her with a rifle butt.

Although Dash was impressed with Savimbi, calling him "the life-blood of the UNITA guerrillas' fight against Angola's Soviet and Cuban supported government," he also found him "an enigma, a man on whom many labels can stick—brilliant, charismatic, affable, unyielding, forgiving, temporizing, Machiavellian, opportunistic, lying, nationalistic, marxist, Maoist, pro-Western and socialist." He also accused Savimbi of denying involvement with the South African army in 1975–76. But despite airing UNITA's "dirty linen," including desertions, drunkenness, looting, the abuse of women in the camps, and summary executions, the articles amounted to a publicity coup for Savimbi. The *Washington Post* editorialized that UNITA's alleged control of the Angolan countryside justified the U.S. decision to withhold recognition of the government. Right-wing columnists embraced Savimbi's cause uncritically, and to rectify mainstream media neglect, his American supporters organized a U.S. publicity tour for the guerrilla leader in 1979, three months after a successful UNITA effort to cripple the Benguela Railway.

Savimbi was not received by the Carter administration, but managed to meet with senators, congressmen, and former government officials such as Henry Kissinger and Alexander Haig. He garnered positive coverage, including an editorial in the *Wall Street Journal* headlined "Meet Jonas Savimbi," which characterized him as "a genuine anti-Soviet nationalist who has a good chance of winning." Savimbi brushed aside questions about his South African connections, exaggerated the strength of UNITA forces and how much territory he controlled, and pressed home his warning message: recognizing the MPLA would mean the United States had accepted being "second to Russia, second in the world." Although he felt snubbed by the Carter administration, he knew that in the face of the growing Soviet influence in Angola, the Western powers would not abandon him. "Geopolitics," he once told Dash, "will force them to come back to me."

At the same time there were important changes in the cast of characters in the long-running Angolan tragedy. Two years before, in May 1977, Agostinho Neto had survived a coup attempt, the so-called *Golpe Nitista,* named for supporters of Nito Alves, the ex–interior minister, who had challenged Neto's leadership and criticized the MPLA's failure to deliver on their promises. His enemies denounced him as a racist opportunist bent on grabbing power; whatever the truth, the Nitists (supported by the Soviets) succeeded only in taking over the radio station and a prison for nine hours. The abortive and bloody takeover was brutally crushed with aid of the Cubans; its leaders were summarily executed. Reprisals went on for days. No one really knows how many were killed, and little is known about Neto's role in this bloody purge, or how the poet-patriot reconciled his empathy for his people with his party's brutality.

But by 1979 Neto had become increasingly concerned about the ongoing conflict and Angola's stagnant economy, and quietly sounded out President Senghor of Senegal on the possibility of settlement talks with UNITA; he also signed a twenty-year treaty of friendship with the Soviet Union. Diagnosed with cancer in Moscow, he died on September 17, 1979. The end was so sudden there was talk of assassination on the operating table. He was succeeded by thirty-seven-year-old José Eduardo dos Santos, the tall, dark, firm-jawed Angolan who had been the MPLA's foreign minister. A bricklayer's son, born and raised in a Luanda slum, dos Santos joined the MPLA in his teens and studied petroleum engineering and military telecommunications in the Soviet Union before returning to Angola and the liberation struggle. He appeared to be a hard-line communist who would run his one-party Marxist state with a firm hand.

The Carter administration was taking a hard line of its own. In 1978 it had supported a UN resolution condemning South African aggression in Angola, but twice in 1979 and again the following year it abstained (along with Britain and France) on similar resolutions. Yet there was significant support for normalization of relations between Washington and Luanda. Gulf Oil advocated the establishment of formal relations. As its president testified at the House Subcommittee on Africa in 1980, "Gulf, as any commercial enterprise, would benefit by U.S. recognition of Angola and the establishment of a U.S. embassy in Luanda." In its effort to harass the MPLA, the Ford administration had forced Gulf Oil to shut down its Cabinda operation in late 1975 to cut off revenue to the government. The company, which had invested heavily in Angola, was finally allowed to start talks with the MPLA on the resumption of oil production in the spring of 1976. In one of the many ironies of the Angolan conflict, Cuban troops were used to guard American oil facilities to ensure the continuation of revenues to the government that many in Washington wanted to destabilize. For many policy makers it was the very presence of those Cuban troops that made recognition politically unpalatable.

By the time the Reagan administration took office in 1981, the effort to topple the MPLA was part of a larger agenda to roll back revolutionary regimes around the world. Covert operations were carried out in Afghanistan, Cambodia, El Salvador, and Nicaragua. For Angola, a complex, dual-track strategy was adopted. Chester Crocker, assistant secretary of state for African affairs, implemented a policy of "constructive engagement" which linked the withdrawal of Cuban troops with Namibian independence, as spelled out in UN Resolution 435. South Africa wanted a Cuban withdrawal in advance, and dragged out negotiations in order to pursue its Angola strategy. The military track, promoted by the CIA and the National Security Council, aided UNITA by encouraging South Africa's destabilization of Angola. The Reagan administration's vetoing of UN resolutions condemning South African intransigence over Namibia independence and its Operation Protea invasion of Angola gave Pretoria a green light to escalate its attacks in that country. South Africa carried out a half-dozen major incursions over the next two years, describing them as "hot pursuits" of SWAPO guerrillas. But the SADF directly engaged the Angolan army, allowing UNITA to damage designated military and economic installations. With massive support from South Africa, UNITA was able to expand its operations along the Zambian border and Moxico Province in the east, throughout Cuando Cubango Province in the southeast, in the central plateau, over the Benguela Railway line, and up into the Luando Reserve itself, the "house of the giant sable."

RICHARD ESTES HAD become increasingly disturbed. The independence struggle had given the biologist cause for concern, but when civil war broke out in Angola in 1975, he knew with sickening certainty that the country's wildlife—giant sable and all—would inevitably suffer along with the country's populace. What protection could there be for the *palanca preta gigante* when the government was preoccupied with a bloody conflict that was destroying the country—devastating its economy and killing thousands of its inhabitants. He could guess the fate of antelopes trapped in a combat zone: at five hundred pounds, an adult giant sable would be protein on the hoof for a platoon of hungry soldiers, a walking feast for a starving village.

During the decade after he and Runi had returned from Angola, Estes had often thought about the animals they had spent a year studying. But there were other things that occupied his time during that period; the couple had two children, a son, Lyndon, and a daughter, Anna, and by then Estes had plunged into the writing of his major work, *The Behavior Guide to African Mammals*, which was finally published in 1991 and has since become a standard reference. Runi assisted him in the research on that comprehensive survey, but between caring for the children and holding a full-time job in publishing, was rarely able to join him on fieldwork in Africa. During the 1970s Estes was also a curator in the Department of Mammalogy at the Academy of Natural Sciences of Philadelphia, and in 1978 became chairman of the Antelope Specialists Group (ASG) of the World Conservation Union (IUCN) Species Survival Commission (a position he now shares with New Zealand–based researcher Rod East). The IUCN, a network of some ten thousand scientists and experts from 181 countries, is the world's largest conservation organization, and as the editor of the ASG's *Gnusletter*, Estes was in a prime position to rally interest in the continuing plight of the giant sable.

By 1980 the reports he'd heard of increased poaching in the reserves had become alarming. As Estes later explained, "A Portuguese friend had told us that our study herds had been machine-gunned. The realization that by helping habituate some seventy-five sable to motor vehicles we had set them up for slaughter was a bitter pill to swallow." He approached the New York Zoological Society to ask for a grant to return to Angola. George Schaller, director of the Society's Animal Research and Conservation Center, wrote to him in Tanzania, where Estes was conducting fieldwork in the Serengeti, to tell him that his request had been approved. He would receive a grant of $2,500 to determine the status of the giant sable, and—presuming there were some left—make recommendations on the protection of the remnant population. In addition, Schaller wrote, he should check on the general wildlife situation in the country, and promote the cause of conservation. He also wished him luck.

Estes would need it. The giant sable lands were split by the warring sides, with the MPLA government in control of Cangandala Park and the northernmost part of the Luando Reserve, and UNITA holding sway in the southern section. He and Runi heard that well-armed bands had holed up in the bush, living off the land and the food stores of intimidated villagers. It didn't sound good. But he thought the size and remoteness of the region and the animals' shyness and ability to fade into the forest might protect the giant sables—unless, as he put it, "their range became a major battleground." Estes knew that the level of instability in the country made the government reluctant to allow travel into the interior, but he had no trouble obtaining a visa and permission. Angolans had come to identify with the beleaguered, proud-looking animal that was once pursued only by their colonial overlords and their guests, and now regarded it as a symbol of independence and nationhood. As such, the antelope continued to be featured on their postage stamps and money, and became the logo of the national airline and the name of their country's soccer team, the Palancas Negras. Luanda was eager to have the giant sable expert visit.

In mid-1982, Estes flew to Luanda and although forewarned, was shocked at the sight of devastated buildings and wrecked vehicles in the handsome colonial city he remembered. The splendid seafood restaurants were long gone; even eggs, bread, and butter were scarce. He was glad to head to Malange city, a day's drive from the capital, with Fritz Holsten, a Danish forester who worked for the ministry of agriculture. There he learned that the presence of UNITA guerrillas would rule out traveling to the northern part of the Luando Reserve; a trip to Quimbango, the village in the middle of the reserve that been his home for a year, would be "out of the question." Still, there was nearby Cangandala. The park looked overgrown, and yard-high grass made it difficult to spot game. But the warden, João Amaro, was passionate about protecting the giant sable. He showed Estes a mural that had been painted on a wall of his home in honor of the American researcher's visit. It featured three giant sable bulls, two on their knees, dueling with their horns, and another with a cartoon thought bubble above his head that read "Welcome, Dr. Estes! Please help me!" Amaro told Estes he could count on seeing a herd of some thirty females and young at a meadow he had burned several weeks before, near the village of Kulamagia.

They woke at 5:00 A.M. to the calls of nightjars. "We drove through the chill darkness and reached our destination at dawn, only to find it socked in by heavy mist," Estes wrote. When the fog lifted at 8:00 A.M., one warthog and a few reedbucks were visible. "A maze of tracks in the ashes showed that sable had been using the burn—so heavily, in fact, I wondered if enough grass was left to interest them in returning."

Several hours later, after driving along numerous trails hemmed in by high grass, Estes began to wonder if he would see the *palanca preta gigante*. Suddenly they came upon a scene that surpassed anything he had witnessed in the entire year he had spent in the Luando Reserve, a group of nine bulls in the open, five of them adult coal-black-and-white males with great sweeping horns. They stood grazing in a small stand of lush green growth surrounded by burned pasture. Amaro drove slowly to within fifty yards of the stately animals, Estes snapping pictures as they approached. "These bulls were as tame as any sable I had ever encountered," Estes recalled. "I was surprised because few vehicles other than the warden's enter Cangandala, and this herd was new to Amaro. Perhaps these animals were naive: a car was a novelty, a slightly alarming noisy moving object, but nothing to fear." South of the park, it was different. There, a maze of car tracks left by poachers explained why the game was shy and skittish, rarely letting vehicles approach closer than three hundred yards. But "these bachelor bulls were so intent on cropping the greenery they hardly stirred from the burn during my five-day stay, except to withdraw into the woods to rest and ruminate."

Searching for other sable that had been recently seen in the countryside between the Cangandala and Luando sanctuaries, Estes and Amaro drove through the region, passing still burning fires that had left the ground scorched and blackened. On returning to the burned meadow where Amaro had first taken Estes, they got out to look for fresh tracks and startled the herd, which galloped for the forest in a billowing cloud of powdery ash and dust; clearly, the giant sables feared the approach of men on foot. The image of antelopes thundering through swirling ashes was a painful reminder of the animals' precarious existence, trapped in a war zone. Still, Estes was relieved that against all expectation, there appeared to be as many giant sable in Cangandala as there had been when he and Runi had visited in 1969–70—perhaps a hundred of them. But what was the status of the animals in the Luando Reserve?

Amaro sent messengers across the deep Luando River to summon the game guards, mostly Songo tribesmen, who, amazingly enough, still carried out bicycle and foot patrols in the very northern end of the reserve. The men spoke of four herds, totaling over a hundred animals, that ranged within a few miles of the village of Gunga Palanca. But they were unable to keep watch over some of the groups because roving bands of heavily armed guerrillas made it too dangerous. They also told Estes that four guards were still stationed at Quimbango, the village where he and Runi had lived. "They named the same men who had assisted in our fieldwork and protected our study herds," Estes wrote. But, he asked them, "hadn't these animals all been machine-gunned?" "Nonsense," they answered. Amaro told a still doubtful Estes that while there had been shooting incidents in the southern end of the reserve, near Mulundo—the settlement that Curtis, Yebes, Keynes, and others had passed through decades before—and a few poaching incidents in the north-central section, "there had been no wholesale slaughter."

The fine for shooting a giant sable stood at half a million kwanzas, then equivalent to over $16,000. But the animal seemed to have something else that protected it, "something intangible and possibly more effective on its side" than guards and fines. From all he'd heard, Estes speculated that there was still a lingering native taboo against killing the animal, one that might have been behind the reticence of the indigenous tribes in the days when trophy hunters and museum collectors came in pursuit of it. Perhaps the same reticence still helped to conceal the presence of the herds from outsiders. Once peace came, so long as the animals' habitat could be protected from "piecemeal settlement," the outlook for its conservation seemed, well, promising. On his return to the U.S., Estes went so far as to write that before the end of the 1980s, it was conceivable that "tourists will be able to see one of the world's most handsome animals in its native haunts."

That assessment would prove wildly optimistic.

THE COLD WAR was not just the context of Angola's civil war in the 1980s; it was its engine. The balance of power seesawed as the major powers poured in weapons and their allies sent in troops to try and tip the scales toward one side or the other. Understandably, the conflict looked better on boardroom blackboards than it did in the bush, where abstract global policy was turned into a living hell for Angolans. Tens of thousands were pressed into fighting each other for causes that became increasingly remote from their lives. UNITA or the MPLA or foreign troops took turns raking over the countryside and ravaging settlements and cities held by their enemies. Millions of the nation's inhabitants tried to escape being swept up in the escalating violence (or were driven from their homes) and fell victim to shootings and shellings, land mines, imprisonment, torture, disease, and starvation.

Jonas Savimbi had wisely relocated UNITA's headquarters to Jamba, his thatched-hut bush capital in swampy Cuando Cubango Province, the southeast corner of the country wedged under Zambia. In that remote location, just above the narrow finger of Namibia's Caprivi Strip that points into the lower middle of the continent, his movement could be readily resupplied by South Africa, which had previously established military bases on the Namibian border at Rundu and to the east along the Caprivi Strip. Jamba was surrounded by a vast ecosystem of sandy soil, yellow grasslands, scattered clumps of dark trees, and muddy floodplains under an empty sky that made travelers squint from the sun and the dust. This harsh landscape, bordered on the north by Angola's Luengue River and the Cuito and

Cuando Rivers on its western and eastern edges, extended down through the Caprivi into Botswana above the Okavango Delta. Only a few tribes, mostly Bushmen, had previously shared this inhospitable corner of Africa with its uncounted elephants and rhinos, lions and leopards, hippos and antelope herds, baboons and bird life and tsetse flies. The Cuando Cubango's near-pristine wilderness had once been a Portuguese hunting concession. It would soon become a battleground between the MPLA's army and Cuban troops, and UNITA and the South African Defense Force, notably its "Buffalo" Battalion, later called 32 ("three-two") Battalion.

This fighting force was welded together in 1975 out of the miserable remnants of Holden Roberto's FNLA forces and an assortment of foreign mercenaries by Col. Jan Breytenbach, the combat-toughened Special Forces officer who formed and led the formidable paratrooper unit, 1 Reconnaissance Commando. Named after the herds of truculent Cape buffalo found near its training base in the Caprivi, the Buffalo Battalion was involved in a series of clandestine missions inside Angola from 1976 until 1988, and gained a reputation for ferocity in battle. It became the most decorated unit in the SADF, and its leader a legend, both feared and respected by his troops. As its exploits and composition (mostly black troops led primarily by white South African officers) became known, it would invariably be referred to in the press as the "notorious" 32 Battalion. It did more than fight alongside UNITA; it fought many battles for it, its white soldiers wearing blackface to disguise their presence, which made it easier for Savimbi to take credit for more victories than UNITA had actually earned.

By 1984 UNITA had failed to tie down MPLA and Cuban forces with effective guerrilla warfare, leaving its bases vulnerable to a government offensive. "To save UNITA's skin," Breytenbach wrote, "it would become the South African Army's lot to go to their assistance." The 32 Battalion geared up to do what UNITA could not: fight a conventional war. When massive government forces advanced deep into Cuando Cubango in 1985, the 32 Battalion came to UNITA's rescue, hitting massed MPLA troops who had regrouped north of the tiny ruined village of Mavinga with rockets and SADF air strikes. Devastated, government forces retreated, leaving a battlefield strewn with hundreds of burned-out vehicles and bodies; two brigades had been nearly annihilated. "The carnage," Breytenbach wrote, "was indescribable." But it was an "excellent propaganda coup for Savimbi, who flew in the press corps. Numerous photographs would appear of UNITA troops in heroic poses standing by the fire-blackened wreckage of trucks, BRDMs [Soviet-made armored cars], and even helicopters, waving their AK-47s at the cameras."

Savimbi was fighting his war not just on the ground but in the media. Exaggerating his military prowess, control of territory, and rural support helped him gain legitimacy and ultimately power. John Stockwell's warning, elicited by Savimbi's first U.S. visit, that "he believes in nothing beyond his own selfish ambitions, and fighting has become his way of life," was largely ignored or deemed irrelevant by Washington policy makers with their own international agenda. On his second trip to the United States in 1981, Savimbi was warmly received by Reagan administration officials and later described in a State Department bulletin as "a legitimate political force in Angola." His trip just happened to coincide with the Reagan administration's first (and unsuccessful) efforts to overturn the Clark Amendment. The United States found means to indirectly support UNITA, however, by encouraging South Africa's Angola operations, even providing military assistance despite a UN arms embargo against South Africa. By the early 1980s, a number of conservative American journalists, some of whom made trips to Jamba for "press conferences" and "exclusive interviews," were promoting Savimbi as the stuff of right-wing dreams, the ultimate "freedom fighter," a virtual Angolan Rambo, whose "powerful frame strains camouflage trousers and a short-sleeved khaki shirt."

When the Clark Amendment was finally overturned in mid-1985, the Reagan administration announced publicly it would provide military assistance to Savimbi, who had by then become a poster boy for the Reagan Doctrine of assisting Third World efforts to roll back Soviet-supported revolutionary regimes. Reacting to the repeal of the Clark Amendment, the Angola's MPLA government broke off diplomatic contact with the United States, dashing prospects for further negotiations with South Africa on Namibian independence and Cuban troop withdrawal. Savimbi reacted by hiring a public relations firm to burnish his image and campaign vigorously for military support.

Angola's President, José Eduardo dos Santos, issued a statement warning that resuming aid to UNITA would endanger U.S. economic interest in his country, specifically oil installations. In fact, South African commandos had tried to sabotage oil facilities in Cabinda—a raid which Savimbi tried to claim was UNITA-led. Although oil revenues provided 90 percent of Angola's foreign exchange, half of these petroleum revenues went to the war effort, badly draining the national treasury. Dos Santos pointed out that U.S. support for UNITA (and South Africa) only deepened Angolan reliance on the Soviet Union and Cuba. In a speech at the UN soon after, he accused the United States of "hypocrisy" for claiming that Savimbi was a "freedom fighter." When talks between Angola and the United States later resumed, no common ground could be found.

But Jonas Savimbi was received with all the pomp and ceremony due a visiting head of state when he came to Washington in January 1986. President Reagan received him at the White House, George Shultz at the State Department, Caspar Weinberger at the Pentagon; he visited congressmen and senators. The day he arrived he heard Assistant Secretary of State Crocker warn that Chevron's Angola operation (formerly Gulf's) was contrary to U.S. national interests. He was fêted and applauded; UN Ambassador Jeane Kirkpatrick gave him an award at one function, calling him "one of the few authentic heroes of our time." She urged he be given "real assistance"; in other words, "real helicopters, real ground-to-air missiles"— exactly what Savimbi had just argued for in an article entitled "The War Against Soviet Colonialism." In it, he bemoaned his lack of real firepower in the attack on Mavinga, and issued an alarm: Angola was the "Munich" of Africa. "That is why I say that UNITA is the key to Angola, Angola is the key to Africa, and Africa is the key to the West. I am not alone in this assessment," he added ominously. "The Soviets agree."

He got the response he wanted. On departing Washington, Savimbi was given assurances that substantial military assistance would be reaching him in weeks; according to some accounts, it already had. Ten years before, when the CIA had sent him a shipment of old World War II carbines, Savimbi had been disgusted. Now, finally, the United States was supplying the "powder" he needed, some $15 million worth just for starters, including the much-vaunted shoulder-fired Stinger antiaircraft missile. Widely considered the most effective portable SAM, it was capable of bringing down Soviet attack jets.

Dos Santos was having a much harder time improving relations with Washington. For most of 1986, government forces, assisted by Cuban troops, withdrew to defensive positions around major cities and battled UNITA along the Benguela Railway. The rail line was a key target for Savimbi and South Africa: disrupting service undermined transport into the interior, and forced Zambia and Zaire to ship their goods through South Africa at greater expense. Angola pulled closer to its allies, and Castro responded by asserting that Cuba was "prepared to stay in Angola ten, twenty, or thirty more years, if need be." Nonetheless, Angola strayed somewhat from the socialist model, and announced major changes in its economic program, including budget cuts, privatization, and foreign investment. In 1987, it even applied to join the International Monetary Fund, but the Reagan administration was unimpressed. It continued to insist on Cuban troop withdrawal coupled with a role for Jonas Savimbi and UNITA in governing Angola.

Once again, critics of U.S. policy wondered if American interests would not be better served by recognizing the Angola government and assisting it with a modest recovery program than by fueling its catastrophic civil war. But Washington was more concerned with ending Soviet presence in Africa than with the fate of a single nation.

SINCE HIS TRIP to Angola in 1982, Richard Estes had been following news of the deteriorating situation in Angola. He had heard nothing but more unsettling rumors, and he became concerned again for the giant sable. Then, while attending a wildlife management symposium in Harare, Zimbabwe in October of 1987, he recognized a delegate from Angola as someone he'd met on his 1982 trip. Senhor N. L. Kingengo was more than happy to talk, but had only bad news to share. The warden of Cangandala Park had died in a "swimming accident." UNITA forces had gained control of the park itself, and burned the warden's house to the ground; what's more, they were said to be shooting giant sable.

Estes returned home, convinced that the situation was desperate. If UNITA was in Cangandala, it must also be in control of the Luando Reserve farther south. Several years before he had dismissed as impractical a giant sable rescue scheme floated by the Game Conservation International Organization. But he contacted his old friend Jeremy Anderson, now director of nature conservation at the Kangwane Parks Board in South Africa, to share his concerns. "It seems clear that the giant sable must now be considered more endangered than ever before," he wrote. "If it is possible to bring the problem to the attention of Jonas Savimbi, then perhaps steps could be taken to relieve the situation." He hoped UNITA forces could be ordered to protect rather than poach giant sable and that Savimbi might allow the capture and translocation of enough giant sable to establish a breeding herd in a neighboring country.

Anderson took the next step, and approached the South African Nature Foundation to enlist their help with the project. "As Dr. Estes has stated, the future survival of perhaps Africa's most spectacular antelope may now lie in UNITA's hands," he wrote them in late 1987. A captive breeding program was essential to guarantee the animal's survival; Anderson had already discussed this with the Pretoria Zoo, which had offered to provide breeding facilities. He suggested the political bait South Africans might take: if UNITA assisted with a capture operation, it could put Savimbi's organization in a positive light. And of course, the operation would have to be done in conjunction with Savimbi's allies in the field, the SADF. Anderson got an interested response—a "high-level" meeting had taken place—and a warning that the entire project would have to remain unpublicized; clearly, there were a number of sensitive political issues as well as military ones. Anderson cautioned Estes, who in turn offered a carefully worded assessment of the giant sable's situation in the January 1988 Antelope Specialists Group *Gnusletter*, hinting at what might be in store. "Why the Angolans in UNITA should be more inclined to squander their wildlife heritage than are Government forces (if indeed they are) is puzzling; and the apparent lack of control over the activities of UNITA forces by Jonas Savimbi and his South African allies is particularly disturbing. Ever since the Angolan civil war began in the 1970's, concern over the fate of the giant sable has often prompted conservationists to propose captive breeding as a hedge against the extinction of this greatly admired antelope. Maybe this is an idea whose time has come."

Six months later Estes learned that Savimbi was returning to Washington. He wrote to Chester Crocker at the State Department: "Everyone concerned with the survival of African wildlife will be in your debt if you can ascertain Savimbi's attitude on Angolan wildlife conservation and bring to his attention international concern over the giant sable."

Nothing ever came of this request. Understandably, Crocker was preoccupied with how rapidly events were unfolding.

ANGOLAN GOVERNMENT FORCES, newly equipped with roughly $1.5 billion worth of advanced Soviet weaponry, including radar, antiaircraft missiles, and helicopter gunships, had been placed under the overall command of Soviet General Konstantin Shaganovitch, the highest-ranking Soviet officer ever posted outside Europe or Afghanistan. In addition, nearly a thousand Soviet advisors were deployed in country. It was a sure sign that the Kremlin was serious about reversing the Angolan government defeats of 1985.

Determined government forces made a second attempt to take Mavinga in mid-1987—with the goal of pushing farther south to Jamba— literally crushing some UNITA fighters beneath the tracks of their tanks in their determined advance. But by September they were halted once again by well-armed South African units, whose flexible tactics and combat experience helped balance the odds against the numerically superior Soviet-led troops. The South Africans used their state-of-the-art G-5 long-range artillery with its twenty-five-mile range to shell the enemy, but it wasn't enough. In a climactic battle that began on the banks of the Lomba River near Mavinga on the morning of October 3, South African soldiers in their Ratels—small armored combat vehicles—outmaneuvered the larger Soviet T-54/55 battle tanks in the dense bush. Swarming tanks sent up clouds of blinding dust, artillery fire rained down, bullets pinged off armor plate, and cannon fire boomed across the grassy openings. Government MIGs, wary of Stinger missiles in the hands of outlying UNITA units, strafed the battlefield in dozens of sorties, but the South Africans continued to inflict tremendous damage. When small groups of government infantry broke cover and ran for the river, they were cut down by machine gun fire that kicked up spurts of black mud before ripping into flesh and bone, or blown away by shrapnel-spewing mortar bombs. Devastated, MPLA forces fell into a disorganized retreat; harried by UNITA fighters, they headed back a hundred miles to Cuito Cuanavale. The South Africans were too exhausted to follow up decisively. As night fell, vehicles burned and billowed thick smoke in the growing darkness. The next morning revealed a scarred landscape that had become all too common in Angola's interior: shattered trees, smoldering grass, burned-out tank hulks dotting the *anharas* and the bodies of combatants sprawled on the ground or tumbling slowly in the river currents.

By some accounts, some eight thousand UNITA fighters and some four thousand SADF soldiers had virtually destroyed an entire brigade and ravaged several others out of a total force of eighteen thousand MPLA troops. Government losses were estimated at four thousand killed or wounded. The campaign was a staggering defeat for Luanda, and a stinging humiliation for Moscow. Pretoria, not wanting to add to the international outcry over its previous incursions, kept silent on its role until a month later, when it had to admit it had intervened to prevent UNITA's defeat; South Africa could no longer pretend to be in "hot pursuit" of SWAPO guerrillas when it was engaged in battles two hundred miles inside Angola. Seizing the moment, Savimbi told a press conference in Jamba that UNITA, with U.S. aid, had won the most important military victory since the war started in 1975. Asked about South African statements to the contrary, Savimbi professed to be "surprised" and "hurt" that South Africa would take credit for his success.

In late November, the UN Security Council unanimously condemned South Africa's "continued and intensified acts of aggression against the People's Republic of Angola and the continuing occupation of parts of that State." Seeing an opportunity to create a bargaining chip with the Angolan government while the Namibian settlement was being negotiated, the Reagan administration supported the resolution. But South Africa had no intention of pulling out of Angola before it had fulfilled its objectives. Its army had been bombarding Cuito Cuanavale for over a month with artillery fire in the hopes that this strategic base would fall to Savimbi's men. If it did, UNITA would be poised to take control of the Benguela Railway, which would allow American supplies to reach it directly from Zaire.

Once more, Fidel Castro came to the rescue. He dispatched fifteen thousand troops to augment the twenty-five thousand already in Angola. By February 1988 the Cubans were on the front lines and managed to stop the South African–UNITA advance on Cuito Cuanavale, and on March 23 forced the attackers to retreat after a ferocious fifteen-hour battle, the last of three attempts to take the fortified positions to the east of the city. South Africa and UNITA had driven their enemies back to their July 1987 starting point, but they could not dislodge them.

The African continent had not seen warfare on this scale since the battle of El Alamein in World War II. But complex negotiations, at first tentative, and then more substantive, had already begun among South Africa, Cuba, Angola, and the United States and would soon overtake the fighting, although not soon enough for many of the troops. While the diplomats balked and talked, soldiers died in last-ditch efforts to defend or extend the Angolan soil under their command and create the required leverage at the bargaining table. For by now, the Soviet Union, Cuba, and South Africa each needed an Angolan exit strategy. Mikhail Gorbachev was seeking to reduce the Soviet Union's military commitments in order to free up resources for his planned domestic reforms under perestroika. Castro, in turn, had created his own Vietnam in Angola: over a period of thirteen years, some four hundred thousand Cuban troops had been in Angola at one time or another and far too many of them had never returned home. Supporting the cause of revolution in Africa resulted in drastic austerities at home and widespread disenchantment with the foreign adventures of the "Maximum Leader." The South African government feared that mounting white casualties would further alarm the South African electorate, which had been deliberately misled about the scale and nature of the conflict, and possibly trigger a political backlash. Part of the process of extraction involved everyone's claiming victory, although no one had really won. South Africa lost comparatively fewer men, but "the butcher's bill" was still too high. Its forces also had to face the fact that for the first time a mostly black army had withstood its military machine, even if its field commanders had been largely restrained by Pretoria's insistence on victories without casualties. Later, the South Africans would say they were happy to let the Cubans claim victory if that gave Castro the fig leaf he needed to withdraw with dignity.

The talks, in which the United States acted as facilitator, culminated in the New York Accord, which was signed in late December 1988. It called for South Africa to pull its troops out of Angola and cease support for UNITA, and for Angola to cooperate in the Cuban withdrawal of its fifty thousand troops over a two-year period. South Africa also had to prepare Namibia for independence, in accordance with UN Resolution 435. The United States was satisfied: the Cubans would withdraw, and the Angolans were already dismantling their centrally planned economy. But it was not giving up on Savimbi.

The MPLA would later speak of the battle for Cuito Cuanavale as Angola's Stalingrad. Although militarily stronger, it needed peace to concentrate on economic recovery. It was all too aware of the staggering human cost of a war that had now dragged on for thirteen years. The statistics were numbing: from 1981 to 1988, some 60,000 combatants and 435,000 civilians (three-quarters of them children) had died. By 1988 the vast number of mines that had been sown like dragons' teeth by both sides (but mostly by UNITA) gave Angola the distinction of having the largest percentage of amputees per capita in the world. Some 40,000 of its citizens, mostly women and children, staggered on crutches into an uncertain future. One million people—12 percent of the population—were displaced. Most had fled to provincial capitals, which were now ringed with miserable shantytowns lacking water, electricity, or sanititary facilities. Half the urban population was malnourished, and nearly half a million others had streamed across Angola's borders. Ten thousand classrooms, two hundred bridges, and a long list of factories, health clinics, and power plants had been destroyed—billions and billions of dollars' worth of physical damage. But Savimbi's supporters looked at Angola's crumbling infrastructure and saw only evidence of Marxist misrule, as if the impact of Portugal's scorched-earth exodus and the devastating decades of war that followed had nothing to do with the state of the nation.

ON OCTOBER 16, 1989, a dusty ten-ton refrigerated truck carrying vegetables was stopped by the South-West African Police at a farm near Okahandja, a bush town some forty miles north of Windhoek in central Namibia. Inside, under a garnish of greens, officers found 980 elephant tusks weighing a total of seven tons, the largest haul of illegal ivory ever seized. Twenty-two men were arrested. The truck belonged to Joaquim da Silva Augusto, a wealthy Portuguese-speaking Namibian businessman who supplied food and fuel to UNITA's Jamba base from his warehouse in Rundu near the Angolan border. Two weeks later Augusto was at the controls of his light aircraft when it crashed on takeoff at Jamba, injuring one of his passengers, the son of Portuguese President Mario Soares. UNITA quickly moved to counteract spreading rumors that the plane had been overloaded with contraband ivory by inviting the press to view elephants roaming wild in the "Freelands of Angola" (in reality, herds were left unmolested for just such photo opportunities), but they were barred from visiting the crash site.

That was it, as far as Col. Jan Breytenbach was concerned. He would go public with what he knew. "I am all for a just war," he later wrote, "but I have great difficulty in reconciling the justness of war against the wholesale rape of the African savannah's last outpost." Breytenbach was not only a soldier, he was an ardent conservationist who had become passionate about the wildlife of the harshly beautiful Cuando Cubango and western Caprivi during his years of service there commanding 32 Battalion. Alarmed by mounting evidence of his military's involvement with widespread poaching and ivory trafficking, and worried about the potential damage to the SADF's reputation, he had tried to warn the high command for years that elephants were being massacred in the Cuando Cubango, but no one would listen. The previous year the U.S. House of Representatives had heard testimony accusing South Africa of supporting the slaughter of elephants to help finance Angola's civil war. "A massive smuggling ring has been operating for years," claimed environmental activist Craig van Note, "with the complicity of South African officials at the highest level of the government and military, to funnel ivory and other contraband out of Africa." These stunning charges created an embarrassment for Pretoria just at the moment when sensitive negotiations with Cuba, Angola, and the United States were underway. The SADF quickly commissioned an inquiry into the matter, and issued a report in early December that found no evidence to support the allegations. "However," the SADF admitted, "small quantities of ivory, captured by UNITA from poachers and others in Angola, were transported by the defense force on behalf of UNITA over an 18-month period from mid-1978 to the end of 1979." The practice, they concluded, was ended in 1979. Jan Breytenbach thought the defense force probe was nothing more than a whitewash.

The secrecy that had always surrounded South African operations in Angola made perfect cover for corrupt army officials—those, as Breytenbach later put it, who regarded an elephant as "a huge piece of worthless, mobile meat, carrying towards its front end valuable tusks under its ludicrous hose-pipe nose"—to personally profit from it. The clandestine conduits that had been set up to bring supplies in to UNITA were also used to smuggle UNITA's ivory out to the Far East. By 1989, with the implementation of UN Resolution 435 (and Namibian independence) looming closer, contraband shipments of ivory, rhino horn, and diamonds increased dramatically.

A week after the news of the seven-ton Okahandja ivory haul broke, Col. Breytenbach sent a letter and an impassioned statement to the *Sunday Times* in Pretoria. The accusations might have had less impact if they hadn't come from him. Recently retired as a colonel seconded to military intelligence, Breytenbach was the most decorated soldier of the SADF. He also happened to be the brother of the exiled poet Breyten Breytenbach and had a vivid prose style of his own. He wrote that after South Africa's Operation Savannah campaign, UNITA forces moved into the remote Cuando Cubango to elude the MPLA. "Savimbi had hardly settled down, however, when he saw the potential riches in hundreds of thousands of tusks, flaunted innocently all around him by hundreds of thousands of elephants . . . Volleys of shots rippled through the region, not the single heavy shot of the discerning hunter, but the tearing rattle of automatic fire from AK-47 rifles and machine guns. Elephants were mowed down indiscriminately," he charged. "The hundreds of thousands of elephants became thousands, the thousands became hundreds and the hundreds only a very few."

Three years before, when Breytenbach had crisscrossed UNITA's territory, he had seen little wildlife. Even the birds had been barely noticeable. "Today, a deadly silence has settled over the Cuando Cubango," he went on. The elephants and rhinos were gone, the herds of buffalo "shot, skinned and cooked to feed thousands of UNITA troops and their dependents. The other animals went the way of the buffalo." A follow-up story based on his revelations ran in mid-November under the banner headline "WAR VETERAN LINKS SADF TO UNITA IVORY SLAUGHTER," and received international attention. UNITA's representative in the United States simply scoffed at the report, although the year before Savimbi had told a *New York Times* reporter that UNITA was in fact trading ivory with South Africa — but only the tusks of elephants that had died of "natural causes."

And now Savimbi was firmly in control of the giant sable lands.

OVER THE NEXT decade, Angolans had reason to wonder why their country had to be taught such a long and grim lesson in twentieth-century geopolitics. Their modern history seemed caught in a loop, doomed to repeat the same exhausting sequence of open warfare, followed by lessenings of hostilities, leading to cease-fires and flare-ups, then behind-the-scenes diplomacy giving way to talks, and eventually to negotiations and peace conferences, the signing of accords followed by subsequent misunderstandings, the inevitable breakdown of agreements and the return to open warfare, over and over again. One could point to segments on the Angolan timeline in which there were fewer hostilities than others, but the simple truth was that for as long as most Angolans could remember, there had been no real peace.

But there were a number of attempts to bring it about. The 1988 accords won independence for Namibia and forced Cuban troop withdrawal, but did not directly address Angola's civil war. The new Bush administration talked of reconciliation in Angola, but despite dos Santos's interest in normalizing relations, continued to support UNITA militarily to the tune of $50 million a year. In mid-1989 President Mobutu Sese Soko of Zaire hosted a meeting of eighteen African leaders at Gbadolite, his lavish country residence northeast of Kinshasha, at which dos Santos and Savimbi met for the first time. Talks between the two sides led to commitments which called for a cease-fire between UNITA and the MPLA.

Although no document was signed, the two shook hands. It proved to be a fleeting moment of reconciliation because disagreements immediately arose over what had actually transpired. Savimbi underscored his dispute with the dos Santos regime by sabotaging Luanda's electrical system and later shooting down an Angolan plane with forty-two people aboard. The United States continued to push for negotiations between UNITA and the Angolan government "without preconditions," which, from Luanda's point of view, would have meant capitulation under foreign pressure. And yet another MPLA offensive to take Mavinga from UNITA was launched and succeeded, but then bogged down in the rainy season. The United States and South Africa continued to supply Savimbi, and the overextended government forces retreated; UNITA claimed a "resounding victory."

In December of 1990 Savimbi made another trip to Washington, where he met with President George H. W. Bush. By now he had the routine down pat. A photograph taken at the meeting shows the broadly smiling Savimbi shaking Bush's hand firmly. What is most striking is the careful mix of signals the bearded guerrilla leader's dress sends off: his dark tailored jacket is part nonaligned Nehru, part militant Mao; the insouciantly folded silk handkerchief poking out of his breast pocket sends the message that he is his own man; the discreet black cockerel pin on his collar reminds everyone that he is the living embodiment of UNITA. Savimbi once dismissed Holden Roberto as a tool of the United States. Of course, Savimbi had been one as well, but by the time of the visit he was also a master at manipulating the United States for his own purposes.

A round of difficult and protracted talks in Bicesse, Portugal in mid-1991 led to an agreement that called for integration of the two Angolan armies and internationally monitored elections to be held in 1992. Resource-starved Portugal, knowing it would never be a world power again, eagerly embraced its role as an intermediary. Its part in these negotiations seemed to assuage the country's residual guilt over the way it had abruptly abandoned its greatest colony. Jonas Savimbi and José Eduardo dos Santos shook hands again, this time with less enthusiasm, and signed the accords. Every church bell in Lisbon was rung to mark the event. Portugal may have harbored hopes it would find a new role in Angola, but until then it would take the precaution of joining the United States and the Soviet Union in agreeing not to supply the combatants with war matériel. The

United States took the attitude that it had achieved all its objectives, except Savimbi's obtaining power, but it was widely assumed he would win the election.

Savimbi returned to Luanda sixteen years after independence with UNITA's general staff to throw himself into the electoral process. At the airport little girls holding doves waited with a curious crowd of some seventy thousand for UNITA's leader to exit his plane and stride down the waiting red carpet, but the doves of peace, groggy from being held too long, fell ominously to the ground when they were thrown in the air. Savimbi, in full battle dress, had to sidestep the birds to avoid crushing them under his boots. It was the biggest crowd he would draw in Luanda, despite his much-vaunted charisma.

The two candidates campaigned for support very differently, Savimbi running up to the microphones at political rallies like a boxer entering an arena and whipping the crowds into a frenzy with his rhetoric and fist-pumping showmanship; the gray-haired, somber-suited dos Santos, repackaged by a Brazilian public relations firm as a distinguished African leader, projecting presidential presence at his soothing speeches, which underscored the MPLA's campaign slogan O Futuro Seguro—the secure future. Both sides distributed T-shirts, hats, headbands, food, and cooking oil and bussed in supporters for rallies. A sense of excitement over this exercise in democracy was partly tempered by uneasy feelings among the populace over the choice, perhaps best expressed by the graffiti scrawled on city walls: "MPLA steals, UNITA kills." Many thought Savimbi would win—he was sure of it. "If UNITA does not win the elections, they have to have been rigged," he said. "If they are rigged, I don't think we will accept them."

Over 90 percent of Angolan voters showed up at the ballot box. Several days later, when the final tally was announced, President dos Santo had received 49.6 percent of the vote, Savimbi 40 percent.

The UN certified that the elections had been "generally free and fair," but UNITA declared them fraudulent. The UN and the United States urged acceptance of the results, but little was done to quell rising tensions on both sides. Fighting broke out when the MPLA, claiming UNITA planned to overthrow the government, began hunting down and executing UNITA officials comfortably ensconced in Luanda's diplomatic quarter. Savimbi, fearing an attempt on his life, fled the capital curled up on the floor of the backseat of a South African intelligence officer's Range Rover to reach a waiting jet at the airport. Thousands died in the vigilante violence, their bodies bulldozed into mass graves. Armed clashes broke out across Angola and UNITA unearthed the weaponry it had hidden before the election and seized important cities and key diamond mines. The government had firm control of Luanda, but having demobilized under the Bicesse Accords, had to scramble to rearm and confront UNITA. João de Matos, an experienced military hard-liner, was picked to spearhead the effort. Angola plunged back into full-blown civil war, punctuated by sporadic negotiations. Knowing it had the military edge, UNITA used such talks to gain time. Meanwhile, Huambo, Savimbi's headquarters, would be pounded into rubble as both sides sought control of the highland city once called Nova Lisboa, its surviving inhabitants reduced to hiding in cellars and eating cats and rats. UNITA won that round, but there was a difference now. Because the international community had accepted the elections, UNITA was now widely viewed the way much of the world had always seen it—as a rebel group trying to topple the legitimate government of Angola.

BY 1992 THERE were fifty thousand rural Angolan refugees in camps in the western and northwestern provinces of Zambia, but the actual number who had fled over the border was probably twice that high. Hopes had risen among them that after the elections they would be able to return to their villages and start their lives over. Some did not wait for the results, and went back early. When the war broke out again, those that were lucky enough to be able to escape the fighting and return to the Zambian camps told appalling tales. Many of the elders there blamed UNITA for Angola's troubles, but the young people thought Savimbi was a heroic figure; at least, that is the impression they got from UNITA's radio broadcasts. But everyone acknowledged his fearsome power and determination; it seemed superhuman. In fact, he came to be regarded much like the *makishi*, those reanimated spirits brought to life through the use of masks and costumes during the all-important tribal rituals and ceremonies of *mukunda*, the circumcision of young boys.

The *makishi* are not to be confused with the mask or costume itself, or with the performers, even though they incarnate these spirits; for the masks and the performers merely give expression to these shades, which embody, among other things, the deepest unspoken fears of the people. Savimbi was identified with the frightening, aggressive *Utenu* spirit that emerges wearing the branch and fiber costume, and his name (along with UNITA's) could be found emblazoned on the intimidating yard-long crested mask for maximum effect. Stamping and whirling like a swooping airplane, *Utenu*-Savimbi would threaten his audience with a tree branch or machete, beating the women and scaring uninitiated boys to remind everyone of the old social order, while giving form to the new, heart-sinking horrors of their now unpredictable lives.

"IN THE LAST couple of years," Richard Estes wrote in 1991 to Willie Labuschagne, director of the Pretoria Zoo, "I have come to consider the status of the giant sable possibly precarious enough to justify the disturbance and expense of capturing animals for a breeding herd," although he wondered if a captive breeding program near the Luando Reserve, rather than one which would involve translocating them far outside their normal range, wouldn't make more sense.

Labuschagne had proposed a giant sable captive breeding program that would involve both the National Zoo at Pretoria and the Angolan government, and would be endorsed by the National Zoological Gardens of Cuba. In follow-up letters to Estes and Jeremy Anderson, he stressed that they were trying to save an endangered species, and the longer they took to take action, the less chance of success they'd have. He suspected trophy hunters were paying considerable sums to the government to hunt the animal. (Just how much trophy hunting was still going on was unclear, although rich Portuguese were apparently going on covert safaris in UNITA-controlled territory.)

Anderson quickly drew up a straightforward plan, incorporating several of Estes's suggestions. It proposed that a survey of the giant sable lands take place in July 1992 and the capture program in September. He wrote

Estes: "If there are only a few animals left, then the threat of extinction will be so great that we 'must' catch some. Alternatively, if there are many (say over a hundred), then we 'can' afford to catch some."

Labuschagne now had IUCN support in addition to approval from the International Union of Zoo Directors, and wrote to the Angolan ambassador in Namibia in March 1992. There was no immediate response; the Angolans were gripped with election fever. A month later the IUCN was making its own contacts in Luanda. Achim Steiner, the organization's program coordinator for southern Africa, found the government highly interested in any number of environmental issues, from retraining demobilized soldiers into park rangers to investigating the status of the giant sable, whose numbers were said to be dropping fast; estimates ranged from a maximum of six hundred to as few as twenty. The only credible sighting in recent years had been by air in November 1991; only three animals were seen. Steiner found a willing sponsor for worthy environmental missions—British Petroleum. BP wanted to enhance its image and improve its chances to obtain oil concessions. Steiner suggested a study of Cangandala Park that would assess its potential as a UN World Heritage Site as well as the fate of the great antelope. BP agreed to provide funding, even a vehicle. It made sense to have Anderson do the survey, and Steiner planned to involve the Frankfurt Zoo in the project; it had sponsored some preliminary work on a survey of its own. The whole thing would cost $44, 722.

But in May of 1992 a Portuguese family was killed in Cangandala Park. BP requested that the survey be postponed, and the IUCN put it on hold. Anderson hoped it would still go through despite the local shootings. But the military situation continued to deteriorate, and the IUCN pushed the survey date back to October in the hopes of a peaceful outcome to the elections. The delay was a matter of concern; the issue of the giant sable was heating up, as Steiner made clear in a memo to IUCN headquarters in Switzerland. There were a number of dubious individuals, particularly South Africans, trying to buy cooperation from the Angolan government for clandestine exports of giant sables to foreign destinations.

But the IUCN survey, like the Pretoria Zoo's rescue project, was shelved after the disastrous denouement to the 1992 elections; it was now too dangerous to venture into the giant sable's haunts.

MY DESIRE TO know what happened to the giant sable had grown far beyond historical curiosity. In February 1994 I reached Richard Estes by phone in New Hampshire and had a long conversation with him. He gave me Jeremy Anderson's number in South Africa, and Anderson and I talked. I asked if I could participate in the planned survey. He laughed—didn't I know that there was a war going on? Sure, if the survey ever got off the ground I could go with him, but I'd have to clear it with Achim Steiner in Zimbabwe. Steiner was agreeable to the idea, to my great relief, and suggested I also talk with Simon Anstey, the Angola/Mozambique program coordinator, with whom he shared the IUCN regional office in Harare. Over a crackling phone line, Anstey told me it was likely that there were only several hundred giant sable left in Angola, as few as there were in 1934—an alarming drop from the 2,500 Estes had estimated still roamed the reserves in 1969. He pointed out that UNITA had been in control of the habitat areas for the past five years and relatively little fighting had actually gone on there.

"But there's no question that they could have been shot out if that had been permitted," Anstey said. I asked him why that hadn't happened. He thought that it wasn't only the Angolan government that regarded the animal as a national emblem; UNITA also saw the giant sable as a potent symbol. He'd been told that the *palanca negra* appeared on the badge of its elite military units. "And there's another thing," he added. "I've heard that Savimbi has declared the killing of a giant sable a capital offense."

Could that be the reason why there would be any giant sable left at all? I found a passing reference in Fred Bridgland's biography, buried in a long interview in which Savimbi described a typical day in Jamba in 1979: "We export ivory, rhino horn and leopard and antelope skins to help pay for our war," he told Bridgland, as if such trade were commonplace, "but we have declared some conservation zones where hunting elephant, giraffe and black sable is banned. The black sable is a rare species and it is a UNITA symbol on our coat of arms."

The fact that Savimbi's shadow had fallen across the giant sable made me uneasy. Could a man who had done all he had be believed? The answers would only be found in Angola, and I was finally going there. Anderson, Steiner, and Anstey had all said they'd be pleased to have me participate in the Cangandala survey as an "attached journalist/ reporter"—Anstey's phrase—when and if it was revived. Some months later Anstey sent me a formal invitation in which he emphasized the point that the project was on hold, given the resumption of hostilities (including the recent shelling of the town of Cangandala), and was unlikely to take place before 1995.

But there had been peace talks in Addis Ababa the previous year, followed by the Abidjan talks, which led to preliminary talks in Lusaka and then the open plenary session of the Lusaka peace talks. All this talking had been interrupted in December 1993 by the alleged assassination attempt on Savimbi in Cuito, but since then the mediators had met with President Nelson Mandela, and President Bill Clinton had sent letters to dos Santos and Savimbi. At long last the Lusaka Protocol was initialed, and—after government forces quickly seized Huambo and several other provincial capitals—it was finally signed in November 1994. It provided for a new cease-fire, the release of prisoners, a UN peacekeeping force, the quartering of UNITA troops and their integration into the Angolan national forces, and eventually, new elections. The survey expedition would surely take place in 1995, and I would be part of it.

FIVE YEARS LATER, the IUCN still had not undertaken a giant sable survey. It had been postponed every year for "security reasons" until it had been permanently shelved in disgust at the turn of events.

But I was going to Angola anyway. In October of 1999, two days before my departure, I had a chance to meet with Col. Fred Oelschig, who had been the SADF's senior intelligence liaison with Jonas Savimbi from 1986 to 1989. I wanted to hear what he knew about Savimbi and the giant sable. Now retired from the military, Oelschig had recently returned from a de-mining project in Iraq to his farm halfway between Pretoria and Johannesburg. He drove up on a Saturday morning in his *bakkie*—Afrikaans for pickup—to meet me at the guest house in Pretoria where I was staying. Oelschig wore a denim vest over his solid frame and greeted me with a firm handshake.

We sat on the garden terrace in the shade and ordered tea. I knew that he'd spent considerable time in Angola, having been with Operation

Savannah in 1975 and Operation Protea in 1981 before he was assigned to work with UNITA. Oelschig helped train UNITA's guerrillas in how to fight a conventional war. Unused to tackling tanks, their tactic had been to run from them; by 1988 they were going into battle riding on Olifant tanks driven by South Africans. Over a thousand were killed in the fighting for Cuito Cuanavale. "There were so many UNITA dead that the Olifants were riding over their bodies, which were crunching beneath the sprockets," Oelschig had written in a brief account of those days. "It was a horrific job to clean the tracks. . . ." He was reluctant now to discuss the war in Angola; it was in the past. "I've done some things of which I'm not proud, and other things of which I am very proud," he said simply.

I asked him about Jan Breytenbach's claims that Savimbi conducted a large-scale trade in contraband ivory. He leaned back. "I have no quarrel with Breytenbach," he said, making it clear that he wanted to stay away from controversy. "I'm an ex-soldier," he says, "just trying to get on with his life." He conceded, however, that some of the things that are said to have happened could well have happened, "but," he adds, "let's just say I had a somewhat different experience." In previous E-mails to me, he'd written that he'd seen more elephants in southeast Angola in 1991 than when he'd first arrived there in 1979. Hunting in the region was deliberate, not indiscriminate; it was under Savimbi's firm control. Yes, he had specific hunting teams to shoot elephants, but it was done very selectively. He told me that in 1989 he saw several UNITA soldiers being punished for hunting without permission. They'd been caught by UNITA's internal police unit, at that time headed by Nzau Puna, one of Savimbi's companions from the early days. I asked for details. He shook his head almost imperceptibly as he circled a thick finger around the rim of his teacup. "Let's just say it was wartime," he said quietly.

And what of the giant sable? He said he once saw a small herd of five animals in the Cuando Cubando on a helicopter trip from Mavinga to Neriquinha and circled around them. The males, he noticed, had much larger, swept-back horns than the typical sables he was familiar with. Another time he spotted similarly impressive sables in southwest Zambia, just over the Angolan border. Again, he thought they might have been giant sables, but he couldn't be sure. But he knew about Savimbi's attitude toward them, and reiterated what he'd written me, that Savimbi had a great regard for these animals and considered them the Angolan people's heritage. In fact, one of UNITA's training bases was named Palanca, and so was his 4th Battalion. He wasn't aware of any *palanca* emblems, however, and couldn't tell me whether Savimbi had made the shooting of a giant sable a crime punishable by death.

I asked him what he thought about Savimbi. He repeated what he had told me in his letters: that some "will always love to hate" Savimbi and seek to discredit him; others "will never see the bad things and will remain blind to those matters that chill the blood."

Oelschig asked me when I was leaving for Angola. I told him I planned to go in two days. I intended to find out what happened to the giant sable.

He smiled at me, but his eyes weren't smiling. "It'll be quite an experience for you."

PART 2

SIX

A CONFLICT OF CRUSADERS

What happened next began with a letter that came to Richard Estes in New Hampshire, in November 1996. There was nothing in it to suggest it would raise questions about the very existence of the giant sable. What it first suggested to Estes was a straightforward case of animal smuggling. The Office of Scientific Authority of the U.S. Fish and Wildlife Service had received a permit application from the San Diego Zoo for the importation of *Hippotragus niger variani* from South Africa, and had faxed him to ask for comment. Estes had been expecting something like this. The month before, at the IUCN Species Survival Commission meetings in Montreal, he'd heard unsettling reports that there was a captive herd of giant sable antelope on a game ranch in South Africa, and that some of the animals had been offered for sale to U.S. zoos eager not just to exhibit, but to breed the endangered species.

Estes is an early morning person. He rises at 5:00 A.M. and makes a thermos of coffee before sitting down at his crowded desk to read and reply to his mail. But this letter was not so easy to answer. He was convinced that if the animals in South Africa were giant sables, they must have been brought out of Angola illegally. There was another possibility, however. These so-called giant sables might be *Hippotragus niger kirkii*, the typical sable north of the Zambezi, a subspecies in which mature males are similarly black and whose females also remain tan to chestnut in color. The mystery herd, Estes learned, was at Sable Ranch, a large game-breeding facility not far from Johannesburg, and the breeding stock, according to the ranch's managing director, came from two dozen sables caught in western Zambia, "near the Angolan border." Estes had his suspicions about what that really meant, but meanwhile all he could do was inform the San

Diego Zoo of his concerns and suggest that hard evidence on the origin of the founder group of animals should be obtained before going ahead.

Given what he knew about the animal, he regarded the idea of a population of giant sable in a neighboring country as implausible. "But," he told me later, "I realized that the story was a perfect cover for smuggling. Someone could claim that these giant sables had been conveniently found in Zambia, when all along they would have been taken from the existing remnant Angolan population." A single live giant sable, he pointed out, could command $50,000—sufficient to persuade some people, in Angola and elsewhere, to look the other way. Such sales could lead to a devastating level of live-capture poaching, particularly if there were also some level of complicity on the part of the Angolan government.

Sable Ranch apparently had sables with *variani*-like facial markings; proving that they were *variani* was another matter. The ranch had already approached Terrence Robinson of the Department of Zoology and Entomology at the University of Pretoria and asked him to undertake a project on sable genetics—something that had never been thoroughly investigated before. DNA confirmation that their sables were the genuine article might allow the lucrative sale of this rare antelope to the San Diego Zoo (and doubtless others) to go forward, despite lingering questions on how such giant sables came to be found in Zambia. Robinson had assembled tissue samples (skin and ear clippings) and blood from various sable populations and subgroups, including the sables at Sable Ranch, and obtained a tiny snip of *variani* skin from the Natural History Museum in London. For completeness, Robinson expanded the study to include the sable's close cousin, the roan antelope, as well. But the tests would take months.

Because giant sables are found only in Angola—he was certain of that—Estes thought Robinson would find evidence of a clear genetic distinction between the Angolan race and other sables, evidence that would provide a subspecies litmus test. In the fall of 1997 he contacted Robinson to ask if he'd come up with any proof that the Zambian border sables were giant sables. Robinson explained that he had DNA samples from Sable Ranch's herd but nothing from a known giant sable, which he'd need for comparison. "Terry tried obtaining some from a patch of giant sable skin sent from the British Museum, but it didn't work," Estes recalled, and the museum had balked at his request for further samples. "He E-mailed me that a tooth would be perfect, if I knew where to get one. I got up from my chair, walked out to the hall, and stared up at the Curtis head. Then I E-mailed him back: 'I may be able to put my hands on one.'"

Did he know it had a tooth in it? "Well, I didn't feel like tearing it apart to find out," he said. "So I called my dentist and asked if he would X-ray something for me." He laughed. "I tell you, it was a strange sight to see a giant sable head propped up in a dentist's chair—but it worked." The teeth were there. Estes pried one out and sent it on to Robinson, and rehung the Curtis head, now sporting a small jagged tear in the corner of the left upper lip that gave it a crooked smile.

Estes had more than enigmatic Zambian sables to worry about that fall. He was trying to keep track of the disparate international efforts to save the giant sable that had been revived with the recent lessening of hostilities in Angola's civil war. After the Lusaka accord was signed in 1994, the MPLA offered to create two vice president posts, one of which was offered to (and rejected by) Jonas Savimbi. But the peace process, overseen by 6,600 UN peacekeepers, continued to inch forward and by April 1997 a Government of National Unity and Reconciliation was inaugurated in Luanda at a ceremony attended by numerous African heads of state. Seventy UNITA deputies were sworn into the National Assembly and the movement was given four ministerial portfolios. Savimbi had even been given legal status as "leader of the largest opposition party," a salary, an official residence, and bodyguards, all at state expense, but, ominously, stayed in the UNITA stronghold of Bailundo during the events, citing fears for his safety. Things were not going in the guerrilla leader's direction. He had been steadily losing ground to government forces since 1994. He still had control of the country's richest diamond deposits, the vast resource he'd been tapping to fund UNITA after cold war aid had dried up. But his old Congo ally, Mobutu, was about to be toppled by Laurent Kabila, a move openly supported by the MPLA, and one which would cut off an estimated half-billion-dollar-a-year trade in illicit diamonds—and his pipeline for fuel and weapons.

Although Savimbi was balking at further demilitarization, an Italian firm started rebuilding the Benguela Railway anyway, shrugging off the fact that most of it ran through UNITA-held lands. There were still a few functioning engines and carriages plying the first twenty-two miles of intact track from Lobito to Catumbela to Benguela, including, amazingly enough, locomotive number one, a venerable antique that had pulled Frank Varian himself by steam into the interior. It would take an estimated fourteen years to completely restore the line. Bringing back the plush cars that once carried Europeans deep into the continent would be the least of it. The line would have to be de-mined to start, and eventually every mile of its torn-up tracks relaid. Some thirty bombed-out bridges, thousands of missing cross ties used for firewood, and the ghostly ruins of twenty-two passenger stations would have to be replaced, and the sabotaged communications systems would have to be reestablished. But everyone agreed that reopening the railway would reinvigorate the economy of central Africa, and Angolans wanted desperately to renew their hopes for the future of their country.

So did the conservation community, but some of the new efforts to preserve the *palanca negra* were not received with much enthusiasm. Victor Fasano, a popular Brazilian actor with a zoo for endangered species in Rio de Janeiro, traveled to Luanda and sparked angry reaction with his offer to bring giant sables to Brazil to start a captive-breeding program. "I have always said and am making it clear," declared João Serodio de Almeida, the deputy minister of the environment, "that the protection of the animal must be done on national territory, in its natural habitat." He had a low opinion of the various offers to breed the animals in other countries. "What is the point? For what? Only because human ego wants to have this animal to see? Ecologically there are no advantages. If the habitat is intact why take the animals out?"

In contrast, the Swedish government approached the IUCN and offered support for a giant sable survey of the reserves, provided local people could be involved. Jeremy Anderson, the Antelope Specialist Group's regional chairman, drew up yet another working plan for an aerial and ground survey—six weeks of fieldwork in all. Now an independent wildlife consultant, he was free to take on the project himself. "If there are enough animals," he argued, "the first option must be to conserve them in situ. If the Swedes will support this, the project could become the catalyst in getting the Wildlife Department on its feet." He now regarded the capture option as a strictly last-resort measure. "Only if we find that the sable occur in relict ones and twos should we consider capture and translocation to a breeding facility elsewhere." But the effort soon sputtered to a halt in the uneasy peace; Savimbi began dragging his feet on the extension of state administration to his long-held (and diamond-rich) territories, precipitating threatened UN sanctions against the movement that would restrict travel by UNITA officials, cut off their supply flights, and force the closure of its offices abroad. But there were others interested in doing something for the antelope who remained undeterred by events.

"Some of the rumors I'm hearing are pretty upsetting," Estes told me when I called him again a few weeks later. We talked about the behind-the-scenes maneuvering and the increasing number of "giant sable players." Each new cadre of self-appointed guardians had a stake in the antelope, but how much of a say they would have in shaping its future was unclear. Estes was all too familiar with the politics of conservation, and quick to recognize the implications of a piece of research, who was behind the winning of a grant, or the real motives of an interested party. Money, he told me, was always the key—no research can be done and no conservation steps can be taken without it. "The unsavory side of scientific research in biology," Estes once complained, "is the competition for funds. It's like hyenas at a kill." But things had become hard to read.

What worried him the most was the Kissama Foundation.

The year-old organization of South Africans and Angolans was under the patronage of President dos Santos and underwritten by Angolan and international oil company money. Its announced objective was nothing less than the rehabilitation of Angola's national parks, starting with coastal Quiçama Park south of the capital, Luanda. Given the devastation those parks and reserves suffered under years of warfare and the loss of perhaps 90 percent of the large mammals in Angola, "ambitious" hardly describes the scale of such a project. The brainchild of its president, Professor Wouter van Hoven of the Centre for Wildlife Management at the University of Pretoria, the Kissama Foundation could already point to wealthy Texans, Swiss bankers, and Prince Anton von und zu Liechtenstein as honorary trustees, and had produced a glossy brochure for fund-raising purposes and a five-year plan of development for Quiçama Park.

Estes had first met van Hoven after an ASG meeting in Pretoria two years before, and heard of his plans for Angola. Estes had been suitably impressed. But privately he was already having qualms about some of the people involved in the organization. He and Anderson were disturbed that half the foundation's executive board were Angolan army generals, and alarmed that the board also included Johannes Nicolas van den Burgh, the managing director of Executive Outcomes (Pty) Ltd. in Pretoria. The press invariably referred to this firm of "security consultants" as a mercenary organization, providing training, equipment, and yes, troops for governments with urgent problems requiring "private peace-keeping," including Sierra Leone, and reportedly Burundi, Kenya, and several other African countries. Its founder and chairman, Eben Barlow, had served with 32 Battalion in Angola, and started the company in 1989 after leaving the South African military. It was widely credited with having given critical aid to the underequipped Luanda government against UNITA in 1994. When their two-year-plus contract with the Angolan military ended in early 1996, departing members of the firm were thanked in a farewell speech by Gen. João Baptiste de Matos, chief of the Defense Force, before flying out of Cabo Ledo, the military base on the coast in Quiçama Park.

Estes and Anderson were not the only ones who found the Executive Outcomes connection questionable. Roger Ballard-Tremeer, then South Africa's ambassador to Angola, originally named as an honorary trustee, promptly dropped his affiliation; subsequently, his and van den Burgh's names were taken off the reprinted brochure. But the whiff of suspicion that the Kissama Foundation had dubious connections would continue to linger.

The ASG biologists' primary cause for concern, however, was the Kissama Foundation's sweeping plans. Virtually overnight, Wouter van Hoven had become the biggest player of all in Angolan conservation. The role he had carved out for himself was summed up in the name he gave to the restocking effort at Quiçama: Operation Noah's Ark. Wildlife, from elephants on down, would be brought by ship from South Africa to Angola and off-loaded into the park at the mouth of the Cuanza. That was just for openers; the foundation's plan was to "reintroduce wildlife species that have disappeared, to nurture back those that are on the brink of extinction such as the Giant Sable (our national symbol)." Both Estes's and Anderson's antennae shot up at that: reintroducing wildlife from, say, overpopulated reserves in southern Africa to the denuded parks of Angola was laudable on the face of it, but what exactly did van Hoven have in mind for the giant sable?

Anderson made some inquiries. What he heard from Brian Huntley was unsettling. Huntley, head of the National Botanical Institute of South Africa and an internationally respected biologist, had been a research ecologist for the Portuguese government in Angola for several years before independence and stayed in close touch with developments there. He had strong opinions on conservation in Angola and was not hesitant about sharing them.

Huntley told Anderson that van Hoven intended to bring giant sable to Quiçama, where they had never been found. Such a move would fly in the face of the IUCN's position that the goal of any country's national parks is to protect ecosystems and the animals that are naturally found there. The dangers of introducing species into alien habitats are well known: the translocation of nonnative species can cause ecological imbalance and high rates of mortality, and risks hybridization of subspecies, blurring their distinctions and muddling their gene pools. Years before, the Esteses had warned that "until the vegetation of the region is known in greater detail, it is difficult to know whether the habitats where the giant sable is found differ in some essential way from habitat where it does not occur." In their view, none of the existing parks in Angola had appropriate environments, although there might be areas reasonably near the reserve that could provide suitable habitat.

If there were only a few giant sables left Estes was willing to concede that a captive-breeding program might be necessary. But only a survey of the reserves would yield that vital information, and van Hoven was poised to take the lead on that front too, leaving the IUCN and ASG biologists behind. When Anderson contacted van Hoven, the Kissama president told him that he intended to fly over some of the giant sable areas in October in a large helicopter, taking along some members of the *Conseil International de la Chasse et de la Conservation du Gibier* (CIC)—the Paris-based hunting and conservation organization. Its president, Dr. Nicolas Franco of Spain, was one of Kissama's honorary trustees. Anderson asked if he could accompany them. Van Hoven told him if the Swedes paid for the entire flight, he could go along. Anderson was flabbergasted. He wrote to his ASG colleagues that if they were paying for a survey, they should be in charge of it. "The

Kissama Foundation seems to be a bit of an enigma. I hope I am wrong, but my gut feeling is that the CIC are after some sable."

When Estes returned in early September after ten weeks in Tanzania monitoring Ngorongoro Crater and Serengeti ungulates, he found another fax from Anderson expressing reservations about Kissama: "I don't know much about it yet, but it seems to be more of a business venture than a conservation effort. This is not for us!!" Anderson also wondered if van Hoven's flight into the reserves would take place, given the level of tension in Angola. The UN Security Council had threatened to impose additional sanctions on UNITA at the end of the month for failing to live up to its obligations under the Lusaka Protocol. Apart from the risk, however, the flight would probably be pointless. Estes wryly noted that van Hoven may not have realized that with the coming rains, the trees in the reserves would be in leaf and the giant sable would have withdrawn into the woodland, making them difficult if not impossible to spot from the air.

The upcoming ASG meeting scheduled for mid-December at the University of Pretoria might have been an opportunity for some fence-mending between these biologists, but van Hoven couldn't be there. Anderson had an E-mail from him explaining that he'd be on holiday then, adding cryptically that the Kissama Foundation—and the giant sable—were doing just fine. Van Hoven had taken charge of the animal's fate, but Anderson still hoped to get the Swedish-sponsored survey off the ground. He'd been offered a two-year contract in Mozambique to start development of the new national park on the border with South Africa's Kruger. He saw it as an opportunity to pick up some basic Portuguese language skills for the survey planned for next July—if UNITA cooperated. But he knew the Swedes would not support such a project without the involvement of an appropriate Angolan nongovernmental organization (NGO). Unfortunately, there weren't any, except for the Kissama Foundation. Matters seemed at a standstill, at least until the ASG meeting.

Then Estes received a startling E-mail from van Hoven:

> We had a team out into Luando recently to make a ground survey of the Giant Sable. The team covered a small area—about 10% of the surface—and found 253 specimens in good shape. All indications are that there are substantially more. We will make a complete air census

using two Allouette helicopters from June 20 to July 10 1998. The Songo tribe actively protected these animals. On the whole the war actually saved them but the peace is threatening them. We do not wish to go public until such time that proper protection measures for these animals are in place. Therefore the confidentiality.

But the story's cover was blown by the December 1997 *Safari Times*, the newsletter of Safari Club International, the prominent and powerful prohunting group, which ran a front-page story under the headline "Herds of Giant Sable Sighted in Angola." Van Hoven had previously given Anne and Bill Dodgson, keen trophy hunters and members of SCI's Utah chapter, a helicopter tour of denuded Quiçama Park and sold them on his vision of rehabilitating Angola's wildlife areas, and darting and relocating Angola's great antelope from its war-threatened habitat. When the Dodgsons were tipped off by van Hoven that this majestic animal survived, they were thrilled. They went into high gear raising funds for giant sable conservation and spread the news—prematurely, from van Hoven's point of view.

Estes was now free to break the story to ASG members, which he did in the next *Gnusletter*. "Talk about welcome news!" he wrote. "Surveying the Luando Reserve of the giant sable and Cangandala National Park has been one of the highest priorities of the ASG for a decade." He swallowed his misgivings about the Kissama Foundation and made an effort to establish a united conservation front. "Clearly the Kissama Foundation is playing a leading role in reviving wildlife conservation and tourism in Angola. The IUCN and the Antelope Specialists Group have finally found an influential ally and a qualified Angolan NGO with which to cooperate in the giant sable and other conservation objectives." He told the membership he looked forward to collaborating; van Hoven had extended an invitation and he hoped to join the upcoming survey. He added wistfully that it "would be a sort of homecoming."

THERE WAS YET another surprise in store for Estes in late 1997. Nearly a dozen ASG members from several countries and guests—wildlife professionals of one sort or another, from microbiologists to safari operators—met on December 15 in the National Parks Board boardroom in Pretoria. Organized and chaired by Jeremy Anderson, the group was anticipating regional and species reports on bontebok monitoring, bovine tuberculosis, and the like. Then Terry Robinson spoke. He began by deferring the report on the recent results of his DNA analysis of sable subspecies to his research associate, Conrad Matthee, and added some prefatory remarks reminding the ASG that conservation of biodiversity is of the highest importance. Then he dropped a biological bombshell, wrapped in a recommendation. Given what had just been learned about sable genetics in his laboratory, conservation efforts for the species, he argued, should be focused on the East African subspecies *Hippotragus niger roosevelti*, the only population with significantly different DNA, rather than on the giant sable, which genetically did not differ appreciably from the typical races.

Estes was floored. He knew Robinson's presentation would have something to do with the differences between sable subspecies, but he didn't realize that he would claim there were no significant differences between *variani* and common sables.

He had reason to be rattled. Although Estes considered himself as dispassionate as the next scientist, the giant sable had been a substantial part of his life's work, and he could hardly react with indifference to these claims. Robinson was a laboratory-based theorist who'd do his research and let the species fall where they may. If unchallenged, his views could be the opening shot in a campaign that could lead to a taxonomic delisting, much the way zoologists decided that the "king" cheetah (classified as *Acinonyx rex* in 1927) was just a differently spotted version of the typical cheetah (*Acinonyx jubatus*) and should never have been given separate status in the first place.

Matthee's overview of the results of his and Robinson's research had everyone's attention. Yes, he explained, comparison of mitochondrial DNA control region sequence data showed there were differences between the accepted sable subspecies, but, as Robinson had pointed out, apart from *roosevelti*, the differences were too slight—roughly 2 to 4 percent—to justify distinguishing the other populations as subspecies (unlike the roan populations, where the DNA differences were much more pronounced, justifying the accepted taxonomic subgroupings). Only the Roosevelt sable of northeastern Tanzania and southeastern Kenya was an undoubted sable subspecies. Although *Hippotragus niger variani* (Angola), *H. n. kirkii* (Zambia, Malawi), and *H. n. niger* (South Africa, Zimbabwe) were geographically diverse, genetically speaking, they were all minor variants and could be lumped together.

Consternation broke out in the room. Estes, joined by Chris Thouless of Botswana's wildlife department, objected to this "radical taxonomic revision." Mitochondrial DNA tests only applied to the maternal genes, they argued. The results may have established that *roosevelti* has long been isolated, but phenotypic (visibly characteristic) differences between other sable populations surely indicated genetic selection for thousands of years during the Pleistocene. In fact, Estes maintained, a whole array of genes, perhaps located in the male chromosomes or in yet to be sequenced female genes, might be responsible for these differences. Robinson responded that mitochondrial DNA is an extremely sensitive marker; the results could not be dismissed. He reminded them that conservation authorities have to decide where to draw the line in regard to preserving species variation — which is more important: phenotypic or genotypic differences? From a genotypic point of view, the highest priority in sable preservation was unquestionably the Roosevelt sable.

Estes underscored his view that the subspecific status of the giant sable was justified by its distinctive morphological features, notably the longer horns of males. Besides, he declared, "it was an important conservation icon inside, as the national animal, and outside Angola." He capped his remarks by pointing out that the giant sable happened to be the ASG's logo. Robinson was unmoved.

What all this had to do with the status of the animals at Sable Ranch was driven home by Anderson's comments. He'd spoken with the man who had done the helicopter capture operation for the breeding ranch. The animals had been taken in Barotseland near Kafue National Park in Zambia. Once you added in the fact that their DNA clustered with typical sables, it was clear that they weren't the giant variety. Estes agreed to inform the San Diego Zoo.

Estes was still brooding on Robinson's results on his return to New Hampshire. Conservation of the endangered giant sable had been one of the ASG's highest priorities for over a decade. Now the latest genetic research threatened to undermine this long-held goal. If it wasn't a subspecies, why bother? There were plenty of ordinary sables. But something about the results just didn't seem convincing to the veteran biologist. In a subsequent *Gnusletter*, he put his finger on a weak point of Robinson's and Matthee's research. Their conclusions about the giant sable rested on a single tooth: "DNA from more specimens need to be compared to substantiate or refute the seemingly minimal divergence of this population," Estes declared. "A sample size of one doesn't hold much water!" But he knew nothing further could be done for the time being. Further research might have to wait until tissue samples could be obtained from Angola. "So, in trying to get at the truth about the giant sable," he fumed, "we have only succeeded in opening Pandora's box!"

High up in the dim stairwell of Estes's house in New Hampshire the Curtis head wore its new, wry grin. Or was it really a half-smirk?

IN MAY 1998 I boarded a flight to South Africa. I hoped finding out more about these new approaches to the giant sable—the study of its genetics and the plans to rehabilitate Angola's parks and reserves—would bring me closer to the creature.

My first stop was Terry Robinson's office in the stone and stucco zoology building on the University of Pretoria's campus, tucked in the corner of a laboratory suite cluttered with microscopes, centrifuges, refrigerators, sinks, racks of test tubes and trays, computers, and coffee mugs. A trim, sandy-haired man, Robinson had a sharp-featured, youthful face, and wore a cardigan sweater over an open-necked shirt. He smiled and said, up front, that he was a little surprised by the stir created by his yet to be published research. He cleared some papers off the sagging couch so I could sit and opened the door to call out into the lab. He had invited Conrad Matthee and Kobus du Toit, a wildlife veterinarian and game catcher, to sit in. Matthee perched quietly on a stool, observing, while du

Toit joined me on the couch. Du Toit was stocky and tanned, and pushed his black hair off his round face with a thick-fingered hand. Robinson came right to the point when I raised the DNA issue, as if he'd been thinking about his answer.

"We had no idea what to expect. We got contrasting evidence. The genetic study on the roan showed that each of the recognized subspecies based on morphology is supported by the genetic evidence." But the sable data—checked and rechecked, he assured me—showed "that there's not much genetic variation to support the claim that the giant sable is a valid subspecies."

Was one tooth enough of a sample to support this conclusion?

Robinson smiled. "There can be no doubt about the science. And it *was* a giant sable tooth."

"Are you sure, Terry?" du Toit interjected.

Robinson looked surprised. "Dick Estes sent it to me."

Du Toit launched into an involved explanation of how lower jaws of antelope trophies are often lost in the field and why taxidermists commonly substituted the jawbone of similar antelopes when doing head mounts. The Curtis head might have the jaw of a common sable and thus everything depended on whether the tooth came from the upper or lower jaw.

Robinson looked dismayed at the thought that detective work was needed to validate pure science.

"I am telling you, Terry, protect yourself. Get another sample."

I commented that some people would be very unhappy if the giant sable were a taxonomic fiction.

Du Toit slapped his knee. "If the giant sable isn't a valid subspecies, Angola hasn't got a national animal!"

At this intrusion of politics into biology, Robinson and Matthee threw up their hands in horror.

I returned to the question of sample size and asked Robinson why he couldn't get additional giant sable teeth from the Natural History Museum in London. He explained that museums have strict destructive sampling policies; they don't let researchers nibble away at their holdings willy-nilly. When the skin sample didn't work out, Robinson asked Paula Jenkins of the mammal section for a tooth. He'd only drill a tiny hole in the root and remove a trace of powdery residue for analysis before send-ing it back, but she turned him down. He shrugged. "Besides," he says, "she may have got wind of where the research was heading." I thought of the portrait of Oldfield Thomas I had seen in Jenkins's office, and what she said about the work of "splitters" like Thomas being dismantled by taxonomic "lumpers" eager to discard many of their distinctions.

Like a magician threatening to make his stage assistant vanish with a snap of his fingers, Robinson was on the verge of making the giant sable disappear. Not the actual snorting, smelly, tick-picked, strutting and rut-ting beast, but the very idea of the animal. Scientists are supposed to shake the taxonomic tree every so often, eliminating unsupported findings and pruning back the multiplicity of unnecessary entities. But already his re-sults seemed to have sucked the reality out of the animal, turning the most magisterial antelope of all into a shadowy, incorporeal being. . . .

Du Toit had another angle he wanted to discuss. He pulled out a map—the same Michelin map of central and southern Africa I'd brought— and unfolded it to expose Angola and Zambia. He'd highlighted Cangandala National Park and the Luando Reserve in yellow. Stubbing a finger into the map, he argued that, given enough time, giant sables could have migrated farther south and east, following the flow of rivers through the watershed into northern Zambia, a distance of several hundred miles. He suspected interbreeding. He'd been doing independent research on sables—he was vague about why—and had been to Zambia, seen sable there, and was familiar with the Sable Ranch animals. Many Zam-bian sables have *variani*-like facial markings, he said, and are far more ag-gressive than ordinary sables, charging right into fences to try to get at people.

"Maybe they're touchy about their subspecies status," I joked. Du Toit smiled and pulled out some slides of Zambian sables. "Look at these," he said with a note of triumph.

Robinson and I squinted at them; the presence or absence of cheek stripes wasn't always obvious. But some looked like *variani*. Du Toit told me I should examine the photographs of the top common sable antelope trophies in the Safari Club International record book; most of them are from Zambia, he said, "and have *variani* face markings." Later, I did and found that he was right: the number one animal laid out next to the kneeling, smiling hunter is a dead ringer for a giant sable—big hoops of horn, black face, no cheek stripe.

"You can't have a subspecies that isn't a geographic and physically distinguishable entity," Robinson pointed out. "If you have within one herd animals which look like giant sable, and animals which don't look like giant sable, that means that the criteria used in defining giant sable are fallacious." I suddenly remembered a disturbing detail: the Curtis head had a faint suggestion of a cheek stripe.

Du Toit left, Matthee went back to work, and Robinson walked me out of the building. He conceded it was unfortunate he had only a single *variani* specimen to study. If he had more individual giant sable specimens, say five more, and they showed greater sequence divergence from the typical subspecies than the Curtis tooth did, and if they formed a separate cluster the way *roosevelti* had, then "there would be some support for the recognition that *variani* has been genetically unique, which would be hellishly important for its conservation—if it were valid." There seemed to be a lot of "ifs," and they all depended on more teeth.

"Look, it would help to have another source of giant sable material," he said. "Do you have any museum contacts?"

I told him I'd see what I could do. I wanted a definitive answer myself.

I REACHED WOUTER VAN HOVEN on his cell phone on a Saturday morning at his home in Pretoria. He'd been busy, as you'd imagine a man who oversees some thirty wildlife projects worldwide would be. A few days before, he'd returned to South Africa from a wildlife conference in Prague to testify as an expert witness in the damage phase of a trial of someone who'd had his wildlife management contract canceled by a tribal council in the eastern Cape. And he had to leave shortly to go to the Kalahari Desert to meet with his graduate students from the Centre for Wildlife Management at the University of Pretoria. He suggested I come over for a chat.

Van Hoven met me in the driveway of a large, multilevel ranch house built into a hillside on a winding street in the upscale suburb of Waterkloof Ridge. A tall, heavy-browed, strong-featured man in his early fifties, he had an incipient paunch and dark gray, just-thinning hair. He was dressed in a track suit and running shoes, and extended a large fleshy hand while simultaneously directing the excited family dog. His blond, two-year-old son scooted out on a plastic tricycle, followed by his wife, Suzanne, who was slim, pretty, blonde, and as tall as he was. He spoke to his boy in Afrikaans, of which I understood nothing but the phrase "high five." Right on cue, the smiling toddler raised his hand and slapped mine gleefully, and then looked up at his father with an ear-to-ear grin.

Van Hoven seemed rather genial for someone who was thought to be up to no good. He took me to the kitchen and made us instant coffee in the microwave. He was intrigued that I would be so interested in the giant sable. "There's something about an animal that no one can get to," he mused, "and that no one can have, isn't there?" I followed him into the second-floor living room, where several mounted heads of various antelope and an enormous white rhino hung on the back wall. "I'm not a trophy hunter," he said. "That rhino was part of my nutrition research for years and finally died of natural causes." He got his Ph.D. in wildlife studies from the University of Potchefstroom and taught big-game management in Colorado for a year in the 1980s. His specialty is analyzing the turnover of food sources into animal energy, and hence the carrying capacity of various environments—"nutrition on a broad scale," as he put it.

I asked how the Kissama Foundation came about. In 1995, van Hoven explained, he was invited to come to Luanda to discuss what could be done with Angola's national parks. Years of war had wiped out almost all the wildlife, which meant that any restocking effort would be enormously expensive. And, with the Angolan countryside riddled with land mines, and so many roads, schools, and hospitals in need of rebuilding, there was no way, politically, to justify putting any of the country's substantial revenues from oil and diamonds toward conservation. "I was asked to advise, but I thought maybe I should do more." He shrugged. "You could say Angola grabbed me.

"I think one of the reasons I got more involved with this thing is that Angola is like Vietnam. With the cold war going on, well, as you know, the United States supplied South Africa, and helped South Africa to move in. The Soviet Union put in Cuba. There were South African families I know that lost their sons fighting Cubans in Angola. Not only did South

Africa participate in that war, but it participated in the destruction of the wildlife in that country. The killing of elephants and rhinos . . ." He shook his head. "It was almost like policy at that time, because the revenue of those sales was to support UNITA. I know of troops that were there who told me they saw containers full of ivory crossing the border. Okay, well, with that background—I just wanted to make a contribution."

He leaned forward in his chair. "I saw that the way to move ahead with this thing would be to create a foundation, and get some government support in terms of logistics. I selected a group of South Africans, and on their side the Angolans selected others, to be founder members. I was asked to be president." He handed me the glossy information kit I'd heard about. It had a photo of a giant sable on the cover; even the foundation's logo was a propellerlike whorl of four giant sable heads. Inside were maps, an overview of the Angolan economy, analyses of the country's parks and wildlife, and an ambitious five-year plan.

"It's working. Quiçama itself is such a huge undertaking—it's over a million hectares—and it had something like three thousand elephants and six thousand red buffalo. Now you don't see a thing. But we've had teams up there, doing research on the ecosystem. We've already produced two thick documents on the management planning for the park and its eco-tourism potential. We've invited the private sector to invest in that side. Sonangol, the Angolan oil company, has pledged a million dollars. Chevron should do the same."

He was now into what sounded like a fund-raising speech, but it was impressive all the same. "Our next big step is what we call our Operation Noah's Ark. And that is to relocate wildlife back to that park. South Africa has surpluses. In Kruger National Park we don't know what to do with the elephants and in Angola we need them. So the obvious answer is, move them there by ship."

Why ship? I asked.

"It's a practical way of doing it. By road is too far and the roads are in poor shape. There would be lots of mortalities. Kruger is close to the ocean, and Quiçama is on the ocean. So it's an option we're looking at." He was thinking big—aircraft carriers. I soon found myself caught up in his vi-sion of a ship's deck full of animals: elephants, giraffes, rhinos, two by two . . . Van Hoven grew more animated. "Can you imagine a television ad

217

showing an oil tanker going one way, passed by a ship carrying animals going the other?" In addition to selling this seductive sponsorship idea to an oil company, he planned documentary coverage, and was already in talks about a possible television series.

But there were some dubious associations I wanted clarified. What about the Executive Outcomes connection? He waved it away, explaining that at first it was "useful for logistics"—they had a plane available—but the connection was now severed. What about Angolan military involvement? Several generals sat on the executive board, including Gen. Luis Faceira, the deputy chief of the army, and his brother, Gen. Antonio Faceira, head of the Special Forces—the commandos. Van Hoven said he found these military men not just helpful, but essential to get anything done in war-ravaged Angola; they provided vehicles, helicopters, and where necessary, protection. And they were conservation-minded, van Hoven assured me, pointing out that Antonio Faceira grew up in the Quiçama region and had fond memories of what it used to be like before the war. What he sees there now upsets him, and he would like to contribute to the park's rehabilitation. The professor and the generals remained on excellent terms; when he went to Luanda, an army major picked him up at the airport, and he often stayed at Gen. Luis Faceira's seaside villa in the capital.

Finally, I asked what his plans were for the giant sable. They were grand plans, it turned out. Safeguarding Angola's national animal was part of Kissama's "primary mandate," as van Hoven put it. "From the start I knew we must take a proper survey of the Cangandala and Luando Reserves. Even prior to the civil war, the numbers were only estimates. Even Estes only had estimates," he reminded me. "He was never able to conduct a proper aerial census, but he had a fairly accurate estimate—about two thousand. Unofficially, I would say that today, close to that number may—I say 'may'—exist. But I don't want to publish that yet." And the brief survey that took place late last year? He was coy about the details. It consisted of "just two or three people and one vehicle," he said. He wasn't on the survey, but assured me that giant sable were sighted. I decided not to press him further. Instead I asked about the upcoming helicopter search scheduled for July.

Van Hoven sighed. "During the twenty-two-year civil war those reserves were left alone. Nobody looked at them, nobody tried to monitor them. UNITA came into control there, and that is still the case today. So we still can't make an aerial census the way we'd like to because they are going to shoot us down. Simple as that. You might go to Jonas Savimbi, and he'd say 'Okay, it's no problem—go.' But their communications, the chain of command down to those guys on the ground that sit there with bazookas is not reliable." He shook a finger for emphasis. "And they see this aircraft and they don't know what the hell it is, and boom!"

He had another appointment. I followed him to his home office. In the hallway, there was a charming child's drawing of a crowded Noah's Ark, heads of happy animals poking out of the hull, floating on a gentle blue sea scalloped with little smiley waves. In his paper-choked office an impressive baboon skull (they have longer canine teeth than lions) sat on a bookshelf next to a novelty spray can labeled "Bullshit Repellent." He shoved some reports into his briefcase and offered to drop me off at my guest house on his way to the university. On the way there, while we waited at a traffic light, I took the plunge and asked if I could go along on any upcoming survey expedition he might be planning. Sure, he said. I was thrilled, and told him so. "You know, I've never seen a giant sable either," he said. "So I have to go, of course, and soon."

Van Hoven pulled in the driveway of my guest house. I had one last question: did he have any qualms about relocating giant sables to Quiçama? He fiddled with the gearshift before speaking. "No. The northern end of the park is the same latitude as the reserves. Why shouldn't they adapt to the environment? But we're still studying it. Well, more than studying it. It's central to our plan."

We promised to stay in touch, and I returned to the United States a few days later.

I HAD BEEN thinking there might be two separate surveys—the IUCN's, led by Anderson, and Kissama's, led by van Hoven—racing to be the first into the reserves. But I could see the field had been left to van Hoven. Anderson agreed with my assessment. "Van Hoven's in the driver's seat now," he said with resignation when I reached him by phone. With the backing of the Angolan military and the funds he'd raised, Wouter van Hoven had not just taken charge of Angola's wildlife, he had become the giant sable's keeper, able to control access, study, even the possible relocation of a breeding herd. If, at long last, an expedition into reserves was going to take place, van Hoven was going to be the one to make it happen. If I wanted to find out what happened to the giant sable, I had to stay on friendly terms with the ambitious professor of wildlife management.

I thought that might not be too difficult; van Hoven had a raffish charm and was very persuasive. I was impressed with him and yet remained skeptical. He was complex, not easy to read. He had strong feelings about the natural world, but I wasn't sure what they were. I later learned that he had kept rabbits and doves as a boy, and once bitterly criticized his father for cutting down a diseased weeping willow in the family garden. But he was far from a tree-hugging purist, even if the audacity of his plans made him look like a dreamer. Van Hoven was a realist, willing to work with the world the way it was, and a self-promoter to boot. The combination clearly got on some people's nerves. Thinking on a grand scale looked more like grandstanding to those used to taking small steps and making incremental progress. And to scientists living from small grant to small grant, his charisma, salesmanship, and ability to raise substantial funds—not to mention the kudos he'd get if he pulled off Operation Noah's Ark—could only rankle. But the snubs were surely the hardest to take. When he planned a survey of the giant sable reserves without consulting Estes, Anderson, or anyone else, van Hoven put the IUCN on notice that he could ignore it. In the closely knit world of conservation, such unilateral moves looked like end runs, if not outright affronts.

But van Hoven had come to realize that it was pointless to alienate the IUCN. Its involvement with his Angolan project would bring international credibility to the endeavor. Needing some giant sable expertise, he found it politic to invite Estes to join the planned expedition. Estes would go, I knew that, if for no other reason than to bring his influence to bear on what van Hoven and the Kissama Foundation might have in store for the giant sable. It would be the least he could do for the animal he had studied in more detail than anyone else.

Van Hoven seemed unfazed by the challenge of juggling the interests of Angolan generals with the interests of those in the conservation community, just as he hadn't hesitated to hit up organizations who would normally be at each other's throats, like the antihunting Fund for Animals and the prohunting Safari Club International, both of which he thought could kick some cash into Kissama's coffers. But it was his political high-wire act that had been the toughest trick of all. Surely he must have known that his grandiose ecotourism plans would inflate the expectations of some highly placed Angolan officials. Why would they be content to build a modest tourist industry around the biological requirements of parks and reserves devastated by decades of war, when his far-reaching plans to move animals around the African map had probably already given them the idea they could manipulate wildlife to suit the demands of tourism and generate some much-needed revenue?

The man who ran Angola, José Eduardo dos Santos, would surely have the final say. The graying, sober statesman in a tailored suit and silk tie who looks out from the picture on the Kissama Foundation's brochure had offered his patronage to van Hoven's dream, announcing his "full support" for the "laudable initiative" of van Hoven's Operation Noah's Ark. But behind that visage is a hardened leader who fought the Portuguese and then UNITA for decades, and has only recently softened his doctrinaire stance since the worldwide collapse of communism. His hated enemy, Jonas Savimbi, had for years occupied the giant sable reserves, making him their de facto guardian. But with van Hoven as his instrument, dos Santos could soon be in a position to take charge of the animal that meant so much to the Angolans. He could give his blessing to an effort to relocate the *palanca preta gigante* to a government-controlled haven south of the capital. This might seem a modest—and to some, dubious—environmental achievement, but as the protector, master, and savior of the species, he would assume a mantle more symbolically important than any non-Angolan could easily imagine.

THE CONTROVERSY THAT surrounded the Kissama Foundation continued to deepen. Back in January 1998, at the annual meeting of Safari Club International in Reno, Nevada, van Hoven had given a presentation on

Operation Noah's Ark and the giant sable to a rapt audience, most of whom had supposed this sovereign of sables had become a casualty of war. Interest in the conservation of the plucky surviving specimens ran high, and many attendees reached for their wallets. The Dodgsons sent $5,000 to van Hoven and planned a raffle to raise more funds. The Safari Club International Africa chapter was also highly interested in contributing to the restoration of elephants to Quiçama, and wrote van Hoven about it. But they wanted to see a detailed technical and financial proposal, covering the capture, translocation, and safeguarding of the animals. Van Hoven's reply was couched in generalities and curt on the issue of feasibility studies — if it hadn't been feasible, he asserted, they wouldn't have undertaken it. His response to their request for audited financial statements and budgets was rejected by the chapter as too vague — it was unclear how much had actually been spent on conservation. Nor could van Hoven provide any recent photographs to support the claim of several hundred surviving sables, much less point to a report on the sightings in a reputable scientific journal. By mid-May the Safari Club International Africa Office in Pretoria was waving a warning flag. Andre de Georges, the manager of SCI's Africa Office, faxed the Dodgsons to tell them not to send any more money to the Kissama Foundation. Keep raising the funds, he advised, and his office would help them find a viable alternative to which they could contribute the money they'd worked so hard to raise.

The Dodgsons wrote to van Hoven. He sent an upbeat reply at the end of May, telling them that the revival of Quiçama Park was progressing (he hoped to release the first batch of new animals in October) and that the giant sable survey was still scheduled for late July/early August (although the only way to do it safely would be with an unmanned spy plane) and expressing his gratitude for their contributions, reminding them that the money they had raised would be a great help. But they had sent him their last check.

But the biggest blow of all to Kissama's and van Hoven's credibility came in the form of an E-mail from Brian Huntley to Richard Estes at the beginning of June. Huntley told Estes he was "fully aware of the very strange relationships being developed between certain military generals and South African 'conservationists.'" He'd been invited to serve on Kissama's board some years back, he said, but had not responded. "Its real versus published aims are, I would say, not very related. The South African mentioned is an opportunist and I would leave my description at that. Of course, there are no records of giant sable, wildebeest, kudu, giraffe, zebra (nor polar bears or reindeer) ever occurring in Quiçama. Golf courses have been attempted along the road from Luana to Barra do Cuanza, using oil and bitumen for the greens—strange sights among the baobabs and dry grassveld of this arid savanna, where water is nowhere to be found. " He drove the nail home. "I would suggest that you alert the ASG to the plans of van Hoven and his cronies. They offer nothing to real conservation in Angola—I see it only as a platform for financial gain."

Estes's early misgivings about the Kissama Foundation had returned in spades, and now matched Anderson's growing doubts. Huntley's objections were fatally clear, and by mid-month he would come out into the open with them. Huntley wrote a letter to his old friend, Dr. João Serodio de Almeida, the deputy minister of the environment, who had worked with him during the years he'd been in Angola. Huntley carbon-copied Estes, the World Wildlife Fund, the chair of the IUCN's Species Survival Commission, and van Hoven himself. He was blunt:

> I write this letter to express my concern that the Kissama Foundation is planning to create a zoo and golf course in Quiçama under the banner of rehabilitating Angola's national park system. The document that they use for fundraising has the Giant Sable on its cover (you know as well as I that this species never occurred in Quiçama) and they have plans for an 'Operation Noah' to take kudu, wildebeest, giraffe, zebra, waterbuck, etc. to Quiçama. It is not clear to me what the real objectives of this group are—a lot of money seems to be involved, with very little genuine conservation knowledge or commitment. I hope that you are able to clarify the situation . . .

If van Hoven hadn't recognized Huntley as his nemesis before, he couldn't mistake it now. His response came in short order, in the form of a letter to Serodio de Almeida (and Estes et al.) signed by Dr. José L. Guerra Marques, the Angolan copresident of the Kissama Foundation. Marques was appalled by Prof. Huntley's accusations and assured the minister that golf courses and zoos were not the foundation's goals. It was a nonprofit organization dedicated to wildlife conservation. Further, Professor van Hoven contributed his time gratis and his scientific reputation could hardly be questioned. The letter closed with a flourish, requesting de Almeida to reply to Prof. Huntley and defend the foundation's honor. The repercussions from this heated exchange would be dramatic, but not immediate; nothing more was heard on the matter for several months.

Estes received these dueling diatribes as he was getting ready to leave New Hampshire for Tanzania. I was traveling to Kenya myself to do a travel article on a tented safari in the Masai Mara, and called him to find out if we could meet there. He suggested Nairobi, where he planned to get together with his son before heading to the Serengeti to spend two months studying wildebeest. The wildebeest, or gnu, is one of those animals that looks as though it was put together by a committee, and its goofy behavior, breaking out into a frenzied, kicking dance on the grassy plains when it gets sufficiently wound up, matches its ungainly appearance. I joked that it was a long way from the giant sable to the gnu—like going from the sublime to the ridiculous. There was a pause; I could sense Estes's disapproval over the phone. He finally selected an epithet and said he found that view "quite trite." He regarded the gnu as a beautiful animal, "marvelously adapted to its surroundings." I told him I wasn't on his level of biological connoisseurship.

A few weeks later we met for dinner one evening at the Horseman in Nairobi. He was accompanied by his twenty-six-year-old son Lyndon, who worked at the Mpumalanga Parks Board in South Africa as a reserve manager. With his blond crewcut, rugby player's build, and khaki shirt and shorts, Lyndon certainly looked the part of a game warden, and clearly shared his father's passion for the natural world. I had been trying the local game dishes on safari, and noticed eland was on the menu. It's often described as the tastiest antelope, so I ordered it. Estes selected the zebra, which sounded about as appetizing as donkey meat. But my entrée turned out as tough as a leather wallet, while his—he shared a morsel to prove the point—was as tender as aged porterhouse.

Estes told me he had become increasingly suspicious of what the Kissama Foundation might be up to. "I've come to the conclusion that the IUCN cannot afford to get into bed with van Hoven," he said bluntly. He knew that if he didn't get something else going, Wouter van Hoven and the Kissama Foundation would end up in charge of any giant sable conservation efforts—and he was afraid of what that might mean for the animal. "I'll work with van Hoven to the extent I can. I don't particularly want to be his adversary," he said. He set down his beer mug and looked at me. "But if I have to be, I will."

THREE DAYS AFTER I met with Estes in Nairobi, a plane carrying Alioune Blondin Beye, the United Nations special envoy to Angola, crashed in a mangrove swamp on its approach to Abidjan airport in Côte d'Ivoire. The day before, Beye had met with Jonas Savimbi, who told the diplomat that despite the threat of wider UN sanctions, UNITA would not meet the deadline to hand over control of the central highlands to the government in Luanda. Hoping to hold on to the lion's share of the country's diamond wealth, Savimbi had been making strategically insignificant concessions during the peace process in an attempt to deny the increasingly frustrated government an excuse for launching a full-scale military assault. At the same time, UNITA had been trying to convince the international community of serious flaws in the implementation of the peace accords, including atrocities committed against its supporters. Savimbi's discussions with Beye did not go well. The special envoy had been running out of patience with the rebel leader for some time, and had recently pushed for punitive UN sanctions in the hopes of forcing compliance. Some believe that Beye may have signed his own order of execution with that action. Discounting the death threat he received before his departure from Luanda, he first flew to Togo to urge pro-UNITA government officials there to plead his case with Savimbi. Beye then flew to the Ivory Coast, whose government was also sympathetic to Savimbi, but his small jet never made it. Local witnesses reported seeing it explode into a fireball and crashing six minutes before its expected arrival at the airport, leading to suspicions that a bomb had been planted aboard.

Meanwhile, General de Matos had been touring his frontline units, a clear signal to many observers that the government was preparing for war. But the chief of the Defense Forces also took the time to attend a celebratory dinner in Luanda in July, and, on behalf of the Kissama Foundation, accept a check for $400,000 from Shell Oil toward the rehabilitation of Quiçama Park. Oil company contributions had put the foundation "firmly on track," as its newsletter put it. The latest plans now called for erecting a thirteen-mile-long fence to create a secure area some twenty-three square miles in size in the north of the park to accept the first shipment of animals in March 1999. A separate forty-three-mile-long fence dividing off the northeastern region of the park would be erected by the end of the year.

Van Hoven E-mailed Estes on his return to New Hampshire in September and told him what Estes had already guessed: that the survey had been postponed to next year due to armed clashes in the region (the plan to use a drone never got off the ground either). He also wrote that the fencing in Quiçama was going forward. Estes was resigned. There didn't seem to be much the IUCN could do in response to the Kissama Foundation's moves. At this point, he said, "we're just an ad hoc watchdog committee." Anderson, however, had not been idle. He managed to arrange a meeting in Maputo with Ebenizario Chonguica, the IUCN representative for Mozambique, and Serodio de Almeida, at which the minister assured him that no sable would leave the country. Apparently, responsibility for the national parks, which used to fall under the agriculture department, had been shifted to his ministerial portfolio. De Almeida told Anderson that his department had distributed a questionnaire in Cangandala the previous year asking for information on sable sightings. The figures, when tabulated, indicated some 230 animals, which made Anderson wonder if that had been the source of van Hoven's information. According to Anderson, the deputy minister was prepared to offer all the assistance he could for a survey. But the problem of how to channel funds remained unresolved, and now, unfortunately, Savimbi had rendered the giant sable areas unsafe yet again.

Brian Huntley's accusation that van Hoven was bent on developing nothing less than a Disney-style safari park in Angola still sounded all too convincing, despite denials. And van Hoven himself had told me he would bring the giant sable to Quiçama. I made plans to meet with Huntley in early December 1998.

YOU COULD TRAVEL to Cape Town just to see Kirstenbosch. It's one of the great gardens of the world. Over a thousand acres in size, it lies in the gray-blue shadows of the southeastern slopes of Table Mountain, and boasts a dazzling diversity of indigenous plants and trees from the botanical riches of the South African, or Capensic, Kingdom. There is a hedge of wild almond planted in 1660 by the first Dutch governor of the Cape, and an avenue of camphor trees planted in 1898 by Cecil Rhodes, the last private owner of Kirstenbosch. But I wasn't there to look at the grounds. I had the taxi drop me off at Pearson House, a small, white Cape-style building tucked in the trees that housed offices of the National Botanical Institute, which administers the garden.

Brian Huntley, the institute's chief executive, holds the Harold Pearson Chair in Botany at the University of Cape Town. He was tall, lanky, and graying, with dark eyebrows, a long aquiline nose, and a direct gaze. He wore a crisply pressed shirt and perfectly knotted tie and spoke in a dry, laconic English drawl. As I followed him upstairs, he asked me, "How many people you've talked to have actually seen giant sable—besides Estes?" I could only think of Keynes, but that was in the 1950s. "Well, I've seen them. But that was some time ago."

His spare, orderly office, with its view of rugged mountain gorges, was all neatly arranged bookshelves and organized files and symmetrically hung botanical prints—none of the usual clutter or compost heap of papers that betray an overwhelmed administrator, although he serves on the boards of a long list of international scientific bodies. He offered me a chair, sat behind his blond wood desk, and tapped his finger on a stack of papers and reprints he'd put together for me. "This will answer some of your questions," he said, but he knew I'd have others.

His vituperative attack on Kissama made me think he might have a volatile personality, but he was very self-contained. I asked about his experiences in Angola under the Portuguese, and he told me how he went there in 1971 as a twenty-seven-year-old ecologist to develop national and regional environmental policy in the Serviços de Veterinária, which in those days administered wildlife in the colony. It must have been a heady experience for a young man. He made a number of visits to the giant sable reserves— the Esteses had left their house to him—observing and photographing the great antelopes and was the last wildlife professional, other than the game warden, to have been in the reserves before the civil war broke out in 1975. Most of the people he worked with in those years were shot or died tragically, although he has remained good friends with João Serodio de Almeida, who worked under him and later with him in Quiçama National Park. "He's an honest and serious conservationist," Huntley said.

He remembered Quiçama well. He had worked to put a stop to illegal cattle ranching and oil development in the park, which in those days featured elephant, lion, red buffalo, and numerous other species. At the time he left, he had been overseeing the construction of administrative offices, a lab, and what would have been his home on the coast there, and recalled how he had to argue with the Portuguese architect to redesign his residence to take advantage of the ocean views and the four o'clock sea breeze. In the end, the changes didn't matter; the civil war broke out and the MPLA used the half-built structures as mortar targets. Many years later, on a visit to the site, he picked up shell casings among the shattered ruins and remembered bitterly what might have been.

I brought the conversation back to the *palanca preta gigante*. He smiled. "There's a grand mythology around the giant sable," he said. In 1972 he had outlined a plan for the colony to ensure the future of the giant sable. He agreed with the Esteses' assessment of potential habitat loss due to population growth in the reserves, but drew a darker conclusion: "The long-term solution to the giant sable's future can only be found in making an extensive area of habitat, unoccupied by man, available to the species." In the same report, he had rejected the rescue schemes that were already being proposed, such as transferring herds from the reserves to other national parks. "This suggestion is untenable," he wrote, "not only on ecological grounds—the national parks do not contain the specialized habitat requirements of giant sable—but also because it would be foolish to think that their future would be any more secure in Quiçama," or any other park. He'd held this view for a quarter of a century, and saw no reason to change his mind now, although he said that when hostilities intensified in 1975, he considered taking a breeding group to Zambia as an insurance policy for the subspecies—but the civil war intervened.

Huntley was optimistic that their numbers remained the same. In his view, the conflict between the government and UNITA might have indirectly helped the sables. He pulled out a long, rolled map, and uncurled it on the desk. It showed Cangandala Park and the Luando Reserve in minute detail—every village, settlement, and track, all the rivers and tributaries. It was covered with clusters of dots indicating giant sable sightings. But this treasure map only showed what the situation had been in 1974. Huntley said there had been some seventy log bridges in the Luando Reserve. Without upkeep, they would have all rotted away by now, and since the population there had all fled to the cities to escape attack and conscription, he was sure many of the roads were impassable. He went back to the reserves in May of 1992, when the prospect of elections made travel in the interior somewhat less risky, and flew over the Luando Reserve with de Almeida. But, "it was the wrong time of year, the wrong time of day, the wrong kind of plane, and the pilot was too terrified to fly low. I'm not surprised we didn't see anything," he said. I asked him about the implications of Robinson's research. "I wouldn't lose any sleep over the giant sable subspecies issue," he said dryly. "It's a unique population, and a distinct one. There are strong conservation and ethical grounds for protecting their uniqueness."

We walked through part of the grounds so he could see for himself what the maintenance staff was up to, but maybe it was really about letting them see him on an inspection tour. The vistas were lovely, and the lawns were impeccably kept. The visitors walked quietly among the specimen trees, as if they were in an art museum. Huntley stopped and pointedly picked up a discarded candy wrapper on the walk and dropped it in a trash can a few yards farther on.

The difference in personality between Brian Huntley and Wouter van Hoven was obvious enough—an oil and water contrast—but it wasn't enough to explain Huntley's virulent opposition to the Kissama Foundation, which was surely based in part on his emotional attachment to Angola. When he was there it was hardly the "good old days," but toward the end of colonial rule, the country had something like national parks and wildlife regulations and a semblance of enforcement even if it was far too desultory, and Huntley had been at the forefront of conservation there. I imagined it was hard for him to think about what had happened to the Angolan environment after that. Certainly it would be difficult to convince him of the value of a gigantic, multimillion-dollar project to resuscitate that war-torn nation's blasted parks, especially a scheme that involved a government widely regarded as corrupt, with generals who had presided over years of protracted conflict.

I brought up the Kissama Foundation, and expected him to reprise his previous attack. But he confined himself to a few weary remarks, as if he didn't want to dwell on it. "The Kissama Foundation has some well-meaning people in it," he said, "but I'm extremely cynical about 'gardeners of Eden' in Africa." To him, they were all self-styled consultants chasing money. I asked about the charge that he would have consulted for Kissama if they'd paid his fee, and he answered that when he found out more about it he simply didn't want to get involved, although he happily sent them various papers he'd written on Angola.

Had he ever heard anything about a native taboo surrounding the giant sable? Not exactly, he said, but on one of his trips into the reserves, he visited the villages and questioned the local tribespeople on the distribution of local species by showing them photographs of various birds, animals, and reptiles. The answers varied, as expected: *Not many of these now; yes, many found by the river; don't know this one; you have to hunt hard, but they are there,* and the like. But whenever he showed them a picture of the giant sable, "they always shook their heads."

The answer they gave was very different, and always the same: *There is no such animal.*

TWO DAYS LATER, on a sunny Saturday morning in Pretoria, I shared the cramped cab of a white flatbed truck with Wouter van Hoven as we headed toward the northern suburbs of Johannesburg. His graduate assistants, Willy and Martin, were riding in the metal mesh animal pen built on the back of the vehicle. Van Hoven was dressed for the occasion in a dark green workman's jumpsuit, and he was trying to keep up with the speeding traffic on the busy highway while juggling a ringing cell phone, shouting second thoughts to Willy, and carrying on a conversation with me. Our destination was The Woodlands, an office park an hour away in Woodmead, where he had a contract to maintain a miniature game park on the grounds—one of the smaller wildlife projects he was currently managing.

The owners of the multistory building complex contacted van Hoven because they wanted something more scenic than a central garden on their seventy-five-acre hillside for their corporate tenants to look at. Could he put in some animals? He came up with a plan, devising security fencing, plantings, and a program of supplemental feeding for three species: some small, dainty antelopes—blesbok and springbok—and a trio of visually appealing zebras. Unfortunately, the latter had proved problematic. Recently, when one blesbok gave birth, the zebras, perhaps feeling crowded, kicked the calf to death—much to the horror of the office occupants, who had become keen observers of the animals' doings. They wanted an idyllic scene on view, not a nature drama, and now it was van Hoven's job to restore their little Eden. He had some ideas about what went wrong. "Zebra are funny, unsociable animals," he explained. "They're always kicking and biting each other. They were the first guys I off-loaded, the only ones on the terrain. Then the moment I brought in the blesbok they started chasing them. After two days, they accepted each other. Then I introduced the springbok, and the same thing happened—the zebra chased them." One was driven into the pond and drowned. "The end of the story was we only had two springbok; they should really have five or six. So I thought, 'Let's see if zebra can count.' I smuggled in some at night. But they started chasing them the next morning." The recent blesbok calf stomping was the last straw.

Like a landscape designer revising his scheme, pulling out trees that won't take and pruning back fast-growing bushes, or an aquarium owner removing pugnacious tropical fish who aren't behaving in the tight little world of the planned community tank, van Hoven was going to make some "adjustments." He's been known to stop his car to pick up injured house cats and rush them to the local veterinarian, but he's not sentimental about animals. This morning he planned to dart, immobilize, and cart off all three of the striped troublemakers.

Van Hoven was doing this on the weekend when none of the office workers would be around to be agitated by the operation. The zebras had their fans, too, and he expected more complaints over the missing zebras than over the little antelopes' "biting the dust." He planned to take the hooved offenders to his own small game ranch, which he runs on leased state land nearby and uses as a kind of holding pen for animals that will end up being shipped to one or another of his projects. In recent years, lots of less productive South African farmland has been returned to bush and native species reintroduced—but not always with a concern for historical accuracy. Van Hoven wanted me to know that there are many private game reserves in South Africa with species that never naturally occurred there. "Ecotourists want to see diversity!" he emphasized loudly above the road noise. "As long as it doesn't have a negative effect on the habitat, or on the animals, what's wrong with it?"

Clearly, he'd been thinking about the hot button issue that had Estes and Anderson and Huntley so exercised—the translocation of nonnative species to Quiçama—and he had an answer for all the questions I'd tried to raise about it. At a *braai* the previous evening at his home, I had asked him why it wasn't enough to restore the natural environment in Quiçama and put back only the animals it used to have.

"Let's debate it for a second," he said then. "Why should we only put in what we know was there? For what reason? And not add some animals that we do not know were there, but might have been there? What are we trying to achieve?" He grew more animated. "If you've got giraffe, which didn't occur there—it's such an attractive animal. You're dealing with people from Africa, you are dealing with Angolans, not intellectuals of the First World. These people come and say, 'Ah, look at the giraffe!' Tomorrow, they want to come back, they tell all their friends. Schoolkids in buses—they're going to say, 'Look at these animals!' We want to teach the people, these kids who live in Luanda, something about nature, spread the message. Tourists that come in want to see wildlife. And they want to see diversity of animals. If we bring in money, we can protect those animals that used to be there as well as those we've brought in. Is it such a sin?"

We turned off onto an exit ramp. I brought up the argument he had made the night before, and he jumped in right where he had left off. "There are two reasons why I say it's not such a sin to bring in a giraffe or a giant sable," he said. "We are not sure that they were never there. The habitat, the vegetation—I have no doubt in my mind that these animals would adapt wonderfully and survive there. Look, they might have been there, but nobody ever recorded it." Why be limited, he asked, to only those species that "the recently written records dictate were there"? Besides, "it was only in this century that the giant sable was discovered—who knows what was there in the seventeenth century?"

I asked how many giant sable he would need to have a viable breeding group.

"At least two males and perhaps fifteen females."

He reflected. "Ideally, if I could have my way, I'd use them as a breeding colony, manage them well. We know what sable antelopes need for successful living and breeding. There are people who have taken sable antelopes out of the northeast part of this country and moved them to places where there is no record that they have ever occurred and they've flourished. . . . I was just two weeks ago in a place in the Kalahari where it gets bloody cold in the winter and horribly hot in the summertime and the man there has got a fine production." He told me that if the estimated numbers of giant sable were what he'd been led to believe, it would be a good thing to diversify the herd, not just have it in Malange Province. "I support the view that people shouldn't have to travel to Malange to see a giant sable."

But van Hoven was opposed to letting the *palanca preta gigante* leave the country. "Look, you've got something which is unique. There's a mystique about them, and a lot of talk about them. You can have a park where the real wildlife lovers of the world can come to see the giant sable antelope." For them, he said, "it would be like a Moslem going to Mecca. It would be a great experience. So why dilute that experience by exporting them to zoos? Why let them outside of the country?"

What's the preferred method of capturing sable? I asked.

"Darting."

We arrived at The Woodlands, and pulled up to the security gate. Several guards in white shirts, gray slacks, and black berets were waiting for us. They let us into the grounds past a cluster of modern brick buildings, and through the security fence. We parked on the service road, and could see the zebras already, grouped on the green tree-dotted slope in the distance; the timid antelopes stood farther away against the skyline of suburban Johannesburg. Van Hoven and Willy broke out the necessary

233

equipment; they intended to capture those critters by chemistry. A narcotic cocktail consisting of M99 (etorphine hydrochloride) and Azaperone would immobilize them; the antidote, M5050 (Diprenorphine), would revive them. Van Hoven looked up the proper M99 dosage in a thick capture and care manual on the front seat. One has to be careful with the dosage; too little, and it has a mere tranquilizing effect on the animal; too much and you can bring on cardiac arrest. Interestingly, the same dosage it takes to subdue a small, high-strung antelope might do the same for a phlegmatic rhino—it all depends on the nervous system. Mere humans have to be careful handling this stuff—a needle nick could be fatal.

He wondered if 4 millimeters would be enough for zebra, and consulted with Willy. "Let's give the sucker five millimeters," he muttered, and Willy helped him ready the delivery system, which consisted of a long-barreled German CO2-powered air rifle that fired a needle-tipped plastic dart. The dart was seven inches long, with a Day-Glo red tail like a miniature feather duster to stabilize it in flight and make it easier to spot when it's stuck in an animal. On impact, an internal valve releases the air pressure that's been pumped into it prior to loading and injects the solution into muscle. The only drawback is that you have to get very close—about twenty yards. This isn't so easy to do with alert animals, and it could be risky around ill-tempered ones. And it's not a foolproof method. Van Hoven said there was a 4 percent mortality rate in these immobilization operations, even under ideal circumstances. You can't keep jabbing the animal—that might lead to an overdose—but on the other hand, if you miss, or the needle falls out, you'd have to redart or give up. Since it makes a difference whether they're peacefully grazing or excited and pumped full of adrenaline, it's helpful not to rattle the intended target. The zebras were already watching us, and I suppose that's what led me to expect an impressively stealthy, belly-crawling stalk by the professor of wildlife management. Instead, van Hoven spent a lot of time walking around in the open in the hopes of encountering one of the confused creatures already zigzagging across the small property.

On the other hand, the animals were somewhat habituated to people, so maybe it wasn't as haphazard a way to zap zebras as it looked. But it took a couple of hours to down a pair of them. The first one, a large male, was shot in the hindquarters, but the dart fell out. I looked for the telltale signs outlined in the capture manual: a staggering gait, or conversely, a high-stepping knee action as confusion sets in, impaired vision as evidenced by collisions with trees and the like, and finally, loss of fear of humans. The ears can droop with enervation, and while some animals stay standing, others collapse on their sides. Total time for the dosage to take effect: three to six minutes. It had been twenty minutes without a visible reaction, so van Hoven let fly with another dart. The second dose worked like a charm, but unfortunately the stallion staggered off and collapsed in the wet reeds and lay twitching on its side. Eight of us pitched in, but it wasn't easy to move an inert, 500-pound ungulate out of a muddy marsh, and we were wet and dirty by the time we dragged it onto dry grass. Van Hoven draped a handkerchief over the animal's staring eyes to prevent sun damage, and went off to immobilize zebra number two. I squatted down to take a close-up photo of the animal and study its iron-solid musculature. One security guard, who'd been leery of getting near to these equids, drugged or not, shook his head. "These things can kill you with one *kick*," he said, chopping his hand for emphasis. It was obvious he was a complete urbanite, despite his tribal ancestry. I'm no horseman, but to me these zebras didn't seem to be behaving any differently than skittish ponies would. A zebra mare ran up to the downed stallion and stood a few yards away, bewildered. The guard beat a quick retreat to the truck. Van Hoven was on the other side of the property, and I raised my hands to shoo her off; she galloped away, but not in the desired direction.

I looked down at the fallen animal. It was ignominious, this leg-splayed, flank-heaving, nostril-quivering, blindfolded posture of defeat. Still, it wasn't the "blood and slop that attended the death of a zebra" that Robert Ruark once described, "the automatic voiding of the bowels, the pumping seminal ejaculation, the great spilling of hot stinking white shiny-bulging intestine" when the animal got gutted. This one wasn't going to be turned into a black-and-white moiré throw rug; unlike a trophy, it would remain alive and intact, kicking and biting, but it struck me it was still being treated as a form of movable décor.

After flopping the beast over onto a blue plastic stretcher, we hauled it to the truck and dragged it up onto the bed of the vehicle. Van Hoven cradled its head to make sure it could breathe easily. The second striped delinquent was finally immobilized and heaved onto the truck, but the last one was scared out of its wits after shaking off a dart, and neither van Hoven nor Willy could get close enough to land a solid hit. The morning was long gone, and we needed to take the two downed animals expelled from this little green playground back to his farm; it's not good to keep them immobilized for hours. Van Hoven decided to leave the third one until the next morning.

Our truckload got a few stares in traffic, but otherwise little reaction on the way out to his 375-acre farm. We turned off the paved secondary road and bumped down a dirt track, opened a locked gate, and backed up to a hillock with a vertical face reinforced with logs—an animal off-loading dock. We tugged hard on their legs, but the four of us were not enough to haul out the animals, so we opened the back gate of the cage. I climbed on the metal frame to watch while van Hoven administered the antidote. He felt for a vein in the leg of the nearest zebra, stuck in the needle, injected the M5050, and removed it. Blood spurted, and he rubbed the spot. There was no reaction. He waited, and then straddled the animal, and quietly slid the needle into a vein in its ear. The zebra exploded to life and van Hoven vaulted out of the truck like a scalded cat—an impressive leap for a large-framed man—just as the beast, kicking and drumming its hooves against the sides of the truck, decorating it with dings and dents that looked like hammer blows, bounded out of the vehicle into the open field. It stood there and shook itself, nickered loudly and nipped a few blades of grass, then galloped into the bush. Van Hoven was already administering the antidote to the second zebra, neatly sidestepping the animal as it scrambled to its feet on the metal truck bed, fell, and finally leapt out of the truck to circle around the clearing before returning to deliver a parting fart.

"That's what you call gratitude," van Hoven muttered, and tossed his hypodermic on the dashboard before climbing back in the cab. "I think we could use a beer," he suggested.

On the highway back to Pretoria I started thinking about something I had heard the night before that now made me think I might have just witnessed a rehearsal for another animal translocation planned for the other side of the African continent.

Van Hoven and I had been drinking beer and watching the steaks sear on the grill as the sun set. "If there ever was an animal that was a piece of art on four legs, it's the giant sable," he said. "It's living sculpture." Then he asked me if I knew that game breeders were offering enormous sums for giant sables that could be bred with their own sable stock to "improve" it. He explained they hoped to develop *variani* look-alikes in, say, three generations—but it wouldn't be the real thing, he assured me. "Fool's gold," he called it. I asked how much the going rate for a genuine giant sable would be, and he said a game rancher in the eastern Transvaal had told him he'd pay a million dollars for a breeding bull. I hoped he was exaggerating, but the idea that such sums were being talked about added to my fears that the lure of financial gain was now a part of what fueled interest in the giant sable.

ESTES HAD ARRANGED to return to the United States from Tanzania via South Africa so he could see his son and attend a meeting on giant sable conservation Jeremy Anderson hoped to organize but had to call off when none of the others he wanted to invite could make it. Instead, he'd planned for Estes to talk with researchers at Kruger National Park, so he could be brought up-to-date on a recent outbreak of bovine tuberculosis; I'd be welcome to come along. Estes and I decided to drive up to White River to meet Anderson and go on to nearby Kruger.

We met up with Jeremy Anderson at the offices of the Mpumalanga Parks Board in Nelspruit. Anderson proved as affable and easygoing as he sounded over the phone. A short, stocky man dressed in shorts, he had curly brown hair, white sideburns, and a tanned, lined face. He shook my hand and grinned at me. I was wearing an old khaki bird-shooting vest stuffed with notebooks, pens, a pocket tape recorder, a camera, and rolls of film. He poked two stubby fingers into the cartridge loops to tease me. "Planning on going lion hunting, are you?" The three of us headed to a nearby outdoor café for lunch. Anderson and Estes caught up on news and gossip and traded good-natured insults.

I asked Anderson for his latest thoughts on the giant sable. He laughed. "At this point," he said, "I'll believe in them when I get in there and see them." I mentioned what I'd heard about game breeders' interest in the *palanca preta gigante* but wondered if anyone would dare undertake a capture mission in a war zone, no matter what the critter was worth. Anderson said that you wouldn't have to bring out animals—someone could fly in, dart a bull, shove an electric prod up its rectum, and collect a semen sample. Kept frozen, the sperm would be worth a small fortune. My head spun at the prospect.

Then they cornered me. The two of them knew I had met with van Hoven—what were his plans for the giant sable? I didn't want to share everything with everybody, but now I was stuck: I needed to stay in their confidence as well. I told them the minimum, that van Hoven was thinking about bringing the giant sable to Quiçama. It confirmed their fears. I mentioned that Brian Huntley told me that Serodio de Almeida, who'd been meeting with parks management educators, might still be in South Africa. Anderson thought it important for Estes to talk to him. In any event, we'd confer in the morning. It was now midafternoon and hot and humid, so Estes and I picked up some cold beer to bring along to Lyndon's and drove off to meet him. I was hoping there might be lions roaring in the Mpumalanga bush after dark, but the most frightening noise I heard that night was the buzz of mosquitos, not the most welcome sound in a malaria-ridden area.

The next day we drove over to Anderson's home in suburban White River. Estes called the Angolan embassy and learned that Serodio de Almeida was in Johannesburg. He reached him at his hotel and made arrangements for the two of us to see him before he left the country. Feeling upbeat, the three of us climbed in Anderson's battered little Toyota, and headed for the park. We entered through Paul Kruger Gate, which features a giant bust of the South African president who founded the park in 1898. Much expanded since its establishment, South Africa's flagship national park now covers nearly 7,700 square miles along the border with Mozambique, an area about the size of Wales. According to my guidebook, it boasts the greatest variety of wildlife of any park on the continent—147 mammal types, 507 birds, and 114 reptile species. Turning off a side road past a trotting warthog, we pulled into the courtyard of a low, stuccoed administrative complex in a grove of trees. We walked down a hallway of offices and stopped to talk with senior scientist Ian Whyte.

Whyte, a heavyset man in khaki shirt and shorts, gave Estes an overview of bovine tuberculosis in the park. Most of it I already knew from news reports: first detected in a Cape buffalo in 1990, the disease had now spread through a number of species, including lion, leopard, cheetah, baboon, and kudu. Buffalo are prime hosts, and lions that dined on infected animals came down with the fatal disease themselves. The outlook was gloomy; whole prides had succumbed, and hundreds of buffalo were being shot in an effort to get an accurate statistical picture of the problem, as well as to keep it from spreading. In fact, a tubercular leopard, apparently too sick to bring down its normal prey, had killed a park tour guide at night several months ago and managed to drag the body away before it was shot.

Disease, however, wasn't the only thing that prompted the shooting of animals in Kruger. Even in an ecosystem its size, culling is necessary to keep the wildlife and the vegetation in balance. I looked at Whyte's bulletin board, which was full of the usual bureaucratic notices and cartoons and photos—not snapshots of red-eyed friends celebrating, but pictures of elephants, huge magnificent bulls. One photo, labeled "Duke," showed an elephant with stupendous ivory that reached the ground, making him look like a hairless mammoth. "140 lbs" was written underneath—the estimate per tusk. Whyte noticed my interest. "Elephants are wonderful things," he said, "but such a headache." A single one can eat over 500 pounds of vegetation daily. Natural bulldozers, they often topple trees just to get at a few tender leaves, usefully opening up the bush to other plants and animals. But too many elephants in too small an environment can create a near desert, dooming other species as well as themselves. Should one let nature "take its course"? That is, adopt a hands-off policy on disease and desertification, and let a park go through catastrophic boom-and-bust cycles in its animal populations? Unless one is prepared to do that, there's no choice but to intervene and fine-tune the environment to ensure that lots of different charismatic mammals will be on view to bring in tourist revenue, which means more money can be put back into the park environment.

Politically, and biologically, it's hard to argue against that. The carrying capacity of Kruger is thought to be around eight thousand elephants; right now there are several thousand too many, although some dispute that. But there's not enough demand from zoos or other areas to soak up the surplus pachyderms, and translocations cost thousands of dollars per animal, so the park has to resort to reducing its elephant numbers the only way that's practical: by shooting them. The park stockpiles the ivory, sells the hides, and cans the meat for local sale. Nonlethal schemes to scale back their numbers, such as birth control, have yet to prove effective or practical, but the unpopularity of elephant culling has forced the park to halt the practice from time to time; currently there's a moratorium. But I saw there was a map of the 230-mile-long park on the wall next to Whyte that showed prospective culling zones and no-culling zones. "We hate to kill our ellies," he said. "It really hurts to have to kill them."

On the way out, we stopped to say hello to Danie Pienaar, the manager of scientific services. A tall, lean, soft-spoken man in bush khakis, he had survived a number of interesting scrapes in his job, including a bite from a black mamba. Several barrel-sized rhino skulls took up much of the floor space in his office. While he and Estes and Anderson talked, I thought about the fact that even Kruger isn't big enough to permit the unrestricted movement of wildlife. For some years now the large private game reserves on the park's western border have been removing their game fences to allow free movement of animals and adding to Kruger's effective size. I asked him why this fence-dropping process couldn't gain momentum. Talks were already underway about combining Kruger with neighboring Bahine and Zinave National Parks in Mozambique and Gonarezhou National Park in Zimbabwe to form a transfrontier megapark of some 36,000 square miles, and to the west . . .

"But eventually, there has to be a fence," Pienaar said quietly. Not far from Kruger there are farms, highways, power lines, houses and schools and shopping centers, and lots of people—none of which are compatible with wildlife the size of elephants, buffalo, or lions. You can read in any African newspaper stories of lions eating villagers or hippos stepping on tourists, elephants flattening farms, and so forth. I suppose it's no different from reading about grizzlies mauling hikers in the Rockies, moose trotting down Maine highways, or alligators emerging from canals to snap up poodles in Florida, but the animals are bigger in Africa and the encounters much more frequent and more often unpleasant. Parks that don't need fences are the ones surrounded with vast, underdeveloped, underpopulated buffer zones, or geographic boundaries that work as well as fences. But bring people and farms right up to the boundaries of a park in substantial numbers, and there is no choice: there has to be a fence.

TWO DAYS AFTER visiting Kruger, Estes and I had a tour of Sable Ranch, a 7,500-acre private game reserve near Brits, an hour west of Pretoria, with Ollie Coltman, the managing director. He's a tall, deeply tanned ex–game ranger from Zimbabwe who came to the ranch a decade ago when its owner, M. F. Keeley, a South African granite-mining magnate, decided to get serious about game breeding. I was curious to see the ranch's giant sable—or whatever they were—and had set up the visit in advance; now, with Estes along, I hoped for some precise answers to the questions that surrounded their herd of mystery sables. We arrived at the ranch with Jaco Ackermann, a wiry, genial conservationist and ex–game ranger himself, who'd invited Estes and me to stay in his Pretoria home, a high-ceilinged bachelor's pad stuffed with marvelous Africana.

I sat in the back of Coltman's Land Rover with Ackermann as we bumped over dirt roads lined with green bush and game fencing. We drove slowly past a black rhino and her half-grown calf, who stuck close to mama as she trotted off, matching her abrupt turns perfectly. Estes, riding up front, imitated their characteristic snort but they ignored him. The population of black rhino has been hammered by years of poaching, plummeting from 65,000 in 1970 to 3,000 or less now in sub-Saharan Africa, and private ranches in South Africa are one of its last redoubts. But Sable Ranch isn't run as a wildlife charity; it's a business.

When we pulled into the ranch's main compound, a cluster of buildings, hangars, and holding pens, it was clear that we had arrived at a kind of giant pet shop. Lorries of giraffes destined for Mexico City rumbled out as a truck carting a juvenile rhino arrived, and Coltman took a few minutes to supervise the youngster's transfer to a large cage. Instinctively, he had backed into the container to protect his rear. Although he stood no higher than my waist, no amount of prodding could prompt him to budge. The little tank had to be induced to rush a few feet forward to scare off a flapping rag so that pipes could be quickly slotted through the bars of the cage behind him before he retreated. After a drawn-out two-steps-forward, one-step-back routine, he was finally safely penned. He might have been headed to Germany or Brazil. These special request exports to zoos were an important part of Sable Ranch's business, but the operation's main income derived from an annual auction of a selection of their animals.

Sable Ranch obtained its stock from farms, parks, reserves, other breeders all over southern Africa, even European zoos, and bred and sold them back to other farms, parks, reserves, breeders, and zoos. "If someone wants four hundred impala removed from their farm," Coltman said, "I'll make an offer for say three hundred rand per animal on the veld. I'll go in with a capture team and the portable kraals, load them up and take them away, and market them to somebody else."

At one time some two-thirds of South Africa's animals were found in the national parks; these days two-thirds are outside the parks, even though the park population remains the same. Previously, many farmers turned to raising game for meat because it made more efficient use of the land than cattle did, but wildlife is now far more valuable alive than dead. Six thousand farmers now raise game. Coltman told us tourism drove the whole business—there is an ever-growing need for animals to look at, observe, and hunt. "We've found that a lot of people are moving out of the cities," Coltman said, "buying country property north of Johannesburg, putting up a little bed and breakfast—and then discovering that they've got to show your overseas tourists some wildlife."

The key to successful game ranching, as practiced at Sable Ranch, is to put wildlife in protected blocks and farm them—especially lucrative species, rare and endangered ones, notably sable, roan, and rhino. Currently, roan are actually more expensive than sable because they are particularly scarce in South Africa; still, ordinary sable fetch $6,000 each. A giant sable, of course, would be the rarest of all—a genuine one, at least. Coltman knew what we wanted to see, and we climbed back into the Land Rover. As we passed through the gates of one fenced area after another, he told us that even though 16,000 bales of hay a year were used on the ranch, the animals weren't totally dependent on artificial feeding; they still grazed and browsed and hence could cope in the wild. "We have an obligation to our buyers," Coltman said, "that when they buy one of our animals, they're getting a wild animal that will survive if introduced to their range."

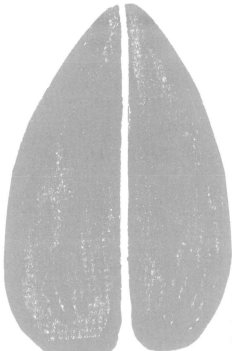

The track of a giant sable (shown actual size, 90–110 mm in length) is no different from that of an ordinary sable.

Intrigued by a five-foot length of horn he saw in a Florence museum, hunter-explorer Frederick Selous searched in vain for the animal in the late 1800s.

A new subspecies of sable antelope from Angola was recognized in 1916 and named after H. F. Varian, an engineer on the Benguela Railway, who first supplied specimens to the Natural History Museum in London.

Quentin Keynes (*left*) in 1954, the year he made the first motion pictures of the giant sable, visiting Varian in Cape Town.

Anita Curtis with Richard Curtis's giant sable trophy in 1923.

Arthur Vernay collected mammal specimens for the American Museum of Natural History and other institutions.

The museum's giant sable diorama.

Author's sketch of a specimen skull from the 1925 Vernay-Angola Expedition.

A 1953 Angolan postage stamp
depicting the giant sable.

Quentin Keynes's 1954 photo of two giant sable bulls fighting.

Richard Estes takes a pontoon ferry across the Cuanza in 1969.

Runi Estes admires a flowering uapaca plant in front of her home in Quimbango.

The Esteses tracked the movement of the herds in open grasslands and forest.

"Patriarch," a master bull that easily intimidated rival males.

UNITA soldiers in the bush in the early 1980s.

UNITA founder and leader Jonas Savimbi addressing the National
Press Club in Washington, D.C., December 7, 1981.

Wouter van Hoven (*second from left*) inspecting the progress of a fence being constructed across the northern tip of Quiçama National Park in Angola in 1999. The Cuanza River is in the distance.

The thirteen-mile-long fence took months to complete.

Containers of antelopes are unloaded from a Russian Ilyushin-76 cargo plane at Cabo Ledo on the coast in the first phase of Operation Noah's Ark.

Angolans watch as elands are released into the bush.

Student researchers and game guards at Caua in Quiçama National Park.

José Eduardo dos Santos, president of Angola, and Wouter van Hoven, after the ceremony reopening the park in December 2000. Gen. João de Matos, chief of the Defense Force, is visible on the right.

Richard D. Estes in Luanda, July 2000.

Gen. Luis Faceira, the former Angolan army chief, checks out Gen. van Hoven's tranquilizer rifle.

General Hendrik (*in beret*) confers with Cangandala Park game wardens Jovette and Domingos in Malange.

Col. Kanzenze Umbari Marinheiro, a traditional Songo chief, at Malange airport, 2001.

Flying low over the *miombo* forest in search of giant sable antelope.

Van Hoven waves to Songo villagers.

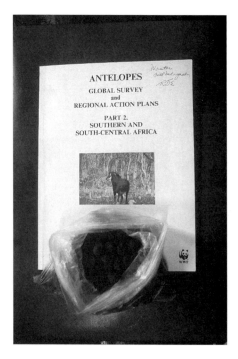

The bag of giant sable dung presented
by the game wardens.

We saw some of these bush-wise animals as we rode the dirt tracks paralleling the electrified fences, including impala, kudu, and an ostrich that raced alongside us. Ackermann shared a story from his game ranger days about trying to escape one of these kick-boxing birds, and that led to swapping stories on arcane wildlife topics, and an argument over which antelope leaps the highest—eland, kudu, or waterbuck. I learned that sable don't try to jump over fences the way kudu would; they attempt to crawl under them. Coltman had a great respect for sables. His left biceps was nearly severed at the elbow by a bull's slashing horns during a capture operation. He's given a great deal of thought to the successful propagation of sables on the ranch, which is prime habitat for the animal—Cornwallis Harris recorded his first sighting of sable not far from here in 1838. It boiled down to three things, he said. The first was the elimination of predators. We stopped along a section of fence bordering one of the 1,000-acre sable "camps" used to keep the Malawi, Zimbabwe, and Zambia "giant" strains separate and looked at a small break where a predator could wriggle through. Caracals—a kind of African lynx—are especially hard on small antelopes and sable calves, whose mothers are not very watchful. Ranch staff live-trapped fifty-six of the cats in the past two years. Since there was no demand for caracals, Coltman said, "we simply knock 'em on the head." When they catch the odd leopard, however, the ranch donates it to a park or reserve.

The second key to successful sable ranching, according to Coltman, was to eliminate the competition on the range. No other large animals—no zebra, no wildebeest—are allowed to compete for food. In fact, he said, "we keep the young sable bulls separate so the big bulls can get down to the business of breeding instead of fighting the young bulls all the time." A simple fence, however, isn't sufficient because the males would get down on their knees and try to spar with each other through the wire mesh. He pulled into an open paddock, dotted with a few trees, to show us some sable from Malawi, *Hippotragus niger kirkii*. A group of sorrel-colored cows began gathering, snorting, and poking each other aggressively as they sorted themselves out. Coltman explained the third requirement for breeding top-quality sables: getting rid of strength-sapping ticks. He had devised a special metal lip to fit on the edges of the raised tin feeding drums to hold cattle tickacide so that the sable dosed themselves when they fed. We climbed out of the truck to deliver a bucketful to each of the feeding stations as the sable sauntered up. They weren't shy, and we snapped a few close-ups. In my fascination for statuesque sable bulls I'd largely ignored cows, so I made an effort to study them. Each had a red tag stapled in one ear. The other sables, Coltman said, had tags of a different color.

Doubtless because of supplementary feeding and their good condition, the ranch's sables give birth all year round—unlike in the wild, where they typically give birth seasonally. They lived longer too; he had a cow that was nearly seventeen years of age, a sable senior citizen. Normally, he sold them much younger—"before they become fertilizer on my property," as he put it. On the other hand, a breeder doesn't want to unload a female too soon. "Look at that prime cow over there," he pointed. "An animal like that you would be very reluctant to sell because you know you're going to get a lot more babies out of her."

Back in the Land Rover, Ackermann reached over and scooped a handful of Epol brand #4610 *wildsblokkies* (antelope cubes) out of the bucket on the seat between us. "You can eat these," he said, shaking them like dice. I looked dubious. To reassure me, he popped a bunch in his mouth, like a kid eating a handful of granola. I chewed cautiously on one small dry kernel, a token sharing with the animals, I told myself, but I really did it to prove to Ackermann I wasn't a wimp. (I should have let the opportunity pass. At his house that night I was awakened by alarming abdominal gurglings while my sleep-fogged brain tried desperately to recall where I packed the antidiarrheal pills.)

We drove down another dusty track and pulled up to a massive green-painted iron gate in the game fence with an orange sign that read "Giant Sable Angola" on it. It slid open on an electronic signal from Coltman's remote, and we drove through some bush into an open clearing. He turned off the engine. The field was dotted with trees, the sky was blue with puffy white clouds; birds twittered. Right on cue, some sable cows and juveniles slowly ambled past, heads bobbing. Estes squinted at them from under his bill cap.

"They don't look like *variani*," he announced.

"Among your younger animals and your cows," Coltman said, "you do find a bit of white on the faces."

"Uh-huh," Estes replied.

"You see, these come from the western tip of Zambia—"

"Is that where they were captured—in the general management area of the Kafue?"

"No, on the western side of the Zambezi."

Estes was silent; that wasn't what he'd heard. We saw a handsome young black bull with modest horns approaching. He looked *variani*-like to me.

"How old is this bull—five years? Estes asked.

"No, no," Coltman said. "He's only three and a half, four years old. But see that cow in the background over there? She's got her head down now—now she's got a good face."

"But," Estes replied, "the giant sable in Angola are *all* like the ones you're picking out."

"What I have found, Dick, is that—ah, look at the bull." They drifted off into a discussion of distinguishing *variani* features, including brown hocks. I squinted at the bull, who was now lingering close by in the shadows of the bush. Coltman brought up the "Angolan drift" theory that Kobus du Toit, the vet I met at Terry Robinson's lab, had proposed. "You see, I think that as you move across Zambia your ordinary sable overlaps with your giant sable. What you've got *here*"—he pointed out the window—"is a different form, which is why you've got a lot of white faces."

Estes looked dubious, and said that there was a lot of empty land— the "Hungry Country"—between the Zambia border and the giant sable reserves. Coltman politely suggested that researchers tend to concentrate on the "reservoirs" of their study animals' habitat rather than their "periphery." I pulled out my Michelin map, folded to Angola, and handed it to him.

"With the war that's taking place in Angola," he said, "when you look at the reserve, and the direction of the rivers, I believe the animals could move up and down like so . . ." He poked the map. Ackermann said he didn't buy the antelopes-driven-out-by-war hypothesis; he remembered that when he was in the South African military he saw that antelopes were reluctant to abandon their habitat even if it was used for a bombing range. They run away from mortar fire, he said, but then they come back.

I asked Coltman if he had any mature bulls. He said they were after young animals that would have a longer chance to breed, and considering the risks—they captured fifteen in Zambia in 1993 and lost seven, a rather high mortality rate—they didn't want to try to translocate older ones. But there were big bulls out there on the border. They darted, measured, and released one that had fifty-seven-inch-long horns. I was impressed; those horns would be longer than record-book *kirkii* by half a foot, and well up into the giant sable rankings—in fact, four inches longer than the Curtis head.

Had he sold any of these animals? "A couple," he said, and added that Kobus du Toit had a breeding bull. I made a note of that.

The animals settled down and we got out of the car to take some pictures. They kept their distance, but let us approach within twenty yards. Ackermann and Coltman filled up their feeders, and I asked Estes what he thought. He said there were certainly variations in sable populations— sometimes you come across *variani* face markings in *kirkii*, but it's an oddity, in the same way that in a population of giant sables cheek stripes are an oddity. In fact, he planned to check his old Angola photographs to see how frequently those variations occurred. But few of these border sables had giant sable face markings, and he was convinced they weren't the real thing. Estes and I took a couple more snapshots and I sketched a few cows and the black, thick-chested young bull as he picked his way shyly through the brush, his head held low.

I was puzzled by these creatures. I didn't know what to think of them. Estes was surely right—they were just Zambian zircons, *variani* wannabes, even if there were fifty-seven-inch bulls out there somewhere. Although they were as sleek and glossy as show ponies, they were disappointing even as ordinary sables. Maybe it was because they seemed practically domesticated. Their complex food-gathering and breeding strategies, honed as survival behavior over millennia, were superfluous in this protected pasture. They had learned to come at the sound of a truck, ate from a tin trough, and through lack of predation, began to lose alertness. A whiff of the bovine hung about those ear-tagged, cud-chewing ungulates. I thought I'd feel I was getting closer to the giant sable if I looked over these imposters and dismissed them, but as I continued to stare I saw the *palanca preta gigante* eerily trading places with these antelopes. I don't really know if it was because I found them uncomfortably close to the real thing in appearance, or because I hated the idea that someday there would be a half-tamed, ear-tagged herd of the royal, or giant, sable somewhere, feeding in a similar field.

I WAS SURE I'd meet Angola's vice minister of the environment in an old Portuguese colonial office in Luanda with half-drawn blinds and a slow-moving ceiling fan. Instead, I was waiting for him in the atrium lobby of the Johannesburg Airport Holiday Inn with Richard Estes, watching the shuttle vans pull up and leave, the sliding glass doors open and shut, and the flight crews check in and out. Dr. João Serodio de Almeida was scheduled to fly back to Angola in the afternoon, and he had just enough time to meet with us before his departure.

De Almeida entered the lobby, walked over briskly, and apologized for keeping us waiting. He looked like and had the manners of a courtly Latin businessman. He was medium height, just graying, and wore slightly tinted glasses and a subduedly patterned sports shirt. We took an elevator up to his room.

De Almeida had spent his entire life in Angola. His father, a Portuguese forester, began working in the colony in 1943, the year he was born in Luanda. His family moved to Moxico Province on the border of Zambia in 1949. De Almeida wanted a career in wildlife, which in those days was the responsibility of the colonial Serviços de Veterinária, and obtained the required veterinary degree. In the early 1970s he worked with Brian Huntley, who was then fighting to eliminate oil drilling and cattle ranching in Quiçama. Later, after independence, de Almeida was put in charge of the park; there was little food and no meat in the capital in those days and he hunted some of the abandoned and now feral cattle that remained and sent the meat to President Neto. At Caua, the old Portuguese rest camp in Quiçama, he had a small house lower down the hill with a view of the Cuanza. Neto visited him there from time to time, and even stayed overnight. Much later, these visits would give rise to the idea that Neto had a house in the park, and the derelict building was now treated as a kind of shrine.

Estes shared his concerns about the Kissama Foundation's sweeping plans for the rehabilitation of Angola's parks. De Almeida cut in to say that he was a founding member of the Kissama Foundation. "My friends, the generals, invited me," he said. But after attending a few meetings he decided not to become involved with it, and given his current position as vice minister of the environment, was careful to keep his distance to avoid any conflicts of interest. But, Estes asked, had he heard of their plans for development in Quiçama Park—hotels, golf courses, riverboats? The introduction of nonnative species?

"Talk is free," de Almeida said. "From the talk to the reality is . . ." He stretched out his hands. He explained that the Kissama Foundation could come up with all the projects it wanted for the rehabilitation of parks, Operation Noah, tourism, and so forth, but only the government could decide whether or not to let such plans go forward. "Look," he said. "Professor van Hoven is not in the government of Angola. It is not his work, his . . ." Responsibility? "Yes, to make those decisions."

Everything had to happen in accordance with the environmental laws now on the books, which de Almeida had helped draft and that had been adopted unanimously by the Angolan parliament earlier in the year. He pulled out a copy of the impressively thick document from his briefcase. But had he heard of the plans to fence off a section of the park to introduce nonnative animal species? Yes, and he was adamant: there couldn't be any change or alteration in the status of the national parks without parliamentary approval. "Quiçama is a national park, not a zoo!" de Almeida said emphatically.

Estes was visibly relieved. But what about the possible export of giant sable? De Almeida brushed off the idea. "Only the parliament could decide such a thing." Estes looked concerned; couldn't it—and he—be overruled on these matters, considering that the generals have dos Santos's ear? "It is true," de Almeida said with a shrug. "But, even the president must consult with his ministers," he added.

I wondered if he wasn't placing too much faith in the letter of the law.

On his return to Luanda, de Almeida intended to clarify who had responsibility for setting policy for the national parks and reserves; confusingly, the parks themselves were overseen by the ministry of agriculture. But three weeks ago he had been effectively put in charge of them. He'd been thinking about Angola's environment for most of his life and was eloquent on the subject. "Our history after independence in Angola demands that we work with the people. The main philosophy of the MPLA is that government without the participation of the people is not possible, and this idea is also true in the national parks and protected areas." The parks in Angola were a Portuguese idea, and under the colonial administration the Africans who were living in them had to get out. He wanted to develop a more sensitive approach that would balance the goals of the parks with the needs of the people, and show them how preserving the environment would benefit them and their families. "But I don't hope to see results next year," he said. There were only a handful of people in the government who had any environmental training, and few resources to accomplish anything. Still, he wanted to start environmental education in schools and on military bases. He wanted to reopen Iona National Park and permit tourist access through Namibia, as well as renovate the old rest camp at Caua in Quiçama.

De Almeida showed us a stack of photos he had taken of some spectacular geological formations and huge waterfalls. He spoke poetically of Angola's wealth of rivers flowing outward in every direction from the rounded breast of the central highlands to water its neighboring countries, and ticked off the remarkably different biomes found in Angola: desert, forest, dry forest, coast, and mountains. To the outside world this raw, beautiful land was nothing more than a battleground—or a source of mineral wealth. But there was one advantage to the country being so underdeveloped, he told us: there was relatively little pollution or environmental degradation.

"I'd like to live long enough to see some of these places," Estes muttered, and handed the photos over to me.

I saw what he meant as I flipped through them.

Estes asked if he could make a phone call, and de Almeida put the photographs back in his briefcase. I thought he must have been an astute politician to have been made vice minister of the environment in the Luanda government, but all I saw was the knowledgeable and passionate conservationist Huntley had told me he was. I asked him how he balanced what he knew should be done with the realities of an impoverished nation and a woefully understaffed ministry. In all these matters, he said, there was a difference between "having a dream and a delirium." What he wished to accomplish was one thing, he explained, but he knew he must not fool himself about what could be done.

When Estes got off the phone I asked de Almeida what he knew of the *palanca preta gigante*. He said that he first went to the reserves in 1974 to investigate reports of a cow sable that was showing signs of hoof-and-mouth disease. It was during the rainy season and it took him four days to reach Quimbango, where he stayed in Estes's old house. Fortunately, the limping animal proved only to have an infected foot, which healed on its own, lifting the threat of having to shoot it to prevent the disease from spreading to cattle. That had been a great relief to him. "I talked with a lot of people—the farmers, the old game guards—and I came away with the idea that the people respected this animal. Perhaps," he shrugged, "they think the spirits of the ancestors reside in it."

De Almeida spent a total of three weeks in the reserve, viewing giant sables with the warden, José Alves, who was still there in those last days leading up to independence. At first, he had trouble seeing the *palancas*; they seemed invisible in the forest, almost wraithlike, even when close. "If you haven't the training, you don't have the eyes to see them," he said. "They—what is the word?—blend into the trees." When he could distinguish them from their background, he was able to take photographs. It was calving season, and he caught on film the newborn sables, so young their umbilical cords still trailed from them. One territorial bull in particular stuck in his memory, a great black beast with heavy sweeping horns and a regal carriage to his step; the locals called him "Dom Pedro," after the last king of Portugal.

"There used to be almost thirty thousand people in Luando Reserve," he said. "Now I believe there is no one. In 1992, I went with Huntley and we flew for two hours over the reserve." From what Huntley had told me, I guessed what he would say next. "We didn't see one person—not one!" The rural people had fled to the cities to try and escape the all-consuming conflict, and the forest had reclaimed the abandoned fields and villages. Estes's and Huntley's reluctant recommendations of nearly three decades ago that subsistence farmers in the reserve be gradually relocated had been accomplished with brutal thoroughness by the civil war. But he remembered a detail. "Only . . . near the river, the Cuanza, we flew very low, a fisherman waved at us." Was he a lone holdout who had refused to flee, or some strange isolated survivor who didn't know to be afraid of an approaching aircraft?

Estes leaned forward. "But did you see any *palancas*?"

De Almeida spread his hands. "It was not possible from the airplane," he said. "Two hours crossing the park, and we saw nothing!"

Estes made his pitch. "Could we work with you to make a survey of the reserve?" He could find funds for an aircraft, bring it from South Africa if necessary. Jeremy Anderson would lead the team. De Almeida listened carefully. As far as he was concerned, the giant sable didn't need saving, at least not in the way most people thought it did. The first rule of giant sable conservation was to leave them alone. That was essentially Estes's, Anderson's, and for that matter, Huntley's idea as well: they should be protected where they were — in situ. And, like everyone else, de Almeida understood how important it was to determine how many might be left.

If there were outside funds available, he said, "I will prepare the project. But it is necessary to go by helicopter, not road. I don't know the conditions of the roads—"

"Land mines?" Estes interjected.

"I don't know. Perhaps. By helicopter it is easy. "

Estes reminded him how the *palancas* would be easiest to spot from the air in July, when they were out in the *anharas*, feeding.

"We prepare a project for next July," de Almeida said, and he would take us. "We will go for fifteen days." Both of us were dazzled at the prospect. For Estes, this was the chance he'd been waiting for. It meant that he and Anderson would no longer have to take a backseat to van Hoven; they'd be able to fly above the *miombo* forest to survey the reserves themselves, the way they'd always planned, and armed with what they learned, be able to make their voices heard when conservation plans were drawn up for the giant sable. But excitement gave way to questions. For one thing, weren't the reserves in UNITA's hands? De Almeida said UNITA operated where there were people and farms to exploit and strategic targets to tackle. He didn't expect guerrilla activity in the Luando Reserve, the way there would be farther north, near the city of Malange, and possibly Cangandala.

"But," he cautioned, "it is not good to say anything about this." He had several concerns. First, there must not be any publicity about the survey or its results before measures for the protection of the animal were in place—he knew there were South African game ranchers who would go to extraordinary lengths to capture giant sable breeding stock. Second, he feared that announcing a survey might give UNITA a reason to shoot some *palancas* to embarrass the government by demonstrating that it couldn't protect the national animal. This appalling thought had hardly sunk in before he mentioned something equally chilling, but for a different reason. If UNITA heard about the aerial survey, they might decide, as he put it, "to prepare a surprise for us." So he'd make quiet preparations within the government for a presumed survey of Cangandala National Park. But when we took off, we would actually fly over Luando Reserve instead. It would be safer that way.

There was a war going on, after all.

SEVEN

The Hunter's Bargain

"Situation . . . you're on safari. There's a poor shot placement. 2,500 lbs of inferiated [sic] animal. Your friend is down . . . *Now* it's up to *You*. TAKE CHARGE! That's What Life's All About!"

So read the explanatory sign that accompanied a life-sized taxidermy vs. a manikin display showing an enraged Cape buffalo about to gore a hapless fallen hunter who'd bungled his shot. There were other full-scale tableaux of equally colorful confrontations—a grizzly swatting timber wolves, a lion dragging off his dinner of zebra, embattled bull moose— but the crowd didn't linger at any of them; there was a lot to see at the Safari Club International convention in late January 1999. SCI isn't the largest prohunting organization in the world, but it boasts 32,000 members in 170 chapters in 37 countries, and nearly 14,000 of them had come to the convention center in Reno, Nevada. They spent several days meeting and greeting fellow hunters and guides, looking over hundreds of exhibits, booking hunts, buying guns, attending seminars, and listening to speeches. Some were here to get awards.

I was here to meet the Dodgsons, the Utah couple who were raising money for the giant sable, and also because I wanted to know more about something that strikes many as an unexpected or even unholy alliance: the involvement of prohunting organizations like SCI in conservation. Could trophy hunting be used to support conservation ends, as its proponents argue? If so, did it have a role to play in saving the giant sable?

Most of the crowd, like most of the membership, were Americans. There were the expected booming-voiced men in cowboy hats accompanied by big-haired women in leopard-patterned blouses, but if anything the crowd was older and somewhat less flashy than I thought it would be.

But then international trophy hunting is a rich man's sport, and many serious SCI members have more than a touch of gray in their hair before they retire to recycle their business fortunes into trophy collections. The crude stereotype of hunters as slack-jawed yahoos cruising backwoods roads in pickup trucks, guns at the ready, was nowhere to be found; this was a different demographic, not the gentleman's world of southern quail plantations or Scottish grouse moors, exactly, but the more assertive one of self-made money and competitive egos.

The convention hall was so cavernous I needed to study a floor map of the exhibits and booths. I decided to take "Lion Lane" to "Grizzly Gulch," and made a left on "Elephant Walk" to explore the side aisles. I was encircled by enough taxidermy to fill several natural history museums—cougars crouching on tree limbs, snarling polar bears, trumpeting elephants, and on and on. Front-end segments of big-game animals were hung like shop signs to entice browsers to pause at various booths, talk, pick up a brochure, and perhaps put down a deposit on yet another dream chase. There was an entire brothel of possibilities, hundreds of hunting fantasies waiting to be fulfilled, from pursuing familiar creatures in famous hunting fields to seeking exotic specimens in obscure corners of the globe. If an elk hunt in Wyoming seemed too obvious, there was argali in Tajikistan, ibex in Spain, Kamchatka brown bear in Russia, mouflon sheep in Hawaii, tahr in New Zealand. And there were always the fleshpots of Africa. Professional hunters from all over the continent, some sporting elephant hair bracelets and native beads, greeted prospective clients with bone-cracking handshakes and reminders that they were almost fully booked for the coming season. Taped tribal music and animal noises lured me into one safari tent that showed a continuous video of sunsets in the bush and drinks by a crackling acacia-wood fire. I picked up a flyer on a twenty-one-day "full-bag" Tanzania safari. Three dozen shootable species were listed. I added up the per diem charges, trophy fees, various licenses, and air charters, and stopped counting when I reached $65,000. And that didn't include tips, international airfare, weaponry, or taxidermy.

There was something for every taste. You could get your portrait painted on an elephant ear, order a standing lamp made out of moose legs, or pick up a buffalo scrotum tobacco pouch. There were lurid videos on sale with names like "Sudden Death," "Death on the Run," and "Shot to Death." One TV monitor played a continuous slow motion loop of a leopard catching lead just as it sprang out of a rock cave in a whirl of paws and claws. But not everything for sale was garish. I gravitated to some of the ultrarefined weapons on view, including an array of London-made sidelock shotguns, sleek as whippets and as expensive as luxury automobiles. I hefted one, admiring its flawless fit of warm walnut and discreetly engraved metal, and it floated up to my shoulder and cheek with seductive ease. For a moment, I was a country squire squinting at heather-covered hills for incoming grouse.

I wasn't entirely immune to the allure that surrounded me. That's because I'm a hunter too, though it's an intermittent passion. On various travel writing assignments I've been able to stalk highland stag in the Hebrides, hunt wild boar in Sonoma, shoot geese in the pampas of Argentina and sandgrouse in Botswana, among other adventures. They were all experiences I savored, but I can understand why some would find them distasteful.

These days, when hunters are asked why they hunt, they aren't really being asked to explain its appeal. They're being challenged to come up with a rationale that would excuse their behavior. The answer depends in part on who's framing the question. Most of the people milling around the hall with me would agree with Theodore Roosevelt, who claimed "there is no need to exercise much patience with men who protest against the field sports, unless, indeed, they are logical vegetarians of the flabbiest Hindoo type." Meat eaters, in other words, are not in a position to condemn hunting for food. It's interesting that Peter Singer, the prime theorist of animal liberation, concurs. "Why, for instance," he wrote, "is the hunter who shoots wild ducks for his supper subject to more criticism than the person who buys a chicken at the supermarket?" Of course, answering objections to hunting by meat eaters who can't stand the idea of animals being killed is one thing; answering objections to trophy hunting by "logical vegetarians" is quite another, and in the middle of this vast, buzzing hall where the word "overkill" took on new meaning, the issues seemed more complicated, tangled, and vexed to me than ever.

The Dodgsons found me. They looked like a retired older couple, sensibly dressed for touring the exhibits. Bill—William W. Dodgson V—

was short, had a trim white beard and glasses, and was wearing jeans, a work shirt, and a worn leather vest. Anne was shorter, had a plump figure and dark bangs, a round soft face, and a quick smile. She was dressed in a gray jumpsuit, jacket, and track shoes. Both were as unpretentious in person as they were over the phone, and delighted to find someone so interested in the giant sable. Bill offered to track down additional museum specimens for me. Anne was upbeat, enthusiastic, and very chatty. In fact, she carried me along in a torrent of ideas, spilling what seemed to be the entire contents of her mind in the process, like a woman dumping out her purse. But as I talked with her and watched her in action on the floor of the convention hall, I saw there was a method to this: she laid out all her cards to find out which ones made your eyes light up, and then discarded the rest.

Bill had owned a successful Toyota franchise before starting to build his vast trophy collection a decade ago. Anne had adopted her husband's passion and by now the two of them had collected hundreds of species. It was Anne who found the giant sable—or rather, the antelope found her. "This animal just stepped out of the record book for me," she told me in our first conversation. In the SCI record book of African trophies collected by its members, there was only one entry for the giant sable, a magnificent bull with fifty-nine-inch horns collected in 1952 by George Parker, an Arizona big-game hunter who lucked out on a license. "I kept asking about the animal. I started writing letters," Anne told me. She wanted to rescue it. "It's an emotional thing with me. Look, I'm ninety-nine percent green. We're responsible hunters—we want to save animals, too."

One contact led to another until Anne finally located someone who was doing something for wildlife in Angola: Wouter van Hoven. She and Bill went to Luanda with the Kissama Foundation's president, toured Quiçama Park, and became converts to his vision, fired with thoughts of doing something to prevent the last remaining specimens of this beautiful antelope from ending up as war rations—or as Anne put it, "sable on a stick." When the Dodgsons returned to Utah they started raising money in their local SCI chapter for giant sable conservation. They auctioned off bear and cougar hunts, and made plans to take their campaign to the annual convention, all with the idea of turning the funds over to the Kissama Foundation. But after the story in the December 1997 *Safari Times* that giant sable had been sighted, Anne kept being pressed for more details or pictures—some evidence that there were any left. Although the SCI Africa Office grew suspicious of the Kissama Foundation and told her not to turn the funds over to van Hoven, she still thought highly of him. "Van Hoven is a one-man show. He's Dr. Dolittle on a shoestring."

The Dodgsons showed me a custom "giant sable magnum rifle" they'd commissioned, a showpiece bolt-action .338 engraved with the animal's portrait in gold. They had been doing a brisk business in $10 raffle tickets that morning, and Anne was hitting up everyone she recognized. "Hey, where are the bunny huggers now that we need 'em?" she joked. I decided raffling off a rifle in Reno to raise money for the conservation of the giant sable wasn't really any odder than some other fund-raising ploys for animal protection—in fact, a few months later actress Kim Basinger would donate a set of her lacy bra and panties to be auctioned off for PAWS (the Performing Animals Welfare Society) in Las Vegas.

It was nearing lunchtime and traffic seemed to be slowing down, so Anne took me over to the World Hunting Awards booth at the corner of "Whitetail Way" and "Elephant Walk." There I met two past presidents of SCI and the awards chairman, who tried to explain how their record book and awards system worked. SCI may be "a non-profit organization representing hunters' interests in conservation and sustainable use," but what appears to make it tick is the manic eagerness with which its members work their way up the ladder of distinction, earning recognition for their hunting achievements. Shooting animals that are outstanding specimens of their species—say, as measured by size or horn length—gets members' names and their trophies into the club's fat record book, but they can also earn a dizzying number of awards by hunting on several continents and bagging scores of animals in various categories. Serious members constantly circle the globe on hunts in their quest to check off the requirements on dozens of lists—the "big five" of Africa, various sheep species, spiral-horned antelopes, even pigs and peccaries of the world. Then there are levels of distinction from "copper" to "diamond" and a hierarchy of honors: "grand slam," "inner circle," "pinnacle of achievement," "crowning achievement" (Bill Dodgson got his in 1996, an honor he shares with only twenty-nine other members), as well as a "world hunting award" (a Super Bowl–style gold and gemstone ring), and a Hunting

Hall of Fame. I got a little lost in the intricacies, but it was clearly a means by which the men could separate themselves from the boys—although there were plenty of women's names on those plaques and pedestals, too.

Anne Dodgson has earned a score of these awards, including a "Fourth Pinnacle of Achievement." She has also knocked off the world-record Maral stag (think monster wapiti) in Russia, bringing it down with a single shot from her .300 Weatherby Magnum. She had to be coaxed into telling me the story, and broke it off to introduce me to C. J. McElroy, the organization's foundering father and the man who invented its pecking order of prestige. Once a compulsive international trophy hunter, he was now in his eighties and just out of the hospital. McElroy was bent over in the electric cart he was using to move around the convention floor, but with his wave of gray hair, powder blue jacket, and string tie, he looked like an alert old rancher. He perked up considerably when he heard I was on the trail of the giant sable.

"Years ago I got a call from a man who asked me if I wanted to shoot one," McElroy offered. "He said he knew someone who'd sneak me in and out of Angola." He frowned. "Hell, everyone would like to shoot one . . . but I turned it down." He got up slowly from his cart, and adjusted his cane. "You know, I've done a few things in my life I shouldn't have. But I didn't want that to be one of them."

THE IDEA OF anyone shooting Angola's great endangered antelope had made Anne Dodgson livid. "I'd like to post a reward on the Internet for turning in anyone who killed a giant sable!" she told me.

If she was talking about poachers, Richard Estes would certainly concur. If she was talking about a blanket prohibition against hunting them, he wouldn't be so sure. "It would seem to fly in the face of everything we've stood for," he once told me, "but . . ." He was open to the idea of allowing someone to pay an extravagant sum to shoot a bull, so long as the money went directly back into the conservation of the species—providing, of course, that there were enough giant sable left that a few could be shot without putting the herds in jeopardy.

Estes had long wanted Cangandala Park and Luando Reserve to be joined into a single giant sable habitat. One way to do that would be to turn the land between into hunting concessions, and allow a strictly limited "offtake" of the odd trophy animal. Anderson and Estes had discussed it for years, and Estes mentioned it to Serodio de Almeida, who thought it made good sense.

Estes was all too aware that the giant sable wouldn't be safe just because it said somewhere on a piece of paper that killing the animal was prohibited. Poachers aren't deterred by wildlife regulations. Protecting the antelope would cost money, and lots of it. Why not take advantage of the fact that there are people who'd pay handsomely for the privilege to go on a hunt for the "finest horns in the world"? It wouldn't be to Estes's taste— in fact, he'd find it distressing—but he understood the advantages. Lots of money was badly needed for game guards, patrols, study, and monitoring— money that Angola didn't have, or more to the point, couldn't put toward its animals even if it had it, considering the dire situation of its people and its devastated infrastructure. And even if money could be raised from other sources for giant sable conservation, why not supplement it with some generous hunting fees?

I started on this train of thought after I came across Fred Duckworth's booth. Duckworth, a grizzled former game warden in Malawi and an experienced professional hunter, now books safaris from his base in the Netherlands. He also has a keen interest in developing conservation schemes for endangered species, and had been in correspondence with Estes about several of them, including Aders' duiker, one of the rarest species of this Africa-wide tribe of small, spike-horned antelopes. Now confined to the island of Zanzibar, this shy, reddish-tawny, stocky little creature, all of twenty-five pounds when mature, is quickly disappearing into local cook-pots as the island's forests come under increasing human pressure. There might be only hundreds left. Duckworth persuaded the Zanzibar authorities to consider raising funds for an ongoing Aders' duiker conservation project by offering a small number of hunting licenses, and was granted five. He was selling them at $5,000 each, $2,000 of which would go to the project to fund a survey and a management scheme and the balance directly to the villages in the project area to encourage the locals to leave the diminutive duiker alone. Bill Dodgson, Duckworth told me, liked the idea and immediately bought one, even though without a special permit he wouldn't be able to import the trophy.

A duiker is hardly "glamor game," so maybe offering a prize for collecting such critters isn't a bad way to get needed conservation money into neglected corners of the world. It might be counterintuitive to think that obsessive trophy hunting can support biodiversity. But the idea that there might even be an argument for legal hunting of endangered species startled me even more. Rod East, the ASG's cochair, was convinced that carefully monitored sustainable trophy hunting can be a positive factor in antelope conservation. "The fact that Aders' duiker is endangered," he wrote Estes, "doesn't preclude this option," though he agreed that trophy hunting would have to be stringently regulated. "Outside Zanzibar," he complained, "I doubt that many members of the general public have ever heard of Aders' duiker. If there is really a significant body of public opinion out there which is concerned with the fate of this species, how come I have had to spend some of my recent weekends writing grant applications to try and raise a lousy few U.S. dollars. . . ?" Instead of letting the little animal go extinct while wringing one's hands over how to raise funds to save it, why not use the money from the sale of a few licenses to stanch the decimation of a species no one but biologists and obsessive hunters seem to care about?

Call it the hunter's bargain: sell off a few rare animals to trophy seekers to help save the species. And there's a sweetener in the deal — the impact of hunting on the environment will be wonderfully low for the dollars received. In one of van Hoven's studies, he calculated that on the average trophy hunters spend seventeen to twenty times more than the typical tourist. Over a one-year period in the Pilanesberg Nature Reserve northwest of Johannesburg, the nine white rhinoceros hunts permitted there generated more money than the 45,000 tourists who visited the park during the same period. There's more: hunters want unspoiled wilderness and are happy in tents; tourists want scenery too, but also roads and flush toilets and parking and lodges and restaurants — in other words, development.

Prohunting groups like SCI and CIC raise millions outright for conservation too, and while most is spent to ensure the future of huntable species, other wildlife in the environment and the environment itself benefit: you can't have ducks breeding in polluted ponds. But so long as the public largely regards hunting and conservation as incompatible, the hunters won't get the respect they crave. The harder they try, the more their achievements are dismissed as an effort to sanitize their unsavory hobby. But this is nothing new. The big-game hunters who founded the first international conservation organization in 1903 in Britain, the Society for the Preservation of the Wild Fauna of the Empire, were quickly satirized in the press as "penitent butchers."

THE GRAND FINALE DINNER at the Reno Hilton pavilion was long sold out, but I finagled a press pass and found my seat at one of the many circular tables that filled the hall as the lights dimmed. The sound system had been murmuring a kind of safari Muzak, a blend of bird shrieks, tribal drums, hippo belches, and hyena cackles to accompany the wraparound slide show of African sunsets on the walls and the full-sized mounts of giraffe, lion, and Cape buffalo onstage. Then the sound track switched to rock and jumped in decibels as spotlights swept the ceiling, panels dropped open, and ropes fell out and dangled. Showgirls in clinging cat girl costumes slithered halfway down, gyrated and kicked, then dropped to the floor and raced up on stage. The routine segued to a secret agent dance number, whose point I didn't get until Paul McCartney's "Live and Let Die" came on at top volume to whoops of approval from the audience. Somehow I didn't think Sir Paul, an ardent vegetarian and animal rights supporter, would have found it so amusing.

But I might have guessed this would be an unusual evening. On the shuttle bus to the Hilton, I was seated behind two women, one a stylishly dressed silver-haired matron, the other a dark-haired woman with a Scandinavian accent, as they discussed their favorite calibers for elephant hunting. The older one reminisced about her .500/465 Nitro Express ("a beautiful weapon"). Then a loud-voiced Southerner described how he "bowled over ducks" on his last outing, and when he finally faded out I overheard a diminutive woman talking quietly about how she'd nailed her Kodiak bear with a single shot.

What sticks in the collective craw of many animal lovers is that some people actually take pleasure in an activity that revolves around the demise of other creatures. At this dinner, I was surrounded by people who not only enjoyed this behavior, but were busy celebrating it. All eyes were on the stage as a succession of prizes were given out, videos were shown, speeches were made. There were prizes for young hunters, disabled hunters, and hunters who'd done it all. It was the Academy Awards for the shooting set, with drumrolls, young women in evening gowns escorting speakers to the podium, and winners apologizing to their families for having taken so much time away from them on their lonely road to hunting status. They were not exaggerating. They have to slog through swamps, cross deserts, climb mountains. It takes about five years afield and several million dollars to amass the kind of mammalian necropolis necessary to reach true prominence—at least the kind that fellow SCI hunters can bestow.

Keeping mementos from the hunt must be nearly as old as the hunt itself, but we're a long way from the first Ice Age hunter who wore the canines of a saber-toothed tiger around his neck, or even Selous and his era. The hunting trophy that used to be regarded as a souvenir of an experience, a means to conjure up old memories of the chase, is close to becoming the entire point of the pursuit. Hunters like to say that a tale hangs on the horns of every one of their trophies, but once the deadly idea takes hold that only the possession of a record book specimen can confirm that their experience was worth it, the entire undertaking gets whittled down to the head on the wall. How it gets there becomes less important, and finally irrelevant. Soon it no longer matters if it was brought home after a long, hard hunt, a patient stalk, and a clean kill. The original possessor of the head can be shot from a car, shot in a pasture, or even shot by somebody else and still passed off as something you "earned." In the scramble for top trophies, guides may be bribed to ignore animals brought down that don't measure up, just so another can be put in the telescopic sights.

It's not that I supposed anyone in the room that night was guilty of such transgressions, but it's happened. Once a trophy starts to carry more of an air of accomplishment than a personal nimbus of meaning, then it's just a chip, a counter, a checkmark on a list; it's number fifty-two in the book, or number nine, or even *numero uno*. There are species you have to get at all costs because you're in a contest to determine who has the most, the biggest, the best heads. After scandals involving members who tried to import trophies of specific endangered species in violation of U.S. law, SCI removed mention of any animals improperly taken after being listed as endangered. One member, who was subsequently prosecuted and jailed, resigned before he could be expelled. Several awards, I noticed, were now listed as rescinded.

And then there's outright fakery. A sixty-two-inch giant sable listed in Rowland Ward's *Records of Big Game* is credited to a famously competitive trophy hunter who was never able to get a permit to hunt the animal he so coveted. Undeterred, he is said to have borrowed a single museum horn and had it reproduced twice in fiberglass and mounted on the scalp of an ordinary sable.

Yet more speeches and presentations followed. Gen. Norman Schwarz-kopf (Ret.), who had roused the troops with his exhortation to take charge of the future of hunting the evening before, introduced the keynote speaker, former president George H. W. Bush, as a man of "un-*impeach*able integrity," a line which got a thunderous response. Bush, an SCI life member, had been out of office six years. Now that his days were no longer filled with staff meetings and photo ops with congressmen and Girl Scouts and people like Savimbi, he's had time to fish and hunt dove and quail—not, he added, that he's suggesting that any of his "little personal exploits" compare with Theodore Roosevelt's 1909–10 East African safari. He quoted T. R.: "Game butchery is as objectionable as any other form of wanton cruelty or barbarity, but to protest against all hunting of game is a sign of softness of head, not soundness of heart."

Among the people who filed out after dinner was Robert M. Lee, who had just been given the C. J. McElroy Award for his contributions to hunting and conservation. He was talking with Prince Abdorreza Pahlavi, the brother of the late Shah of Iran, whose former palace in Tehran once housed his vast worldwide trophy collection. The prince looked unhealthily pale under the spotlight where the two of them paused to look at Lee's custom 1962 Land Rover on display in the foyer. It was the vehicle Lee designed for use forty years ago when he opened Angola to the safari business. He's one of the last people alive to have shot a giant sable on license.

I wanted to know what it was like.

A TEN-MINUTE taxi ride from Reno brought me to an unmarked street in Sparks where it dead-ended at a huge warehouse complex surrounded by a vast empty parking lot ringed with a barbed wire fence. I spoke into the call box while being scrutinized by a security camera, then walked across the lot and around to the back, where I found a couple of parked cars and an unmarked door to what looked to be a no-nonsense shipping office. Inside, three young women were busy at their desks. A few posters of Hunting World products decorated the walls above the bookshelves, filing cabinets, photocopiers, water cooler, and bulletin board with posted Nevada workplace rules. My eyes came to rest on several blocky gunstock blanks of top-grade walnut resting on an opened rifle case.

Two dark doors faced me. One had a substantial lock on it. The other had a sign: "Please knock before entering/Keep door closed at all times." Behind that one, obviously, was the boss.

I'd seen Bob Lee a couple of times before in his store, Hunting World, on East Fifty-third Street in New York, but never introduced myself. Lee started the business in 1965 as a catalog of his own designs of outdoor equipment and luxury luggage and opened his first outlet two years later; there were now over fifty such shops and boutiques worldwide. He also began trading with China during the cultural revolution and in 1980 was given an extraordinary opportunity: the chance to hunt Marco Polo sheep at high altitudes in the Chinese Pamirs, the first Westerner to do so since T. R.'s sons, Kermit and Theodore, Jr., went there on an expedition in 1926. In the late 1980s he became particularly active in conservation, setting up his own foundation to make contributions to wildlife groups and an endowment for graduate studies in sustained wildlife management at the University of Montana.

I was ushered into the small windowless room. It was a working office, not for show, but among the framed documents I noticed a signed photo of President Bush on a bird shoot. Lee was behind his desk, dressed in a tweed jacket and tattersall shirt. He has an aquiline nose, dark blue eyes, and black, thick, just-graying hair slicked back from his face. He looked younger than his sixty-one years. He also had a brusque manner and didn't smile much. When I asked if I could tape our conversation, he said *no*. "I don't like journalists," he explained. But he didn't mind if I took notes. We were off to a flying start, but after I asked him if he'd always been involved with the outdoors he softened a bit as he recalled his early fascination with nature.

An only child, Lee grew up on Long Island and began horseback riding with his mother when he was five. He bought his first rifle, a .22, by selling magazine subscriptions, and took shooting lessons, again with his mother. She also drove him to trout streams so he could fish. By twelve he was tying flies professionally and selling them to the old Abercrombie & Fitch on Madison Avenue. He took his fly tying supplies to prep school, along with his horse, and was able to buy his first high-powered rifle, a .30-06—and later, his first Ferrari—with his earnings. Lee still has both. He went on safari in 1955, at the age of eighteen. Smitten by Africa, he gave up a promising career in building construction to start Lee Expeditions, Ltd., in 1959, forming a partnership with a Portuguese businessman who had obtained a hunting concession just above the Caprivi Strip in Cuando Cubango. But first he had to convince the suspicious colonial administration that he wasn't there to spy on the Salazar government.

At an age when he might have been forgiven a few years of directionless drifting, Lee was already running his own safari firm. "I was a kid," he says, all of twenty-two, but he spent six to eleven months a year on safari for the next several years, guiding clients like Prince Abdorreza. I mentioned that I saw the two of them looking at Lee's old vehicle. "He spent a lot of time bumping around in that car," Lee said. There's an old photograph of the two of them in the Angolan bush, the Iranian prince in the floppy hunting hat he always seemed to wear, and the youthful Lee, his shock of black hair swept off his face, smiling.

How did he get his giant sable license?

"I got one because I helped Angola. I brought a lot of businessmen there, encouraged investment. The license was a way to say thanks," Lee said. "But I was told not to publicize the fact—there were well-connected Portuguese who had been refused a license." I asked if the prince had tried to get one. "Well, the prince could have asked the Shah to ask Salazar to grant permission, but he didn't want to do that."

It was September 1960—or maybe 1961, he'd have to look it up—the start of the rainy season, when he set up a fly camp on the road that runs from Cangandala to Capunda in the Luando Reserve, hoping to spend a week filming in the *miombo* woodlands and open *anharas*. But the rains came and he cut his visit to three days. He remembered one night when it rained and then abruptly stopped. He left his lighted tent to retrieve an item from his car. As he walked back, he became aware that a leopard was padding softly alongside him, a short distance away. He made it back to his tent, shaken but unscathed.

Lee made films and took photos of the numerous giant sables he saw there, then on his last day took up his rifle and stalked them. He was able to get surprisingly close to a large group grazing in the open. Once there, he found it difficult to decide which one was the biggest bull. "They all looked huge," he said. Finally, he singled one out and shot it through the lungs at fifty yards with his .270. The horns were sixty and three-eighth inches, although he thought they might have shrunk a bit since.

Lee's description stirred my dormant hunter's heart. I had brought down big game myself with that very caliber and I saw the bull in profile, the .270 coming to my cheek and the crosshairs settling on his shoulder, felt the awful final squeeze of the trigger and the crack/smack of the rifle, the beast's shocked flinch and doomed sprint, faltering, stumbling, the heavy, flopping collapse into the grassy stubble . . . and the triumph tinged by regret.

What had happened to the trophy? Lee said he had the entire skin removed for a life-sized mount, and was persuaded to leave it with Dr. Abel Pratas, the head of the Serviços de Veterinária, who assured him it would be properly cleaned and prepared. Unfortunately, by the time he received it, all the hair had slipped; it was wrecked, useless. But he had the horns.

Lee left Angola in 1965; the widening war of independence meant he could no longer guarantee the safety of his clients. A year after his departure UNITA was founded and would soon base itself in Cuando Cubango. He thought it horrible that millions of land mines now dotted the landscape he once knew, and said the conflict would never end. In fact, Lee hadn't been back to Africa since 1970; he didn't want to see what had happened to it.

Recently, Lee decided to put his giant sable horns in a full-sized mount using a common sable skin—its face markings judiciously dyed to remove the cheek stripe—so that he could display his rare trophy as it was meant to be shown. It was just back from the taxidermist, and he offered to show it to me. He took me through the other door into what he called his "toybox." I thought the rest of the massive building was a warehouse full of Hunting World gear, but he flicked on the lights to illuminate a huge open hangar with several long gleaming rows of angle-parked rare automobiles—Ferraris, Bentleys, Rolls-Royces, and who knows what else. How many cars was I looking at? "That's like asking a cattleman how many head he has," he said dryly. There were walls of sporting art and a collection of Bohlin saddles, too, which looked a bit lost in the vast automotive treasure trove. But an entire corner and considerable floor space of the hangar was filled with animal trophies that more than held their own against the four-wheeled sculptures. There were hundred-pound ivory tusks, Lord Derby's eland, various Iranian rarities, a double-shovel woodland caribou, and scores more. He shrugged. "I'm not a 'species collector,'" he said. "I've never even had a lot of my trophies measured. There are guys who want to collect every little subspecies of duiker—I could care less." He had no interest in SCI's record-keeping or medallion system, either. "The Fourth Pinnacle of Achievement . . . hell, I don't even know what that is."

His giant sable was a full museum-style mount on a platform. The proud sable's face markings would pass scrutiny as *variani*, but the impressively hooped horns were the only visible features that were actually what they purported to be. The rest of it was a re-creation of the idea of the giant sable—Lee's giant sable. Even though it was a superb approximation, I couldn't seem to see the animal of my imagination in it.

I got another *no* when I asked if I could take a photograph it, so I contented myself with a quick furtive sketch in the margin of my notebook. I wanted to remember the slight asymmetry in the flare of one of the horns; it was the only imperfection. We went back to his office to look at his old giant sable films, which he had transferred to video. Lee popped a tape into the VCR and we watched as the *palancas* grazed, their tails flicking while tick birds fluttered around them and hung on their sides. Even when their heads were lowered, the horns of the bulls were higher than their withers. Footage followed that showed them viciously thrashing bushes. After a few minutes of the same, Lee got impatient and put the video on fast forward. The giant sables began darting back and forth across the screen, grazing with rapid-fire speed, their heads bobbing like frantic woodpeckers, and then abruptly rocketing out of view. He zapped it off.

What did he think someone would pay to shoot a giant sable? Fifty thousand dollars, perhaps? Lee said that sounded cheap. Hunters were more than willing to pay for the unique privilege of playing predator. "Hunters do the necessary culling," he said, "at their own expense." Lee reminded me that at conservation fund-raisers, scarce permits to hunt desert sheep in Mexico have been auctioned off for five- and six-figure sums. He'd bought one himself. So why not ask $100,000 or even $250,000 for a giant sable license? Surely that wasn't too high a price to put on the head of a priceless animal. For some hunters, it would be a bargain.

It would be a win-win situation for the hunters and the giant sable — well, the species, anyway. I couldn't think of an unsentimental argument against it.

EIGHT

WAITING FOR ANGOLA

The fragile peace process in Angola came apart after the UN special envoy's plane crashed in the Ivory Coast in mid-1998. Clashes between both sides had escalated by then, precipitated by UNITA's refusal to allow the extension of state administration into the central highlands and the government's subsequent three-day bombing of the UNITA strongholds of Andulo and Bailundo. But Luanda underestimated the rebel movement's strength; Gen. João de Matos discovered that UNITA was as well armed as it ever was. The government army advance was pushed back, and UNITA laid siege to the government-held cities of Cuito and Huambo and targeted the city of Malange to the north. Cuito, the once important junction on the Benguela Railway that had been shelled into rubble during the 1992–94 round of fighting, was pounded again. On Christmas Eve, in the heaviest rebel attack on Cuito since the fighting resumed, thirty people were killed and thirty-seven wounded; nine of the casualties occurred when a Catholic church was hit by mortar fire. Some thirty thousand refugees streamed into the city from the surrounding area, but relief agencies were unable to airlift food and medicine to those trapped there.

Frustrated by the turn of events, I pondered my map of Angola and the giant sable's territory in the dead and dying center of the country. I drew hatch lines in the reserves to shade them darker and tracked the progress of battles up and down the key cities in the adjoining highlands just to the west, from Cuito to Andulo to Malange city, and glumly faced the fact that there was little hope of a giant sable survey expedition into the reserves in the coming year—not with open warfare in the interior.

As many had warned, Jonas Savimbi had been loudly talking peace while quietly rearming his movement, even flying in almost a hundred

Ukrainian-made T-55 tanks to UNITA's landing strips. UN peacekeepers (as well as the troika of observer nations, the United States, Russia, and Portugal) had shrugged off UNITA's token fulfillment of the demobilization and handover of arms called for by the peace process. It was an old-men-and-muskets charade that surrendered no armored vehicles and less than a truckload of ammunition. But Savimbi had never made a secret of UNITA's determination to keep control of the key alluvial diamond fields in northeastern Angola, where the gems could be dug from riverbanks, "for the sake," as he put it, "of its own survival."

The government, burdened by billions in foreign debt, desperately needed access to the glittering wealth which had earned UNITA nearly $4 billion since 1992—doubtless motivation enough to try to seize control of these regions. After two aircraft were shot down over UNITA-controlled areas, the UN Security Council expressed its usual "grave concern," demanded "full cooperation by all," and pronounced itself "actively seized of the matter." But there didn't seem to be anything anyone other than the combatants themselves could do about the return to civil war.

. The war was no longer a conflict fueled by foreign powers; it was a conflagration stoked by the very riches of the land it was so busy devastating and presided over by two sharply contrasting figures. No one has ever accused José Eduardo dos Santos of having a scintillating personality. An engineer by training, he maintained a carefully calibrated balance of power around the presidential palace by shuffling ministers, generals, and cronies. He now ruled a regime increasingly accused of skimming off substantial amounts of the nation's income from its huge oil revenues before it ever reached the state treasury and of having a chilling human rights record, rife with extrajudicial killings, summary executions, abductions, forced conscriptions, and torture. But now that dos Santos had successfully retooled himself into a semblance of a democratic leader by carefully shaping his statements and policies to meet minimum international expectations, Western nations had not let their reservations about the Luanda government interfere with any number of lucrative oil, diamond, or arms deals. On the other hand, the charismatic Jonas Savimbi, having lost the support of the UNITA parliamentarians in Luanda in the national unity government several months before—and branded a "war criminal" by the entire National Assembly—had lost much of his attraction and what little international support he still had as evidence of his savage crimes mounted.

Fred Bridgland, the British journalist who had once proclaimed Savimbi "a key to Africa," had been steadily losing faith in the leader UNITA now called O Mais Velho (The Eldest One). Years before Bridgland had accused him of believing "his own Messianic propaganda about himself." By January 1999, he openly attacked him as a "murderous dictator." Bridgland had turned on him after Tito Chingunji, who rose to be Savimbi's senior international spokesperson and became Bridgland's close friend, was murdered on Savimbi's order; prior to that, Savimbi had apparently ordered the killing of Chingunji's parents, four brothers, and a sister. Eliminating those around him who had fallen out of favor—including various of his many wives—had become a familiar pattern with Savimbi. Bridgland declared that "executions, tortures, forced marriages and abuse of women were almost the least of Savimbi's excesses. He also began burning women and children to death in public." Chingunji had told Bridgland he had seen a group Savimbi had accused of "witchcraft" publicly immolated in a bonfire. "A lady named Judite Bonga was called first," Bridgland said. "She was so shocked that she was unable to move. Commandos grabbed her and threw her into the flames. Eyewitnesses said she jumped from the bonfire and begged for mercy. Savimbi drew the ivory-handled pistol he always wore at his waist and, together with one of his generals, forced Judite back into the fire . . ."

Bridgland had more to say about the man who had once impressed him as a revolutionary patriot: "Savimbi's sexual practices went beyond most usual concepts of lust. He chose wives for his senior officers and slept with them in a bizarre rite of passage before they were married." Savimbi's growing harem came to include his own niece; her parents were executed when they protested. Over the years the stories of his rapaciousness had all served to wrap Savimbi in mythic power, but to many they now appeared for what they were—the crimes of a cruel despot. Although Savimbi's propaganda machine still pumped out his "Pátria ou Morte!" ("Homeland or Death!") diatribes on the "war machine of Eduardo dos Santos and his oligarchy," they were sounding increasingly stale. A communiqué on the occasion of the thirty-second anniversary of UNITA's first military success, the Christmas Day attack on the Benguela Railway stop at Teixeira de

Sousa on the Congo border, announced that "the standing committee of the political commission of UNITA, in the name of all combatants of our glorious party, reiterates firmly in letters of gold, that the programme that started on 25 December 1966 has been kept on track and is in a real and dynamic state today." Having backed UNITA-Renovada, the parliamentary UNITA splinter group that broke with Savimbi, the government now referred to Savimbi's rebel movement only as "armed bandits," "Savimbistas," the "terrorist group of Jonas Savimbi," or "the black cockerel gang," a reference to UNITA's flag that showed a *galo negro* crowing at the bloodred dawn of a new day.

The Angolan government news was suspiciously upbeat and consistently vague about what was happening in the rebel-held center of the country, so I tried to glean information from those who had long had contact with UNITA. But in Pretoria, the government had taken a strong anti-Savimbi position, and I found little interest in discussing any former (much less current) involvement with UNITA. One government official explained that some of those who could have supplied me with answers had previously sought amnesty from the South African Truth and Reconciliation Commission and would not want to talk for fear of compromising themselves.

In Washington, D.C., there was widespread amnesia about UNITA. Former government officials, lobbyists, and diplomats were happy enough to talk about the current conflict (it was a change of subject from the presidential impeachment talk that was then consuming the capital), but when I brought up Savimbi's name, those who had been among his ardent supporters often became uncommunicative. In the Reagan and Bush eras he had been hailed as a hero, but now that the cold war was over, Savimbi was an embarrassment. But not everyone was hesitant to discuss him. Paul Hare, who had been the U.S. special representative for the Angolan peace process from 1993 to 1998, and was now executive director of the U.S.-Angola Chamber of Commerce in Washington, blamed Savimbi for the breakdown of the Lusaka peace process. The UNITA leader had really expected to come to power in the 1992 elections, Hare told me. But his control of the bulk of the country's diamond production gave him an alternative means of achieving that goal. Savimbi's current strategy was to make Angola ungovernable and to create a humanitarian crisis so ghastly the international community would be compelled to intervene and demand negotiations. "Because UNITA would have to be a party to any such meetings," Hare pointed out, "Savimbi would be able to reach his objective of getting back to the negotiating table. The act of sitting down with the government for more peace talks would legitimatize him all over again."

By the end of March the UN had given up peacekeeping in Angola; there was no peace to keep. I reached Chester Crocker, the former assistant secretary of state for African affairs, by phone to ask him what he thought of the current conflict. He was not encouraging, and expressed an equal lack of enthusiasm for dos Santos or Savimbi. "Personally," he said, "I wouldn't want to live under either of them." He faxed me a recent op-ed piece in which he argued: "Opportunists with a Leninist sense of power are in charge on both sides in Angola. Neither places a high priority on peace or people. Barring victory, they prefer war over peace."

Dos Santos is not quite a Mobutu or Emperor Bokassa, to name two recent examples of African despotism, but he is hardly a Julius Nyerere, either, who may have pursued ill-conceived economic policies in Tanzania but died without the stench of corruption that clings to many contemporary African leaders. Savimbi, on the other hand, now seems destined to join the ranks of such bloodthirsty tyrants as Pol Pot, Augusto Pinochet, and Idi Amin. Branded a war criminal and deservedly demonized, he'd relinquished whatever claims to legitimacy he ever had.

In early 1999 the prospect of these two men ever reconciling looked more remote than ever.

THERE WERE OTHER developments by then. With SCI's encouragement, Anne and Bill Dodgson had decided to turn over the funds they'd raised for giant sable conservation to the IUCN's Antelope Specialists Group. They'd been in touch with Richard Estes, who wrote to them to explain that he had hoped their financial support would allow Angola's vice minister of the environment to arrange an aerial survey of the giant sable reserves. Unfortunately, he wrote, "the window of opportunity slammed shut again" as fierce fighting had now resumed in Malange Province. Nonetheless, he would establish a special fund with their contribution to enable the ASG to develop and pursue a conservation action plan for this "spectacular subspecies"—when it was possible to do so. The Dodgsons left for Turkmenistan to pursue Trans-Caspian and Afghan urial, and Estes left for Tanzania. When he returned to New Hampshire several months later, a check for $10,000 was waiting in his pile of accumulated mail; a month later the Dodgsons sent an additional $3,200. He wrote to thank them and to reassure them that he didn't "believe for a minute that the giant sable has been shot out or even reduced to a critical level." While the Cangandala population might be vulnerable, he believed that the size and remoteness of the Luando Reserve meant that "it would take a concerted, deliberate effort to hunt and kill all the different sable herds."

Brian Huntley told me over the phone that he hoped to give a presentation on the giant sable at a biodiversity meeting in Cabinda he planned to attend with Serodio de Almeida; it was scheduled for March, but considering the hostilities in the country, he doubted it would come off. Wouter van Hoven replied to my E-mail inquiry for news. "The war has certainly hotted up in Angola, but it is far from Quiçama. I have a board meeting of the foundation in Luanda on 18 Feb. and will then be in a better position to see about the giant sable survey. I am not too optimistic because a lot of action is taking place in the Malange area."

As expected, the biodiversity conference Brian Huntley thought would be canceled never took place, but I was startled by the news that Serodio de Almeida was no longer vice minister of the environment. In a reshuffling of government posts that dos Santos announced earlier in the year, de Almeida had lost his portfolio after twenty-two months in office. Now only one possibility for a giant sable expedition remained: the Kissama Foundation. But those plans too had been scuttled by the conflict.

The timetable for Operation Noah's Ark also had to be scrapped several times in 1999. Wouter van Hoven had hoped the fence would be up in Quiçama by February, which would allow the first animals to be introduced in May or June; by late April, however, he admitted "things were at a standstill because of the rain." In mid-July, when I reached him by phone, he told me that he was hoping to off-load some animals into the park in September.

By contrast, a Kissama Foundation media event planned for Washington, D.C., was only postponed by a couple of months, and finally took place there August 17. The foundation's press release cordially invited me "to a reception with the First Lady of Angola, Her Excellency, Ana Paula dos Santos," joined by Their Excellencies, the ministers of travel and tourism and environment and fisheries, "for a discussion and visual presentation of The Noah's Ark Project, the largest movement of animals in the world." Van Hoven would not be there, but I didn't want to miss it, and together with a handful of press, assorted dignitaries from the Angolan embassy, and a few oil company executives, I attended the late afternoon event. It unfolded predictably; the canapés were snapped up by staffers, cards were exchanged, a few photographs were taken of the attractive, smiling First Lady in her colorful Angolan dress standing with various officials, and we gathered in an adjoining meeting room to listen to speeches.

The presentation was familiar—I'd heard it all before from van Hoven. The first shipment of animals, now scheduled for September 30, was billed as "the largest and most unique operation of its kind ever mounted, a modern Noah's Ark of giant transport planes and great ocean-going barges, bringing animals back in breeding pairs—two by two—to restock a land destroyed by war." A ribbon-cutting ceremony involving dos Santos was in the works. I looked at the five-year draft budget handed out: $13 million plus, including $2 million for the capture and relocation of five hundred elephants and another $2 million for thirteen more species. The concluding pitch seemed to be aimed at the oil companies: get credit by getting on board now. As the audience filed out, I found myself behind two oil company executives conferring quietly; the key word I overheard was "premature." I paused to pick up a couple of the glossy Kissama Foundation press packets showing a resplendent giant sable on the cover.

THE NEXT DAY I had a breakfast meeting with Jorge Alicerces Valentim, Angola's minister of hotels and tourism, at the Courtyard Marriot in Washington. He was dark-complexioned, heavyset, and medium height, had close-cropped, just-graying hair, and wore gold-rimmed glasses and a light beige suit. His English was fluent, as I knew it would be. Valentim is an ex–UNITA man, a veteran of the movement from its early days who went to university in Belgium and later joined Savimbi in the field. Bridgland described him as having a "manic" quality. He was accused of being responsible for summary executions in Lobito after independence—a charge he has long denied—but later rose to become Savimbi's information minister, adept at modulating his rhetoric to suit the political needs of the moment.

Valentim helped represent UNITA's side in the negotiations over the 1994 accords. Hare remembered him as "loquacious, even strident" at the meetings, but "constructive and creative" in private. He, along with others in the UNITA leadership, including Abel Chivukuvuku, General Ben-Ben, Jakka Jamba, N'zau Puna, and Eugenio Manuvakola, joined the national unity government. When Savimbi's return to military action forced UNITA parliamentarians to sever relations in order to stay in the government, Valentim was one of the leaders of the break. Now the former fiery revolutionary used his eloquence as an enthusiastic booster of tourism—not an easy job in one of the least likely vacation spots on the globe.

Valentim warmed to the subject of ecotourism. To him, it was a key element in the new effort to diversify the economy. "You can't rely on petro dollars," he said. "A country that does that thinks it's rich, but it gets poorer as it sinks into debt buying foreign goods." He stressed the importance of "thinking past the war," and thought the Kissama Foundation's Operation Noah's Ark one of the initiatives that was helping to do just that. It bothered him that Angolans who could afford to take vacations went to South Africa or Portugal. "They don't experience their own country," he lamented. But the rehabilitation of parks would keep tourist spending inside the country, as well as make Angolans realize that they didn't have to escape their borders to find scenery and enjoy nature. It also distressed him that most children in Angola had never seen some of the country's indigenous animals; they had lost contact with their heritage, and he wanted "to bring back that experience for them."

A few days before I came to Washington, UNITA had announced on its website that it controlled Malange Province, and thus was in charge of Cangandala Park, where, the communiqué pointedly remarked, one could find the especially rare *palanca preta gigante*. I asked Valentim what he could tell me about rebel control over the giant sable. "There was a tradition among the local people that it was sacred," he said. "UNITA always respected that tradition. Any guerrilla army must respect local traditions if it is to gain support from the people." Did UNITA have a specific policy against shooting it? He smiled at the word "policy." There was nothing that formal, he explained. "It was just a decision. That's how we did things then." Valentim recalled that sometime in the 1980s there were discussions with Savimbi in Jamba on utilizing wildlife. It was concluded that "any animal could be hunted but the *palanca negra*," he told me. It would have been "antipatriotic" to let it be harmed. "It had become a national symbol and no one who hoped to lead Angola could have allowed that to happen."

What did he think of Savimbi's prospects now? Valentim sighed. "People say he has all this war matériel. But he has no cause left but himself." He ticked off UNITA's former causes: fighting the Portuguese, fighting the Cubans and Soviets, fighting for multiparty democracy. "But the government took all these causes away," he said. UNITA received ministerial posts, seats in the national assembly, got control of local administrations, and the like. Savimbi even got special status, rights, and privileges written into law, and a personal bodyguard of four hundred men. "And even that wasn't good enough!" Valentim threw his hands in the air. "He wants all the power. But that is not enough of a cause—and it takes a great cause to motivate a soldier." He leaned forward on the table. "You can't win a war with matériel but you can win a war with a powerful political message. We're doing that by keeping democracy open while we fight the war." He was proud of the fact that the First Lady asked him, an opposition party member, to be part of her delegation to Washington; it sent a strong message, he felt, that Angola was a functioning democracy.

I mentioned that Savimbi didn't seem to have any of his old comrades around him now. Valentim explained that Savimbi got rid of those who had been with him the longest. "They know too much," he said quietly.

His tea finally came. Valentim picked up a packet from the sugar bowl and frowned. A waitress waddled slowly past with a carafe of decaf. "Don't you have proper sugar?" he asked, and wiggled the saccharin packet in the air to demonstrate the weak, sifty little sound its contents made.

"Hon," she sighed, "that's all we got."

He shrugged. For a man who had traded camouflage fatigues for a business suit and bush battles for boardroom debates, it was a minor irritation.

MARIA DE FÁTIMA Domingas Monteiro Jardim agreed to meet with me briefly at the Angolan embassy. She was an engaging, full-figured woman with an easy smile, dressed in a black skirt and colorful blouse. Jardim obtained a degree in biology from the University of Lisbon in 1974, and after independence joined the fisheries ministry, becoming *ministra* in 1991. Since January, when dos Santos reshuffled the ministries, her portfolio had included the environment. She proved enthusiastic about the Kissama Foundation, assuring me that it could work within the framework of the government's environmental policies, implementing and realizing its environmental goals. (I was getting the picture that the foundation's independence from the underfunded, understaffed environment ministry was a plus, as far as the government was concerned; it put no strain on limited resources.)

And what did the *palanca preta gigante* mean to the Angolan people? I pulled out a copy of a photograph of the animal that showed a bull coyly looking over his shoulder, his horns arched over his hindquarters. Jardim had been talking to me in English, occasionally clarifying a point in Portuguese with a staffer. Now she studied the picture intently and slipped into heartfelt Portuguese, underscored with gestures, and the staff translator had difficulty keeping up and finding English phraseology that didn't sound overwrought. But I understood that Jardim was making it clear that Angolans are passionate about their national animal. Her hands framed the image as she spoke of how the *palanca negra* was a symbol of her country's people and culture, its very profile signifying strength, force, power, dignity. It stood for the wealth of Angola's wildlife. It was unique. I was a bit surprised by the strength of her reaction; maybe I shouldn't have been.

ON THE TRAIN back to New York that afternoon I read through the Kissama Foundation press kit. It was a typical slick mix of plans and promises, hard facts and hot air. One of the releases proclaimed "a mission of this scale has not been undertaken before nor may it ever be undertaken again." I wondered if van Hoven had ever vetted the copy, which located Kruger Park (from which elephants were to be obtained) on the west coast of Africa, listed "water buffaloes" among the species to be reintroduced to Quiçama, and claimed—disturbingly—that "money is needed to capture wildlife still present in Angola, such as red buffaloes, elands, and giant sables," and that habitat suitability for giant sable introductions into Quiçama "must be assessed." But clearly the fat packet was aimed primarily at getting the attention of media and potential donors; most of what was being proposed, such as a "luxury lodge of world-class standards" in Quiçama or a television documentary for worldwide distribution, would require substantial sums. Still, money could materialize.

I wondered what Richard Estes would think about all this. I reached him in New Hampshire the next day by phone. He'd returned several days before from Tanzania, and was eager to hear what I'd learned in Washington. He seemed resigned to the eventual introduction of animals to Quiçama, despite his concern that the project would not meet IUCN guidelines on environmental integrity in national parks. "But the red line," he said, "is moving the giant sable." De Almeida's dismissal had been a dismaying development for him, but I gave him Maria de Fátima Jardim's contact details and said I'd mail him an extra copy of the Kissama press kit.

It may have been a mistake for me to send it on. Estes E-mailed me (and Brian Huntley) a couple of days later.

"Jesus! I've never read such garbage as the description of the Noah's Ark project," he wrote. "There's actually going to be a 1.5 hour documentary wildlife special about it? The proposal by the Kissama Foundation to capture giant sable for exhibition in Quiçama NP, despite all the drawbacks pointed out by the ASG, is just one of the ecological outrages in their program. To think that Van Hoven & co. may be given responsibility for all of Angola's wildlife preserves makes me shudder. The question is, what can be done to wake up the international conservation community and through them convince the Angola Ministry of the Environment that introducing exotic species into national parks violates all accepted international standards? We've got to get the IUCN and WWF involved."

Estes sounded the alarm by firing off E-mails to his contacts at both conservation organizations, but the reaction from IUCN headquarters in Switzerland was to turn it back to Estes, with the suggestion that he write a letter to Minister Jardim, making reference to "The IUCN Position Statement on Translocation of Living Organisms: Introductions, Reintroductions and Re-Stocking" and "IUCN Guidelines for the Prevention of Biodiversity Loss Due to Biological Invasion"—hardly the response that could check the Kissama Foundation's plans. But Huntley, having been alerted, would soon take matters into his own hands.

On September 7 Wouter van Hoven wrote Gen. Luis Faceira, head of the Angolan army and a Kissama board member, to say that he'd had no reply to his letter inquiring about the planned September 9 meeting in Luanda; since he was presumably busy with military matters, he'd postpone his visit. This would force him to put off the first shipment of animals planned for the end of September, he added, but considering the war situation, a delay would be prudent. Van Hoven forwarded a copy of it to me, explaining in a follow-up conversation that he'd received information from reliable intelligence sources that the civil war was moving in the direction of Luanda and a "culmination." Although work would proceed on fencing, training, roads, and the like, he intended to put off the delivery of animals until he could be more assured of their safety. "We're the custodians of these animals," he said. "We must guarantee their well-being."

That same day Estes and I received an E-mail from Huntley: "So, it seems my compatriots are still trying to raise funds to set up a zoo in Quiçama. What a sorry story—adding to the confusion and exploitation of the desperate situation in the country." Estes's heated letter had relit Huntley's fuse, and he was about to explode again. Several days later, he sent an acid, antagonistic letter to van Hoven, with a copy to Estes and several other prominent conservationists. "My 30 years of close association with Angola is filled with knowledge of many hare-brained schemes to 'rescue' the giant sable—sometimes even from well-meaning conservationists. I have recently been approached again, by international agencies, for an opinion on a new 'Noah's Ark' scheme. Once again, some organization (Kissama Foundation?) talks of plans to 're-introduce' kudu, zebra, giraffe, sable, rhino, etc., to Quiçama." He informed van Hoven that "such animals have never been recorded from Quiçama." He feigned ignorance of the foundation. "It has been hinted that you are leading this scheme, and that a fund-raising meeting was recently held in Washington, D.C. This latest rumor may be unfounded. I would find it difficult to believe that a South African authority on wildlife management" would "undertake or support or in any way be associated with a scheme that goes so clearly against international best-practice in African wildlife management." Huntley asked for confirmation that van Hoven had "nothing to do with this," or if he did, and felt that "all components of the proposal are sound and professionally defensible," Huntley wanted a copy so that he could "refute suggestions that South Africans are giving Angolan colleagues poor or misleading advice."

I'd E-mailed van Hoven earlier to ask if he had plans to go to Angola in October; if so, I wanted to accompany him there. He E-mailed back to say he'd try and arrange a visit that month; he was also faxing me a copy of a "rotten" letter he'd got from Brian Huntley. He asked if I had been feeding rumors to Huntley. Taken aback, I sent off a quick response to assure him I didn't deal in rumors. I reminded him that I had contacted a number of people, including Huntley, to ask about the giant sable, Angola, and various conservation efforts there, including Kissama's.

I got a copy of Huntley's letter from Estes as well. Estes, forgetting his own intemperate E-mail, was surprised at its incendiary tone. "Better put on your oven mitts before you handle this letter!" he warned; "I'd say it doesn't pay to get Brian riled." I called Estes and said that I was trying to stay neutral and above the fray. He told me, dryly, that I had "dipped my oar" into murky waters now, and that I couldn't pretend otherwise. He was right; my probing and questioning and sheer interest in the fate of the giant sable had already begun to shape the unfolding story, and now it had revived a bitter biological disagreement among the key players.

Fortunately, van Hoven's reply to Huntley's virtual declaration of war was surprisingly even-tempered. Van Hoven explained that in order to reintroduce wildlife into Quiçama, the first shipments of animals would be confined to a fenced-off, protected area in the north of the park. "A detailed management plan has been drawn up by the Centre for Wildlife

Management, University of Pretoria. How is it that you now claim to be unsure if the latter Centre is involved, when you in fact made some articles available to the research team when they asked you for it?" He assured Huntley that "the species which used to occur in the area are to be reintroduced," and that "the policy of the Kissama Foundation at this point is to oppose any form of 'rescue' for the Royal Sable Antelope (*Hippotragus niger variani*), but rather to assist in and encourage their further protection and management in the Malange Province." He asked Huntley to join the foundation's board, and added, "I would like to invite you, at my expense, to visit the area you call a 'zoo' and be a guest at a board meeting." He even suggested a date: "Would 20–24 Oct. 1999 be suitable?"

Estes was relieved at van Hoven's remarkably cool reply. "I must say that Wouter has made a reasoned and reasonable reply to your letter," he wrote Huntley two days later. "The news that plans to captive-breed the giant sable have been scrapped is particularly welcome. Please do take him up on his offers. If you become a Trustee, you can make sure this project will have minimal adverse effect on Quiçama." He reminded Huntley that he could always resign. "Wouter's invitation to visit Quiçama with him in October is a golden opportunity to see just what's going on. I do hope you can accept."

Estes's diplomatic encouragement might have helped moderate Huntley's stance toward Kissama. Huntley replied calmly to van Hoven's letter two days later, thanking him for his "clarification." To explain his original concerns, he quoted several of the misleading statements found in the Kissama press materials and said he was "glad to learn" that van Hoven agreed "that the giant sable should be conserved in its natural habitat." When he'd first been approached about the Kissama Foundation, he "was not prepared to join other than as a consultant." But in view of van Hoven's "clarification of the nature of the plans for Quiçama, and the assurance that exotic species will not be introduced," he wrote, "I would be pleased to accept your invitation to join the Board," and to accept his offer to come to Angola "should my schedule allow."

The biologists had reconciled—or so it seemed. Van Hoven suggested I could go out with him to Angola sometime during the second half of October. It would take me that much closer to the giant sable.

THE PALE, YELLOWISH tooth resting on soft white tissue in the clear plastic box looked like it could have been the relic of a saint. To some, it was just as precious; locked within it was a code that could be broken, revealing clues that might help solve the zoological puzzle surrounding the giant sable. *Hippotragus niger variani* specimens are hard to come by, and this one, marked ANSP 14322, was one of three teeth sent to Terry Robinson's lab from the Academy of Natural Sciences of Philadelphia some months before, the only ones he had been able to obtain in addition to the Curtis tooth. They were from skulls of specimens obtained on the 1929–30 Gray Expeditions; the first was from the splendid bull on display in the African Hall, collected by Gray himself near the Cuanza on the first expedition, the second was from a juvenile female collected a year later by H. T. Green. The tooth I was looking at was from another female collected then—curiously, the very one whose skull I sketched in the academy's storerooms the year before.

I had flown to South Africa in October 1999 to meet Wouter van Hoven, but purposely arrived in Pretoria a few days earlier to talk with several people, Robinson among them. I was apprehensive about what the molecular geneticist might uncover. Since he had been preoccupied with working out the details of relocating his laboratory to the University of Stellenbosch, he had only recently resumed work on the giant sable and had given the task of extracting the DNA to Bettine van Vuuren, a Ph.D. candidate in zoology. Robinson asked van Vuuren, a slim young woman with short, straight blonde hair, to walk me through the procedure. She took me to a stainless steel bench under a ventilation hood in the back of the laboratory, where I found a plastic box with the tooth, a small electric drill, and a clutter of tubes, trays, tweezers, and bottles of various chemical solutions.

Van Vuuren had already extracted the DNA from the Gray Expedition teeth several days before, using sterile techniques.

"When you extract DNA material from giant sable teeth," she said, "you need to know that what you have there is really giant sable, and not something else." As long as the provenance of the teeth was reliable, what else would it be? She explained that contamination of the samples was a serious concern. There's always "lots of DNA floating around," as she put it, not just human contamination from handling the specimens, but also mouse DNA that can be introduced by little rodents scurrying around the back rooms of museums and coming into contact with bones and skins. She took a number of precautions—washing the teeth in a weak acid bath, using sterile solutions, drill bits, and gloves, and working under an air filtration system—to reduce the risk of foreign DNA contaminating the samples, and, like an argument built on a faulty premise, invalidating the results that would follow. There were further checks at each step. "In the whole process of the extraction of the DNA, we build in a lot of what we call negative controls," she said. "I know then that if I do the amplification of the giant sable, that it is in fact giant sable that I've started off with, and not some other contaminant that was introduced from a dirty solution."

Van Vuuren pointed out the dot-sized hole she had drilled in #14322, and then showed me how it was done, demonstrating on an old kudu tooth. She turned on the noisy laminar flow hood and the rotary drill, and pushed the tiny .05mm bit with its minute burred tip into the bottom of the tooth to reach the root canal. The grinding noise reminded me of a dentist's slow-speed drill. "That little hole that I drilled here now, that's all that you actually need," she said, and agitated the bit delicately, just enough to loosen some of the softer material inside. It produced a tiny pinch of powdery dust that fell onto the small rectangle of aluminum foil she placed on the benchtop. But it was enough. She switched off the drill, picked up the foil, folded it into a V-shaped trough, and shook the powder into an Eppendorf tube, a clear plastic bullet-shaped container about an inch and a half long with a snap lid.

The rest of the procedure became rather involved. She explained that the methods used for DNA extractions from seventy-year-old museum samples are basically the same as the ones used on fresh material; the main thing was that many of the steps are prolonged. "If I were doing it with fresh material, I'd start in the morning and I'd have my DNA by the afternoon," she said, but this would take days. The giant sable tooth dust had already been soaked overnight in a sterile solution to break down the tooth enamel and then spun in a centrifuge for five minutes (at 12,000 g's) to remove the solution and reduce the dust to a hard pellet. After that it went into an extraction buffer. "What that does is basically break up the cell, to allow the DNA inside the nucleus to actually come out," she said.

My notes became sketchier as the explanation turned technical. I scribbled down a complicated series of steps, things like adding proteinase K to remove most of the protein from the DNA solution before it was incubated in an oven at 55–65 degrees Centigrade then adding a dash of potent-smelling phenol chloroform before giving it another spin or two in the centrifuge and a bath in ice-cold ethanol—the laboratory recipe was over my head, although the purpose was plain enough. By the time the giant sable tooth dust had been shaken, stirred, whirled, heated, and cooled, the deoxyribonucleic acid, or DNA, will have been separated out and made ready for analysis.

To make useful comparisons, however, requires sequencing. DNA is composed of four chemical subunits, or bases, the order of which provides coded instructions for everything the cell does; sequencing decodes the order of the bases along the DNA strand. Researchers amplify matching sections of DNA from individual specimens within an animal species or subspecies for comparison, and then use computerized techniques to align matching sections to determine their degree of relatedness. In the end, what could be extracted from the teeth of the Gray Expeditions would be expressed as impressively long strings of symbols on a computer monitor that should, hopefully, yield a few answers.

But I was going to have to wait for them. The sequencing had to be put off for a while, Robinson told me over lunch. The movers were coming in ten days and he had to pack for his relocation to the University of Stellenbosch. But he would be taking Matthee, van Vuuren, and the giant sable teeth with him.

THE FRONT DESK called and said Kobus du Toit's car was being buzzed through the gates at my guest house in Pretoria. He'd come that morning to drive me out to his game ranch and show me an animal that no one else but he and his partner knew about; he was willing to let me see it because I'd know what it meant.

Since first meeting at Terry Robinson's lab the year before, we had seen each other again at Jaco Ackermann's the previous December. Back then we talked mostly about the Tuli elephants, some thirty animals that South African game dealer Riccardo Ghiazza bought from Botswana's overpopulated Tuli Reserve in August 1998 to train and sell to zoos and circuses as an alternative to starvation or being culled. Ghiazza, who once sold elephants to pop star Michael Jackson for his private menagerie, became a center of controversy when secretly taped videos of cruel treatment of baby elephants in his care were shown on television, provoking an international outcry. Animal rights activists and animal welfare organizations, schoolchildren, and the Spice Girls alike implored President Nelson Mandela to intervene. After a protracted court case, the elephants eventually ended up in the custody of the South African SPCA. Du Toit had seemed embarrassed by the whole thing. A wildlife veterinarian by training, he handled game translocations for a variety of clients and had captured the Tuli elephants for Ghiazza. He agreed with van Hoven, who told me the footage of baby elephants being "trained" was appalling. But du Toit wondered about the larger issue of what could be done with excess elephants. "Personally, I think I'd rather be put to work than put to death," he confided. "What about you?" Months later, I was still thinking about that question.

We shook hands in the driveway and I climbed into the passenger side of du Toit's little cream-colored Nissan *bakkie*. When I picked up a windbreaker on the seat to make room for my camera bag, I uncovered a stainless steel .357 magnum revolver. He shrugged, and said apologetically, "We have a terrible crime problem in this country." I covered it back up. We drove several hours under cloudy skies to Hoedspruit, a small town and airfield near the western edge of Kruger and the game reserves that border it. He owns a game farm nearby with a partner, Chris Mostert, who has his own adjoining game business and collaborates with du Toit on wildlife capture operations.

At Mostert's farm we found him supervising the final stages of construction of steel and concrete corrals for Cape buffalo, although by the look of their massive steel piping and thick walls, they could handle rhino as well. Mostert, a big, barrel-chested man in olive green shorts, shirt, and bill cap, took us for a brief tour of the two game farms in his *bakkie*. We drove out along dirt tracks lined with game fencing and pulled into another compound to look over a herd of glowering Cape buffalo in a pen, many of them with thick, sweeping, heavy horns, and then rolled through acres of bush to catch a glimpse of a colossal white rhino sporting a horn that looked a yard long. Past another farm, owned by Mostert's father, I was startled by the sight of young white lions that looked like stone statuary come to life. But that was all a buildup to the real prize, and as we lumbered in low gear toward another large paddock, du Toit explained that he and Mostert had set up a specialized operation to breed endangered animals, largely financed from the profits of breeding disease-free buffalo.

They now had thirty-two Livingstone's eland, forty-odd nyala, and nine sable. It was the sable we were heading for, and after passing through a gate, we slowed to a crawl and rolled through thick grass and around clumps of low bushy trees before encountering a half-dozen chestnut-colored sable cows, lying at rest in the shade. Some of them got up to watch us. Mostert steered us around several more trees, and turned off his engine when we saw a young jet black bull with a quarter-circle of horn. He was fat and sleek and had perfect *variani* face markings—short splashes of white under his eyes. He watched us curiously as I snapped some photos, then he turned to nip at his shoulder. He was four years old, du Toit said, and had forty-inch horns; he had kept quiet about the animal, but he wanted me to see it.

I knew that du Toit had obtained a Zambian bull from Sable Ranch; he confirmed it, but remained cagey about the details of the transaction. He and Mostert were stock breeders, selling to other game farmers who wanted to improve their herds. They were especially interested in ultrascarce rarities like the bongo, Lord Derby's eland—and the giant sable. He explained that if the ancestry of the Angolan subspecies could be traced to the Zambian population—which after all, was the only likely story—then the *variani* characteristics (large horns, lack of a cheek stripe) that show up here and there in the mother population could be bred for, using the same careful selection techniques as cattle breeders. He could have virtual "giants," in several generations; in effect, fast-forwarding an evolutionary process that took millennia the first time around.

Correct face markings were one thing—I was looking at a perfect example in the animal in front of the vehicle—but what about horn length? "Well, it might be a function of genetics and environmental factors," he suggested, arguing that by giving a bull the right food, all the inherent maximum potential for horn growth could be realized. "He's young," du Toit said, gesturing out the car window. "Really big bulls are probably eight to twelve years old."

But what was the point of going to all the trouble of re-creating the giant sable, when the real thing was still there in Angola? "I cannot see how the animal survived all those wars," du Toit said. Even if some remained now, he was sure there wouldn't be any left in twenty years' time. "But we'll have a hundred." He turned to me and smiled. "It's our pension plan." Mostert nodded. I pulled out my binoculars and studied the young bull. His fur was wonderfully black and looked glossy, except for two symmetrical patches on his chest where the fur was so soft it looked matte. His underbelly was snowy white. He was in immaculate condition.

Of course, breeding Zambian sable for *variani* traits would be possible but close selection could lead to problems such as enhanced gene frequencies that lead to congenital disease (like hip dysplasia in German shepherds). One could never replicate the original, right down to every gene. Still, if it looked like a giant sable, and walked like a giant sable, and sparred and defecated and rutted and bellowed like a giant sable—then where would the difference lie? It would be a classic case of the identity of indiscernables, and in all the ways that counted—the majestic form, the noble carriage, the proud profile—the Zambian stand-in would be just as good as the Angolan original. Or would it?

Back at the farm compound, we looked at two younger sable males that were being kept in a separate pen away from the older bull to prevent them from scrapping with him. Their face markings weren't quite pure *variani*. They stood facing away from each other, like bookends, and I did a quick sketch while they held their pose. Then the one on the right twitched, snapped his tail like a fly whisk, and stamped his forefoot; the one on the left flicked out his pink tongue, shook his head from side to side by pivoting it from his shoulders, and urinated vigorously. I wondered what they would look like in six or eight years.

Behind Mostert's house was a feeding paddock, and as dusk gathered, the three of us leaned on the railing and drank beer and watched the antelopes come in to feed from the hay troughs, the way farmers have always looked out over their fields and herds at the end of the working day. The first antelopes to arrive were the small, lightly striped, lyratehorned nyalas, their silhouettes outlined by shaggy fringe, taking their mincing steps, as if on tiptoes. The stately Livingstone's elands were next, heavy yet graceful, the mature bulls' approach announced by the curious clicking—really a kind of loud knuckle-cracking—that their walk produces. They headed right for the hay and scooped it up, using their horns like pitchforks, leaving a wreath of straw on their heads. They reminded me of the beautiful Brahman cattle depicted in Indian paintings, but their heads were handsomer, and the old bulls' coats were slate blue, with just a hint of stripes, like several lightly traced chalk marks on their withers and ribs. It was an entrancing pastoral scene, heightened by the golden glow the low African sun cast over the field and Mostert's little blonde girls collecting guava leaves around the yard to feed through the fence to the gentle antelopes. In the distance I could hear a low rumbling.

"It's the Kruger lions," Mostert told me. The Timbavati Reserve was not far away, and there are no barriers between it and the park, which meant the fence we drove past earlier in the day was the last one between us and Mozambique.

As night fell, Mostert fired up the *braai* and his wife brought out a tray of meat. He threw a sausage the size of a fireplace log on the grill and buttressed it with yet more slabs of beef. Appetites sharpened, we heaped our plates, poured ourselves glasses of sturdy South African Pinotage, and gathered inside around the television. A rerun of *Baywatch* was on, and Mostert asked me if American women really looked like the young mammals on the show. I told him they were a rare California subspecies. After dinner he popped in a videotape to show me the equipment he had designed for elephant translocations. Once the elephant was darted from a helicopter and went down, a special mat and crane were used to slide the drugged animal up onto the waiting truck with minimal handling, making the move decidedly less traumatic for the huge creatures.

Du Toit and I spent the night at Mostert's. Although I didn't hear the lions anymore, I had trouble getting to sleep. Thinking of the big cats reminded me of a project already underway to breed back the Barbary lion, an extinct race last found in the Atlas Mountains of Morocco. The plan was to selectively breed zoo lions with partial Barbary ancestry and eventually resurrect the subspecies from the dead. I stared into the dark. "If it can be done for the Barbary lion," I thought, "it can be done for the giant sable."

THE NEWS REPORTS I'd read on Angola before I left for Africa hadn't been particularly encouraging. At the beginning of August 1999 the World Food Programme reported 160,000 people in Malange were completely dependent on whatever aid could be flown in. Half the children under five in the city were malnourished. It was hard to look at the photographs of the tiny wide-eyed stick figures with their shrunken buttocks, their hair frighteningly orange—a sign of kwashiorkor caused by lack of protein. The population of Malange, along with those of government-held Cuito and Huambo, had been swollen by rural Angolans fleeing the renewed conflict, but sporadic attacks by UNITA made arrivals of badly needed relief shipments unpredictable. The government's military offensive had been talked about for months, but only now had begun to win back territory from UNITA. By the end of the month, the Central Committee of the MPLA was urging the government to "annihilate the enemies of peace and democracy once and for all."

In early September UNITA continued to shell Malange, Cuito, and Huambo dismayingly close to the western borders of the giant sable reserves. Heavy fighting even broke out in Cangandala, south of Malange, forcing UNITA troops back to their central highland strongholds. Troops on both sides had to be crisscrossing the animals' territory. At the end of the month, word broke that the government had captured Bailundo from UNITA. Gen. Luis Faceira told journalists that the army had the situation there under control, but the government itself had no immediate comment. UNITA acknowledged fierce fighting in several regions of the country, but at first denied that Bailundo, the traditional seat of the Ovimbundu, who had always been the rebel movement's main supporters, had fallen into government hands.

I was only going to Luanda and the park a few miles to the south— far away from the war zone and land-mined roads—but after reading the U.S. State Department's warning against travel to Angola, I decided it would be a good idea to stick close to van Hoven. According to the consular information sheet, travel there "remains unsafe due to bandit attacks, undisciplined police and military personnel, sporadic high-intensity military actions," and the like. Foreign nationals "are subject to arbitrary detention"; soldiers and police are "unpredictable," and "frequently participate in shakedowns, muggings, car-jackings and murders." That travel outside Luanda was "inadvisable" seemed superfluous to add. On arrival in Pretoria, I found out UNITA guerrillas had made hit-and-run attacks on the towns of Catete and Caxito, each no more than thirty miles from Luanda.

I met van Hoven at his office in the Centre for Wildlife Management, a small low building close to the University of Pretoria's playing fields. He waved me into a chair in front of his desk while he finished up a call. He looked a bit thinner and grayer than the last time I had seen him, but he hadn't slowed down a bit. In fact, he now had a wire dangling from an earplug to free up another hand while talking on his cell phone, which seemed to ring every ten minutes or so. He was busy arranging the sale and shipment of animals to China for a safari park near Beijing, and exploring the possibility of setting up a wildlife foundation along the lines of Kissama for Dindar Park in Sudan. While he answered a second call, he handed me a faxed copy of a letter he'd just received from Fátima Jardim in Luanda. At his urging, she'd written to her ministerial counterpart in Botswana to ask him to consider the donation of three hundred elephants from the excess population in Chobe Park to aid in Angola's restocking effort of Quiçama. He finished off his call and said that there was a hitch: after the scandal of the Tuli elephants, Botswana was touchy on the subject of donating its pachyderms. "I've been told I might have to get certain animal welfare groups to approve this," he said, "before Botswana would go through with it." He was worried about setting the precedent of allowing animal rights groups to "vet" conservation projects—it would turn them into de facto regulatory agencies passing on the validity of wildlife work.

Talk of projects reminded him that he had a student waiting in the hall who needed to talk to him about his third-year courses. While he advised the student, I looked at his bulletin board. There were maps and charts and an 8 × 10 enlargement of a photograph he took in Luanda. It showed a destitute child standing next to a crumbling hovel against the skyline of the capital and the bay beyond. The student left and van Hoven joined me and put his finger on the photo. "This child lives in trash and eats garbage and knows nothing else. Can you imagine what the impact of seeing animals in Quiçama could mean to him?" He expanded on one of his favorite themes, the bussing of schoolchildren from Luanda to a restocked Quiçama so they could not only encounter their country's wild-life heritage but see something that would excite them and open their imaginations.

I asked what eye-opening things he had planned for our trip. We would fly out tomorrow afternoon, he said, arrive at night, stay over at the Shell Oil compound, then visit the park the next day to check the progress of the fence. There would be a board meeting of the Kissama Foundation that evening. Although he had to return earlier than planned and would fly out the next morning, he'd made arrangements for me to stay on and would put me in good hands, someone who would not only take me around Luanda for a couple of days but would drive me to the airport: the foundation's treasurer.

"You can't plan too far ahead with these things," he reminded me.

I WOULD HAVE felt better about the Johannesburg-to-Luanda flight if the cabin attendant hadn't used masking tape to keep one of the overhead bins in business class shut. The 737 seemed a bit worse for wear, so I focused on the one outstanding feature of Linhas Aéreas de Angola (TAAG Angola Airlines): its orange and black circular logo, a stylized silhouette of the head of a giant sable. It was everywhere—the tail of the aircraft, the bars of soap in the toilet, even on the airsickness bags.

When I poked at my tray of heavy airline food, van Hoven joked that I better eat it all—we were going to Angola. That led to a discussion of animal nutrition, van Hoven's area of specialization. He had long been intrigued by the chemical defenses of plants, which can be as effective an adaptation as thorns in keeping the plant from being eaten. "Look, if you're a plant and you want to survive in a land that's full of plant eaters, the best strategy is to taste lousy." Giraffe in the central district of Kruger Park consume twenty-seven different tree species, he explained, but the one whose leaves they eat the most of is a variety of acacia that is particularly low in tannin. "These critters select a diet not so much in what is protein-rich, but what is tannin-poor." So they are actively avoiding tannin in their diet? "Exactly," he said. Tannins not only taste bitter, but bind with stomach enzymes. "Excessive tannin," he said, "interferes with a browser's digestion."

But more than dietary conditions have to be met to ensure that a given animal will flourish in a particular area. Had I heard of the sitatunga, a splay-footed, spiral-horned, semiaquatic antelope? "Well, you take that sucker out of the Okavango Swamps and you put it in the Kalahari Desert, it can't survive. You dump the desert oryx in the swamps, it's not going to survive. So those are extreme things." But even subtle habitat changes can be important. He brought up the sable, which occurs naturally in the northeastern part of South Africa.

"Well, that's what they say is the number one habitat for those animals. But things have started changing there, and the biggest thing that's happened is that elephant disappeared off the scene when so much of it became private property. People didn't want elephants around. With that disappearance, bush encroachment took place. The density of trees increased, in some cases up to two thousand trees per hectare. And high tree density is not on the preferred list of sable antelopes. There were ranchers there who had problems," he said. "They contacted me to find out why their sable were not breeding well. It was obvious on the farms where they had zero or negative growth that the habitat had changed. Some of those guys had too many trees and too many other animals. Those are two things that sable don't like."

So, he summed up, if suitable habitat and dietary conditions for a certain species can be found in a given area, "there's no reason why that animal will not survive there." I saw where this line of argument was going. But even if animals could be moved to suitable habitat, if they hadn't occurred there naturally, it wouldn't be representative of the local environment, would it?

"You know it really wasn't my idea to bring giant sable to Quiçama," van Hoven said abruptly. "The Kissama Foundation's board thinks it would be a good idea because it would be a great tourist attraction, and attracting tourists is what we need." He'd already said he was opposed to translocating giant sable, so I figured he was letting me know that he was getting pressure the other way, too.

I tried to look at it from the board's point of view. They knew that lots of other exotic endangered species—pandas, mountain gorillas, snow leopards—were on exhibit in zoos. Why shouldn't Angolans derive some tangible benefits from their national animal, the way the Chinese turned their pandas into profitable pawns, while seeing to it that they were bred and fed and protected? On the other hand, if there were another population of giant sable in Quiçama, it might not seem as urgent to protect them from poaching or their historic range from encroachment. But van Hoven wasn't interested in looking at the giant sable, or any other animal, in a vacuum. To him, the *palanca negra* existed in a political context as well as a biological habitat. It was an Angolan animal and an Angolan responsibility, and its fate was theirs to decide.

Out my window, to the north of our route somewhere, were the giant sable reserves. But all I saw was cloud cover and my reflection in the double-thick glass. It was getting darker; the sun's rays were almost horizontal. Up to now we'd been cruising at 35,000 feet, and I started to feel our descent over Angola. The coastline was still visible in the growing darkness, and I thought I saw the silvery ribbon of the Cuanza just before we reached the lights of Luanda. It was night when we landed, and as the tires screeched on the rough runway the passengers broke out in applause and shouting, as if astonished the flight had made it. Van Hoven shook his head.

"They do that every damn time," he muttered.

Nine

Luanda & Quiçama

Desculpe, não compreendo. I am sorry I don't understand. I tried to review some phrase-book Portuguese as our plane taxied up to the terminal, but it was too little too late; the seminasalized diphthongs and gnashed consonants weren't sticking with me. In the harsh airport lighting I picked out a World Food Program jet and several military craft before we came to a stop and shuffled off the plane onto the waiting bus. Standing in the bottleneck of passport control I had an extended opportunity to study a leak in the ceiling and some dangling wires, but soon followed van Hoven through and found him in the baggage area shaking hands with a round-faced, dark Angolan in a white shirt and tie with tie clip, who beamed delightedly.

"Meet Dodo," van Hoven said. "He's our driver." I hoped his name was undeserved. His English was hardly better than my Portuguese, which limited our communication to body language supplemented by a few *palavras.*

Outside the terminal a motley, milling throng of young men was kept off the sidewalk by airport security. Out of the dark several youths rushed toward us eagerly, but backed off when two uniformed private guards stepped forward to greet us. There was some confusion about who was supposed to pick us up and where we were supposed to go, which initiated an animated, polyglot curbside conference. For a while, it sounded as if we were expected in Lobito, but that turned out to be another driver's name. Van Hoven sent Dodo off, and we rode in the guards' roomy van through the dimly lit slum streets of Luanda to Condominio de Belas, the Shell Oil compound on the city's outskirts.

Inside the compound's guarded gates was an apartment complex that looked like it had been transported from Boca Raton in its entirety, right down to the clipped grass, palm trees, and lawn furniture. There were curved streets and walkways, a clubhouse with a swimming pool, two-story tile-roofed buildings with verandas and soft lighting that accented the landscaping. It also had its own water supply and massive generators for electricity—even its own satellite TV and phone system, rendering it independent of Luanda's unreliable utilities and decidedly more attractive than local housing for oil company executives on a tour of duty in Angola. Van Hoven and I had a four-bedroom condo to rattle around in. It was a little surreal, but the air-conditioning was pleasant, and had the added virtue of rendering invading mosquitos from the malarial capital too somnolent to bite.

FRAMED IN THE backseat window, a wavering landscape of gouged and eroded red earth rushed past, punctuated here and there by clusters of collapsing shacks, torched car wrecks rusting by the roadside, unblinking, dust-covered children, and startling vistas of quiet bay and open ocean beyond. We were speeding south the next morning in a two-car convoy down the coastal road from the capital, one of the few stretches of recently repaved highway to Quiçama National Park.

Not much is left of Angola's parks and reserves other than their names and locations. Their shaded borders look impressive on the map, but now that the once vast herds of animals are gone, all they enclose are hosts of problems and a few faint hopes. Quiçama, the three-million-acre national park an hour's drive from Luanda, occupies a chunk of the Atlantic coast one-third larger than Yellowstone, providing plenty of scope for unfettered optimism. Free of land mines and presumably safe from antigovernment incursions, it is the obvious first candidate for resuscitation by the Kissama Foundation.

When the scarred scenery started repeating itself like a short, monotonous loop of video footage, I stopped taking photographs and sank back in the leather seat to listen to Cape Verde pop music pulsating on the CD player. Van Hoven was up ahead with Peter Osborne, head of Shell Angola and our host at Belas, in his Range Rover; I was in a plush air-conditioned

Nissan Patrol with Fillipe de Freitas, a lean, Luanda-based Portuguese South African who had been a translator for the SADF and had close connections with several Angolan military figures, which was the reason we were able to borrow Gen. Luis Faceira's vehicle with its Angolan driver and his sidekick.

The SUV braked abruptly. There was a police roadblock ahead, and we waited, engine idling. The drivers of the vehicles in front of us were being questioned. I rolled down the window and the air pushed in, hot and thick; the sky was gray and low with clouds. The rainy season had not yet begun.

We were waved through the roadblock—we had the right credentials—and continued south. I was eager to see the Cuanza, but the dark, deep river that the Portuguese used as a route to the interior, and whose southern bank forms the northern border of Quiçama Park, was hidden from the road, and it wouldn't be visible until we crossed it. The driver slowed again, this time to a dignified parade pace. The fortified military roadblock that guarded the narrow suspension bridge built in the early 1970s was coming into view, and it would be unwise to rattle the heavily armed soldiers by rushing up precipitously. Van Hoven once tried to show a visitor Quiçama Park from the river but made the mistake of racing his boat toward the bridge. The soldiers opened fire, making the excursion more exciting than originally planned. Now he avoids investigating the park from the water, at least near the strategic crossing.

I started to raise my camera, but de Freitas pushed it down and repeated a well-worn joke. Question: What do you call an African boy with an AK-47? Answer: *Sir!* The soldiers gave us the once-over, and we drove over the span—I got a momentary look at a wide river between two jungly banks—and passed a manned .50-caliber machine gun emplacement on the other side.

A few miles south of the bridge the paved road runs through a varied landscape of grassy swamps and dry, eroded coastal badlands. We turned off onto an unmarked dirt road and pushed on into the top end of the park in low gear, bumping along the track that cuts through the stunted scrub bush and raising billows of choking red dust. When we paused, it was eerily silent; once thick with elephants and other game, there was now no sign of wildlife, not even birds. Solitary baobab trees, their twisted branches thrust up as if in resignation, stood watch under a leaden sky. Apparently, anything bigger than a rat had been shot out years ago to feed the coffers of whatever side, provide meals for soldiers or starving locals, or simply serve as target practice.

At the fence we climbed out of the cars to take a close look. I walked over and joined van Hoven and Peter Osborne, a tall, genial, black-haired Irishman. We should all have been in shorts instead of slacks and golf shirts—it was midday and already 97 degrees Fahrenheit. Depending on the shifting cloud cover, the light alternated between blindingly bright and shadowlessly diffuse. Van Hoven inspected the barrier with Osborne. A twenty-foot-wide swath on each side of the line had been bulldozed clear of bush and trees, and the soft, red-brown earth showed every footprint and outlines of dropped tools. I traced a tentative finger along the silvery strands of the as-yet-unelectrified boundary. The eight-foot-high metal fence looked absurdly delicate—slim upright rods holding a wide-spaced grid of twenty-seven bright thin wires, only five of them electrified—but the 8,000 volts it would carry would be sufficient to deter anything living, short of an enraged elephant going full tilt. When complete, it would be twenty-two kilometers long, over thirteen miles, slashing straight across the bush to cut off a huge loop of the Cuanza, creating, with the barrier of the river, a roughly fifteen-thousand-acre park within the northern tip of the larger one. "It's the most land for the least fence," van Hoven said, and at $6 or so a meter, total length is a prime consideration. Only the ends where the fence met the river remained unfinished, but work had been agonizingly slow in the stultifying heat, and it wasn't even summer yet.

Van Hoven wanted to see how things were progressing at the western end, so we followed the line of posts down to where a South African game fence firm and a gang of Angolan workers were clearing brush at the riverbank and digging holes to sink the fence supports into concrete. The sandy-haired head of the crew was sensibly dressed in shorts and sneakers. He had the deepest tan I'd ever seen on a Caucasian—his back was nearly the color of mahogany. Van Hoven listened to a list of various problems, such as the difficulty of extending the fence across boggy ground, which can be overcome, and the fact that the workers can't take the heat, about which nothing can be done. In fact, they had stopped working altogether and were gathering palm fronds to make temporary sun shades for their midday break. But if all went well—which was a big if—there were some three weeks of labor left to finish the fence.

Then van Hoven wanted to visit the eastern end of the fence, so we climbed back in the cars and followed the posts the other way. He was annoyed to see that creepers and vines had already filigreed the wires in some spots, which can cause shorts when the system is operational. It was a typical problem: decisions made in Pretoria, or for that matter, Luanda, failed to be implemented at the work site. I hadn't realized we had been slowly climbing, but as we stopped at the last fence post, an extraordinary view spread out before us when we walked on to the raw, red-earth edge of the hillside.

Below us the blue Cuanza River split and coiled across a green, marshy plain, curving back on itself in oxbow fashion. Plumes of smoke from bush fires rose in the middistance. Over the far gray horizon, hundreds of miles down that same river, were the lands of the giant sable, but van Hoven was focused on what the future would bring to this spot. He gestured like an impresario toward the vast arena of the Cuanza floodplain and invited us to see elephants splashing in the river, antelopes darting through the forest, predators pouncing. . . . Well, not predators in the fenced section, he cautioned. The herds would have to be established first and then released into the park itself before any large carnivores would be needed to keep the herbivores in balance.

To inspect the terrain at the foot of the hill, we drove down a steep, bumpy switchback, parked, and then climbed past an immense bulldozer that was stalled under spiky euphorbia trees whose sap is caustic enough to cause blindness. Van Hoven pushed on into the bush—there was no fear of running into anything large in this empty landscape—and we all followed, collecting dozens of thorn scratches and clinging, thistlelike seeds in the process. The edge of the marsh presented a problem. How could the fence be anchored in this spongy vegetation? There were plenty of ideas, but no obvious solutions.

"We'll organize something," van Hoven said confidently.

We took a break at Caua, the old Portuguese tourist camp on the hillside above, just inside the fenced area. It looked largely dilapidated as we drove up, but van Hoven envisioned it as it would be once the *rondavel* huts were renovated, and waved grandly in the direction of the river where excursion boats would ply the waters with hordes of tourists. The workers living in the surrounding squalid housing watched us curiously from a distance. Osborne had wisely brought along a cooler of beer and soft drinks. As we dragged some plastic chairs under the shade trees in the center of the compound, two small chimpanzees shuffled up, a male and a female, clinging to each other like forlorn orphans. In fact, they were, having been dropped off several weeks before by Gen. Luis Faceira. His troops in Cabinda picked them up following armed clashes with the tiny, largely ignored separatist guerrilla group that has fought unsuccessfully in that enclave for years. The little apes had become the camp's mascots. The male pursued van Hoven, while the knee-high female, grinning toothily, dragged her florid rear in the dust, sidled over to me, and pursed her lips as if to hoot or coo; then she shyly slid her leathery little hand inside mine and hung on like a wide-eyed toddler.

"She's a pickpocket," van Hoven warned me.

He shared part of his sandwich with the male, but had to fend off the chimp's roundhouse swipes at his beer. Foiled in his efforts, the chimp screeched and flailed in frustration. The crew boss warned us not to give him any beer, or he'd climb up in the trees and try to piss on us. Eventually both primates made complete pests of themselves and when they got shooed off, retreated to the branches above, where the male chimp threw handfuls of leaves at us in disgust.

It was time to push on. I switched cars to talk with Peter Osborne. He'd been the head of Shell's Angola operations for less than two years, but he knew the country well. Right out of university, he had spent three years in the early 1970s prospecting for De Beers, traveling throughout the colony and panning for diamonds in river gravels, before it all fell apart. "I've seen it from top to bottom, east to west," he said. In remote areas, he sometimes had up to two hundred workers with him, and has vivid memories of some of the extraordinary things he saw, including a twenty-seven-foot python that had strangled and swallowed a man. "We cut it open, and there he was. I have pictures to prove it," he assured me.

I told him I'd like to see them sometime, but not right after a meal.

Eventually Osborne became disillusioned with the diamond business and joined Shell as a petroleum engineer. In 1997 he had a chance to return to Angola with the company, and took it. Shell had filling stations in Angola in the 1950s but lost them all after independence and only returned to the country in 1992. Although Royal Dutch Shell is a global giant with substantial African investments, it hasn't had much success in Angola—several of the offshore oil license blocks it developed haven't panned out. But Block 18, developed with BP Amoco, looked promising. Osborne hoped so; Shell had already invested $240 million in Angola. He believed the potential was there. "Angola," he said, "could be a new Nigeria." Angolan oil is attractive because it's highly desirable light sweet crude; it's also offshore and thus not affected by civil unrest, the way oil production in Nigeria has been. Here, shuttle tankers take oil directly from platforms at sea to refineries or coastal oil terminals elsewhere.

Angola was producing some eight hundred thousand barrels of oil a day. At the then-current price of some $30 a barrel, a lot of money flowed along with the petroleum, providing up to 90 percent of government revenue. Some claim that only half this wealth ever makes it into the official budget—though there's no way of telling, short of a look at the closely kept accounts. But such skimming would help explain why there are so few government funds for social services. I asked Osborne about the issue of transparency in the oil industry. He said it was easy enough to figure how much goes into Angolan coffers, but what happens after that is "anybody's guess." Still, he was convinced that it was better to be involved in a country like Angola, with all its problems, than to "wash one's hands of it."

We barreled though the opening in the fence—the gates would go up last—and bumped back through the park, leaving plumes of clay-colored dust rising behind us to settle on and rouge the low bushes lining the track. Why did he arrange a donation of $400,000 from Shell to the Kissama Foundation? Osborne's response told me he'd answered this before: "First, nostalgia. I'd seen what Quiçama was like before war destroyed it," he said. "Second, our corporate policy requires us to be good citizens." He said there were some complaints that the money should have been given to the local hospital or some other worthy cause, but, he pointed out, Shell does that as well. What he saw was the opportunity to help Angolans in a different way, by contributing to the "touch of normality that's coming back to their lives; that's worth supporting, too." Their heritage, after all, "includes the flora and fauna they once had."

He had been captivated by van Hoven's grand plan after being given a river tour of the park, and asked how much money would be needed to make it happen. Van Hoven told him "lots." He smiled. "I've always said that Wouter was a visionary or a madman, or both. One of the things I like about him is that he doesn't act like an academic, even if he is one. He's not petty and his outlook isn't narrow." Osborne liked van Hoven's can-do attitude. "If you are going to change people, you've got to give them role models. And who better for the Angolans than Wouter van Hoven? As far as I can see, he's a principled man." I mentioned the conservation objections to bringing in nonnative species, the idea that the whole project may be premature, and that the involvement of the military raises eyebrows. Osborne wasn't impressed. "Single-issue people," he said, "can always sharpen the moral needle." But he'd been careful to ensure that Shell's contribution would be restricted to wildlife acquisition and transportation—in other words, Operation Noah's Ark.

We made a detour to visit the old colonial outpost at Catalangombe, a hilltop cluster of salmon-colored stucco barracks now used as the headquarters for the park's antipoaching patrol. There's no sneaking up on it; the site commands uninterrupted views of bleak open grassland and a few solitary baobabs. As we climbed toward it, it was clear that these buildings had also fallen into disrepair. In fact, pulling into the compound gave me the impression I had arrived on the set of a postapocalyptic film. Our new 4 × 4s looked distinctly out of place next to half-stripped military vehicles from long-ago battles baking in the sun among scattered tires and oil drums. Thin baby goats the size of cats emerged from doorless openings of crumbling tile-roofed buildings to bleat weakly, like faintly played kazoos. Then the soldiers stepped out, one by one.

It was an elite Special Forces unit, contributed by Gen. Antonio Faceira to assist the foundation, but they looked like bandits in their filthy military castoffs, torn T-shirts, loose shorts, bandoliers, and mixed headgear. Some were in boots, others sandals, the rest unshod. Their leader—at least the one doing most of the talking—wore a camouflage undershirt, baggy trousers, and a floppy hat. His dark eyes glittered under the brim and I noticed his oddly long fingernails were filed to sharp points, like claws. De Freitas did the translating, and van Hoven started shaking hands. I went to the car to retrieve my camera bag and contrived to take several surreptitious photos. An ancient truck, leaking oil, roared into the compound and a soldier back from patrol climbed out of the cab with his AK-47. I walked back to join the group, which had gone into the rear courtyard.

Van Hoven was carrying on a tense conversation with Peter Osborne, explaining that he had just asked the soldiers if they'd found any poachers. "Yes, a few, they said," he went on. "What were they doing? I asked. Cutting trees in the park and making charcoal. Well, that's not good, I said. When was that? Oh, a week ago. So what did you do? We put them in custody." Van Hoven pointed over his shoulder with his thumb at a chain-link and metal cage with a low tin roof attached to one of the buildings. He shook his head, and walked over to the soldiers guarding it. The door to the cage was open, and de Freitas was inside with the commander and a couple of his lieutenants. They were all talking heatedly. Van Hoven, Osborne, and I walked in. It smelled. Two men were standing in tattered filthy clothes, one of them old and grizzled, the other a bit younger, and behind them, huddling in a small recess in the corner of the cage, were seven women of various ages, several of them with babies. A little boy with a runny nose, his dark matted hair frosted with dust, stood close to one woman with an infant. He filled out his shirt so pitifully it might as well have been hanging on a nail. All of them were barefoot and dressed in rags and looked fearful, their eyes sliding around the cage. They were rural refugees, fleeing from the war and drawn to the relative safety of the park, hoping to make some charcoal to sell or exchange for food. On the bare concrete floor a puppy with a distended, wormy belly twitched in his sleep. But the place wasn't fit to be a dog pound.

We followed van Hoven outside.

"These people were caught making charcoal. They've been locked up for a week," he said, fuming. "This guy's keeping them here to show them off to his colonel when he gets back from carousing in town. Okay, these people shouldn't be cutting down trees in the park, but what's the point of locking them up? They could rot here before that guy gets back—"

Osborne cut in. "You're the president of the Kissama Foundation. Can't you tell them to let these people go?"

Van Hoven rolled his eyes; he knew it was not going to be easy to persuade their leader to let prime evidence of his usefulness walk away. We followed as he marched back inside the cage and conspired with de

Freitas in Afrikaans. A long and loud argument in Portuguese got under-way, punctuated by gestures, bluster, appeals to authority, and some shout-ing. The two male prisoners stood at attention, awaiting the outcome with what little dignity they could muster, but their cowed shoulders gave away their deepest fears. The frightened women clutched their babies tightly and rocked them to keep them quiet. Finally, the confrontation broke off abruptly and everyone but the prisoners walked slowly out of the cage. But the wire mesh door was left open.

What had happened? "He's letting them go," van Hoven said qui-etly as we returned to the vehicles. "They've got a long walk back to their village." I looked back. The charcoal burners were still standing there, as if they couldn't believe they'd been set free. We wound down the hill in our cars, and as we reached the bottom under the side of the barracks where the cage was, shouts and claps and cries of joy broke out. Above us I saw the freed prisoners cheering their liberators and waving, their arms thrust out through gaps in the chain-link cage.

We drove on. None of us felt like talking for a while. Finally, Osborne said, "I'm no longer moved by pictures of starving babies on television. I've seen too many, I suppose. But that shook me." He looked out the window. "It was hard to see those two men, standing there wondering what their fate was, how they would keep their families intact."

Van Hoven, who was riding with us in the front, was unusually quiet. Somehow we got on the subject of elephant conservation in Kruger—it was a welcome distraction—but eventually that conversation petered out. I braced myself to keep from whacking my head against the window as Osborne's driver negotiated ruts and dips and fishtailed around the soft, sandy curves. A lone vulture hovered in the empty gray sky. At the coastal road, we crossed over; van Hoven had one more thing to show us that afternoon.

There was no track on the dry clay pan on the ocean side of the road, but we picked up one in the palm-dotted bush. It took us across a grassy hillside to a derelict building—just a foundation and a few standing walls, all blasted and pockmarked with bullet holes. We got out and poked through the ruin, and took in the view of the sea in the distance framed by a couple of baobabs. It was the spot van Hoven had picked out for a luxury lodge. We were standing in a yard of rubble and old shell casings, but he saw it as an outdoor dining area, and in truth the view was spectacular, perfect for watching the sun set over the water. The rolling plain below to the north, he pointed out, was an obvious location for a golf course. Kruger has golf courses, and brags about it; why shouldn't Quiçama? From his point of view, the park needed a variety of tourist facilities, from ultraluxurious to basic camping, to appeal to a range of tastes and travel budgets in order to earn tourist dollars. I was leaning on one of the walls when I noticed that they weren't the remains of typical colonial architecture. This concrete shell was what was left of the half-built house and park headquarters Brian Huntley planned to live in before Angola collapsed into civil war. I decided there was nothing to be gained by bringing up this little historical detail and kicked idly at the broken masonry.

"There's a good view of the Atlantic just there," van Hoven said.

Looking at the sea sounded appealing. We drove a little farther on, and stopped partway up a faint track in the thick grass. Leaving the drivers with the cars, we climbed the rest of the way to a reddish, sandy hill sparsely covered with scattered brush. The footpath up the hill took us closer to the water's edge, where the slight protrusion of coastline had been savagely sea-gouged for thrusting out into the Atlantic. Its cliff face was spectacularly raked and eroded with an alarmingly vertical drop of several hundred feet to the smashing surf below. Unlike a rocky overhang, whose solidity underfoot helps you fight down a sense of vertigo, this lip of loose earth invited disaster.

"Don't get too close to the edge," van Hoven cautioned. "It could give way." He stamped his foot to demonstrate, sending down a shower of sand and pebbles. But I was drawn to the sweeping view: the gray Atlantic to the west, the slack-jawed mouth of the river—the Barra do Cuanza— opening into the ocean to the north, and the suspension bridge, tiny in the distance to the east, and beyond that the serpentine course of the Cuanza trailing off in a green haze.

We trudged the last few yards to the very top and found a crude circle of tall timber posts in the sand, the cold remains of a fire, and a torn, soiled mattress and wretched blanket on a rusted bed frame facing the magnificent seascape. Whoever dragged that rubbish up here and pounded in stakes planned on staying. Van Hoven was furious at this squatter's camp in the making, in one of the most scenic areas of the park no less, and started pulling on the posts, rocking them back and forth to dislodge them, and we all quickly joined the effort. De Freitas started pitching the posts over the cliff, caber-tossing style. I threw a couple, running to give them the heave-ho and then digging in my heels to stop in time. Van Hoven and Osborne slung cans and bottles into the air and de Freitas trundled the bed to the precipice, its rusty springs squeaking in protest, and flipped it over into pure space. Its blanket gaped and flapped, like a bridge jumper's overcoat, before it smacked the cliff wall, broke apart, and disappeared from view.

We did get a little carried away with the hilltop cleanup. I don't know why that small-scale littering of a scenic headland seemed so outrageous, considering that so much of Angola had been trashed already. Perhaps it was displaced anger at what we saw at Catalangombe, but afterwards I felt that there had been no real rush to deprive the owner of that miserable rack of a bed or his million-dollar view and the cool sea breezes that came with sleeping under the stars.

I took a last look around. The late afternoon light glared off the calm ocean; there was nothing visible on the horizon.

THAT EVENING VAN HOVEN invited me to sit in on a Kissama Foundation board meeting at Gen. Luis Faceira's high-walled seaside villa in Luanda. I followed van Hoven and de Freitas through a large planted atrium entranceway, a long hall, and a room with fat leather couches and a large-screen television, escorted by a little black chihuahua, its nails clicking on the polished stone floors. Luis Pereira Faceira, deputy army chief of staff, was waiting for us in the white-walled dining room. He was short and stocky, with a shaved head, mustache, and a bit of bristle under his lower lip, and wore wire-rimmed glasses. He welcomed us warmly and gestured toward the Scotch and beer. The air-conditioning was on full blast.

Others arrived soon after, including Gen. Antonio Emilio Faceira, the head of the Special Forces. Like his brother, he was short and compact, and also wore glasses, but had close-cropped gray hair and a matching mustache. Gen. C. A. Hendrik Vaal da Silva and Brig. Gen. Domingos Wilson Melgaço came in together. General Hendrik, as everyone called him, had a dark, chiseled face, while General Melgaço's was round and open with a neatly trimmed beard. I wasn't expecting the Kissama Foundation's inner circle to look like the college of cardinals, but I didn't realize I'd see quite so many military men, either. All the generals wore camouflage fatigues, berets, heavy silver or gold watches, had one to three stars on their epaulets, and carried cell phones. These Angolans were an interesting ethnic mix; their skin tones varied from pale Portuguese to dark African to a shade between, like that of the Faceira brothers. I took a seat at the table next to Christo Roelofse, the general manager of Gray Security Services, a South African firm that has close relations with the military and provides private protection to corporations and various institutions.

It wasn't a very structured meeting—there was no chairperson, no reading of minutes, no handouts, and no one was taking notes except for me. The discussion proceeded jerkily, bouncing back and forth between Portuguese and English, and a lot got lost along the way when people talked too long before translation. But the generals seemed comfortable; I surmised that they all knew more English than they let on.

The fence dominated the discussion. Without a solution to extend it out into the marshy eastern end, the game barrier would be useless. Van Hoven drew a diagram on his notepad to explain the problem. A crisscross of railroad ties sunk in the spongy ground was proposed; others argued for a floating pier.

"Let's talk logistics," van Hoven said. "Who's going to supply the materials?"

A four-way conversation ensued in Portuguese that seemed to revolve around cement. There wasn't any resolution, so van Hoven dropped the topic and brought up the idea of constructing a *boma*—a smaller fenced stockade that can be used to familiarize wild elephants with an electrified game fence. But they won't always need the *boma*, he added; someday they'll want to release animals directly into the primary park, even lions.

Antonio Faceira smiled and shook his finger. "No lions."

Van Hoven assured him this wouldn't happen soon. "*Palanca negra* before lions," he said. This got satisfied nods all around, I noticed with dismay. Van Hoven added that a survey would have to happen first. "We wouldn't want to take the last ten out of Malange Province." If he really was against moving them, why was he always talking about captures?

Then van Hoven said he couldn't bring in animals this year. *Porquê* . . . ? The generals looked surprised. "I want to explain the reality," van Hoven said, and ticked off a number of unsolved problems; in short, there was too much work that remained to be done. The Faceira brothers looked very unhappy. What about November 11, Angola's Independence Day? The fence can be finished in three, four days, no problem, they said. "It's not that easy," van Hoven answered. He explained he needed to coordinate finishing the fence with the construction of the *boma* and the arrival of the animals. The Faceiras took turns trying to pin him down: if everything is made ready, when can the animals come?

Van Hoven explained that the best time would be May 2000. The generals got agitated; it seemed that they'd already told everyone that animals would be introduced this year. Mutterings, frowns, and side conversations broke out. Van Hoven said he didn't even know Angola's veterinary requirements for animal imports. That got a laugh. "There are no requirements!" Van Hoven considered this and said, "Then I'd need a letter stating that." The generals all agreed: Fátima Jardim would send a letter, no problem.

Van Hoven pointed out that the biologists would object. In May or June, the animals would be in better condition and the juveniles would be three or four months old; right now the animals were weaker, and in many species the females were pregnant. At this time of year in South Africa, game breeders would be reluctant to catch animals because helicopter chases often cause the females to abort.

The generals thought he was stalling. Van Hoven offered to investigate the possibility of zebra and giraffe, which don't have seasonal births. General Melgaço asked, "Why can't we have ostriches? Ostriches are very nice." He put his fingers and thumb together to make a beak, and rotated his hand on his wrist as if making a shadow puppet, which got a chuckle. Van Hoven coyly suggested the generals give him a call when the work was done and he'd bring in animals. Luis Faceira wasn't buying it. Give us a date when the animals arrive, he countered, and we'll do it. Van Hoven said he didn't want animals standing on the airfield tarmac because there were no trucks or cranes. Neither wanted to budge; it had become a pissing match.

The generals exchanged some sharp words. De Freitas translated. "The generals say that if you don't bring animals, they'll put goats in there." This got laughs all around, and helped break the tension. The generals shrugged and said, Okay, maybe it will take three weeks to finish the fence. Van Hoven shrugged and said, Hey, take three weeks and finish off Savimbi—that would help tourism. We passed around the Scotch.

Van Hoven asked casually why it is was so important to have animals in the park this year. The Faceiras exchanged glances. Luis Faceira leaned forward and explained that they couldn't look the president in the face anymore—for months they'd been telling him animals were going to arrive, animals!

Van Hoven said, "Let's look forward gentlemen, not back," and called South Africa on his cell phone. He talked in Afrikaans for several minutes, then announced that the five giraffes that couldn't fit into the 747 bound for the Chinese safari park would be available, if a cargo plane in which they could stand upright could be rounded up.

I thought I had learned earlier in the day just how difficult rehabilitating Quiçama would be, but now I realized that van Hoven was not just juggling problems, he was also juggling people. In fact, he was presiding over a volatile mix of powerful personalities, events beyond his control, and biological principles that could only be bent at his peril, in a country where hardly anything works and what gets done is accomplished at a snail's pace. He was not just playing ringmaster, he'd taken on the job of lion tamer, too.

It felt more than a bit strange to be sitting around a table with a quartet of Angola's top brass—four of the most powerful men in the country, as Roelofse told me afterwards—discussing the resuscitation of a national park. They had a war to wage, which is why they were all in uniform, but they'd made the time to meet and talk about anchoring fences, shipping wildlife, raising money, and the like. Of course, the Angolan civil war wasn't an ordinary war. It had been going on for decades, which meant it was more like a career than a crisis to these old pros, some of whom had been in uniform most of their lives. I knew next to nothing about these military men, but they had to be both battle-hardened and politically adept to be holding the positions they did in the Luanda government. And clearly, they were keenly interested in Operation Noah's Ark. There's no intrinsic reason why a general, even one fighting a war, couldn't be concerned about his country's environment, but I wondered how all this fit together. These generals would want to show their support for anything the president had given his blessing to, and dos Santos was the Kissama Foundation's patron. But there had to be more to their involvement than that.

I didn't know if they were contributing any money, but they openly helped the foundation with men and matériel. In the West, a general who used a few soldiers from his army base to paint the porch of his house would be thought to be abusing his authority for personal gain. Here, it seemed to be taken for granted that these commanders could and would divert substantial military resources—helicopters, trucks, planes, men, various supplies—to assist in the rehabilitation of the park. It was just the way things got done in Angola.

As the meeting broke up, Gen. Luis Faceira gave me his card. I gave him mine. Roelofse leaned over and said quietly, "Hang on to that one. It's your 'get out of jail free card.'" He offered to drive van Hoven and me back to the Shell compound in his van. We passed through several dimly lit, ominous-looking street scenes, but Roelofse assured me that Luanda was not all that bad. I was curious; he was with a security firm—did he feel the need to travel armed when he was here? He shook his head. "Violence begets violence," he told me solemnly.

"Great," I thought. "We have a pacifist for a bodyguard."

Back at the Shell compound, Osborne said I could stay on for a couple more days and look around Luanda, for which I was very grateful. Van Hoven had to leave for the airport early in the morning, and we agreed to meet after my return to Pretoria. "Don't worry," he said, stuffing some papers in his briefcase. "Dodo will drive you around."

But wasn't the treasurer of the Kissama Foundation going to do that? I asked. He turned and looked at me. "Didn't I tell you? Dodo is the treasurer."

JUDGING FROM OLD photographs, Luanda used to be a lovely Portuguese colonial seaport, all pink stucco and palms, but except for a few important buildings, most of what was left from those days was crumbling away and easy to miss among the ugly and in many cases unfinished Soviet-era structures. What was not easy to miss were the slums. The capital has always been ringed by its *musseques,* or shantytowns, but these, now swollen by several million war refugees—a full one-third of the nation's population—threatened to overwhelm a city built for several hundred thousand residents. Not surprisingly, there were regular outbreaks of cholera, polio, and other scourges. Locals joked that the only reason AIDS figures are so low in Angola in comparison to other countries was that there are no reliable statistics.

Dodo drove me in his battered blue sedan toward downtown Luanda, talking on his cell phone and winding his way through areas that looked more like gigantic dumps or landfills than neighborhoods, except that they were inhabited—crawling with people, in fact. They spilled out into the streets from sheds, shacks, and bunkerlike stores to step in front of traffic with utter indifference to danger, leaning to pull their backsides out of harm's way at the last possible second. Perhaps it was to show their disdain for the few who could afford automobiles. But they also crowded around any vehicle that slowed in the hopes of selling something. In any large city in the world, newspapers, fruit, and flowers are hawked, but here anything and everything was proffered, no matter how slim the hope of enticing a driver: a reeking fish, a wire coat hanger, a near-empty roll of toilet paper, a single toffee, an old flashlight battery, a pencil stub, a paper clip.

We passed young men holding up what I took to be heads of lettuce, but when we got closer I saw that they were money changers with fistfuls of kwanzas, the local inflation-bloated currency—the exchange rate at the time stood at 5 million kwanzas to the U.S. dollar. We slowed to a crawl behind a truck and I spotted a man in a trash-filled lot, sprawled out in the dust under the gray bowl of the Angolan sky. Maybe he was just dead drunk, but there was something about the way his arms and legs were twisted that made him look more dead than drunk. I could have looked for the hordes of children that live in Luanda's sewers, but I didn't, because I decided I would rather skip the sight of a child's head popping up out of a grate as we drove by.

There was heavy congestion on the garbage-strewn Rua Ho Chi Minh, and the line of army trucks, exhaust-belching busses, and impossibly packed minivans finally congealed at a traffic circle. Dodo joined the other drivers in honking, shouting, and gesticulating, but it had no effect. Crowds milled around the cars. I ignored the peering faces of hawkers hoping against hope I would show interest in their pathetic wares. But I couldn't ignore a blind man in a torn shirt who staggered out into the vehicular sprawl, his contorted face and filmy, rolling eyes raised up to the sky, tapping with his white cane, alternately clutching at and pushing a frightened little boy by the shoulder. The child was his eyes and beggar's hand as they worked their way down the line of cars, the boy holding out his tiny palm timidly, eyes darting back and forth. He led the man closer toward us through the surrounding horde. I began digging frantically in my pocket for coins, but Dodo, who was looking elsewhere, rocketed forward into a hole that appeared between two trucks and shot up the avenue, pleased at his display of deft driving. I slumped in the seat, defeated by the hopelessness of it all. He looked over, and shrugged as if to say, "What can one do?" "*Pouco trânsito*," he said—there's always traffic in Luanda.

Moral numbness was setting in. I felt I should be doing something other than just letting these miseries wash over me, but couldn't think of anything more meaningful to do than record my impressions. I knew I would see these kinds of scenes if I came here—I had been reading about Angola's agonies for years, and thought I might actually seek some of them out, perhaps by visiting Papa Kitoko's Traditional Medical Centre on the outskirts of Luanda, where Angolans who have gone insane from the war are chained to old engine blocks in the courtyard to keep them from running away and harming themselves further. But already, without looking for it, I'd had my face shoved into the country's sufferings, and what had I learned? Only that it was just as bad as everyone said it was.

THE *MUSEU DE HISTÓRICA NATURALES* (Natural History Museum) was officially closed—I gathered there weren't enough funds to run it—but my press credentials got us inside the colonial building, where, using Dodo as interpreter, I explained to the woman in charge that I wanted to see the diorama of Angola's great antelope. She turned me over to an assistant who took me into the darkened mammal hall and flipped on a single flourescent fixture to illuminate the *Sala da Palanca Negra Gigante*. In the green-blue light the diorama looked eerie and depressing. The glass front was gone, and so was the foreground foliage evident in the old photograph I had of it. Dust and chunks of plaster had rained down on the three animals in the group, and a broom had been left leaning against the backdrop painting of an *anhara*. Despite his dried-out, splitting skin and his shabby surroundings, the big bull still projected a vaguely regal air.

We pushed on to the *Museu Nacional de Antropologia* (National Museum of Anthropology), where I met the young and personable director, Américo Kwononoka. I asked if he could share any details of Songo and Lwimbe beliefs about the giant sable with me. He knew these tribes, he told me; they were related to his own ethnic group. "I am Chokwe," he said proudly, placing his hand over his heart. But unfortunately, he couldn't add to what I already knew. "If those peoples had a cult of the *palanca negra* in past times, well, I don't know anything about it," he said.

On the way out I lingered in the cool halls of the pink colonial building to look at the splendid masks, chiefs' chairs and divination baskets, and an enigmatic Chokwe figure carving. She had a painted, half-smiling face, but her eyes were slits, mere knife nicks, like the creases in coffee beans. Alas, the museum's most famous treasure, the Chokwe carving *O Pensador* (*The Thinker*), had been stolen, like most of Angola's patrimony.

I instructed Dodo to take me to the Agostinho Neto monument. By this time, Dodo's endless cell phone conversations were getting on my nerves. Sometimes they seemed businesslike, but now he was making back-to-back hysterical calls, moaning in distress and shrieking tearfully and banging on the dashboard for emphasis. Oddly enough, he seemed perfectly calm when he got off. I asked if he was in trouble. "Girlfriend trouble, Mister John!" he said, and smiled from ear to ear. He'd been keeping her in line, that's all, and dialed up again.

On the way we passed a high-rise apartment building whose front had fallen off, but it hadn't discouraged people from living there, on open shelving, as it were. As we hurtled down a wide, tree-lined avenue, I spotted the silhouette of a giant sable set in brown tile on the sloping facade of a building across the street. Excited, I told Dodo to stop. He screeched to a halt without interrupting his latest harangue, and I grabbed my camera and dashed out into the traffic, dodging a couple of cars to reach the median and an unobstructed view. As I fiddled with the zoom lens a heavy hand grabbed my shoulder and I turned into the large face of a frowning, blue-uniformed policeman questioning me in rapid-fire Portuguese. I stepped back, but he stuck to me like a pickpocket and hefted his truncheon as I offered useless explanations in English, all the while walking backward across the street. When we reached the car, I grabbed my press pass out of the camera bag on the seat. Dodo, who'd been shouting into his cell phone and rocking back and forth in a rage, noticed nothing.

The pass was snatched away by a much larger policeman who had materialized behind my back. He held up the little laminated card and stared at it with contempt; it looked very small in his meaty hand. I composed my face to match my sullen expression on the *carte de impreza* in case he thought of comparing them. Traffic roared past. Finally, without so much as a glance, he thrust the card back in my direction and walked off, the junior officer right on his heels.

I jumped in the car and slammed the door.

"*Problema?*" Dodo asked, plucking the cell phone from his ear.

"A *monumento Neto!*" I said, vigorously stabbing a finger at the road ahead.

I was more annoyed at Dodo's obliviousness than rattled by the incident, but he saw that I was agitated and snapped into action. Clamping the cell phone to his head, he screamed more invectives, threw the wheel hard to the left, and floored the accelerator, sending us into a stream of honking vehicles. We whipped along past a shabby-looking colonial building that either was or wasn't Savimbi's headquarters in 1992—I couldn't untangle Dodo's multilingual explanation from the tongue-lashing he was simultaneously giving his lady love—then swung down a curved hilltop street with a view of the monument to the revolutionary hero in the distance. I took some photos on the sly as we approached the sad spire, now just another example of Angola's failed aspirations.

In the mid-1980s, while the proxy war raged, the MPLA government embarked on a gigantic Soviet-style building scheme intended to house Neto's mortal remains as well as a government office complex. An entire low-lying neighborhood was destroyed to make room for the project. Eighty million squandered dollars later, the government abandoned it. All that's left now is a shantytown that's crept back to reclaim the mosquito-ridden area, and the half-built tower of the gray mausoleum, still partly clad in scaffolding fused with the rusted arm of a crane like the cross of a lower-case "t."

From a distance, it looked like a mock-up of a booster rocket, which may account for its local nickname: "Angola's Sputnik." Up close, the nearly two hundred-foot-tall concrete excrescence looked more like a bundle of pointy, futuristic spikes. The government, embarrassed at having Neto's body on their hands (when he died in Moscow in 1979 he'd been embalmed for eternity, like Lenin), sealed it up some years ago in the abandoned monstrosity, where without benefit of cooling, it now rots away. Neto's tower is a monument to waste, but it's nothing compared with Angola's landscape of loss, the *panorama de morte*, of its civil war.

Extravagance in the midst of misery is hardly news in Angola. In the weeks before I arrived, the government reported that the number of needy people in Angola had increased to 3.2 million. This followed an earlier admission that 129 container loads of foodstuffs, including pork, maize meal, and milk powder, sitting at the port of Luanda since 1993, had finally deteriorated. But the flow of oil keeps the party going. ESSO announced the discovery of a new oil field in Block 15, north of Luanda, the week after dos Santos's fifty-seventh birthday party, at which well-fed, carefully groomed schoolchildren sang for the president before he hit the dance floor with a Brazilian soap opera star flown in for the festivities.

There was a guardhouse up ahead with the inevitable rifle-toting soldier. I wasn't interested in further tests of the powers of my press pass, so I tried to tell Dodo I had all the pictures I needed, but he interpreted this as encouragement to penetrate the weed-choked grounds. We came to a stop and a guard pointed the muzzle of his AK-47 through the car window at us. A long conversation ensued, and finally the soldier went off to find his commander. I tried again to make plain that we must, alas, leave this fascinating spot. Dodo finally caught on and we departed, slowly and respectfully, before anyone returned. As we climbed the hill I took one last look. Considering the way the father of the country had been treated, it was a little naive of me to be surprised that plaster was falling on the national animal in the Natural History Museum.

ON MY LAST night in Angola, I returned to my condo in the Shell compound, popped open a can of South African beer, flopped on the soft leather couch, and zapped the satellite television on with the remote. The BBC science fiction spoof was funny, but probably not the wildly amusing, head-slapping, slide-down-to-the-floor-and-wipe-my-tearing-eyes sort of funny I first thought it was. I could tell I was overwrought and ready to leave lovely Luanda.

I decided I'd go upstairs and pack after flipping around the dial one last time. Clicking to the state television broadcast, I found scenes of tanks rolling down sandy tracks in the countryside. Commanders reviewed troops and saluted each other; a soldier shinnied up a flagpole to rip down a UNITA banner. Fists were thrust in the air. There was a smiling four-star general—de Matos himself, the chief of staff. I heard the word "Andulo" in the rapid Portuguese sound track—that key rebel base was only fifty miles west of the Luando Reserve. The "casa blanca de Savimbi" was invoked as the camera panned around empty meeting rooms, zoomed in on a double bed, and then lingered on an exercise bicycle—was that how the sixty-five-year-old guerrilla leader kept in shape? There were many minutes of footage devoted to showing piles of captured weapons, heavy artillery, vehicles. I stayed with it to the end, hoping it might be repeated, but it was time for *Torre de Babel,* a Portuguese soap opera.

But it was clear enough. Andulo, UNITA's highland headquarters, had fallen, and Savimbi had fled.

WHEN I STOPPED in to see van Hoven in his University of Pretoria office after my return from Angola, he was buoyed up by news of the Angolan government's military advances against UNITA. Maybe Dodo was right;

"Savimbi finish!" he had told me before I left Luanda, underscoring his pronouncement with a slicing motion across his throat.

Van Hoven had more plans for Quiçama. He wanted Kobus du Toit and Chris Mostert to capture the hundreds of Botswana elephants he expected to be donated to Angola, and he was looking into the possibility of using a huge landing craft for a dramatic D-day-style drop-off of family herds right on the beach. He was also planning a new, much longer fence below the first one and showed me on his pinned-up map where it would slice off a third of the park. That way he could introduce animals into the first fenced section, then release them into the second, and eventually into the park as a whole, at which point the second fence would be dropped. I pictured trumpeting elephants marching southward as the fence fell, ears flapping, heads swaying, the other animals following in the swirling dust.

But after having seen the Kissama Foundation board in action, I was amazed at his optimism and his working method. It could be maddening to get things done in Angola, but van Hoven hardly helped matters along with his indifference to details. He waved them away like bothersome gnats, or let them trail after him while he went off in one direction or another, figuring they would sort themselves out eventually, conveniently fall by the wayside or end up in someone else's lap. But maybe this was what came of having grandiose ideas; if he allowed himself to dwell on everything that could delay, complicate, or sabotage Operation Noah's Ark, he wouldn't have the nerve try to pull it off.

His willingness to work with a rather unlikely group of conservationists—Angolan generals—to rehabilitate the nation's parks impressed me. Actually, it wasn't so much that he was willing to work with them, it's that he *could* work with them. But he was very adroit at relating to his audience. He could spin a charming tale at dinner, deliver an impressive lecture from a podium, or dip into his stock of vivid off-color jokes to bond with the military boys. He could get on their wavelength and fine-tune it. A couple of years ago, they would go for a helicopter ride over Quiçama with him and think nothing of throwing beer cans out the window. Now that they had been given tours of Kruger and had come increasingly under his sway, they were starting to think environmentally. But they still set the agenda, and van Hoven, persuasive as he was, had to reconcile their blunt demands with sound conservation. To do that, I saw that he often stalled for time. He'd tell people what they wanted to hear, not so much to deceive them, but to humor them and keep them in line until they could be persuaded to see things his way. Still, underneath the surface salesmanship, there was a wildlife man. He would bend his own principles, but at the point where he thought he might be violating good conservation practices, he stopped short.

Van Hoven had now arrived at one of those points: there would be no wildlife shipments that year. "It's not a responsible thing to do," he said, and the generals would just have to put up with it. Van Hoven was thinking May 2000 for the first release. I looked surprised. "I know, I thought we'd be finished with the fence," he said. "But that's thinking along Western lines. I sent a team up there. They left here in September. They should have done most of it by now. Then this doesn't arrive and that doesn't work and the bulldozer breaks down and then you are dependent on the Angolans, and well . . . ."

So when did he expect the fence to be finished off—realistically? "February," he said. Did he feel discouraged? He frowned. "I don't like to turn around," he said. I wasn't sure what he meant. "I'm stubborn," he explained. "I want to see the thing through." He was convinced he could help "uplift" the Angolan people by restoring their wildlife heritage. But the effort couldn't depend on government money, because there wouldn't be any. In fact, he believed that all national parks in Africa should be run by private enterprise, not government. In many cases money allocated to wildlife disappeared before it ever made it to the parks; it would make far more sense if any monies generated in a park stayed right there. "That's why," he said emphatically, "Quiçama must be self-sufficient."

He leaned back in his chair. "So we are going to bring wildlife there, protect it, improve the infrastructure, make it attractive." In fact, he confided, the private sector already wanted to invest in the tourism industry. On land surrounding the park?

"No, they are interested in the hotels and lodges right inside the park. We will give out concessions to the private sector to put up those game lodges," he said. "They get the land for free. They just have to build the structures." But, he added, "we want a percentage to put back into the foundation to protect the wildlife."

I asked what sort of financial stake the generals had in Quiçama. He said that they had the rights (how wasn't exactly clear) to develop tourist facilities in the park. The foundation was set up as a separate, nonprofit entity, and was concerned solely with restoring the environment. Did he himself stand to gain financially from his involvement? The generals had offered him two choices, he said, a consulting fee or a 10 percent interest in future concessions from the park. He might end up someday with a fractional interest in a lodge, but, he said, "there's nothing on paper. It's a handshake deal." Meantime, he wasn't being paid for his time, only expenses.

"Believe me, if I was in it for the money, I would have dropped out long ago," he assured me. "There are many more lucrative things I could be involved with." Apart from a unique chance to "uplift" the Angolans, it had to be the prospect of fame and glory as much as any potential financial rewards that made him persist there. If he could pull off Operation Noah's Ark, he would get considerable credit for doing something extraordinary. And if he made it work, why shouldn't he get some financial benefit out of it as well? Angola would get its flagship national park restored in the process—no small accomplishment in an impoverished, war-wracked nation.

And the giant sable survey expedition? I could count on it happening in July, but he was already thinking beyond that to putting up a rustic camp in the reserve, where tourists could fly in to see giant sables the way they now go to look at gorillas in Uganda or Rwanda. Any plans to capture some? "Taking a group to Quiçama would be an emergency measure only," he said. I felt reassured. "Although sable are pretty resilient," he added. "Remember, they're all over South Africa now, in places they never were previously."

Now I was alarmed again. Every time he brought up how easily they'd adapt, it sounded as if he really wanted to bring giant sable to Quiçama and had no plans to dissuade the generals who were for it.

Van Hoven asked me if I'd heard anything from Huntley about the Kissama Foundation. Nothing that he hadn't already said in his letters, I answered. He fumed, and said Huntley was just looking for faults. "Wildlife politics in Africa—get ten guys in room, and nine agree on what should be done and one guy disagrees. Then everyone listens to the negative guy," he said.

Huntley wasn't just opposed to what the Kissama Foundation was planning; he was opposed to there being a foundation at all. "The more money that's thrown at conservation in Angola," he had told me, "the more damage will be done." In Huntley's view, it was better to let conservation matters slide; then the Angolans would do nothing about the parks — they'd be left mercifully alone. But van Hoven couldn't disagree more. He thought that by waiting until there was government money, responsible ministries, and all the rest, it would be too late: someone else would have already sold the Angolans a dubious bill of goods. He would at least steer them in the right direction. "Better to take action now," he once told me, "so that there's something workable in place when peace comes."

I had to return to my guest house and pick up my bags before heading to the airport. Van Hoven offered to give me a lift, and we walked out to the parking lot.

"Professor van Hoven! Are you leaving?" a slim young woman in a sundress called out as she pedaled up on her bicycle.

"I'll be back shortly," he said.

"You had an E-mail from Dr. Estes," she said, and unfolded a piece of paper and handed it to him.

Van Hoven read it over, and muttered to me, "He wants to know if Brian Huntley went with us to Angola." He turned to her. "Send Dr. Estes a reply and tell him that Professor Huntley didn't choose to go."

We got in his station wagon, and he backed out sharply. "You know, Huntley never replied to my invitation to go to Angola," he said. "That guy is just going to stay on the sidelines." He pulled out into traffic and added bitterly, "He's what I call an armchair conservationist. They always have something to say, but never something to do."

BY MID-NOVEMBER 1999, Jonas Savimbi was on the run.

General de Matos had announced that "we know where Savimbi is. We are tracking him, we are bombarding him every day, and we are going to keep going until we capture him or kill him." It was rumored that the army nearly had him once, when two South African–registered helicopters were intercepted in Moxico Province on a mission to evacuate the guerrilla leader and his senior aides. One thing was certain: government forces had stormed a number of UNITA positions, retaking towns long under Savimbi's control and reopening transportation links with the besieged and starving cities of Malange, Huambo, and Cuito, and were preparing to attack Calai, a suspected warehouse for ivory, timber, and diamonds held by the rebel movement near the Namibian border. With twenty-seven enemy tanks, thirty missiles, hundreds of vehicles, and tons of small arms seized so far, 80 percent of UNITA's conventional military capacity had been disrupted. De Matos was ready to extend a hand to those willing to lay down their weapons. "The only one we will not reconcile with is Savimbi," he asserted.

The rains had come and the giant sable had retreated into the *miombo* forest. Where had the guerrilla leader gone?

A day after de Matos made his upbeat assessment, van Hoven E-mailed me that the fence was virtually finished. Everything was on track, and I started thinking of the upcoming survey in ten months. The next day news reports added a touch of apprehension to my expectations. Government forces reported that the rebel movement only held a small triangle of territory between Cuemba, Munhango, and Luando on the borders of Bié, Malange, and Moxico Provinces—right at the foot of Luando Reserve, where Cameron, Serpa Pinto, and Capello and Ivens had crossed, where Varian had put the Benguela Railway through, and where Jonas Savimbi had been born.

The government's striking military successes received important diplomatic support from Britain and the United States. Peter Hain, British minister for Africa, condemned Savimbi in unmistakable terms, saying "the blood of hundreds of thousands of Angolans drips from his hands," and Richard Holbrooke, the United States ambassador to the United Nations, said the Security Council should take firmer action against UNITA, distancing the United States even further from the man and the movement it had propped up during the cold war.

The fighting continued to be savage. Government troops on the Angolan-Namibian border had left burned huts and the bodies of executed civilians—men, women, and children—suspected of harboring enemy soldiers, matching the appalling atrocities UNITA had been accused of

321

in the area. The casualties mounted: over 5,000 of the estimated 60,000 rebel troops had been killed, and another 5,000 surrendered; 2,500 government troops had died so far in the offensive, and 7,000 were injured.

But those numbers hardly compared with faceless figures released by the UN Humanitarian Coordination Unit (UCAH). Over a million "internally displaced persons" were trying to flee the fighting throughout the country, but "security restraints" prevented hundreds of thousands from being reached with any kind of aid. Other sources said the number was closer to two million people forced from their homes, but under the circumstances, a precise head count was not readily available. The numbers of desperate and needy were overwhelming relief efforts—that much was clear—because two hundred people a day, give or take a few dozen, were dying of starvation. Thousands of Angolan rural refugees, mainly women and children, continued to stream across the Zambian border, the biggest influx in six years, to escape the fighting. Most had walked for days, and brought little but tales of young men press-ganged into fighting for the rebels and women and girls abducted for use as sex slaves.

Savimbi's days seemed numbered, but by mid-December, there was still no word of his whereabouts. His propaganda machine had fallen silent, and rumors abounded. There were reports of a mass grave containing the remains of some UNITA generals, executed for losing key battles. Savimbi was said to be in a drunken rage, he was said to be reduced to fleeing on foot; others said he'd slipped out of the country, to Uganda or Togo. De Matos claimed that he had been located in the bush. "The army is following him as he moves slowly with a personal guard of fewer than twenty men," the general was quoted as saying.

The war in Angola never breaks for Christmas, and 1999 was no exception. On December 25, Angolan state radio announced that Jamba, for many years UNITA's bush capital and a key rebel base, had been sacked, dealing a serious military and psychological blow to the guerrilla movement, and giving the government nearly complete control of the country's southern border. On New Year's Eve, Gen. Luis Faceira, now the army's chief of staff, praised the determination and courage shown by the Angolan armed forces during the *restauro* campaign to recapture UNITA's strongholds, and urged government soldiers to press on with determination "to destroy Jonas Savimbi's war machinery." It sounded like a mop-up operation was all that remained, and that expectation seemed to underlie President José Eduardo dos Santos's remarks in a year-end address to political and military leaders and diplomats prior to a gala reception for a thousand guests at Futungo Palace. "Our aim is not to crush the enemy at any price," dos Santos reassured his audience. The statement was taken as an indication of his willingness to deal with a defanged UNITA—so long as it excluded Savimbi.

IN EARLY JANUARY 2000 I reached Wouter van Hoven in Pretoria by phone. "I'm quite encouraged," he told me. "The military situation has improved drastically." UNITA rebels were still hanging on, but if they could be contained in a few "pockets," he thought it looked very promising for a giant sable survey. Van Hoven informed me he had also beefed up the Kissama Foundation's board. There were now three ministers on it— Fátima Jardim, Jorge Valentim, and Albino Malungo, the minister of social integration. And van Hoven had persuaded General de Matos himself to be the Angolan copresident, to replace the ailing Dr. Marques. Operation Noah's Ark was on track, too.

Richard Estes had left for Tanzania the day I returned to the United States, and had only just flown back with Runi after she and their son and daughter had joined him in the Serengeti for Christmas. I called him in New Hampshire and told him of the plans for a giant sable survey. He was cheered by the news and wrote to van Hoven to propose that Jeremy Anderson be invited to represent both the IUCN and the ASG. "May 2000 be a banner year for your conservation efforts in Angola," he added. "So much may be accomplished if only peace could break out at long last."

General de Matos was now talking about using every military means to end the war, a statement which coincided with the announcement in Luanda of a new compulsory draft of males eighteen and over, issued with a reminder that those who tried to evade the order would be considered escapees and punished accordingly. The government seemed determined to prevail, but there was a rumor out of London that UNITA was trying to regroup and establish a base in the Luando Reserve itself. Would the rebel leader many saw as a freedom fighter, now reduced to a petty warlord, make his last stand in the "house of the giant sable"?

As usual, the rumors balanced each other out, so that I didn't know what to think. Gen. Diogenes Malaquias "Implacavel," UNITA's former chief of operations, and a recent defector, claimed Savimbi was in the region where the Benguela Railway crossed the Cuanza, but thought he might commit suicide to "escape humiliation and having to surrender." But an aide to Savimbi told Reuters by satellite telephone from the bush that UNITA had reorganized and would continue fighting "for a very, very long time." The threat was underscored by follow-up propaganda announcing a guerrilla campaign, with troops redeployed to Cuando Cubango Province and north of the Cuanza River between Mussende and Malange—right between Cangandala Park and the Luando Reserve.

When I talked to van Hoven by phone at the end of February, he had just returned from Angola, and was now thinking June was a better time for the introduction of animals. And the prospects for the giant sable survey expedition? The situation in Malange Province was calm (or under control), and it was "on for July." But there was no way he could take a crowd—we would be going in military aircraft. He had heard from Estes about Anderson, but said he'd rather invite Estes himself, who was knowledgeable about the whole area and the animals, and had been there. "You're his neighbor," he said—I supposed it looked that way from South Africa. He told me to pass on the invitation to him.

I immediately called Estes, who was surprised but cautiously pleased. He had come to accept that, for better or worse, the Kissama Foundation had taken charge of Angola's parks. He would work with van Hoven. Although Estes had wanted to step aside for Anderson, he could certainly take his place on the survey; perhaps Anderson could still be involved at a later date. Anderson took the news that Estes would be going instead with remarkable equanimity, considering that he had invested over a decade in the effort to determine the status of the giant sable. There was a part of him that wished he were going, he told Estes, but he was happy that at least his old friend was involved. Estes was going to Tanzania to watch the June wildebeest rut in Ngorongoro Crater anyway, and could tack on the expedition to the giant sable reserves in late July. And he felt he could justify using a small portion of the giant sable fund the Dodgsons had created to pay for a side trip to Angola to check on the status of the animal. He fired off his acceptance that day. "I'm really looking forward to the Angola trip," he wrote in a follow-up E-mail to van Hoven, "though a little nervous about the risks of our helicopter getting shot at by Savimbi die-hards, land mines, and such."

There were grounds for his nervousness. Savimbi's dwindling sup-port and the continuing top-to-bottom desertions from his forces had crippled but not stopped him. While dos Santos was inaugurating the country's first Coca-Cola bottling plant just outside the capital, Savimbi's forces had apparently presided over another kind of ceremony, the ston-ing and crucifixion of six Christian children near the Congo border for allegedly giving information to government soldiers. In fact, UNITA claimed to have killed 800 government troops in several weeks of spo-radic fighting across the country. It also captured arms it was now finding difficult to buy due to tightening UN sanctions, although it was widely believed that the rebel movement was still financing its war effort by sell-ing diamonds from the mines it controlled.

General de Matos had thought that the end of the war was in sight back in November, but even that level-headed commander must have been astonished at Savimbi's ability not just to elude capture but to rise out of the ashes. It looked like he would never be able to mount a conven-tional military offensive again, but he could still wreak havoc and destabi-lize vast tracts of the country by reverting to what he had long been a master of—guerrilla warfare. How could de Matos, with his mechanized forces, fight a foe on foot that faded into the forest whenever it was pursued? Savimbi continued to espouse dialogue to end the conflict while initiat-ing armed clashes with the government, and to accuse dos Santos and his cronies of bottomless corruption while enslaving whole villages and ter-rorizing the countryside. It was confusing on purpose, of course. "I like confusion," Savimbi once said. "Lots of it."

Angolan state television announced further military breakthroughs by the middle of June, disclosing that after the fall of Andulo, government troops had pushed rebel forces back from the central highlands into the eastern bush. The list of villages the army had marched through grabbed my atten-tion: Nharea, Calei, and Dando—where Estes and his wife used to buy supplies—and then after crossing the Cuanza into the Luando Reserve,

Mulundo, the very village the Curtises had visited in the early 1920s and the same one that the Count de Yebes had passed through in the 1950s on his pursuit of the giant sable. In this news dispatch it was described as an abandoned UNITA camp, strewn with damaged and burned-out and abandoned vehicles, including a sinister-looking gray-green Ukrainian long-range multiple rocket launcher, the Uragan, or "Hurricane" 9K57, parked under a wispy canopy of trees. This wheeled monster's rocket tubes, each the size of a drainage pipe, could rain down explosive warheads on targets up to forty miles away. It was an impressive example of the deadly Soviet bloc weaponry UNITA had been amassing in the hopes of building a conventional army capable of taking on the government directly.

But there was another vehicle left behind, this one a truck equipped with a generator and living quarters, believed to be the rebel leader's mobile home. Of course, he wasn't there. Jonas Savimbi was no clumsy, easily cornered bandit chieftain—he was a maddening wraith of a warlord who always managed to slip into the forest ahead of his would-be captors. Without him, it was widely believed UNITA would fall apart, but all the power Luanda could muster seemed not enough to seize hold of the master of the *miombo*.

THE DECODING OF the human genome may have been trumpeted in June 2000 at a White House news conference, but the genetic secrets of the giant sable had yet to be cracked. I had been bugging Terry Robinson for months for word of any results. He'd moved to the University of Stellenbosch in late 1999, but it had taken longer to set up his lab than he anticipated. "However," he reassured me in February, "the giants remain the first order of priority." By April he wrote to tell me that Bettine van Vuuren had now made two unsuccessful attempts to amplify the DNA from the Gray Expedition teeth. "Bettine's results show what looks like a visible DNA pellet after extraction but there seems to be something inhibiting the PCR," he explained. He was going to let Conrad Matthee give it a try, and would let me know if they "got lucky." By mid-June he had to admit failure. "I'm afraid we bombed out with the teeth," he wrote. No one could get amplification and he was sending the teeth back to the Academy of Natural Sciences of Philadelphia. "It's really just too damn bad," he added. The next day, however, he assured me of his determination. "I haven't given up on the beast yet!" But he would need more teeth.

In my imagination I could see a giant sable bull parading through his harem of copper cows, throwing back his great head and peeling his lips over his teeth in a *flehman* grimace that doubled as a sneer.

RICHARD ESTES HAD forgotten his battered old 8×32 binoculars, so Runi sent them to me to bring to him. I was happy to do it; they were the same ones he'd used to observe herds of giant sables thirty years ago in the Luando Reserve, and I hoped they'd prove to be a potent good luck charm. Estes flew in from Tanzania on July 14 and we met up at the guest house I was staying at in Arcadia, Pretoria. Over dinner I told him what I knew of our impending expedition—which wasn't much.

The next morning Estes jogged through the hilly neighborhood before breakfast. Little keeps him from his exercise routine—it permits him to eat double cheeseburgers with impunity—and he finished off with a flourish of chin-ups on the child's swing set on the guest house's lawn. Shamed by his example, I went for a brisk uphill walk and did some push-ups. It was a good idea to get in some exercise; van Hoven had invited us to the wedding of one of his daughters from a previous marriage, and there would be a feast to follow. He picked us up in his car at midday. His two little towheaded, brown-eyed boys, ages two and four, were dressed in crisp shirts and clip-on bowties. They rode in the back with me. Estes, who hadn't seen van Hoven in some time, rode up front.

Estes asked van Hoven if he had any safety concerns about traveling into the interior of Angola. Van Hoven mentioned the recently reported terrorist incident in Malange. Taken aback, Estes asked me why I never said anything about it. I told him no one seemed to know how serious it was. Van Hoven concurred and turned to Estes. "Well, Dick, we have one thing to lose, and that's our lives. If there's any real danger, we'll just postpone, that's all. But we're not going to know what to do until we get there."

Estes mulled this over, then said that if we were going to travel to the reserves in government helicopters, would we be armed or unarmed? Unarmed, van Hoven thought—that way we wouldn't look like we were army. Estes wondered aloud if it wasn't better to go in a gunship; the threat of retaliation might make any guerrillas think twice about firing on us. Van Hoven shrugged. Estes fell silent. The little boys were very quiet, too.

IT WAS A startlingly cold Monday morning in Pretoria. I had to keep my hands in my pockets on a brisk morning walk through a neighborhood of upscale, well-fenced homes and embassies. Over breakfast, I read the morning paper, full of news of a heavy snowfall and bitter cold in the Cape. A man was reported frozen to death, hardly the way one expected people to expire in South Africa. It would be a lot warmer in Angola. Van Hoven picked us up at one o'clock for the drive to Johannesburg airport. There we met up with the latest person he'd recruited for the Kissama Foundation's board, Roelf Meyer, a former member of the South African Parliament. Widely respected across party lines before his recent retirement from active politics, he seemed a solid addition to Kissama's inner circle.

I expected Dodo might be waiting for us at the airport in Luanda, but he was recovering from a car accident. Fillipe de Freitas was waiting instead; there was a management vacuum at the foundation, and he had become the de facto director, shuttling between the Luanda office and the park and "liaising" with the generals. We threw our luggage into the back of his Mitsubishi pickup and squeezed into the cab. It was a particularly quick ride to the Shell compound because we rolled through stops and traffic lights to thwart the thieves who darted out of the shadows to grab whatever they could out of the open backs of trucks.

We met up with Peter Osborne again, and discussed the upcoming giant sable survey over whiskeys and cold beers in the guest condo. De Freitas said he knew nothing about the incident in Malange, although one general told him it wouldn't be a good idea to go there. On the other hand, he opined, General de Matos might say it's a "go." He said the chief of the defense forces was planning to borrow two helicopters from Sonangol, the state oil enterprise, for our foray into the reserves. They were better maintained than the army choppers.

We kicked around the likelihood of UNITA guerrillas being present. Osborne thought it highly unlikely they would be hanging out there on the offhand chance that something interesting might fly by for them to shoot down. Van Hoven said that if an air survey was ruled out we could still fly to Malange and then make an excursion by road. It would take two to five hours, depending on conditions, to drive to Luando Reserve from Malange. "We must push to the limits of acceptability and safety," he said. This led to a discouraging discussion of land mines and ambushes and whether it was better to be in the lead car or the last car of a convoy.

We turned in. Tomorrow we would learn what was in store for us.

WE MET FOR a ten o'clock meeting the next morning at the *Fundação Kissama* offices, which occupied a third-floor suite in a concrete high-rise building on a busy street. Up close, the building appeared a wreck. Wiring hung from the hallway ceiling, and the stairwell had been used as a public toilet; the stench made me gag. In the unpaved alleyways behind the building women drew water from a filthy well with buckets and did laundry in tubs while men dug holes in the red earth for purposes I couldn't divine. But the office, with its own generator and air-conditioning, was well insulated from the street and intermittent power failures. The white walls of the meeting room were bare, except for a blowup of the $400,000 check Shell had presented to the foundation and a large black-and-white topographical map of Quiçama taped to an opaque glass partition.

Brigadier General Melgaço showed up in camouflage fatigues at 9:58. Gen. João Baptiste de Matos arrived a few minutes later. A solidly built man in his late thirties, he too was in full camo, with rolled-up sleeves, and exuded a distinct air of authority. Van Hoven introduced Estes and me. De Matos seemed impressed with the interest shown in the *palanca negra*, and the fact that we had come all the way to Angola in the hope of verifying its survival.

De Matos took a seat midway down the table, instantly transforming it into the head chair. While we were waiting for others to turn up, he chatted aimiably in Portuguese with a snappily dressed Angolan in a blue blazer, striped shirt, and colorful silk tie, who turned out to be the chief of police. De Matos, like the Faceiras, is a *mestiço*, with a bronze complexion, short-cropped hair, a full mustache, and a bright, even-toothed smile. Depending on who you talked to, he was either the most powerful or second most powerful man in Angola. Some saw him as dos Santos's successor, perhaps even sooner than dos Santos would want. Although he supported earlier peace efforts, de Matos had led the government's forces against UNITA since 1992 with a vengeance, at one point ordering massive air attacks against the crippled city of Huambo in an effort to dislodge the rebels. He had long declared that "only the total defeat of Savimbi can ensure peace." De Matos sent troops into Congo (Brazzaville) in 1997 to ensure a government sympathetic to Luanda, and was also in charge of the Angolan forces in the Congo that had helped prop up Laurent Kabila's shaky regime for the past two years.

There were a few absences, including Jorge Valentim, who was in Europe, and Fátima Jardim, who was recovering from an auto accident, as well as Gen. Luis Faceira, but additional observers from various ministries showed up. At 10:15 Gen. Antonio Faceira walked in and apologized for being late. He sat across from de Matos and pulled out a notebook.

Van Hoven launched into his agenda. "On May 25, Botswana formally offered to contribute three hundred elephants to restock Quiçama. The scale of this operation has never been attempted before. We will bring in the first thirty by air." De Matos interrupted and asked if this wasn't going to be done by landing craft. Van Hoven explained that the fee for the vessel would be exorbitant: $400,000. De Matos nodded. Instead, they would catch elephants near Chobe starting on August 21, and take them to the nearest airport to be flown in separate shipments to Cabo Ledo, the coastal military base in the park.

The generals started talking about elephants among themselves in Portuguese. Couldn't they swim across the Cuanza? Suppose they started raiding crops on the other side of the river. Van Hoven assured them that the jumbos would have no reason to leave the lush vegetation on the north end of the park. De Matos wondered if the ceremony that was planned with dos Santos and the president of Botswana would happen as easily if the elephants came by air instead of ship. Van Hoven replied that a ceremonial release could be arranged on August 28 with the elephants that would be brought in earlier. Kobus du Toit was scheduled to arrive next week to supervise installation of the *boma*. Everyone concurred: the *boma* had to go up now.

A discussion broke out about what sort of aircraft might be available; Kasane airfield in Botswana had a 2,000-meter-long tar strip, but could an Ilyushin-76 cargo plane land there? De Matos waved off the problem: it was a technical issue. Everyone agreed that regardless of how the elephants were brought to Cabo Ledo, getting them to the fenced area in the north of the park meant that the miserable dirt road to Caua needed grading to eliminate any banks—trucks carrying elephant-tall containers could easily tip over. General Faceira said his men would sort out the road, no problem, and made a note with his fat fountain pen. Van Hoven brought up the issue of security. De Matos nodded; it was the biggest concern. If one elephant was lost to poachers . . . He rolled his eyes, and explained, in de Freitas's literal translation, that then the "bad habit of no conservation continues."

There was a rumor that someone had shot an eagle and a serval cat in the park. This was almost good news, an indication there might well be more animal life left there than first thought. More problems were aired: it would be a good idea to crack down on the sale of illegal ivory curios in the roadside markets on the way to the park, and new housing at the camp needed to be constructed. Van Hoven raised the issue of the proposed second fence, the one that was supposed to cut across the middle of the park from Cabo Ledo to Muxima. Now that he had seen the evironmental impact of the current fence, he had become reluctant to put another forty-foot-wide gouge across the sensitive landscape. It would cost $1.6 million to construct an electrified fence that would eventually have to come down anyway. Instead, he proposed a "human fence," linking the refugees now squatting in the park with the villagers who have always lived there, giving them some "voltage" through environmental education and hiring them to watch the elephants.

General Melgaço jumped up, grabbed a pointer, and started tapping noisily on the map of Quiçama. General Faceira whipped out a laser pointer and wiggled a red dot around the map to show where the second fence would go. A squabble in Portuguese erupted over how much had been paid out already for the fence materials and whether they could be resold. The generals shook their heads. I couldn't tell if they were unsettled by van Hoven's sudden about-face, the switch in plans, or the potential waste of money. After things calmed down, a consensus emerged that the second fence really was too expensive. Perhaps it was a bad idea all along, this stringing a steel fence across the heart of the park. Besides, the idea of spending the money allocated for the fence on people was very appealing, and everyone agreed that the time to start talking with the villagers was now. Some manioc had always been planted in the park, but it could not be allowed to get out of control. Already there was talk that some people had started using the park's trees to make palm wine.

By this time the meeting had gone on for nearly two hours, and people were yawning behind their hands. I was losing track of the tangled discussion and getting distracted by details of dress, such as the fact that one-star Brigadier Melgaço had a brown beret, two-star General Faceira had a red beret, and four-star General de Matos had a purple beret. But mostly I was getting anxious that van Hoven had yet to mention the survey.

At long last, he brought up the subject of a survey in Malange Province. But de Matos immediately cut in to give a short speech explaining that the army had occupied the now depopulated Luando Reserve, but unfortunately, none of the air patrols had seen any sign of the *palanca negra*. Of course, they weren't looking for them, so it was not necessarily a bad sign, just not encouraging, and while the security situation did not make the survey expedition impossible, the real stumbling block was logistical: there were no planes, vehicles, or accommodations available for us to use now.

Stricken, Estes and I slumped in our chairs. De Matos added that after the introduction of animals and the ceremony on August 28, it would be possible for him to organize a "proper program" for us. Estes made a heartfelt speech about how he had waited eighteen years to get back into the area he had first studied thirty years ago and had come all the way to Angola for the sole purpose of seeing the *palanca preta gigante*. De Matos was moved by the impassioned plea from this senior scientist *importante*. He looked at the ceiling and then relented somewhat. He suggested it might be possible to get into Malange city and then just possibly Cangandala Park. Estes, in an effort to close the deal, said we'd like to go by the end of the week. De Matos looked at his heavy gold watch and blew out his cheeks. Next week, perhaps. He took out a small map of Angola and put his finger on the giant sable areas. Estes smiled and said he remembered them very well. De Matos smiled back. Smiles broke out all around, and handshakes were exchanged. The meeting broke up, although I had no idea what had been decided.

It seemed we had a reprieve for our hopes of venturing into the interior, but it was all vague and unsettled—who was getting in touch with the general? Did he understand who was going? Would we have a translator? What day would we leave?

Van Hoven said de Matos would get back to us. "You can't push these guys," he said. "It doesn't work."

I was left clinging to what was promised in the general's smile. On the way back to the Shell compound, we stopped so Meyer could pay a courtesy call at a Mercedes dealership owned by an Angolan businessman he knew. The facility also sold BMW convertibles, and for that matter, enormous refrigerators and wide-screen televisions. In my disembodied mood, I couldn't decide if this sleek showroom of luxury goods in the middle of squalid Luanda was an outrage or a sign of progress. The whole place was surrounded by blue-uniformed guards in black berets, an indication that the customer base here was a select one. The guard blocking the showroom door wore mirrored sunglasses and didn't move a muscle, and it took some time to convince him we shouldn't be brushed off. Once we were inside, the receptionist suggested we wait in the upscale café attached to the showroom. The décor was international coffee bar, right down to a chalkboard list of trendy concoctions. I passed on the "Luanda latte" and opted for an espresso, which came with—surprise—a packet of sugar advertising Palanca Café, complete with the head of a sable. I circled my spoon in the small fat cup and watched the pretty *mestiço* girls in starched uniforms and little white caps behind the bulging curves of the mahogany and glass pastry cases as they waited languidly on a steady trickle of well-heeled customers. One by one they offered for close inspection an alluring array of sticky sweets, sugary cakes, soft rolls, plump éclairs, and various Portuguese custards oozing their fillings.

We conferred. The ideal plan was to visit Quiçama the next day, then leave Thursday for Malange, have a couple of days afield, and return on Sunday. Meyer said he couldn't go with us; he had to leave Luanda on Friday. Van Hoven thought unless there was a chance of flying to Malange by the weekend, he might as well leave on Friday too; he had Operation Noah's Ark to conduct. But Estes and I were more than willing to stay on in Luanda if there was any chance to go. Finally, we were admitted into the genial owner's office and found the chief of police just taking his leave, along with an advisor to the president. Luanda's elite circulated in a very small world.

AFTER A DUSTY day in Quiçama checking on the progress of preparations for Operation Noah's Ark, we returned, tired and dirty, to the Shell compound. Meyer went off to make a phone call, and van Hoven pulled out his papers. The amount of unfinished business left to wrap up would have put most people into a full-blown panic. Van Hoven looked over the list and muttered to himself, as if mildly surprised, "I see we haven't got a lot of time." The fence, which was supposed to have long been completed, was missing the final section and what had been erected needed to be repaired and cleared of weeds. The necessary permits for imports hadn't been secured, the transportation wasn't settled, nor had the road been graded for the twelve-foot-high elephant containers to pass safely—the list went on and on. Van Hoven had sharp words with de Freitas; faxes had been going back and forth between Pretoria and Luanda that had yet to be answered. Van Hoven was overloaded, was keeping too much in his head and relying on others to take responsibility even when they hadn't been given clear directions. But they parted amicably enough; right now, van Hoven needed de Freitas.

Lack of ideas has never been van Hoven's problem. Over dinner he shared his latest brainstorm: put a minicam on the head of one of the elephants that will be flown in to record the daily activities of pachyderm life in Quiçama—eating leaves, showering in the Cuanza, tusking baobabs, hanging out with fellow jumbos, courting, copulating, and all the rest. The images would be picked up by satellite and broadcast directly over the Internet. Why watch some woman in Pasadena put on makeup in real time when you could follow *My Life as an Elephant* 24/7?

The next day de Freitas took van Hoven and Meyer to see Gen. Antonio Faceira about further details of Operation Noah. Estes and I decided to stay put; he needed to finish some encyclopedia entries on antelopes, and my giant sable monomania could only get on van Hoven's nerves. The hours dragged by. Finally they drove up with the makings of a fish barbeque and news that Antonio Faceira would be meeting with de Matos on Monday and promised to "organize something." In the meantime, Estes and I would have to find another refuge; Peter Osborne was expecting other guests.

Friday morning, Estes and I went with de Freitas to take van Hoven and Meyer to the airport, and then stopped at the Kissama office to send off a couple of E-mails. If all went well, we would be incommunicado for several days. De Freitas boosted our confidence by telling us that we could expect de Matos to take us to Malange on his private jet. What's more, he would not let us out of his sight—he wouldn't want anything to happen to an American scientist and a journalist. We asked de Freitas if he would come along as a translator. "Look, I am a fatalist—if you are destined to die, you die, that's all. But I don't want to go there," he said. "Land mines, ambushes . . ." Clearly, he thought we were nuts. When I pressed him about it, he said he'd once been in a military jet that had an engine blown off by a missile when it was landing and didn't care to repeat the experience. He went off to run some errands.

Estes called the U.S. embassy to get an independent view of the sanity of our venturing into the interior and reached the security officer there, who was surprised we were in Luanda in the first place. He gave Estes a disquieting update on the military situation: Malange city itself was secure, but heading into the bush would require a full-scale military convoy. He made it plain that with the ever-present danger of ambush by well-armed rebels, he'd "have a hard time selling seats on that trip."

When de Freitas returned, we went in search of a reasonably priced hotel—most of the major ones in Luanda are several hundred dollars a night. Although it's a toilet of a tourist destination, the city is as expensive as Tokyo because everything—milk, eggs, bottled water, even the plants

335

in hotel lobbies, which sounds bizarre, given the climate—has to be flown in by plane. To make our limited cash go further, we needed to pick up some food. In Luanda, little boys gather when cars back out of parking spots and pretend to give directions in the hopes of being thrown a coin, but older boys are often more ambitious. As we climbed in the pickup after one stop, we were surrounded by a gang of youths who banged on the vehicle and its windows while one of them yanked open the rear door as I was closing it and lunged for my camera bag. When de Freitas burst out of the truck's cab, they all scattered into traffic.

Soon after, de Freitas started complaining of being alternately cold and then hot, and having a headache. He suspected malaria, but seemed rather casual about it; on the other hand, he'd had it several times before. He'd get a blood test at the army clinic, he said, and shoved a Shania Twain cassette into the tape deck. At the Jumbo, a sort of Angolan Wal-Mart for the wealthy, we were frisked at the door for weapons. Estes and I loaded up on cheese, sausages, bread, fruit, and bottled water. Back in the parking lot, a young boy ran over as we were climbing into the pickup. His face was nothing but a suppurating mask, melted down by some ghastly disease or perhaps hideously burned. We jumped back, and I flung the entire contents of my pocket into his open palms before leaping into the cab. De Freitas gunned the pickup and we shot out of the parking lot. I calculated my knee-jerk gift of crumpled-up kwanzas had bestowed the equivalent of one-tenth of one U.S. cent on the street child.

At the clinic, de Freitas was diagnosed with malaria. After dropping us off at a hotel by the bay, he planned to check into the clinic, at least overnight, for observation and more tests; we'd talk in the morning. Estes phoned Serodio de Almeida, who was happy to hear from us and stopped by on his way home from Agostinho Neto University, where he was now a senior lecturer in ecology. I asked why he lost his ministerial portfolio. He shrugged. "Politics!" he said, and waved his hand as if to ward off the distasteful subject. But he was not disappointed to be out of the government. "I couldn't do anything anyway—no money." Estes told him we had just visited Quiçama. "The elephants are not a problem for me, the roan is not a problem, the *pacaça* buffalo is not a problem," de Almeida said. It was the precedent that bothered him. He worried that the northern fence would interfere with the seasonal movements of the animals in the park, who gathered near the Cuanza in the dry season. As far as he knew, no environmental impact study of the fence was ever done, as required by the regulations passed by the national assembly. Now these regulations were being ignored. If a fence could be put up and nonnative species introduced into the north end of the park, what did that mean for the future? He was sorry to admit he was suspicious about van Hoven, because he had nothing against him personally.

"I'm reserving judgment on van Hoven," Estes said. "I don't think he intends to bring giant sable to Quiçama or South Africa. I think he has accepted the idea that no nonnative species should be released into Quiçama"—although some Angolan species intended for restocking of other parks might end up in the fenced area. He added that as far as he could tell, the Kissama Foundation "looked like an up-and-up operation," and that Brian Huntley may have "overreacted" to the first press releases put out by the foundation.

But, de Almeida asked, "after van Hoven, in the future, in another government, then what?" He feared commercialization and disregard for environmental standards for national parks could mean the door would be opened to other commercial enterprises, perhaps a return to the bad old days when cattle ranching and oil exploration overgrazed the plains and ravaged the landscape in Quiçama, the very things Brian Huntley had successfully fought against. If wildlife didn't come first now, what would the priorities be when van Hoven was no longer involved? He said this with evident sadness, as though nothing would make him happier than to be shown his concerns had been groundless.

As he left, de Freitas called. He had been hospitalized; he must have been sicker than we thought.

FOR THE NEXT four days, we waited for some word from de Matos.

Estes took his usual morning run; except for the car exhaust, it was enjoyable, he informed me, and he was pleased to notice that herons were nesting in the Australian pines along the beach. I kept alternating between enthusiasm and depression about our prospects and in any event had had my fill of Luanda's street life. The hotel breakfast had its own Angolan contrasts—delicious fresh pineapple, a stone cold fried egg repulsively congealed. Over coffee, Estes conceded that he'd been having second thoughts about the trip, too; unless we could get some reassurance about going to Malange, we might as well give up. I reluctantly concurred.

I called de Freitas. He sounded much better; it was a mild case of malaria, he said, and he'd be leaving the clinic soon. Gen. Antonio Faceira's meeting with de Matos Monday morning was still on and he would let us know the grand plan that would presumably follow. Estes agreed it sounded encouraging. I wondered, however, about the likelihood of seeing any giant sable from a military convoy. Would we be able to set foot on the soil, or would the possibility of land mines preclude that?

As our cash was dwindling rapidly, we moved from the bayside to the Hotel Avenida a couple of doors down from the Angolan press office. The colonial-era building was well maintained and clean, only $100 a night, and we could share a twin-bed room. The seven-minute taxi ride cost $17, but it was the only taxi service in Luanda that we were assured wouldn't dream of kidnapping us.

Estes proposed that we have our main meal at midday, so that we didn't have to walk around the streets at night. In fact, the same advice has been printed in translation and left in our room: "Do not walk around alone, mainly tonight." But he was keen to explore Luanda, which he remembered from better days. He brazenly wore his camera, telephoto lens and all, hanging around his neck during daylight strolls. The rest of the time we stayed in our hotel room, typed on our laptops, flipped through Angolan magazines in Portuguese, and hoped the phone would ring. We had cable TV too, but there was only the choice of the boring government station, endless coverage of the Tour de France in French, or amateur hour from Oporto in Portugal.

I flopped on my bed and as the complaining springs subsided, reflected on the state of Angola. Too many people came and they all stayed too long. The Portuguese came centuries ago when they could hardly be expected to have behaved any differently than they had. That explained why the proper ladies of Luanda used to be carried to Mass in curtained hammocks by slaves, followed by more slaves bearing cushions, fans, and prayer books, in a lavish display of piety, oblivious to the cruelty they rested on. But fervent beliefs have always abetted colonial exploitation, which is also why the Portuguese hung on so long, and when they finally gave up, Angola was nothing but a broken dream for the *colonos* and a crippled legacy for its inhabitants. And foreign powers, like the United States, who fervently believed their interests were at stake, kept the civil war that broke out at independence going years after it made sense for them to do so, and of course it now grinds on mercilessly without outside help, thank you very much. It had been nearly forty years since the beginning of the anti-colonial struggle, twenty-five years since the civil war began, and for all that time Angola's infrequent periods of peace have been little better than pauses in the hostilities.

By some estimates, a million Angolans have died in the civil war and the nation is sprinkled with roughly 12 million land mines left by various combatants, one for every person left alive. Others say that's a complete exaggeration, there's only half that number of explosive devices, which means Angolans must share this special patrimony, two per land mine. The truth is that the various armies lost count and didn't keep track of where they were strewing them, but there are sure to be enough to surprise generations of truck drivers and farmers and children to come. Angola has bottomed out on most measures of human dignity, from infant mortality on down, for many years now. The conflict has been so protracted and the resulting statistics so bloated that the international community long ago contracted Angola fatigue, a diplomatic condition that makes other humanitarian crises appear far more attention-worthy, if only because they're new.

But it's more than chronic war that has eaten away at the national soul.

I got up and looked out the window at the street filled with money-changing ladies and hawkers and open trucks with armed soldiers and new UN vehicles and the odd amputee hopping down the sidewalk using a branch for a crutch. For every person that strode by purposefully, there appeared to be dozens just standing or sitting or leaning. They were waiting for something to happen, but I doubted many had a sense of expectancy. In Luanda, there is immense wealth for a privileged few and crushing poverty for almost everyone else. Flagrant, open corruption has become pervasive.

Some Western observers say it's not "constructive" to focus on corruption in a country so beaten down by war, but it's impossible to ignore. Angolans have told me that it wasn't that bad before 1990, just the usual sort of bureaucratic influence peddling and hand-in-the-till fund skimming, with teachers and government clerks demanding bribes to supplement their tiny and undependable incomes. Now it had spread everywhere. Taking care of yourself first is just common sense to most Angolans today, given the regime they live under and that the war makes their future uncertain. Not surprisingly, everyone expects to take their cut as soon as they gain access to money. This attitude has penetrated into nearly every transaction. There are always two invoices, the real one and another with the inflated figure built in, and it isn't a 10 percent commission, it's a 200 or 300 percent commission. It's simply the way business is done. There is a term for it: *vertentes*, the Portuguese word for "slopes." In Angola, it refers to the angles required to accomplish anything—who has to be paid off, by how much, and when.

It started at the top, when the MPLA found itself with a country to run and a catastrophic war to fight, and little security even for the leaders. It was then that the politicians began helping themselves to public monies, and by now the habit is practically institutionalized, centered around the powerful, sycophantic group that surrounds President dos Santos at Futungo Palace. There is plenty of opportunity. Oil revenue has been $2 or $3 billion a year for almost a decade, and what happens to it is disguised in a national budget that has been described as fiction. A substantial part of it is apparently dispensed at will by dos Santos himself to buttress his power. How much ends up in his own pockets is unclear. One hears a lot of gossip about dos Santos in Luanda; that he is the largest private landowner in Brazil, that he owns a colossal palace in Portugal, and so forth. Hard facts are hard to come by. But in 1996 he started a private foundation, the *Fundação Eduardo dos Santos*, with funds contributed by oil companies, as well as signature bonuses received by the state for awarding oil blocks. The foundation builds schools and provides humanitarian relief, in effect allowing him to gain a reputation as a philanthropist for what the government he has led for two decades should have been providing all along.

What I have seen for myself is the wealth of the generals. The excuse of necessarily secret military spending can explain away hundreds of millions, and arms deals, by their secretive nature, are ideal for kickback arrangements. But it's apparently diamond revenues that are really fattening the generals' bank accounts, at the same time that many soldiers go unpaid, unfed, and unclothed. It's hardly a revelation that UNITA's control of the diamond areas now funds its operations, but when these mines in the Lunda Provinces come back under government control, only a tenth of the revenues expected from them reach Luanda. Much of it is thought to disappear in illicit deals between rebel leaders and army generals.

But a general doesn't have to do anything that crude to accrue wealth. Rewarding the loyalty of top generals with diamond concessions for a nominal license fee is an easy form of government patronage—it enables them to find wealthy foreign partners eager to have a stake in the industry. Besides, if a diamond mining company wanted to do business in the unsafe interior of Angola, and needed a "sleeping partner," who better than a general? They know how to get things done, how to shake loose permits or bypass troublesome regulations, and they have key connections and access to intelligence and can pitch in with the military's resources when necessary. Given that war is a condition of doing business in Angola, entering into partnership with a general can be a wise move.

The details that had begun to emerge in recent reports from various human rights and political watch groups suggested that the generals I'd met had become astute businessmen. After their mutually beneficial experience with Executive Outcomes, the generals "sought to develop their own methods of melding military activity with entrepreneurial pursuits," as one analyst put it, obtaining diamond concessions (both legal and illegal) and gaining control over the *garimpeiros*, or rural prospectors who risk scrabbling for gemstones in the valuable terrain contested by UNITA and the government to peddle their finds to either side. What's more, they now dominated the domestic private security industry. The top generals are said to require that the diamond mining companies in which they have a stake hire security companies in which they're also involved, in effect profiting from protecting their own diamond holdings.

Was the growing power and independence of the generals making dos Santos uncomfortable? He must have thought he was buying their unswerving support by dispensing diamond concessions to them, but their evident wealth has also given them greater autonomy from the Futungo elite. In 1996, dos Santos had even tried to buy off Jonas Savimbi with diamonds, offering to give UNITA the right to exploit certain concessions through a legally registered company as a "peace-building" measure, in effect rewarding the rebel movement with mining rights. But the proposed deal finally collapsed, and hostilities resumed.

By now there are no causes left on either side in Angola except the control of riches—the war has become a naked struggle for the nation's resources. Meanwhile, the Luanda government has ruled through repression and UNITA through terror, though the difference in emphasis would be lost on anyone catching a bullet from the troops of either side.

Night was falling. It was time to pull the curtains; the mosquitos would be coming out, and besides, it was unwise for foreigners to advertise their presence to the street life below.

DE FREITAS CALLED ON Monday to report that de Matos would make a final decision by 8:30 A.M. Tuesday. He said there was talk of a "program." I took that as a sign that it was really going to come off.

It was back to waiting. I worked while Estes napped, and we traded off recharging our laptops. Outside in the street a pained wailing started, as if someone had been hurt or robbed. I couldn't see where it was coming from, but it didn't seem to elicit much interest from the pedestrians. By this time we were starting to get on each other's nerves. Estes's Yankee tightwad tendencies had emerged, and he insisted on always turning off the light in the bathroom, even though it was only a seven-watt bulb. On the other hand, I had eaten more than my share of the biscuits he was wisely hoarding for both of us. We tiptoed around each other and went to bed early.

The next morning we packed our bags after an early breakfast. De Freitas called us at 8:30 A.M. to report that Antonio Faceira was going to de Matos's office. Estes read about the Unabomber in an old *Time* magazine. I watched a rebroadcast of some decades-old English soccer finals on cable TV with the sound turned off. It matched my mood. Estes and I were both too keyed up to work. It was 9:30 A.M. and we still hadn't heard anything. An hour went by. By eleven o'clock I called de Freitas. His cell phone wasn't working.

From the window of our room the vehicular traffic looked like a demolition derby parade, except for one shiny sports car. I made a list of all the different things I saw women carrying on their heads: buckets of fish, a single yogurt container, whole stacks of eggs, an entire heavy door, long pieces of lumber and plastic pipes, cans of spray paint. It does wonders for their posture, and left their hands free, too. They were remarkably adept and could even break into a run without losing their load when a van threatened to clip them. I sketched one bread-bearing woman with a child tied around her waist, and for a moment, it took my mind off waiting.

By 12:20 P.M. we couldn't stand it anymore and I called the Kissama office to leave a message for de Freitas to get in touch with us immediately. I went back to the window and watched a man riding slowly down the sidewalk on what looked to be an upside-down tricycle. I realized he was pedaling it with his hands, his legs either useless and folded up or missing—I couldn't quite tell. Estes and I were starting to snap at each other. He tried the Kissama office himself and reached de Freitas, who said he'd just arrived and would call in half an hour with a definite answer. We expected him to call before two o'clock but heard nothing. We'd had it with waiting and decided to walk to the snack bar for lunch. The call came in as we were passing through the lobby. I picked up the phone.

"It's not good news," de Freitas said. "General de Matos apologizes, but it's a no-go. The situation in Malange is unstable and under the circumstances, he says he can't risk it."

There was no one to blame but Savimbi.

IT WAS RAINING heavily in Cape Town, and in the shadows of the cliffs at Kirstenbosch Gardens, cataracts plummeted down the rocky gorges. Estes was in Cape Town to visit his son Lyndon, so the three of us met briefly with Brian Huntley at Pearson House. Huntley wore a bemused expression on his face as Estes described our abortive mission. He was not at all surprised at the turn of events, he said, and used a favorite phrase of the continent's cynics: "Africa wins again!"

But there was more to report. On our return to Pretoria, van Hoven had asked Estes for IUCN support for Operation Noah. He had no interest in biologically dubious wildlife management schemes, he said, and the imprimatur of the IUCN would help allay any lingering conservation concerns over the translocations. Estes arranged for the two of them to meet in Skukuza with Jeremy Anderson and Petri Viljoen, a senior scientist at Kruger, to discuss the details of exactly which species and subspecies should be introduced into the park. It was obvious van Hoven would accept their findings. Huntley was interested in that development, but it was clear he was not about to become a convert anytime soon. He was waiting to see what would happen. In the meantime, he had a committee meeting. As we walked outside, he told me he understood how disappointed I must feel about not being able to get into the giant sable lands. "Don't give up," he said with surprising feeling.

I spoke to van Hoven by phone before flying back to the United States. The release of animals was unlikely to happen on August 28, he said. "There are so many factors." He couldn't bring in elephants in the hope that the fence would be finished, repaired, and cleared of brush, and that security patrols will be in place and all the rest—he simply couldn't take the chance. He needed to know that all those things were in place before the elephants were captured. And now Botswana was concerned that Kobus du Toit would be in charge of the operation. Du Toit's experience—he has relocated several hundred elephants—now counted against him. He had captured the Tuli elephants, after all, and while what happened to them afterwards was hardly his fault, it might make the operation look controversial. They wanted it put off until next year. But van Hoven could always obtain several elephants, perhaps a rhino, and a few assorted antelopes from South Africa for the initial release. I was afraid to ask about the possibility of a giant sable survey for fear he'd tell me it was a dead issue.

Back home in mid-August I spoke with Estes in New Hampshire by phone to ask him how the ASG meeting with van Hoven went. He and Lyndon had driven up with van Hoven to Kruger, where the professor of wildlife management had hit it off with everyone. The upshot, Estes said, was that the Antelope Specialists Group would endorse Operation Noah's

Ark so long as it abided by certain restrictions. Jeremy Anderson would send van Hoven a list of species the ASG approved for release into Quiçama; the giant sable, it was made clear, would not be on it. The IUCN biologists were already thinking ahead; Anderson suggested that when lions are introduced, warthogs should be too, so that the big cats wouldn't be forced to dine exclusively on the roan that would be released.

I told Estes it was too bad the giant sable survey never got off the ground. He disagreed.

"Let's face it, there was a palpable risk of being shot down," he said. A survey expedition was just not in the cards—not now anyway. "I think we have to let it ride."

Ten

Flight of Antelopes

"Hundreds of Rare Antelope in Angola Flee Park Toward War Zone" read the headline of the press report that appeared in September 2000. The story had been broken by Angolan radio, and although I could smile at giant sables being described as large black antelopes with "crooked antlers" living only in Cangandala Park, I was alarmed that they were reported to "have run as far as 200 km away from the park near the town of Andulo, in Bié Province," an area that had seen heavy fighting between government and rebel forces the week before. The story concluded ominously: "The giant sable, already on the brink of extinction, could become even rarer if they leave their natural habitat and run into war zones, according to experts from the Institute for Forestry Development. The experts could not explain why the antelope had left the park or how they had chosen their path."

Had the war driven them out of their haunts into even greater danger? I had visions of the *palancas* bolting out of the reserves as rockets exploded around them only to end up in the cook-pots of government or UNITA troops. I queried Estes, van Hoven, and Anderson by E-mail, but unable to wait for a reply, phoned them all the same day. Estes didn't think that the last of the animals were galloping off into the sunset, but because the human population had moved out of the region, the giant sable might be "dispersing once again into what must have been its former habitat." Van Hoven thought the report indicated there were more giant sables in the region than anyone thought. Anderson was suspicious; the story didn't ring right to him, but he said it was just possible that a new population could have been encountered. I didn't like the sound of it.

346

WHEN I GOT back from Africa in early August I had begun planning to return in a matter of weeks, ostensibly to see what would happen with Operation Noah's Ark, but really to advance my chances of getting into the giant sable lands. I called van Hoven. He had an offer of thirty elephants from Madikwe Game Reserve in South Africa's North West Province. They were used to electric fences, hence there would be no need for a *boma*. And he'd lined up some Livingstone's eland and warthog, as well as kudu, but due to ASG/IUCN concerns, those would be kept in the fenced area for later relocation to other parks. He had just been out to Johannesburg to check on the suitability of the containers for elephants. "All the parts of this jigsaw puzzle are falling into place," he said. So far, he was planning on capturing entire family groups and flying them in on September 9 and 11, and the other species on the 16th. Of course, he warned me unnecessarily, those dates were subject to change. I E-mailed him a few days later to ask if I could fly in on the last airlift, and, naturally, inquired about the possibility of de Matos taking us into the reserves the following week. He said yes, and promised he'd bring it up the survey expedition with the general.

In a late August phone conversation, van Hoven told me that the park opening was scheduled for September 17, and an antelope release a day later. He needed to be there for the opening—dos Santos might come—so he was flying to Luanda on the 16th. He suggested I go on the cargo plane with the antelopes that would depart from Hoedspruit near Kruger early on the 17th and arrive at dawn at Cabo Ledo in Quiçama. I'd be there in plenty of time for the opening of the park. And Willy, his assistant, would be driving up the night before and could give me a lift from Johannesburg airport. This sounded perfect; de Matos would be there, and I'd have a chance to push the survey again. But van Hoven cautioned me that there had been another rebel attack on Malange, and the Angolans were overstretched as it was with Operation Noah's Ark. "Look," he said, "on a scale of one to ten, the likelihood of their organizing a trip into Malange is about three."

I offered to write to de Matos. He thought it was a good idea, and gave me the general's fax number. I got off the phone and immediately composed a letter to the chief of Angola's defense forces respectfully requesting his help. If he could take Professor van Hoven and me on a brief foray into the interior to confirm that the animals still survived in their habitat, I wrote, it "would be an extraordinary conservation accomplishment for the Kissama Foundation." I sent it off, with a copy to van Hoven, who also urged de Matos to consider a trip to investigate the status of the animal by the end of August.

Three days later van Hoven was fuming about a *Chicago Tribune* report that suggested Angola was wasting precious funds on the rehabilitation of parks while a million of its people were being kept alive on UN food donations. "Angola isn't spending any government money on this— it's all foreign donors," he told me wearily. The article's claim that it was "bad genetics" to relocate elephants from Botswana to Angola also irritated him. There were no elephants left in Quiçama to interbreed with and Botswana would either have to let its excess elephants starve to death or start culling them—sending them to Angola was a way of saving them. To top it off, the piece quoted Brian Huntley, but van Hoven wasn't surprised at the biologist's remarks. "Investing resources into conservation in Angola today is a waste," Huntley said. "It's like pumping blood into a body that's had its legs shot off."

Van Hoven was on his cell phone at Mafeking airfield near the game reserve, looking over captured elephants, and couldn't talk long. He had scheduled a press conference at the airport, and lined up a film company to cover the translocation.

I saw the tape that resulted some weeks later. It showed small family groups of elephants in Madikwe being tracked by helicopters and then darted from the air; they staggered and finally collapsed on their haunches. Guided by radio contact, the ground crew arrived, and carefully rolled the huge animals over to make sure they didn't suffocate from their own weight; one of the crew held the end of a jumbo's trunk clear to make sure it was breathing. Others hosed them down to keep them cool. In all, four bulls, two cows, and four calves were rounded up. There was footage of ellies in slings, lifted by cranes, a dozen hands guiding the immense loads onto the trucks. Green-painted steel shipping containers had been altered to create stalls for the adults to prevent shifting during flight, but they were left open at the bottom so calves could find their mothers. Because the amount of urine an elephant voids is enough to play havoc with a cargo plane's wiring, special waterproof trays had been fitted to the bottom of each container, but they failed to prevent an alarming amount of sloshing. The first flight took off with seven pachyderms on board, but on landing at Cabo Ledo, a large cow stumbled and wedged herself in the corner of the container and suffered respiratory failure. Efforts to revive her were useless, but fortunately her calf was nearly weaned and would be accepted by the others.

At the off-loading in Cabo Ledo the generals were there—I spotted de Matos, the Faceiras, and Hendrik as the camera panned around—with squads of soldiers. The Angolans were all visibly excited. Apparently, many had never seen an elephant before; some of the generals actually became teary-eyed at the sight. There was much fussing with the containers, and it was 11:00 A.M. before the containers were loaded on the trucks. It took until two o'clock to get into the fenced area of the park and up to the off-loading ramp, which was too low. As the elephants began to overheat in the containers, the generals rolled up their sleeves to pitch in themselves and after much shouting and digging the ramp was ready and the container doors opened. There was a shot of one young adult elephant backing out cautiously, kicking up red dust, and scooping up some with its trunk and tossing it over his head. It was quickly joined by others, some wearing radio collars, all with white numbers spray-painted on their hindquarters. A pair strode off into the bush, ears flapping, trumpeting loudly, a calf scampering to keep up. The crowd cheered wildly.

The second flight a few days later went more smoothly and brought the total number of elephants to fifteen. I planned for my departure. Estes E-mailed me to let me know he'd written Brian Huntley to tell him he'd concluded the Kissama Foundation "deserves support." He cited the sound management plan that van Hoven had drawn up for the park, and addressed a key issue. "The composition of the Kissama Foundation board, with three top generals, the chief of police, etc., has raised some concern about what they expect to get out of it," he admitted, but said the presence of so many important ministers suggests something else, too: "Isn't it a plus that the most influential leaders in Angola are involved? That's quite an accomplishment." Cooperating with like-minded people could only assist the restoration of Angola's wildlife. He finished with a plea: "I really wish you would reconsider working with the Kissama Foundation."

349

The next day—the same day the story of giant sables fleeing into the war zone broke—van Hoven told me the opening had been rescheduled for the 16th. But rest assured, he said, there would be someone to pick me up at the airport when I landed the day before and to drive me directly to Hoedspruit, where a team of South African sky divers hired for the park opening would fly with me to Cabo Ledo. When we spoke a few hours later, he said I could forget about the sky divers; my fellow passengers now included a film crew and a French student who was going to work in the park for a month. And yes, he'd try to "twist de Matos's arm" on the subject of the survey.

The day of departure, my New York–to–Johannesburg flight was delayed four hours, which meant I wouldn't arrive until 6:30 P.M., too late for a ride to Hoedspruit. Then disaster struck: van Hoven E-mailed me that the animal shipment was canceled—the antelopes weren't ready, it was too hot to capture them, they might be too stressed, and it wouldn't be any good to open a cage at the ceremony and find a dozen dead animals sprawled inside. Unfortunately, there was no way for me to get to Angola in time for the park opening. I agonized over this, and called van Hoven back to see if someone could pick me up late Saturday in Luanda, only to find out the cargo flight was back on: after van Hoven canceled it, the generals called up and put enormous pressure on him to bring animals to release at the opening of the park.

I WAS EN ROUTE over the Atlantic, trying to get some fitful sleep, when van Hoven nearly decided to give up once again. Everything was in place for the animal airlift except for specialized rubber mats for the containers. Ordinary rubber mats become slick with urine, and he couldn't take the risk of delivering a planeload of antelopes with broken legs. But he couldn't obtain the right mats. His wife Suzanne saved the day by tracking down a specialty rubber supplier in Johannesburg who agreed to open early on Friday and meet with van Hoven. He spent the morning cutting up the mats himself to fit the containers.

Deon, a tall, lanky, long-haired blond Afrikaner who'd been work-ing on the airlifts, met me in the arrivals hall and warned me we didn't have much time to spare. In minutes, it seemed, we were racing along the N4 through the moonlight landscape in his Mercedes at 160 kph. Deon informed me the reopening of the park had been postponed, and the cere-monies that would accompany the release would be minimal. Van Hoven must have been furious, I thought—he'd pulled off something amazing, and now the Angolans had fumbled it. But when Deon told me he thought van Hoven was not planning to return to South Africa until Thursday, I leapt to the conclusion that General de Matos had agreed to take us into the interior for a few days.

The two of us hurtled down the highway, slowing down only for stretches of cottony fog and later, some sharp curves as the road twisted through the Drakensberg Mountains. The veld fires in the distance, like snaking lines of burning torches in the black night, sent up billows of smoke and made the craggy hills look like the red lips of active volcanoes. South-ern Africa smolders with these blazes at this time of year, which are al-most always set to clear off brush, or simply by tradition, but these days often just for the hell of it.

We arrived at the military airfield at Hoedspruit, pulling in behind a waiting convoy of trucks and cars and *bakkies* full of animal handlers and their families who'd come to see the loading of the animals onto the cargo plane. Kobus du Toit and Chris Mostert were standing on the road in the glare of headlights next to two huge tractor trailers. The massive green steel containers held eight Livingstone's eland and ten kudu from Mostert's farm, young healthy animals, he informed me, from the same herds I saw at his ranch. I could hear them shifting inside. The sentries at the gate gave us clearance, and we wound around the twisting roads to a vast runway and the sight of an immense Russian Ilyushin-76 cargo plane lit up by batteries of powerful lights. From behind, its tail towered above us and its open rear cargo doors revealed a twenty-five-yard-deep bay, big enough to swallow three full containers end to end—up to forty tons of cargo.

The flight had been cleared for takeoff along with its Russian crew, but I hadn't, and neither had Guillaume, a young French biology student who was planning to track animals in Quiçama before resuming his studies in Pretoria. We were the only passengers; the animal handlers weren't going—these bovids wouldn't need any attention until they got to Angola. Guillaume, whose English was far better than my French, told me he'd never been to Africa before. He asked me if Angola would be exciting. I told him it would live up to his expectations.

It was 1:00 A.M. Although the South African immigration service had agreed to meet the plane and put exit stamps in our passports, one of the two officers on the scene seemed to think the purpose of his driving out to the airfield was to prevent us from leaving. At this hour, a dozen cell phone calls failed to locate a more senior immigration official to set him straight, although a police administrator, roused from sleep, told the stubborn officer that he should be more concerned with who entered the country than who left it. I sat in Deon's car, tired and depressed, while Deon continued to argue with the officers. It was getting close to 3:00 A.M., the expected departure time, and the two steel containers of antelopes had been loaded into the belly of the plane and chained down to keep them from shifting in flight.

A short, stocky Afrikaner from Mostert's crew called me over to his *bakkie*. I should put my bags on the tarmac near the car, he explained. The entire group there, men, women, and children, would walk en masse with Guillaume and me over to the plane bringing our luggage; the two of us could quietly board in the dark while the others milled around as cover and then walked away. If there were any questions they'd say that the animals were restless and needed sedation. The immigration officers weren't paying much attention anyway—they were sitting in their car, busy with their argument. We sauntered over in a group, invisible in the shadows of the landing gear, and climbed up into the cavernous, dimly lit cargo bay. It looked like the back of an auto repair shop, all wires and dials and fat spare tires and toolboxes and magazine centerfolds taped to the bulkhead.

Deon climbed up and handed me the Northern Province export papers and the veterinary health certificate for the animals. I wondered if this little caper was going to get me into trouble, but there was no other way for me to get to Angola in time for the animal release. I tucked the papers away, and shook his hand, as if being a stowaway on a Russian cargo plane was old hat. Guillame was enjoying the frisson of adventure. So were the children; it was like something out of the movies—they were helping people escape and scampered up the companionway bringing our luggage. We hid between the two chained and shackled containers, and sat on our suitcases staring up at the dangling insulation and exposed wiring in the dim yellow light. There wasn't much space for us; it felt like we were riding between boxcars. Guillame turned to me, grinned, and whispered, "For first African experience, this is not bad!"

The antelopes milled around inside their dark steel confines, shuffling and lurching into the sides of the forward container like inmates rattling their jail bars. Then they started a tremendous racket, a hammering-on-a-Dumpster-with-baseball-bats kind of din that set off the other container's worth of *bovidae*. With all the noise, I couldn't tell if the hatch had been shut. I poked my head around the corner of the container and spotted some Russian crewmen—one smoking a cigarette—and glimpsed several other figures.

The engines started revving, sending a deep, shaking vibration through-out the plane. Sitting between two massive steel containers was obviously no place to be while the plane took off, so we dragged our luggage forward and to my astonishment I found that Dodo was aboard. "Mister John!" he greeted me, pumping my hand. He was on some unspecified "Kissama business," and so presumably were another couple of Angolans, two men and a woman, who joked in Portuguese and clustered at one of the few portholes to see if anything was visible. But I felt movement, and looked for someplace to sit. I thought there might be some additional seating between the pilot's cabin and the cargo bay, but there was only a narrow, fold-down steel tray along each outer cabin wall that looked like a prisoner's berth. Dodo immediately flopped down on the one on the starboard side, huddling completely under his blanket until he looked like a corpse in a shroud. His companions made do with the rest of the space. An Angolan crewman came out of the pilot's cabin and unwrapped a foam mattress, slung it on the port bunk, and lay down. He pointed to what was left of the seating space. By this time the heavy plane was rumbling down the run-way. It seemed to be taking a frightening amount of time to gain any speed, and the sound was deafening. Dodo popped out his head and one arm to give a thumbs-up, and then disappeared again under his blanket. Guillaume and I sat down. There was nothing to hang on to, but it didn't matter—we were airborne to Angola.

I inserted a pair of foam earplugs to cut the noise, and the two of us curled up on the end of the berth and tried to sleep. I kept banging my leg on the bolts that stuck out of the bottom of the forward container, but finally managed to wedge my shoes to keep from kicking Guillaume in the head, and after pushing my folded-up jacket against a pair of Angolan feet, achieved just enough muscular relaxation to rest. I decided I would never complain about economy class seating again. A Russian crewman cut the lights. Lulled by the constant drone, I fell into a fitful doze.

I opened my eyes in the dark and saw a pale moon hanging low on the horizon. I blinked and it became the glowing porthole on the starboard side of the cabin. It was 6:30 A.M. It was light outside, but nothing was visible — only a faint smear of pink on the horizon; cloud cover hid the ground below. My companions began to stir. Without warning, we touched down, the tires screeching. A tremendous roar accompanied violent shaking as the huge plane pounded down the runway, the chains on the containers rattling as we rolled to a halt. Out of the window I could see Cabo Ledo and a welcoming committee of soldiers. The Russians unlocked the hatch, a coastal breeze wafted in, and a trio of South Africans working in Quiçama climbed aboard to introduce themselves — the oldest was James Coetzee, the new warden of Quiçama Park, the two younger ones Andreas and Paul. I clambered down the companionway and threw my luggage into Coetzee's pickup. While we waited for the containers to be lifted by crane onto the trucks, Guillaume pointed out the cargo plane's tires: half of them were completely bald, and the others were ringed with patches, like open rubbery sores. But we had made it.

I GAVE THE import papers to Coetzee, and climbed into his pickup. We led the slow procession of trucks up the empty coastal road. So far, he told me, everything had worked according to plan. Andreas and Paul had been tracking the elephants, who had carefully explored the inside perimeter of their new home, from fenceline to riverfront, as if mapping the boundaries. Coetzee was aware that that the entire undertaking was hemmed in by more than an electric fence. The ministry of fisheries and the environment wanted some credit for what had been accomplished, and the agri-culture department, which still had formal control over parks, wanted to reexert its authority as well. "Let the politicians make the decisions," he said. If he was left to do his job, Coetzee hoped to extend control from Caua down through the vast park, unrolling the new wildlife policies month by month. Tourism needed immediate attention: already Angolans from the capital—those that had SUVs, anyway—wanted to visit. Eventu-ally, Coetzee wanted a staff of fifteen, including sector wardens, and some fifty game rangers. Currently, Gray Security was donating its services to help establish the park patrols.

At the last minute, formal ceremonies had been postponed until at least November. But since the invitations had already been sent out, hundreds were expected to show up anyway, including a busload of students from Luanda. We passed through the gate in the fence, now flanked by armed game guards in bush hats and brown uniforms, and rumbled through the bush to the slop-ing hillside where the earth had been bulldozed into rough ramps among scattered euphorbia trees, the Cuanza was just visible in the distance. The schoolkids were already there, wandering over the slope, as were various in-vited guests, many wearing Kissama Foundation T-shirts and bill caps. Even-tually the containers were jockeyed into position, and aimed slightly downhill. Van Hoven arrived and went into a huddle with Coetzee. A number of im-portant guests had yet to make an appearance, and General Hendrik wanted the opening of the containers to be delayed. But it was getting on to 11:00 A.M., and the temperature was rising steadily. Van Hoven, worried that the animals could get badly stressed, decided those concerns overrode any worries about offending latecomers. "Fifteen minutes more, that's it," he declared. By the time this was announced, most of the remaining guests had driven up. Now several hundred people were milling around or clambering up the red earth heaps for a good view. I recognized Fátima Jardim and several more gen-erals, including Antonio Faceira in safari garb, carrying a video camera, and de Matos in dress camouflage. Van Hoven got the chief of the defense forces to stand with him next to the container doors. Dozens of people standing right in front, unaware that they could find themselves in an antelope stampede, had to be waved away.

A plea for silence was ignored, and the crowd chattered excitedly as the ends of the containers were thrown open. Several frisky kudu leaped out and bounded off into the bush, and the rest rocketed out after them. De Matos grinned and the crowd applauded in delight, clicking their cameras and loudly explaining to each other what just happened. The second crate was opened and several stately eland marched out, paused, and shook their dewlaps before striding off into the forest. In this diffuse but harsh light they looked more beige than slate blue. More eland walked out and stood there considering their options before eventually strolling off. The crowd was impressed; these were big animals. The remaining two eland, who were not facing in the right direction, refused to come out despite being tickled with branches, so the other end of the container had to be opened. They stepped out, blinking at the light, and seemed taken aback by the assembled crowd, cars, and noise. They walked into a clump of nearby brush and refused to budge. Minutes went by before they could be shooed into the bush.

The final shipment of this initial phase of Operation Noah's Ark was emblematic of the entire project—a mix of triumph and farce, bad timing and unclear motives, last-minute planning, and heroic effort—but in the end, was inarguably worthwhile. The animals that used to be here were actually coming back, species by species—no small achievement. Few in the crowd knew just how risky, daring, and ambitious an undertaking Operation Noah's Ark had been, or how many times van Hoven had sustained its momentum by his sheer bravado and an unshakable faith that things would finally fall together. It was a near-thankless, monumentally irritating, often confused, and dangerous task—but he had pulled it off.

Certainly the animal release was a big hit with the Angolans. Everyone piled back in their vehicles to head for Caua to party. There, on the hill overlooking the Cuanza, a large tent had been set up with an open bar and a buffet table with trays of fried seafood and sausage and doughy canapés. A sound system sent pulsating dance music echoing through the camp. I noticed the extroverted chimps had been banished from the festivities. Van Hoven was pleased the release had gone well, but angry at the bungled planning for the festivities. He blamed de Freitas, and said he'd heard he had been giving radio interviews. I grabbed some food and mingled with the guests, but my lack of Portuguese limited my conversation to some oil people, an ambassador, and a few journalists. I talked with Johan Blaauw—"Jas," as everyone called him—a blond South African who worked with Gray Security and was now heading up the force of some fifty armed rangers, who would patrol on horseback and foot. Then I spotted de Matos's purple beret in the crowd, and got Jas, who speaks Portuguese, to go over with me and translate.

De Matos acknowledged that he had received my fax about going into the interior, but said he hadn't had a chance to reply to it. He suggested it might be possible to "organize something in October." I said I would be in South Africa until October 10; would it be possible . . . ? He smiled and shook his head. "Too soon," he told me. "Perhaps later." We shook hands; I told him I understood how busy he was with military matters and how much I appreciated his giving some consideration to the idea. Then I wandered off and tried to face the fact I had just been given a definite rejection. There wouldn't be any survey expedition, no foray into the reserves, not even a flight to Malange this year.

Later, van Hoven returned to Luanda. After a night at Caua I would join him at Gen. Luis Faceira's farm the next day for lunch. I unpacked my bags in a *rondavel* I was sharing with Guillaume. When Caua is fully renovated, it will be a very pleasant spot; but the water wasn't running yet, so the nicely appointed bathrooms—they even have bidets—weren't functional. A sponge bath in river water was all that was available, making it a bit like camping in unfinished housing. But I had a pleasant meal of grilled steaks and mealies that night with Coetzee, Andreas, Paul, and Guillaume. Two of the elephants had working radio collars, and Andreas and Paul had been able to follow them as they explored their part of the park. The jumbos knew when they were being followed, and when they felt pressed, turned and gave mock charges, rushing toward the vehicle, ears out, trumpeting, and then wheeling in the dust at the last minute before crashing off into the bush. The two researchers had also been noting every other form of wildlife in the park, and happily, had determined it wasn't quite as denuded as had been feared. So far they had spotted porcupine, African wildcat, civet, vervet monkey, aardvark, bushbuck, both red and gray duiker, a couple of black mambas and forty-odd birds, among them yellow-billed hornbill, palm nut vulture, black-shouldered kite, various kingfishers and bee-eaters and doves. That's great, I told them.

I slathered myself with insect repellent before turning in. It took me a long time to get to sleep.

IT WAS RAINING gently the next morning. When I walked out to the edge of the hillside and looked downriver I could see the dim outlines of the derelict cottage where Neto once stayed with de Almeida in the days after independence. The soft mist that now dampened my shirt had blurred the banks of the Cuanza curving below, making the river seem as if it weren't fixed in its course, but could, if it chose, follow its own direction. Andreas, Paul, and Guillaume had gone off to track elephants. I could have gone with them but I wasn't sure when they'd be back and was concerned I might miss my ride to the general's farm. In truth, I wasn't in the mood. I packed my bags and walked out to the view again. The light was so diffuse the horizon was confusingly indistinct, so I did a sketch of the view, but couldn't concentrate on it.

I knew it wasn't de Matos who was keeping me from my desired interlocution with the antelope of my imagination, it was Jonas Malheiro Savimbi. I was unlikely to reach the reserves anytime soon, unless Savimbi stepped on a land mine—no worse a fate, to be sure, than the one to which he had consigned so many of his countrymen. There would be a certain poetic justice to it. But these muddled thoughts were getting me nowhere. It began to rain harder, and all that came to mind were a few lines from one of Neto's prison poems:

> The Cuanza overflowing
> with menace and despotism
> advanced over the land
> in a spreading parturition of torrential rain

THE SUN WAS out by the time Coetzee and I squeezed into the cab of Jas's pickup, where an armed ranger sat precariously in the back of the truck. After crossing the bridge at the Cuanza we turned right soon after and worked our way along dirt roads through several huge ranches to the Faceira brothers' farm, which occupies several thousand acres on the other side of the river across from the park. Luis had a house here, Antonio was building one, and they had given a large plot to de Matos.

We passed the large, imposing residence he'd built on the way to Luis Faceira's raised ranch house on a hill overlooking vast fields of pawpaw and tomato crops, with vistas of mango orchards and herds of cattle lowing in the distance, and a nearby pen of ostriches. I was told the handsome wooden retreat, paneled inside and out, was built in Brazil, disassembled, shipped to Angola, and reassembled here. A cool breeze blew through the wraparound veranda, which overlooked a large swimming pool; beyond, the Cuanza was tucked out of sight below the distant hills of Quiçama Park.

A board meeting of the Kissama Foundation was already in progress at a table at one end of the veranda. General Hendrik and the Faceiras were there, all casually dressed, Luis in a bright canary yellow golf shirt and striped shorts. Several people took turns translating, but as usual there were often several simultaneous side conversations.

Van Hoven was asking if the many kilometers of fencing material that were intended for the now abandoned second fence couldn't be used on the eastern edge of the park to create a more definitive boundary. This raised the question of whether Quiçama should be a park without people or a park that included settlements. Antonio Faceira suggested that those people who were born in the park should be allowed to stay, but those who simply drifted in and settled there should go. Luis Faceira said that rules and policies should be established now, ones that the people in the park can understand. His brother suggested that they ought to build on the existing laws that already govern Angolan parks, and add to them what could be learned from the successful operation of national parks worldwide—provided these rules fit the Angolan situation.

Coetzee brought up the idea of developing a breeding and wildlife rehabilitation center in the secure area of the park, perhaps one that would draw a lot of international support by concentrating on endangered Angolan animals, such as the chimpanzee and the giant sable. *Giant sable?* I wondered if van Hoven had shared the ASG/IUCN's views on the matter with the board. Van Hoven responded by saying that the giant sable "is such a valuable animal that one would have to investigate the habitat there very carefully. One wouldn't want to move them and have them die. But, sable are such adaptable animals." He was back to his old flip-flop on the subject, tailoring his remarks to his audience—or was it that he thought bringing them to Quiçama was inevitable, and events would prove him right? "The giant sable issue is an important one," he added. "We have tried to organize an expedition into Malange but security problems have prevented it." De Freitas started to say something about the news report on giant sables fleeing the war zone and van Hoven immediately accused him of starting a baseless rumor. "Negative!" de Freitas protested. "I told the radio people there was no truth to it. It came from some Department of Agriculture guys." Van Hoven looked dubious.

Luis Faceira spoke. "It worries Angolans," he said in Portuguese, "that giant sables have not been seen for a long time." I prompted Jas to ask if any were spotted when the army pushed UNITA out of Mulundo, which historically had been prime giant sable habitat. "No," he replied, "but there are some in Capunda. Do you know Capunda?" To be sure I understood what he was talking about, I pulled out my detailed map of the reserves. The general tapped his finger on the village of Capunda, north of Quimbango where the Esteses lived decades ago, and then circled his finger around it. His troops had been to the east of the reserve, and apparently passed through there and saw some *palancas negras*.

The meeting broke up. Since Faceira's troops would have been looking for UNITA, not wildlife, any giant sable sightings would have been accidental, which suggested to van Hoven that there might be a fair number there. "That is where we must go," he said. I asked the general how safe Capunda was. He smiled and spread his hands. "You must give us more time."

More friends and family members showed up, and it was time to eat. Everyone sat around the veranda and overate. Afterwards, Luis Faceira joined his guests on the lawn, and then wandered down near the pool to inspect a freshly tilled patch of red earth, a future flower bed perhaps, or the start of a vegetable garden. He picked up a shovel and started digging at some stubborn rocks. It was a pleasant scene, this idyllic, bountiful African farm under blue skies, kids splashing and squealing in the pool. But the chief of the army didn't get to enjoy the pleasures of his country house that often; he had owned it for fourteen years but last night was the first time he had ever slept in it overnight. The war only seemed far away.

Later, Coetzee and Jas returned to the park, so I caught a ride back to Luanda in General Hendrik's SUV. Antonio Faceria sat in the back with several friends. We were driving into the setting sun, everyone was quiet, and I had plenty of time to reflect on having spent an enjoyable Sunday afternoon with military men who were up to their ears in a murderous civil war and murky (at the least) financial dealings. It was hardly where I thought my search for the giant sable would take me. But I had to admit that these generals, particularly de Matos and the Faceiras, impressed me—they were sharply analytical, politically adroit, very persuasive, and not without charm. Should I have expected any less of men wielding such power?

I had thought the generals must have viewed the rehabilitation of Quiçama solely as a way to wring money out of their tourist concession. Maybe they started out thinking that way, and maybe they still did, but now, seduced by van Hoven's vision, they seemed genuinely interested in bringing back the wildlife. Were they also thinking ahead to a different future, when real peace and democracy would take a less tentative hold and business dealings would become much more transparent? Questions might be raised then about the sources of their wealth, and whether they might have personally profited from the war. Their role in rehabilitating the national parks and restoring the country's wildlife heritage could help deflect unwanted attention by cloaking them in a mantle of international respectability. They might even be honored for their achievements.

Was that what Operation Noah's Ark amounted to—something extraordinary that had been accomplished by a cast that included some questionable players? Against all odds Angola's parks had started to come back to life, and maybe it couldn't have happened without all the mixed motives at work, from ambition and egotism to greed and chicanery and all the rest—at this point in time, anyway. The generals deserved credit, just as van Hoven did, for all that they had done. And they had just begun.

Still, did Operation Noah's Ark really make sense for Angola, when so many of its inhabitants were dying, starving, sunk in utter despair? It did to many Angolans, at least the ones I had talked to in Luanda, if only because it took their minds off the war, it made them feel good about their country and proud of what they had. They were excited about the prospect of seeing elephants bathing once again in the Cuanza. I understood that; I was, too.

BACK IN PRETORIA I went into a funk, and for days spent much of my time lying on my bed in my guest house room, watching the ceiling fan revolve and replaying recent events. I knew now that the survey expedition should have taken place during the lull in the fighting that followed the fall of Andulo. Once UNITA regrouped and returned to guerrilla warfare, the army was at a loss to cope with this change in tactics, and the bush was once again Savimbi's, too insecure to risk traveling in, or even flying over. It was back to the old standoff: the government controlled Luanda and its environs and the provincial capitals, UNITA held sway over the country-side. Obviously, the government wasn't about to let journalists, missionar-ies, or aid workers travel outside the tight security perimeters that extended no more than a mile or two from these interior cities. If foreigners were killed or kidnapped, it would be an embarrassment to the government and proof that their grip on the countryside was weak.

So how could I get any closer to the giant sable? Clearly, I wouldn't get far venturing out on my own. I sat up and looked at the telephone on the nightstand. There was another way into the house of the giant sable. Through UNITA. For several years now, whenever I had gone to one or another of its various websites, I had stared at the E-mail links, and thought about making contact to inquire about the *palanca preta gigante*. But I feared tipping off the rebels that interest in the animal was building on the government side, much less that a survey might be planned. I remem-bered de Almeida's chilling warnings about giving UNITA an excuse to shoot some animals to embarrass the government, or a reason to prepare a "surprise" for anyone who'd dare to penetrate into the reserves. Until that moment I had never given any thought to going into the interior with-out Estes or van Hoven. But perhaps it was time for me to take the last step of the journey myself.

I had been given the number of a former South African intelligence officer now living in Pretoria who worked in Jamba in the old days. He knew Savimbi well, and was still in contact with the movement. I gave him a call, and introduced myself. We arranged to meet for drinks.

WE SAT AT an outside table of a crowded café in the bright afternoon sun. The ex-soldier was happy to share what he knew—in confidence—of how he spent several years in Jamba, UNITA's bush capital in the late 1980s, and came to know Jonas Savimbi and his family. He described the rebel leader's mesmerizing presence, and we talked about the CIA and the SADF and the Cubans and the Angolan generals and how there were no innocent parties in the Angolan civil war. He confirmed a number of things I'd heard, and understood when I told him I had to find out what happened to the giant sable. He had a great interest in the antelope as well, and said flatly that Savimbi regarded the *palanca negra* as a sacred animal. In the late 1980s he had been personally involved in meetings with Savimbi and "several groups of people" who wanted to capture some to take to South Africa to form breeding herds. But Savimbi refused outright; he wouldn't even consider it. "In hindsight, maybe it should have happened," he said. "It would have been possible then—with the SADF's help. But now it may be too late."

But there was every reason to think the antelopes were still there, I told him. In fact, I wanted to find out if their survival had anything to do with Savimbi's efforts to protect them. But most of all, I wanted to see them for myself.

We finished off our drinks and watched people passing on the sidewalk. He put his glass down and said quietly that he knew how to reach the current head of UNITA's intelligence and would ask him if their troops had seen any giant sables lately. I asked if anybody went into UNITA-held territory. He said it happened all the time. I knew he would say that; others had told me that seven tons of supplies were flown into Savimbi's territory every single day from poorly patrolled airstrips in South Africa.

Maybe it was crazy, I said, but was there any chance of getting into the interior to see giant sable from UNITA's side? It was quite possible, he answered. He would make inquiries, and let me know what he found out; I just had to be patient. I was left wondering just how far I'd go—and who I would be willing to travel with—to see a giant sable.

I FLEW TO Cape Town and found Terry Robinson delighted with his new setup: a brand-new laboratory in the zoology building on the University of Stellenbosch's handsome campus, a full professorship, and the surrounding spectacular wine country at his doorstep. In fact, he'd even found a handsome Tuscan-style house to rent on a hillside surrounded by vines, although there was a catch: he had to feed and fend off the unwanted attention of the absent owners' large and lonely pot-bellied pig.

As Robinson gave me a tour of his molecular zoology laboratory he asked if I knew that Sable Ranch had listed "giant sables" for sale in its upcoming game auction. Yes, a disgusted van Hoven had showed me the ad. Robinson explained that they had to withdraw the offer after numerous inquiries asking for proof the ranch had the genuine Angolan subspecies. We stopped to talk to Bettine van Vuuren (now Dr. van Vuuren) in her office. She hadn't been able to get any answers out of the Gray Expedition teeth because the genetic material was too degraded. Robinson suspected bleaching was the problem. "If we don't get anything from amplification of tooth material," he said, "I always ask 'What did the skull look like?' In the old days, you see, they left skulls on an anthill to be cleaned or just boiled them in water." But whitening the bones in a powerful solution of bleach, a common procedure in many museums, damages the DNA. I remembered now that the handsome skull I'd sketched had been a dead, chalky white.

But Robinson had another source of giant sable specimens now. After months of failing to extract a few teeth from major museums, Kobus du Toit had called some weeks ago and told him that a game ranching friend of his stumbled upon a cache of giant sable skins and skeletons in the Powell-Cotton Museum in England, and was sending him snippets of skin from three specimens by registered mail. I'd heard of Major Powell-Cotton—he shot the second-biggest elephant on record—and knew that he had gone to Angola, but I hadn't realized he'd collected giant sable; none had been listed in the record books I'd consulted, and I hadn't come across any mention of his travels into the interior. But, alerted by Robinson, I had been able to dig out the story before I flew out for the antelope release in Quiçama.

Percy Horace Gordon Powell-Cotton, traveler, collector, hunter, and naturalist, went to Angola in mid-1921 to procure specimens of the country's larger mammals for display in his growing private museum at Quex House, in Kent, England, where he pioneered the exhibition of fully mounted mammals in natural settings. Although he was an exacting collector and kept detailed records of his specimens, Powell-Cotton largely confined himself to cryptic journal entries in the field. Diary no. 61, Book no. 3, January 21 to July 5, 1922, contains the brief distillate of his lengthy expedition into the interior for giant sable and dozens of other Angolan rarities, a trip that took him from Huambo to Chinguar and across the Cuanza into the region Blaine and Statham had traversed. "Tent up, odd jobs, tiff, read label skins, settle as to fetching rice, tub, din, wrote, bed," reads a typical passage. By the middle of February the major had bagged his first giant sable, a male with fifty-five-inch horns, and by the time he departed in July he'd collected several complete specimens and purchased some additional skins and skulls.

Robinson leaned against van Vureen's bookshelves and told me that they had already extracted amplifiable DNA from the initial skin samples and had sequenced short sections from each.

And?

He smiled. "We've confirmed that we have sable DNA and not a contaminant." And—I was leaning forward in my seat—was it different from or similar to the DNA from the Curtis tooth?

"Bettine can show you," Robinson said, and she pulled up the sequences on her computer. She scrolled through *roosevelti*, a couple of *niger, kirkii,* and then *variani*.

"There's the one giant sable we had," she said, pointing to a long string of letters on her screen. "Now I've added another three." The Powell-Cotton specimens appeared as equally long strings. "If you actually look at the sequence here between the different *variani* . . ." She clicked in a few more commands. And the differences? "That's what I'm going to show

365

you now," she said, and hit a key. I was still hoping the Curtis tooth sequence would prove to be a fluke, and the sequences from the new giant sable specimens would form a dramatically different cluster of their own, clearly distinct from typical sables. It would be so much simpler.

But the three new *variani* sequences were remarkably close to that of the Curtis tooth. I didn't have to have it spelled out; Robinson's and Matthee's original conclusion that, genetically speaking, the giant sable wasn't significantly different from the typical sable looked like it was on the way to being confirmed. Robinson was confident that any more specimens he could gather would only further support that contention. He was particularly interested in obtaining sable specimens from southern Angola and the Angola-Zambia border, because they might fill in the genetic gaps between *variani* and typical sables. Thousands of years ago, he explained, sables may have been widely distributed across southern Africa into Angola, but changes in climate since then had left certain populations isolated. The giant sable could simply be a sable population with a high incidence of the genes that are responsible for giant sable characteristics—primarily facial markings and horn length.

"Go to Angola," Robinson said, "and you might see nine out of ten individuals with these characteristics. Go to Zambia, and it might be only one out of ten has these characteristics. But that just means that the population there didn't go through the same bottleneck as the Angolan population." This "fixation of characteristics" is exactly what game ranchers accomplish by selective breeding, developing populations of white lions, king cheetahs, and the like that predominate in the desired characteristics.

"The definition of a subspecies is that it is a geographic variant," Robinson explained. "If you say that the criteria for the giant sable are the facial markings and the horns, well, my original argument was that we don't know how robust that distinction really is because nobody has looked to see how variable it is across the distribution. But now that we know that if you move to northern Zambia and you get the phenotype, that makes the phenotype distinction for the giant sable suspect."

On the way out of the lab Robinson paused in front of a large map of Africa hanging in the hall to reiterate his point. "You can't have the giant sable phenotype here," Robinson said, putting his finger on the center of Angola, "and the giant sable phenotype here"—he tapped on northern

Zambia—"and call them different subspecies. That doesn't work. It means that the criteria used to distinguish these things are flawed." Wasn't all this going to undermine the subspecies status of the giant sable? He didn't answer the question directly. "If you see there's bugger-all difference in phenotype between here (*tap*) and here (*tap*) plus the genetics are identical and cluster together, then it seems a very questionable distinction." I tried to find an objection; after all, it was the *giant sable*. . . . He nodded and finished my thought for me. "I know. It has all this baggage associated with it."

I flew home.

THE NEWS OUT of Angola during the last few months of 2000 revolved around the usual themes. Ten people a day (usually three adults and seven children) were dying of starvation in Luau, which used to be the Benguela Railway's final stop just before the Congolese border in the days when there were trains. Fierce fighting between government and rebel forces had cut off access to the town, and although relief efforts were underway, hungry army troops would doubtless appropriate any fresh supplies. In fact, Angolan army officers had just sent a letter to President dos Santos warning him of serious discontent in the armed forces and protesting that funds allocated for the military had disappeared. "Young soldiers are hungry, going naked, or have no boots and are being driven to quit their units," they lamented. Considering that Angola had recently been singled out as one of the most corrupt countries in the world, it hardly seemed surprising. However, if the new press law proposed in Luanda was enacted, anyone who "publishes, divulges or reproduces news or facts for the national or foreign press which attack the honor or reputation of the president" would be imprisoned for two to eight years, so I didn't expect to hear much more about this minor embarrassment to Angola's commander-in-chief, much less anything about rumored mutinies among government troops in which the army had to fire on its own soldiers.

It was obvious de Matos was too busy to organize a survey expedition. There was the ongoing crisis in the Congo, and the army had yet to pin Savimbi down. UNITA claimed he was in "good health and leading troops from his command post," which was moved daily as the rebel leadership was pursued across Moxico Province. But Savimbi took the time to stop and execute several more of his generals along the way. UNITA also took credit for downing a Russian-built Antonov-26 aircraft which exploded in a midair fireball shortly after taking off from Saurimo in the thick jungles of diamond-rich Lunda Sul Province in early November. The privately chartered twin-engine turboprop was carrying either a Russian or Ukrainian crew and forty-odd Angolans—the details were unclear—and according to UNITA, a cargo of diamonds from the area they had recently lost to government forces. There were no survivors, just a lot of carbonized corpses spread over the ground or found hanging from trees. The government claimed engine failure caused the crash, and in truth, considering how poorly maintained aircraft and airfields are in Angola, it seemed a plausible explanation, but no one doubted UNITA's ability to shoot it down.

I must have been out of my mind to think of going into that nightmarish war zone—from either side.

THE TWENTY-FIFTH anniversary of Angola's independence was marked in Luanda by a number of patriotic events intended to underscore the progress that had been made since November 11, 1975. But with half a million dead from the war and nearly three million forced to flee their homes because of the fighting, the official slogan, "Twenty-five years of dignity, twenty-five years of liberty," rang hollow and the date only served to remind average Angolans how much the promise of Agostinho Neto's declaration of liberation had been left unfulfilled.

President dos Santos unveiled a modest monument to his predecessor in office and reiterated his offer of general amnesty to the rebels. Military actions, he declared, were now "confined to a few regions," and "could no longer impede the country's development." On the other hand, he admitted, the country's economic and financial situation remained difficult and could not significantly improve the living standards of its citizens.

He reassured his audience that elections would be held when "the time is right"—perhaps in the latter half of 2002. UNITA rejected the amnesty offer outright and marked the date by setting off a bomb in the provincial capital of Uige Province. General de Matos shrugged off these guerrilla attacks a few days later. Savimbi's men, he announced on state radio, "no longer stand as a danger to peace in Angola."

One wouldn't have known it from the conditions in Cuito, however, which was plagued with flies and an invasion of black cockroaches attracted to the corpses that still littered the streets there. Even though parks in the city had been turned into makeshift cemeteries, many of the war dead had yet to be buried. In truth, it was hard to keep up; nationwide, some five hundred children a day were said to be dying from malnutrition, disease, or land mines. Some twelve thousand refugees had swelled the camps just inside the Zambian border the month before, a sign that conditions in the bush had become even more hellish than usual. Some of the reasons for that were laid out in a stomach-turning report that Médecins Sans Frontières (Doctors Without Borders) issued just before the twenty-fifth-anniversary celebrations.

The group revealed that in an effort to demonstrate it had established stability in the country, the government planned to "reinstall" populations in the areas they'd fled to escape the fighting. There was one small difficulty: the government did not control "90 percent" of the nation's territory and the conditions had not been "normalized." There had long been reports that UNITA was using rural populations as human shields, but now the government was cynically orchestrating population displacements to areas where there was meager or no protection, or displaying them in humanitarian "shop windows" to elicit international aid funds. Detailed eyewitness interviews told of flights into the bush to escape plunder and reprisals, forced enlistment, mutilations, and murders of men, women, children, and the elderly. "Shunted from one side to another," the report asserted, "the populations have been deliberately manipulated by the warring parties." One displaced man fled with his family from Huambo Province after UNITA threatened to massacre his village and government troops threatened them with death if they didn't follow their units. The most gruesome practices—such as the lopping off of limbs—were perpetrated by UNITA, but the army wasn't far behind, its troops raping women and selecting villagers to carry food and equipment looted from them, under threat of being beaten or killed.

Nothing seemed to have changed. Even the Russians had come back, agreeing to supply their old Luanda ally with military aid and training and offering increased support for its diamond trade, worth $1 billion annually now that the army had wrested some key mines from UNITA.

The West was now "constructively engaged" with a government some of its countries, like the United States, were once determined to destroy. The need for oil and the fact that Savimbi refused to accept the outcome of the 1992 elections—or to fulfill the terms of the 1994 Lusaka Protocol—had virtually guaranteed that dos Santos would be embraced, albeit with some provisos. These ranged from diplomatic finger-wagging at Luanda's repressive rule to a recent agreement between the International Monetary Fund (IMF) and the government to monitor oil revenues in an effort to force Angola to reform its economy and redirect some spending from the military into rebuilding the country's infrastructure. Presumably, Luanda would no longer be able to so easily hide the use of oil revenues in financing covert arms purchases, or cover up the blatant corruption that watch groups and human rights observers had detailed. There was a widespread belief that if Luanda could be pressured into good governance, and the sanctions that had been imposed on UNITA successfully choked off its resources, permitting peace, Angola might have a future after all. There was not much stomach left in the international community for more dramatic interventions in the Angolan quagmire, just the hope that the country would sort itself out somehow—but without endangering the flow of oil along the way, please.

Dos Santos was getting boxed in. Meeting the expectations of the West, the pressures of his own people, and the demands of an interminable war were leaving him little room to maneuver, or to perform financial legerdemain. The man once portrayed by the United States as a doctrinaire dictator now presented himself as a progressive leader. Was there any reality to it? Well, he now tolerated mild political opposition and a more open economy, and had initiated some efforts at resuscitating his shattered nation. Certainly there was more tolerance under dos Santos's rule than under Savimbi's iron fist, where there was none—but Angola was hardly an open society. Whenever dos Santos was criticized for not doing more for his people, he raised the obvious excuse of the ongoing civil war, and then trotted out the soothing bromides the West wanted to hear, extolling the path of peace in every speech and modulating his rhetoric on Savimbi, even holding out the promise of pardoning the man he had once branded a war criminal. While committed to the Lusaka peace accords, he had no intention of entering into a dialogue with his archenemy. Savimbi, on the other hand, would be happy to hold talks—he was after legitimacy.

The fact that Savimbi had broken every agreement he had entered into seemed to let dos Santos off the hook. But there were more and more voices in the country—from the church, civil society, and other political parties—now calling for some way out of the state of chronic war. The military situation was far different than it had been the year before, but the government was unlikely to crush UNITA now that it had fallen back on a guerrilla strategy. Even a trickle of diamonds could fund enough hit-and-run attacks to create insecurity in the countryside. De Matos told dos Santos that this new war was, in his opinion, "unwinnable," and that it was up to the politicians to find a solution. The president could not have enjoyed hearing that.

JOSÉ EDUARDO DOS SANTOS was spending much of his time behind the stone walls of Futungo de Belas, once a beach club for Portuguese army officers and now the presidential compound, emerging infrequently in a convoy of fast cars filled with armed, nervous guards—the "ninjas," as they're known locally. It was something of a publicity coup, then, for the Kissama Foundation when the president of Angola agreed to cut a ribbon at the gate of the fenced area of Quiçama to officially reinaugurate the park on December 16. The invited guests stood in the hot sun as General de Matos, in crisp uniform, made some introductory remarks on the role of the foundation, and then heard from dos Santos, dressed for the occasion in a loose white tunic. The president spoke of the need to prevent the further deterioration of natural resources caused by the war, and hoped that this initiative would expand to other parts of the country, so that conditions of security and freedom of movement could be created not just for animals, but for "visitors." He praised the "noble task" of those involved in bringing Quiçama back to life and hoped the youth of Angola would learn to respect and love nature, and want to protect it from "devastation and acts by men without scruples." A Catholic priest gave his blessing, and with de Matos, Wouter van Hoven, and assorted dignitaries and guests looking on, dos Santos cut a white ribbon.

After lunch at Caua, van Hoven presented the president with a small tabletop bronze statue of a giant sable bull on behalf of the Kissama Foundation, and dos Santos offered his assistance on future conservation initiatives. Van Hoven shared this and the other good news that a baby eland and a baby elephant had been born in the park by E-mail.

He had something else to report, too. General de Matos was excited to tell him that an army helicopter crew near Cangandala had spotted a large herd of giant sables, perhaps as many as a hundred and fifty. De Matos planned to give his men a camera to carry with them in case the *palancas* were seen again. When Estes got van Hoven's E-mail, he wrote a cautious reply before returning to Tanzania. "Apart from the sighting of giant sable in Cangandala, which is already something to celebrate, the estimate of 150 animals is remarkable on two counts: a) the total population of this reserve back in the '70s and '80s was estimated by the park wardens at about 100; b) the largest herd of giant sable Runi and I ever saw was about 75 head, in our Luando study area near Quimbango, i.e., half the size of this Cangandala herd. So," Estes concluded hopefully, "if there really are that many sable in Cangandala, the possibility I have kept in the back of my mind becomes more tenable: that the civil war has actually benefited the giant sable and its habitat." But when the sighting was reported by a Portuguese news agency nearly two months later, the estimate of their numbers had dropped to twenty-five. Soldiers aren't scientists, of course, and at first they must have exaggerated the size of the herd to embellish their story. But it was another indication that the animals were there.

IT WAS JUST after the start of the new year, 2001, and because months had gone by, I hadn't thought anything would ever come of the talk I had in

Pretoria about going into Angola with UNITA to see the giant sable. But then my South African contact told me over the phone that he'd been in touch with "his guys" and he expected to work things out shortly. He would be meeting with them in Togo and would report back. Several weeks later, a few days after Laurent Kabila was assassinated in the Congo, we had another conversation. He reported that UNITA troops had seen a herd of eight to twelve giant sable—with calves—last August, south of Malange city. And he had again discussed the idea of my going into the interior to see the *palanca negra* in person and received a "positive response." Further discussions would be held with the rebel command in the Angolan interior. And then a journey would be arranged, never mind precisely how, but it was not hard to guess it would involve a flight on a small aircraft. I might be able to go in a month or two. He'd be back in touch with details.

I could hardly believe I was thinking of going into the reserves under the wing of a rebel group whose crimes I knew all too well. It was not only foolhardy, it had to be morally and politically suspect to be the guest of these guerrillas. And for what purpose? It wasn't a mission of mercy that was impelling me to go into the interior, just a selfish desire to see an animal and turn a long-held dream into reality.

And what was the price I would have to pay to see a giant sable? To put my life into the hands of a charismatic warlord who long ago may have had a valid dream for his country but decades later was near defeat, clinging to the scraps of his tattered ambitions that have prolonged a national nightmare for a quarter of a century. Savimbi had to be behind this invitation. Where else would this "interest" in helping me come from but the inner circle of UNITA—and that meant O *Mais Velho* himself.

What could Savimbi expect to gain from my "visit"? All I could think was that he might want a journalist to acknowledge the one thread of decent behavior that could go into his near-empty plus column, the fact that all these years he had apparently stayed his troops from shooting the *palanca preta gigante*. In exchange, I would be shown the dark antelope, alive and well in its haunts. Many would scoff at giving Savimbi credit for saving Angola's national animal, arguing his control over his troops could never have been total. At various times, squads of famished guerrillas, even if they didn't dare hose down a herd with automatic weapons fire, must have been tempted to shoot a straggler to eat and bury the leftovers. Yet if he had not, in his long rule of the bush, singled out this animal for special consideration, would there be any left now?

But it hardly seemed an opportunity for a propaganda coup. Did he want me in his *miombo* kingdom for another reason? He wanted to talk to me? I hadn't asked to interview him. Would he insist on a meeting? There was something odd about it; it didn't make sense. But I couldn't tell anyone about it because I didn't want to be told it was madness to even think about it. And I didn't want to examine it too closely, either; I wanted to convince myself that there was every reason to believe I'd return to tell about it, and then . . . what? Well, I could worry about what it all meant later, and whether I had to really take this insane risk to see the beast, on the slim chance that I would learn more than I already had.

Because despite all that I had gone through, an unanswered desire still hung in the air. It wasn't about the giant sable—I knew it survived, there was no doubt now. It was about realizing one perfect dream.

All I had to do was get the word, and get on a plane.

THE NEXT DAY I learned that President dos Santos had sacked General de Matos, his chief of staff. Rumor had it that several other senior generals in the defense forces had been stripped of their commands as well. This shakeup wouldn't be announced until replacements could be lined up, but meanwhile Luanda was swirling with hearsay and half-truths, and it was hard to know what was a credible report and what was gossip. Some say it was a purge against the *mestiços*, whose hold over the military has been long resented by black commanders, and of late, vocally criticized by the minister of defense, Gen. Kundi Paihama. Dos Santos himself may have felt directly threatened by their growing power and influence. But in view of Angola's troop commitments in the Congo and UNITA's ongoing guerrilla actions, the timing of these firings was certain to have a negative impact on the army's morale and its fighting capacity; de Matos was well regarded by his soldiers as a competent leader and strategist. One hypothesis was that these firings were in retaliation for the *mestiço* generals' informing French authorities how deeply implicated the dos Santos regime was in a widening arms sale scandal involving Jean-Christophe Mitterrand that erupted in December, out of resentment at not being given a share of Angolan oil revenues like others in the Futungo elite. Yet another interpretation pointed to a piece of legislation recently passed by the national assembly that would grant amnesty to government officials declaring their sources of income; to avoid compromising themselves when the law takes effect, the general may have decided to take early retirement.

When the news became public, de Matos told the media that his being replaced by Deputy Defense Minister Armando da Cruz Neto was routine and expected. In turn, dos Santos lavished praise on de Matos and thanked him for his patriotic efforts in several speeches, but no one disputed that the general's downfall was hastened by their sharp differences over the conduct of the war. De Matos had resisted dos Santos's demand for more intensive war that might deliver a fatal blow to Savimbi. The general had believed for months that there was no way the army could stamp out UNITA's guerrillas—his soldiers were not trained for antiguerrilla warfare, they were reluctant to get off the roads or even out of their vehicles, their chain of command was top-down and lacked flexibility. He'd initiated counterinsurgency training, but may have had little faith in it.

On the other hand, dos Santos knew that his government could not afford to lose any of the areas it had already taken; it would be a public relations disaster. The last thing he wanted to hear from de Matos was that the only solution to the conflict was political. Yet who could dos Santos turn to now to rid him of his sworn enemy, when his own top general had failed to do it? The Faceiras? It was said that the brothers had avoided the axe by striking a deal with the president to stay on to assist with the upcoming dry-season offensive against UNITA. Yet the financial transparency being forced on his administration would presumably make it harder to funnel the vast majority of state revenues toward the military, increasing the pressure to come to a political accommodation with UNITA.

What these developments meant for the Kissama Foundation, which had depended on these men, was unclear. Van Hoven downplayed the significance of the firings and said that he expected all the generals to stay involved. On the other hand, if they no longer wanted to be, well, others could be invited on board. "Perhaps less military involvement would be a

375

good thing," he suggested. But who besides the military would dare take us into the reserves? He promised to stay in touch on that.

IN CHESS, THE endgame is the concluding stage of play, when the pieces and the possible outcomes of the moves that are left have been reduced to a precious few. A similar finality was gathering around Jonas Savimbi. He had been confounding his enemies for years, but now the noose around his rebel movement was tightening. Dos Santos and Sam Nujoma, Namibia's leader (who decades ago gave Savimbi his first gun) and Frederick Chiluba, Zambia's president, gave a joint news conference in Luanda to pledge the safeguarding of their borders in an unmistakable gesture of anti-UNITA solidarity. This followed on the heels of dos Santos's efforts to patch up relations with the Ivory Coast, which had supported UNITA in the past, but was now cracking down and confiscating the passports it had previously issued to the rebel leadership. It was plain Luanda wanted Savimbi dead or alive (preferably the former), in the belief that removal of the guerrilla leader was the only way to end the twenty-six-year-old conflict. Government news was, as always, upbeat. The new specially trained counterinsurgency units were said to have been deployed in central Angola. Continued shelling of the northern town of Uige was dismissed as a minor setback and UNITA's raid on the Benguela airport the month before was credited to local cattle rustlers. "Mr. Savimbi is kicking his legs," Defense Minister Kundi Paihama said on state radio. "He is at death's door."

The self-styled leader of "Free Angola," who had run collective farms and built hundreds of schools and clinics and sent students abroad to study medicine, virtually running a state within a state, was now rumored to be hiding out with his bodyguards near Camacupa on the Benguela Railway line just south of the Luando Reserve and two rail stops from where he was born. "I love this forest," Savimbi once said of the Angolan bush and the cover it gave him. "Without it, things would be very difficult for us."

It was impossible to know what the rebel leader's situation really was. But under the circumstances, it hardly seemed likely I would be summoned by Savimbi; arranging passage for a journalist to come to his forest hideout to look for an elusive antelope could not have been a matter of much urgency for him.

WHILE WAITING FOR an improbable invitation from UNITA, I had my hopes teased by yet another possibility of getting to see the giant sable reserves. At the beginning of March, van Hoven met with the Faceiras in Pretoria. They confirmed further sightings of giant sable and Luis Faceira suggested it might be possible "to do a quick flight over the area next week," he informed me in an E-mail. "We are still planning on doing the survey in July of this year."

For the next several days I tried to convince myself that it made sense to fly halfway around the world on the slimmest of chances that I could get into the Angolan interior. All I could picture was a waste of time and money I didn't have and almost certain disappointment. Yet I feared that if I didn't go I would have stumbled miserably at the end of my quest. I also felt a hot spike of irrational jealousy at the thought that van Hoven might get to see them without me. Van Hoven told me flatly I shouldn't come—he'd feel like hanging himself if I came out and it was another bust like the last trip. He reminded me how often things are promised and not delivered in Angola, and that even if we got into the interior, there was no guarantee we would see a giant sable; we both knew it was the wrong time of year for aerial observation.

Reluctantly, I agreed. He was relieved, and reassured me that he'd keep working on the generals, and provided the military situation in Malange didn't go up in flames, the long-awaited expedition should take place in July.

Later the same day I learned that dos Santos had relieved Gen. Luis Faceira of his post. When I spoke with van Hoven after his return from Luanda—the side trip into Malange was a washout due to torrential rains—he said there was "nothing sinister" about Faceira's being replaced; he'd been planning to step down the year before, and now would have more time to devote to Kissama matters. His brother remained head of the Special Forces. And de Matos, van Hoven pointed out, was still chairing

377

meetings in Luanda; the foundation would continue to enjoy good access to the military.

I began to wonder about my South African UNITA contact. I E-mailed him and he sent me a reply a couple of days later. "I must say I am a little bit frustrated with my 'friends,' or their lack of communication," he wrote. "I think, however, they have a bit more pressing issues at this stage." I understood all too well. If Savimbi was serious about forestalling the government's dry-season offensive, he would have broken his silence months ago and started—or tried to start—negotiations. But he hadn't given up hope of military victories. He had been in contact with the new Bush administration, hoping there might be some lingering sympathy in a Republican administration for an old cold war ally. But now that the cold war was over and dos Santos was selling oil to America, Savimbi was an embarrassment, the symbol of an unsavory, largely secretive African episode with catastrophic and lingering regional aftereffects that Washington would just as soon forget about. There was no interest in putting him in power; all the United States wanted to do now was "get him out of the equation." Cynics claimed if the retirement package was big enough, he might be persuaded to live out his days in, say, Morocco, surrounded by his bodyguards and his bank accounts and his memories of what might have been.

In the end, it might have been the cheapest solution, not just in monetary terms, but in human lives. But Savimbi had no interest in such an end to his career. At the end of February, when government troops recaptured Quibaxe a hundred miles northeast of Luanda from UNITA, they discovered a ghost town. Nearly eight thousand inhabitants—local residents and the refugees who had been prematurely resettled there—were missing. Some, surely, had been killed when UNITA occupied it, others must have escaped into the bush, but many must have been marched off at gunpoint. A few weeks later in Bié, three thousand people suffering from advanced malnutrition staggered into a refugee camp at Camacupa from their home district of Cuembe, which had been without road access since 1985 due to land mines, and without air links since the previous June. Sixty-six died of starvation shortly after arrival. One hundred thousand refugees swelled Cuito, overwhelming aid agencies, while humanitarian operations had been paralyzed in northern Malange Province due to lack of security.

Savimbi broke an eighteen-month silence to drop hints that the 1994 Lusaka peace accords might be able to be revived. "We would like to come to a national reconciliation phase," he told the Voice of America by satellite telephone without a hint of contrition, "in peace, with calm, with a disposition to accept the errors pointed out to us." He conceded government troops wanted to capture him and crush his movement, but he scoffed at reports that he'd ever been close to capture. He would consider disarming, he maintained, but wouldn't discuss it while he was being hunted down. UNITA had regrouped as a fighting force, he asserted, and his soldiers were within sixty miles of the capital. Although his forces were thought to have been reduced to some ten thousand troops—perhaps half its strength in recent years—no one doubted these fighters, despite being undersupplied and ill equipped, could still wreak havoc across the country. Government troops liked to joke that when they heard the boom of distant cannon from UNITA, it was O Mais Velho farting again. But when the shells started falling around them, it didn't seem quite so funny.

It was obvious UNITA's sporadic attacks around the country were intended as a show of strength, something Savimbi could use in any eventual peace talks. Was dos Santos dragging his feet on negotiations as well, hoping that his troops would get lucky and trap the rebel leader in the bush? Barring that, Luanda was probably interested only in arranging Savimbi's surrender or exile, something the rebel leader hardly seemed ready to accept. Some analysts continued to wonder if the government didn't find the war a convenient cover for its ongoing military spending and the corruption it allowed—so long as the capital wasn't attacked and the oil kept flowing. The war continued to seesaw; UNITA recaptured Umpulo, while government troops finally took the key rebel base of Mavinga—though not without local village chiefs complaining of massacres, summary executions, enforced disappearances, rapes, mutilations, and cattle stealing.

Still, Savimbi did not enhance his image in early May when his troops capped a dawn raid on Caxito that left up to a hundred people dead by kidnapping sixty children from an orphanage at gunpoint and forcing them to carry the goods the rebels had looted back into the bush. The incident provoked international outrage. UNITA gave contradictory accounts of

379

what happened, at first claiming the children were being taken to their homes in rebel-held areas, and then announcing an investigation. A week after the kidnapping, Savimbi wrote a letter to Catholic Church officials drawing parallels between his "mission" and theirs ("We are all serving the same people and sooner or later, we will all be before God for judgment"), and urging the church to "commit itself to creating a favorable environment of trust between the Angolans"—i.e., facilitate negotiations. That may have been why after force-marching them for twenty-one days, UNITA decided to turn the exhausted children over to church officials 180 miles from Caxito.

Savimbi may have had other reasons. He had become increasingly plagued by regrets. At a UNITA conference that month he delivered a strange, rambling speech in which he begged forgiveness from his followers for the hardships he had put them through, and apologized for some of the worst actions that had been committed in his name. Yet they continued unabated. UNITA's attacks on civilians made it clear that Savimbi had completely abandoned the Maoist guerrilla tactics he had once espoused, with their reliance on the masses, in favor of sheer terrorism— knifing adult villagers while they slept was the least of it; there were even reports of bayoneting babies. Were UNITA's actions intended to trigger an international gag reflex at the senselessness of the Angola conflict, a reaction that Savimbi hoped might pressure Luanda into talks?

Even van Hoven, whose hopes for eventual peace in Angola often led him to minimize the conflict, admitted that the war was "flaring up to some degree." Despite that, he wrote, "we are going full steam ahead with the planning to do the survey of Giant Sable in Malange at the end of July." Van Hoven's latest scheme called for a six-seater King Air surveillance plane with infrared detectors and floor-mounted video cameras, a back-up helicopter, and a ground patrol, in case it might be possible to "dart one or two"—to obtain DNA samples, he reassured me. Estes was pleased, but surprised that van Hoven was proceeding with plans to survey the reserves. "Presumably, since all concerned are anxious to avoid being shot with Stinger missiles, the military will be securing the area beforehand," he wrote. But van Hoven was in no position to make promises about what the army might do for us. Estes was getting ready to travel to Zimbabwe to give some lectures and observe mammal behavior at Mana Pools National

Park during the solar eclipse at the end of June, but would delay his return to the United States in the hopes the survey would come off.

IN JUNE 2001 a chartered UN aircraft carrying food aid was hit by a surface-to-air missile in eastern Angola. The clearly marked Boeing 727 was struck at 15,000 feet as it approached Luena in Moxico Province, suffering damage to one engine, but the pilot regained control and landed the plane safely. UNITA admitted firing on the plane, but claimed it was carrying arms. The World Food Program suspended cargo flights to the area, and when a second plane was fired on in less than a week, the UN agency canceled all aid flights in Angola until further notice. Because rebel attacks and land mines have rendered many roads impassable, the cratered and potholed airstrips in the nation's interior constituted the sole lifeline for more than a million of its inhabitants. Without continuing airlifts, supplies would be dwindling fast. Starving refugees were continuing to stumble out of the bush into Camacupa, where over two hundred flights a day would be required to supply the needed aid. Nearby Cuito, swollen with a 150,000 displaced people, adding to a destitute population of almost a quarter of a million, faced utter catastrophe. The mortality rate there had reached 25 percent at one therapeutic feeding center run by Médecins Sans Frontières.

UNITA had not neglected Malange either, having launched several attacks against the city and surrounding towns in the past few months. In the most recent incident, unidentified gunmen opened fire on mourners in a church, killing eight. A few days later, twenty-two civilians were killed and seventeen injured when their truck ran over an antitank mine north of Malange; it was the twenty-fourth such incident in the province since the beginning of the year. The next day, van Hoven wrote to tell me that he was "going to Angola on 25 June for some meetings and to review the security situation. It remains difficult to know the whereabouts of rapidly moving guerrilla forces or their plans since this is the whole object of this type of warfare—surprise attacks to cause frustration and leave you with a feeling of hopelessness."

I knew what he meant. On June 21, the World Food Program announced the restoration of aid flights even though it had not been able to obtain any guarantees of security from the government. It had to. Planeloads of maize and fish were needed for Cuito and scores of other destinations. The UN agency urged all parties to respect its neutrality and its humanitarian mission, but could only hope its white-painted planes would no longer be targeted.

Something else happened that day that briefly seized everyone's attention. It was one of those rare cosmic coincidences in which the dark disc of the backlit moon could be seen from specific earthly vantage points to align perfectly with the sun, blotting out all but the fiery halo of its luminous corona. The umbra, or shadow, of the first total eclipse of the new millennium began off the eastern coast of South America, crossed the Atlantic Ocean, and at midday hit Angola at Sumbe, south of Luanda, which itself fell under the surrounding wider penumbra of partial eclipse. The 125-mile-wide swath of darkness cut across the country to the Zambian border, passing right through the giant sable lands from Quimbango south and intersecting the rusted and twisted tracks of the broken Benguela Railway.

At any point along the path through Angola totality lasted about four minutes. The strange blue darkness of the event, as deep and cool as twilight, is said to be just long enough to trick flora and fauna into behaving as if night were falling. In the interior, as the dappled sunlight on the ground under scattered *brachystegia* trees began to shrink into hundreds of crescent-shaped images before fading, the giant sables would have paused in their grazing. They might have even turned toward the forest before the sun emerged from behind the blackened moon with all its burning power, flooding the *anharas* with light again.

The eclipse lasted an hour over Africa, racing eastward across Angola and appearing above the refugee camps and then downtown Lusaka in Zambia before it swept over northern Zimbabwe, straddled the lower Zambezi in Mozambique, reached the cloudy skies of Madagascar, and then disappeared over the Indian Ocean. Few tourists flocked to Angola, where the viewing was superior. Nonetheless, the government imported six million pairs of protective sunglasses, of which two million were meant to be given out free to the impoverished, who might be tempted to watch the celestial drama and risk permanent blindness. But the supposedly free glasses were soon changing hands for dollars a peek, and the street kids of Luanda, who knew a good scam when they saw one, began hawking phony viewing glasses for even stiffer prices. They had to compete with doomsday sects that preached staring at the sun without any protection to welcome the new messiah, whoever he might be, insisting that Angolans could fill their empty lives by an eye-searing look at a burning hole in the heavens.

Enthusiasm wasn't universal. In African tradition, eclipses are seen as the rotting of the sun, an omen of turmoil and bloodshed and the anger of the ancestors. In Huambo Province there was even talk that the eclipse augured the very end of the world, but government authorities said this was the ignorant prattle typical of those who had been recently freed from captivity under UNITA.

I waited to hear from van Hoven.

ELEVEN

EXPEDITION TO MALANGE

"This stuff is beginning to work on my nerves," van Hoven admitted in late September. But he refused to give up. After consulting with the generals on the Kissama Board in July, van Hoven E-mailed Estes and me from Luanda to report that although Malange Province remained an obvious target for high-profile attacks, military patrols would track enemy movements there and question locals about giant sable sightings in anticipation of a survey. Unfortunately, van Hoven reported, "Any travel by roads to and in the Luando and Cangandala areas is viewed as being too dangerous at this time because of the threat of landmines and ambushes. Tree-top flying by helicopter is ruled [out] as being irresponsible by military authorities." What would be feasible were overflights above 3,000 feet in fixed-wing aircraft using infrared and high-magnification cameras; high enough to be safe from small arms fire—though not surface-to-air missiles.

Estes, who had been staying in Mpumalanga since returning from Zimbabwe, E-mailed van Hoven. "I don't see that the planned over-flights from 1000 m. would require my and maybe not even your presence. The cameras will provide verification of any sable sightings." I was saddened at the thought that he, of all people, wouldn't be on the first scientific foray into the giant sable reserves since his own visit to Cangandala nearly twenty years before. But he had already spent a year of his life studying the animals close up, whereas we'd be lucky to spot any from that altitude. I called van Hoven, who was in his backyard, firing up the *braai*.

"I'm sorry things have to be done this way," he said. "It's like a game of chess; you judge your options, and make the moves that minimize your risks." We would have to bow to the judgment of the military men and be content with an overflight this year, and leave the helicopter and ground survey until next. "Let's face it, you and I are no good at parachuting, and it wouldn't be much fun to have a leg shot off."

A few days after Estes returned to New Hampshire, van Hoven E-mailed us the results of a meeting with Gen. Luis Faceira. Reconnaissance patrols operating in the central and eastern parts of the Luando Reserve had encountered a herd of thirty giant sable southwest of Capunda the week before and a smaller herd farther north. Also, UNITA had been active in the region and their soldiers had shot one of the sable for food at the beginning of July. Confusingly, the local Songos—there were still some in the area—reported little UNITA activity and reported that no local inhabitants had hunted the *Kolwah* in years.

Then the kicker: van Hoven had just received a letter from Gen. Armando da Cruz Neto, the chief of the Defense Force, "offering their full support for a survey of the sable." Unfortunately, because the army wanted to ensure the safety of the survey expedition, the general wanted it postponed to mid-September, when it might be possible to use helicopters. Van Hoven said he'd have more information in a few days. But his plan to begin moving animals to Quiçama at the beginning of September was worrisome—could the Angolan military support an overflight across a forested war zone while simultaneously assisting with another complex animal airlift?

Estes replied by E-mail that he found the giant sable news heartening, a sign that the population had survived "the warfare and turmoil of the past twenty-five years." However, it was "too bad that the survey can't occur before mid-September, by which time I expect the sable will be feeding on the new flush in the woodland while avoiding the seasonal plague of *moscas* (tabanids) on the *anharas*." But, he wrote, "with infra-red sensors to detect animals beneath the woodland canopy, it should be possible to flush, film, and count sable from a helicopter. Herds may also be out on the *anharas* early in the morning and only withdraw into the woodland as it gets hot and the flies become active." He added a note of regret: "I wish I could take part, but it's not feasible for me to come back again so soon. . . . Best of luck and I'll be with you in spirit and E-mail."

The next news item out of Angola, however, was a ghastly report that UNITA had attacked a train. But not on the Benguela Railway. Varian's great achievement had been reduced to a few cars chugging between

Lobito and Benguela, which was why there would be little cause for celebration on November 28, 2001, when the torn tracks and derelict premises and properties, both fixed and movable, of what had once been Angola's great iron road to the interior of Africa reverted to the state at the expiration of the ninety-nine-year concession granted to Sir Robert Williams. Instead, UNITA had targeted the limping Luanda-Malange line, the one Statham had taken eighty years before to reach the giant sable lands.

The train, carrying some five hundred refugees and local passengers crammed in carriages and sprawled on open wagons shared with freight, was ninety-five miles southeast of Luanda when it detonated a waiting antitank mine and derailed. The explosion set off two cars carrying drums of gasoline, engulfing the train in a fireball. Screaming survivors trying to flee were cut down with automatic weapons fire from rebels waiting in the bush. The scores of bodies later recovered from the smoldering wreckage were buried in a common grave nearby. As the burn victims who were hospitalized began to die, the death toll spiraled to 252. UNITA admitted responsibility, insisting that the train was a legitimate target because it "was being escorted by a battalion of the government army with munitions." Luanda denied this, although some survivors said there had been a few soldiers escorting the train. International condemnation was swift and eloquent, and the Catholic Church called for a thirty-day fast.

Van Hoven reassured me by phone that "everything was on" despite the attack. He laid out a complicated scenario involving an elephant capture operation in Botswana and several airlifts to Angola, some carrying other animal groups as well. On September 7, he and I would depart at 1:00 A.M. from Waterkloof Air Force Base in Pretoria on the last cargo flight to Cabo Ledo, accompanied by containers of wildebeest and ostriches. On the morning of September 9 we'd leave Luanda for Malange Province on military aircraft for a week's survey. He was so confident the survey would come off that he had invited a documentary film crew shooting the second phase of Operation Noah's Ark to cover the giant sable expedition as well.

When I arrived in Pretoria I found that the expedition had been put off by two weeks. The giraffes that were supposed to have been caught and acclimatized to a *boma* prior to shipment were never captured, which meant the final animal airlift had to be delayed. Knowing full well that there wouldn't be sufficient logistical support for the survey without

Operation Noah's Ark out of the way, van Hoven postponed the last ship-ment of giraffes (and ostriches) to September 23. Since I had planned to go to Stellenbosch to research an article on the wines of the Cape at some point during my trip, I went early and distracted myself with wine tastings and visits to various estates and producers, hoping the new date for the survey would hold.

On September 11, I returned to my guest house in the afternoon and switched on the television to catch the news. Horrified and shaken by the terrorist attacks on New York and Washington, I made a flurry of calls to family and friends in the United States to make sure they were safe. But I was stuck in South Africa until flights to New York resumed. Left to brood about what it all meant, I was wondering before too long as to why on earth I thought it was so important to go in search of the giant sable. When I finally talked with van Hoven by phone two days later, I found out that he'd been stopped in his tracks as well, glued to his television and hardly able to believe what had occurred. The Angolan reaction to the attacks on the United States, however, was predictably balanced: Luanda solemnly declared that it was all too familiar with acts of terrorism, while UNITA accused the dos Santos regime of dealings with international terrorist net-works. But by the time I returned to Pretoria a few days later, the survey expedition was back on, although now postponed to October 10. I didn't know what to think, and flew home.

Van Hoven E-mailed me on September 25. Despite a few hitches, phase two of Operation Noah had been equally successful—sixteen ele-phants and as many zebra, a dozen ostriches, another dozen wildebeests, and four giraffe had been released in Quiçama to join the animals already there. He was waiting for confirmation for the October survey, which I suspected might not be forthcoming. The same day, UNITA rebels had pulled off an attack on an electrical substation on the outskirts of Luanda, interrupting power supplies in many parts of the capital—including Futungo Palace. It was the first attack the rebel movement had staged there since 1992. At least three died in the ensuing gun battle; soon after, a grim-faced dos Santos toured the scene, then left without comment. It would prove to be Savimbi's last great gesture of defiance.

But van Hoven was determined the expedition would take place, writing me two days later that if we failed to see giant sable by October, "I will not be able to prevent myself jumping off the bridge at Barra do Cuanza." Less than a week later he had to admit that rebel forces had been detected in the reserves, forcing yet another postponement of the "mission to Malange." He would keep me informed. "In the meantime scream and kick the dog, like I did," he wrote, "but don't start traveling until further notice."

SIX WEEKS LATER, the expedition was on yet again, and having received no news to the contrary before my scheduled departure, I flew to Johannesburg. I had grave doubts about this trip, my eighth to Africa in four years. I knew that late November/early December was hardly the ideal time of the year to search for giant sable, as Estes reminded me when he called to wish me luck. I knew, too, that a single incident in Malange was all it would take to scuttle the venture. Yet it was a chance, however slim, to enter the giant sable lands and see what we could find and I couldn't turn it down.

Van Hoven and the documentary film crew were waiting for me at the airport for the start of what he wryly called "Mission Impossible." There were four others who would join the two of us: an American, David Allen, a lanky, gray-haired, chain-smoking former ABC-TV news producer, and three South Africans—Phillip Hattingh, a beefy, genial director; Pierre van Heerden, a grizzled veteran cameraman; and Duane Graham, a slim, quiet film student who'd signed on as an assistant. The first three were partners in a film company that had produced a number of wildlife documentaries, including a short segment on Operation Noah's Ark that had just been shown in newscasts in the United States and Europe. I took their participation as a good omen. We returned to the airport the next day with a sizable pile of film equipment, and flew to Angola on TAAG Angolan Airways.

We stayed at Gen. Luis Faceira's home, not his seaside villa, but his townhouse in the Miramar section of the city, full of dark paneling, marble floors, and impressively appointed bathrooms. That night he took us to dinner at a beachfront restaurant. Faceira told van Hoven that he would rather stay on his farm, where his latest project was raising emus, than revisit the war zone. If we wanted to see *palanca negra* there was a nightclub along the Marginal with a statue of one outside. "That's real," he teased us; the ones in Malange were *"fantasmas."*

After breakfast the next morning, the general cleared up a confusion: we were going to fly to *Capanda*, not Capunda. Instead of heading directly to the eastern edge of the Luando Reserve, we were going to a site near Pedras Negras where Odebrecht, the Brazilian-based construction company, was building a massive hydroelectric dam on the Cuanza, about seventy-five miles west of Cangandala Park. Over maps quickly spread out on the dining room table, van Hoven asked about flying into the Luando Reserve from Capanda. General Faceira rolled his eyes. "No control," he grunted, dismissing the region with a wave of his hand; UNITA was there. Wasn't there some way we could go in? The general shook his head firmly, and to make sure we understood the reasons against it, lifted up his pant leg and then pulled up his shirt to point out old battle scars. But Cangandala Park was a different story, he said. There, the military situation was currently "secure" for helicopter flights over the treetops. We would fly over it in two helicopters lent by Sonangol, the state oil company, for two days (after that UNITA would know we were there) and both he and General Hendrik would accompany us. We would leave first thing tomorrow. So what if it wasn't exactly what we were expecting? The expedition would finally be underway.

Our plans settled, van Hoven headed off with the general to deal with Kissama Foundation matters. There had been considerable turnover in staff at the park; both Coetzee and Blaauw were long gone. Indiscriminate new hirings had created problems, and he wanted to lobby other board members for support to recruit a full-time professional director to run the foundation in Luanda and oversee park administration. With the rest of the day on our hands, van Heerden, Hattingh, Graham, and I went for a midmorning walk. Miramar is an upscale neighborhood by Luanda standards, dotted with well-guarded diplomatic compounds, none more secure-looking than the American embassy hidden behind a high gray concrete wall topped with concertina wire. Van Heerden had brought his video camera for our stroll along the Rua Houari Boumedienne and its hillside view of the bay and the shacks of the squatter settlement below. We paused a few blocks farther for another view of the precipitous shantytown.

It looked like a freshly bulldozed town dump, all raw red earth and hills of trash with children clambering over them.

Van Heerden filmed the children, who waved back, and then zoomed in on a scrawny dog loping along the street. It dawned on me that we were looking at Boa Vista, or what was left of it. Five months before, in an action reminiscent of colonial forced resettlements, riot police armed with automatic weapons, batons, and tear gas had swept through this slum to evict its 50,000 inhabitants. Demolition was preceded by the inevitable clashes, during which two protesters were shot dead. The residents were trucked off to a tent camp twenty miles from the capital on the pretext that several huts on the hillside had collapsed during heavy rains and the area was unsafe. The real reason for the removals was that the seaside site had been earmarked for redevelopment into a luxury market, entertainment, and leisure complex by a Sonangol subsidiary. Many of the former slum-dwellers who had managed to eke out an existence in Luanda could not afford the daily bus fare (about a day's wages) to commute to the capital, but they were put to work building their own shelters. Although they couldn't be paid for that happy chore, the government planned to call on the international community to help feed them — hadn't other countries always stepped in rather than let thousands starve? But aid organizations showed little interest in a humanitarian crisis of Luanda's own making, pointing out that Angola's humanitarian needs already exceeded $200 million a year, although the country pumped that sum in offshore crude every week.

Before I could suggest we move on, van Heerden panned around to the building complex behind us to find several blue-uniformed policemen in wraparound sunglasses and black berets filling his viewfinder. One clamped a firm hand on his shoulder, another fingered the trigger of his machine gun. We had stumbled on Boa Vista all right, and we were in for a long, tiresome confrontation. At one point I foolishly produced my press pass, which only resulted in having it and my passport confiscated. When I protested, the dark-glassed officers invited me to their police post to discuss the matter. I offered $20 to facilitate reconsideration of the matter, and finally got my papers back. We refrained from filming on our stroll back to the general's house.

Luanda is always in your face. Later, when Lobito, General Hendrik's driver, took me and the film crew to a streetside market to pick up some staples, a crowd of ragged youths surged around the general's shiny red SUV in excitement and grabbed at us as we got out of the vehicle. Lobito restored partial order by brandishing his 9mm pistol and shouting threats, but our attempts to purchase the few items we wanted—bottled water, eggs, fruit, bread—set the crowd off again. The rare presence of foreigners with pockets full of dollars made the stallkeepers giddy with greed and crushed when we wouldn't pay the exorbitant prices asked. A snapped photo elicited demands for money, which we ignored, much to the youths' disgust. The afternoon sun was merciless—I could feel it biting into my forearms—and the crowd edged ever closer, thrusting brooms, strings of Christmas lights, fish, toothbrushes, or just their hands in our faces. While Lobito chaperoned Hattingh and negotiated prices, the rest of us retreated to the vehicle, where more faces and hands pressed up to the windows. Surely we must be here for more than bread and water. A child tried singing for us. A man sidled up and offered diamonds. A youth exposed himself and wiggled his penis inquiringly. At last, Hattingh squeezed back in the car with the provisions, Lobito gunned the engine, and the crowd reluctantly parted for us.

When would the misery of ordinary Angolans stop? *Not until the war ends* was the government's automatic response. Cynics said that peace will only come to Angola when Savimbi's widow attends dos Santos's funeral. How it would finally come about was anyone's guess. Perhaps there could be a negotiated settlement, unlikely though it seemed. But would the dos Santos regime finally begin to respond to the needs of its people, once the excuse of fighting the rebels disappeared? The president announced in August that he would not run for reelection, but since it wouldn't be possible to hold a countrywide vote anytime soon, the gesture was largely symbolic; he would probably remain in power for years. Savimbi countered with an unlikely "peace plan" for a transition government that would include UNITA as an equal partner. What if he were to seize the moment and declare a cease-fire, announce his candidacy, and press for elections? I wondered who the MPLA could put up to oppose him. But I was weary of speculating, and preferred to see those latter-day moves as reminders that dos Santos and Savimbi would pass from the scene eventually, making way for the hope of new and genuine leadership in a country that cried out for it and surely deserved it after all that its people have endured.

Back at the general's house we flopped on cool Brazilian leather couches in the air-conditioning and flipped through the TV channels until van Hoven and the general returned. Van Hoven was pleased to report that the board had backed his plan to hire a full-time professional manager. What's more, General Faceira had proposed that the foundation support a ban on hunting throughout Angola until proper conservation could be restored. The board unanimously agreed, and Fátima Jardim promised to take the matter up with the government, which was expected to respond positively to the initiative.

And how was our day? he wondered. We told him we were looking forward to tomorrow.

IT WAS JUST after 9:00 A.M. on November 28, 2001 when the pilots started the engines of the nineteen-passenger twin-engine Beechcraft and we taxied out from the military hangars to the runway for takeoff. Wouter van Hoven and I exchanged grins across the aisle and signaled thumbs-up as the plane rumbled down the tarmac and lifted off under gray skies. Through my yellowish oval window the shack-strewn red-earth landscape surrounding Luanda receded and the silvery Cuanza meandering to the east was briefly visible before being lost below in the cloud cover that masked our steep climb. We leveled out at 21,500 feet—above surface-to-air-missile range—before breaking through to blue skies and wispy clouds over Malange Province.

"Bet you thought this would never happen," van Hoven said. I admitted I'd had a few doubts and still had no idea what was in store for us. "We'll just have to see," van Hoven said. "Nothing happens in Africa until it happens."

The film crew was sitting behind us, along with a few Odebrecht staff returning to the dam site. Ahead of us General Faceira, in civilian khaki, and General Hendrik, in combat fatigues, exchanged jokes. I felt reassured they were leading the expedition—not only would they have up-to-date intelligence, these career military men would hardly take undue risks.

An hour and a half after our takeoff from Luanda the pilot banked the plane into a "modified combat descent"—a tight spiral landing—just over the airfield at Capanda, giving us a dramatic view of the immense half-built dam that would necessitate flooding a vast area of land to supply electricity to Luanda. We landed and rolled up to a reception committee of soldiers and security personnel. I took in the army truck with radar on top, the military helicopters and transport planes, the troops that greeted the generals with snappy salutes and firm handshakes, and the amazing fact that van Hoven and I had finally made it into Malange. We hauled the bulky film equipment onto a waiting bus, which took us through a surprisingly large settlement. Some 3,500 workers, including Brazilians, Russians, and South Africans as well as Angolan laborers, were housed in this giant camp, which had its own road system, dormitories, clinic, mess hall, recreation facilities, offices, vehicle sheds, and an airfield that can handle 727s—everything that was needed to build the second largest compacted cement dam in the world. Work had started in 1987 on *Projeto Capanda*, the single largest building project in the country, but had been interrupted by the civil war several times; in 1999 UNITA had leveled it, stopping construction for ten months. The rebuilt dam site's external security was now handled by the Angolan army, and internally by a private security company, whose guards stood ready with machine guns at the entrance of each building. Still, three soldiers and an employee had been killed by rebels only five months before when an Odebrecht truck convoy was attacked near Malange city.

After locating our rooms, we spent the rest of the day in fruitless speculation, trying to figure out where the helicopters were, who would get to go on them, when we might leave, and where we'd explore. But when thunder rumbled through, followed by lightning and steady rain, it was obvious that nothing would happen until the next day. I walked through the game room of the complex in which most of us were staying, thinking I might as well waste an hour watching Portuguese cable TV, and saw two Angolan military officers in uniform and two local men in worn sport shirts and slacks sitting at a snack table.

One of the officers was Brig. Gen. Manuel de Santos Hilário, the solidly built area commander, who had personally spotted a herd of twenty or more *palancas negras* from his patrol helicopter some months back and was still regretting he hadn't had a camera with him, and the other was Col. Kanzenze Umbari Marinheiro, who also happened to be a traditional Songo chief. Colonel Marinheiro was eager to explain that there were sixteen Songo *fiscals* (game wardens) assigned to Cangandala district under him, some of whom still watched the giant sable herds. He'd brought along two of them, Jovete and Domingos, to give us an eyewitness report. Van Hoven came in at that point and I quickly waved him over to the table.

The two Songo were quiet at first, but became animated on the subject of the *palancas negras*. Jovete explained that in 1993 UNITA had shot some *palancas* and the *fiscals* had all fled. Still, up to 1997 they had been able to track the herds regularly, but after UNITA swept through again, they were forced to relocate to Malange city. There was no one in the park now, but he and Domingos tried to go back in every week or so, hostilities permitting. They knew the animals' favorite haunts, but it was difficult to find them at this time of year; they moved only until midmorning, and then again only in the late afternoon. Jovete's pronunciation of the local name for the animal sounded more like *Kolo* than *Kolwah*, but there was little doubt we were talking about the same creature. "Many big ones," he said through a translator, using the plural term *Jikolo*. He made arcs with his hands over his head to indicate the horns of the big males, while Domingos sketched out the white undermarkings of the antelope with his palms, smoothing down the front of his thin gray shirt. And the white cheek stripe? I asked, pretending the giant sable had them; Domingos said *não*, wiping his own cheek with his fingers—the *Jikolo* had no cheek stripes. Van Hoven and I exchanged looks: these men knew what giant sables looked like, that much was certain. Jovete smiled shyly and brought out a small, dusty plastic sack filled with dry, grape-sized dark droppings. He and Domingos had sighted a herd two days ago, and were now proudly bringing us their scat. I stared at the contents of the bag, which gave off a faint, earthy, grassy odor—the scent of our success. Van Hoven and I hastily conferred: some cells from the animal's gut would certainly have been passed along in this dung, from which Terry Robinson could doubtless extract DNA to compare with his existing giant sable samples to present hard evidence that a living, breathing giant sable was responsible for this splendid shit. The *fiscals'* firsthand account had been convincing enough on top of all we had heard, but this was a bag of solid, neatly rounded proof, a redolent prize that by itself would justify our trip.

Capanda didn't get many visitors and our arrival was celebrated that evening with a festive barbeque. The beer flowed freely and the Brazilian beef on skewers was delicious, but I was too excited to rest well that night and couldn't get back to sleep at all after being awakened at 4:00 A.M. by a DDT truck that sprayed clouds of insecticide around the buildings to suppress the malarial mosquito population. In the predawn darkness it was easy to imagine a forest with indistinct forms slipping silently and seductively in and out of the dark trees.

After breakfast I watched van Hoven get in some target practice with his tranquilizer rifle. The possibility we might be able to flush some giant sables out within darting range and collect skin or blood samples was too tempting for him to ignore and he wanted to be ready. He propped a doormat up outside and fired a dart at it from twenty yards. It hit dead center, its pink tail feathers quivering. The dormitory guards were impressed.

But the dense morning fog refused to lift, and without better visibility we couldn't take off. I repacked my camera bag. The Sonangol pilots watched television. Graham and General Hendrik played Ping-Pong. By 9:30 A.M. the weather finally cleared and we climbed on the bus to the airfield, where an awkward game of musical chairs ensued. There were not enough seats for everyone, even with two French Dauphin helicopters; word of our foray had spread and the generals were compelled to accommodate several unexpected and important guests from the camp, military and otherwise. Van Hoven, Hattingh, van Heerden, Jovette, and I commandeered one aircraft, squeezing in with the equipment and the two pilots and leaving the generals to sort out who they'd take with them on theirs. I noticed they made room for AK-47s and grenade launchers, in case their intelligence on rebel movements proved faulty.

We rose off the runway, one after the other, light rain spattering on the bulbous windshield as we raced over thick forest that gave way to a sparse landscape dotted with a few solitary huts and fields, low clouds hugging the distant hills. We followed the generals' helicopter east to Malange airport, where we were due to check in with General Hilário, both for the sake of protocol and to get any military updates before heading on to Cangandala Park. Half an hour later we rolled up to the shattered terminal building and nearby rusted hangars of the old colonial *Areoclube de Malange.*

Every window in the entire terminal, from the control tower on down, had been blown out and the entire structure thoroughly peppered with automatic weapons fire. Weeds waved in the cracked walkways. On the walls, lizards darted in and out of assorted bullet holes. Inside, mortar shells stuck out from the crumbling cement, against which a crowd of people leaned or milled around, waiting, presumably, for one of the many mercy flights supplying the twenty-nine international aid organizations that operated in the city of Malange. In 1993 starving war refugees here were so desperate for nourishment they picked maniacally at the tarmac for the grains that spilled from maize sacks broken during the frantic unloading of humanitarian airlifts. Eight years later thousands were still trying to flee the intense fighting between rebel UNITA forces and government troops. The government was pursuing a savage offensive in Mexico, where Savimbi was thought to be hiding, causing much of the rural population to flee and seek safety in government-controlled towns like Malange or stream across the border into Zambia. But there were no stick-figured refugees in evidence that day, just a few police, some hawkers with beer and soda, thin children in rags, a wizened man who fervently hoped I needed a ride into the city, and a boy selling, of all things, bags of popcorn.

It was well past 11:00 A.M. when the local commander rolled up to confer with the generals. Finally, we took off again, dipping forward as we circled out and headed east at a hundred-plus miles per hour toward the settlement of Cangandala and the park beyond under puffy white clouds. It was already midday, but our hopes were high—we would be flying over the same land where Livingstone and Statham had led their expeditions long ago and that Estes had last revisited in 1982.

It was hard to talk above the whomping roar of the rotors and we soon gave up leaning forward or backward to shout in each other's ears and lapsed into watching the blurry, pinwheeling shadow of the helicopter as it flowed over the green grassland and then rippled across the treetops of the *miombo* forest. We passed over abandoned manioc fields and patches of faint furrows scratched out of the forest like fading hatchmarks, overgrown remains of burned-out villages and the rusted wreck of a T-55 tank, reminders, if we needed them, that we had entered a land still contested by government troops and UNITA rebels.

Van Hoven sat behind me and Jovete, who wore headphones so he could let the pilot know where to go and alert him if he spotted any animals. From time to time the *fiscal* spoke to the pilot and we swooped down close to the treetops. I was uncomfortably aware that a band of rebels could easily be hiding somewhere in the immense forest, although I knew government patrols had swept through the region and found nothing. But any nagging fears about our vulnerability to attack from below were damped down by the excitement of scanning the forest for giant sable. Once we entered the northern part of the park and began a slow loop of the area, van Hoven slid open the rear door and van Heerden leaned out with his video camera. Open clearings dotted with termite mounds and parklike grassy-green *anharas* appeared like scattered islands in the sea of trees in full foliage. I stared into their dark edges, hoping the shadows in the understory would morph into antelopes. Van Hoven and Hattingh each spotted a small buck, but nothing the size of sable. I glimpsed a colorful bird. As the minutes went by, Jovete started frowning. His familiar landscape must have looked very different from the air and I wondered if he knew where we were. All too soon, the pilot indicated we had to return to Malange airport for refueling.

Back on the tarmac, the generals and the *fiscals* held a conference and consulted their maps and came up with a new strategy for the afternoon: we'd land at a Songo village outside the park and talk with the locals before exploring further. The bad news was that it would be our last chance: the generals, never enthusiastic about treetop flying in Malange, decided we had to return to Luanda with the helicopters the next day. In an instant I went from concern over rebel presence to anguish that we couldn't have more time, but in the end there was nothing to do but get back into the helicopter, with Domingos taking the place of Jovete, who joined the generals.

Once back in the air, we followed their helicopter to a nearby forest settlement and circled above while they landed in a field crossed by a small stream. Several boys who had been filling water jugs threw down their loads and ran in excitement—or terror—back to the cluster of thatched huts. Villagers were already streaming out to look at their visitors, although they

397

stayed well back from its whirling rotors. Several people on board climbed out to talk to the residents and shortly after a series of hands shot up in answer to the inquiries, each pointed in a different direction. I wondered if they were trying to throw us off the trail, the way they had all the others who had come in pursuit of the giant sable. But some consensus was apparently reached, and we followed the generals' helicopter as it lifted off and cruised high over a heavily forested area and then spent an hour on a long, low loop deep into the pristine *miombo* of Cangandala that now completely surrounded us, as if we were in a green sea out of sight of land. "It was just the way God made it" was how van Hoven remembered it later. But it was all too apparent that in the hours we had left, we would be damned lucky to find any of the hundred or so giant sable that might be scattered across the 232 square miles of the park. Still, van Hoven cradled his rifle on his knees in readiness and stared out the open door at the endless forest below as the wind roared past.

So it had come to this, I thought. Those in whose hands the future of the giant sable now rests were descending from the sky into its haunts. Ours wouldn't be their first encounter with humans; the tribes here had cultivated crops, burned the grass, laid traps, hunted, and fished in the rivers for generations and more recently others had come rumbling across the *anharas* in their vehicles. The antelopes saw them all, smelled them, heard the twig snaps of their approach. But pursuers like us would announce themselves by the distant hum of an engine in the sky.

Somewhere in this forest was a herd bull, spiky mane twitching, alerted to the faint, unnatural droning of our approach. If he and his cows were out in the open, and if we were lucky enough to be heading directly for them, they would panic at the thrumming staccato now reverberating through the forest below us. They wouldn't see us until our helicopter leapt into view over the treetops and swooped down on them like an immense bird of prey. Then they'd bolt across the grass, whipped flat from the wash of the whirling rotors, but we'd loop around and cut them off from the trees and van Hoven would lean out of the open hatch with his rifle. The bull might rear up as if to do battle with the mechanical monster bearing down on him, as sable often do, but he'd only end up kicking helplessly when the tranquilizer dart stabbed into his withers.

I looked back at van Hoven, who was staring through his binoculars. I turned to scan the passing trees on my side. If he managed to dart a giant sable—and we didn't lose it in the trees—we would land and cautiously close in. Van Hoven would not risk a lethal overdose. No, it would be better to let the master bull stagger in a circle or try a leg-crumpling charge before collapsing in groggy defeat. We'd rush up, grab his horns to seize control, and throw a rag over his eyes. We'd snip a small piece of his ear, take a blood sample, photograph him, measure him, stroke his fur and touch his horns and walk around him and marvel. Then van Hoven would administer an antidote and we would watch as he shook off his stupor and galloped off to his future, now forever changed.

But why stop at that? It took only a little more imagination for me to picture us, or some future helicopter crew, stuffing wads of cotton in his ears, tightening his blindfold, shoving sections of plastic hose over the rapier tips of his horns, rolling him over onto a canvas stretcher, and then staggering with the load toward the open belly of the helicopter that would take him and others far from this ancestral forest to another reserve, another park, perhaps even Quiçama. There, someday, tourists crammed into a zebra-striped minivan could be thrilled by the sight of a herd of giant sables trotting along the puzzling perimeter of shocking wire and shout at the driver to stop so they could snap photos of their retreating rumps before they plunged into the bush.

Van Hoven slapped the seat ahead to try to get the pilot's attention. He shouted that he saw something, and pointed as the pilot dipped the helicopter sharply, tilting the flat green world below us. I grabbed my cameras before they slid off the seat. *Where are they?* But van Hoven slowly shook his head. He thought he saw something large, but now he couldn't be sure—every part of the forest looked like every other part and there was no way to retrace our route precisely and find the exact shadows that might have been great dark antelopes.

Twenty minutes later the pilot tapped the fuel gauge and motioned to van Hoven to slide the rear door shut: our time was up. I groaned inwardly as we turned westward toward Capanda and picked up speed and then turned to look over my shoulder. Hattingh looked resigned. Van Hoven shrugged and shouted over the thrumming noise, "We've been looking for needles in a haystack. But there's no doubt they are there. We know that now." I nodded, turned around, and stared out at the *miombo* rushing past and the afternoon light flickering through the rotors. Between the rain and fog and the generals' caution, our search had been truncated to a few hours at the wrong time of day at the wrong time of the year, because, of course, there was a war going on. Later I would come to think that the generals may have been right not to push our luck: three weeks after our foray UNITA rebels shot seven civilians and wounded twenty others in a vehicle ambush near Cangandala, a follow-up to their missile attack on a bus there back in August.

But at that moment I was crushed with disappointment; I had wanted desperately to see the animal with my own eyes.

For years now I'd staged scenes of this anticipated final encounter in my head, rewriting them after every setback and incorporating every new whiff of hope. This was supposed to have been the last leg of the journey, the realization of a long-held dream: somehow we would fly over the warlord's forest and find the giant sable. It should have happened, and could have happened, and almost did, but for the war, and because few journeys end the way you think they were meant to end. It wasn't that I had to personally confirm their existence—it was clear from all we'd heard that the giant sable had survived. If Estes and van Hoven believed they were there, who was I to entertain any doubts?

No, it was something else. I had hoped to be vouchsafed a vision of just one master bull shaking his heavy head before the inevitable realization sank in that the antelope I'd been pursuing for so long couldn't possibly have been what I was after. Over the years, each time I thought I had captured its meaning, the beast had given me the slip, shifted shape, and re-formed into something else, as if purposely taunting me. But that never deterred me. Yet somehow, months back, the full implications of what Terry Robinson told me began to take hold. Of course DNA results couldn't alter the animal—it was what it was—but they forced me to see that the royal, or giant, sable had always been a partly invented beast, compounded out of belief in its uniqueness and the dark beauty that made it a walking talisman. It was just an antelope whose small population was wedged between two rivers and a bit north of that in a southern African country, a four-legged thing with hooped horns that happened to attract a whorl of ideas, a nimbus of meanings completely extraneous to it, valued even by warring enemies for its symbolic power. At various points over the years the giant sable had sometimes looked like a chimera to me, but now I knew it was partly fictive at its core—it was a real antelope, and a magnificent one at that, but an illusory creature all the same. What had the tribespeople said to Huntley?

There is no such animal.

As we neared Capanda, the pilot flew close to the huge ominous outcroppings that UNITA used as cover to shell the settlement in previous attacks. Whatever made me think I could pursue an antelope dream with impunity in this landscape of death? The Angolan civil war was far more than the cruel context of conservation in Angola, the looming reality that threatened to blot out the beast; it was the agony of an entire nation, and rightly dwarfed my personal quest. Perhaps the giant sable was destined to remain tantalizingly out of sight until real peace came to Angola. In some ways it would be fitting for an animal whose meaning was so bound up with the country's history.

That was why there would be no prize, no trophy to take home from my long journey—only searing memories, discarded illusions, and the small hope that nature here would survive even the most bitter human battles. Mixed feelings of regret and relief began to take hold as we approached the airfield. Although I had been denied an encounter with the creature in the flesh, I had embraced it as close as possible short of that.

I found myself letting the creature go.

SHORTLY AFTER MY return to the United States I took a day off to go to The Cloisters at the northern tip of Manhattan and revisit the Unicorn Tapestries. Designed in Paris about 1500 and woven from fine wool, metallic thread, and silk, these complex works are brocaded with symbols that easily allow disparate readings—as a tale of courtly love, an allegory of Christ's passion and crucifixion, or an enigmatic pursuit—and are rightly regarded as treasures, though for many years after the French Revolution they were relegated to shielding espaliered trees from frost. Every so often

I like to spend a quiet hour with these strange, compelling tableaux depicting the hunt and capture of the great magical beast of the medieval world and dwell on the riot of flowers and tumult of hounds, the all-knowing maidens and courtly spear-wielding hunters, and the impossible, singular, ivory-pale unicorn.

I find the scene that invariably lingers is the last in the series of seven hangings, a fragment called *The Unicorn in Captivity*. The tapestries as a whole don't tell a coherent story, they rise above one, so despite the fact that the others show the beast at bay and then slain and brought to the castle, it is that one that radiates finality. The image of the unicorn in a bed of flowers, encircled by a little railed fence and collared and chained to a thin little tree, whatever else it might represent, perfectly captures the binding of nature, the harnessing of a dream. The magic beast is brought to heel, tethered and tamed, made subservient to a greater power and compliant to desires other than its own. But the little fence is also protection, for boundaries serve to hold off as well as enclose. Considered that way, its confining space becomes a tiny park for the gentled unicorn.

On much of this planet we are still a world of nature dotted with human settlements, but in many regions we are rapidly becoming a world of human settlements dotted with patches of nature, a few of which will be saved, guarded, and eventually fenced. These nature gardens will have to be maintained, and that means not just watched but clipped and weeded, reordered, and the species balanced out to show off each constituent life-form to its best advantage. How else to maintain biodiversity in spaces that are invariably too small to maintain themselves without intervention? And there will have to be a place for the giant sable; this was their fate too, tellingly woven into a medieval hanging as if it had been foreordained for centuries. These magnificent antelopes are too important to far too many people to be left alone in the house of the giant sable.

Early on I had resisted the idea that the population of giant sables might have to be split, and a captive-breeding program established outside their habitat, not so much on biological grounds, but because I saw it as lèse-majesté, an offense against the very dignity of those antelope kings. Now I saw that eventually some were likely be captured and translocated, held hostage, as it were, to assure the survival of the main herds, whether there was a war or not, and could end up the minor rulers of fenced-in paddocks in far-flung zoos. The giant sable had become another antelope that needed to be monitored and managed and manipulated, and should the remnant population permit a sustainable yield, perhaps even culled, and the dark privilege of executing that task sold to help defray the maintenance of the herds.

The royal, or giant, sable of Angola might someday even be stripped of its subspecies status, dismissed as a relict *Hippotragus* variant living out a twilight existence in the land between two rivers. But a certain mantle of meaning will always linger with the beast, like the persistent odor the old hunters said clung to the drying skin of a giant sable trophy, if only because the Angolans see the *palanca preta gigante* through different eyes. For them it will always be the noble animal whose uncertain fate echoed their own, a creature kept hidden from their colonial overlords for centuries and which escaped extermination even in war—and whose future, like theirs, hinges on the peace that they hope will finally follow after years of conflict.

IN EARLY FEBRUARY 2002, I heard from Bettine van Vuuren. Terry Robinson had given her the sable dung to analyze, but the dried-up little turds refused to talk. "Am afraid that I have bad news," she E-mailed me. "The giant sable DNA extraction from the dung pellets did not work. We tried various things over the weekend (used only the supernatant, different times in the buffers etc.), and nothing amplified. The primers that I used for the PCR are very conservative primers which work on fresh material (I included a positive control in the amplification which worked). This shows that the problem definitely lies with the extraction (cannot get DNA from the dry pellets) and not with the PCR amplification. Pity . . ."

Robinson had warned me that DNA extraction from old dung was a long shot. The *Kolwah* had appeared to the faithful Songo, but further proofs would await developments in Angola.

THE ANGOLAN GOVERNMENT continued to pursue its grim strategy in eastern Moxico Province. For months, army units had been forcibly removing thousands of rural peasants to depopulate the region and deny UNITA forces support or supplies, shoving them onto helicopters with only the possessions they could carry and dumping them in government camps near Luena, the provincial capital, without regard to the limited aid available, outraging humanitarian relief organizations. Angolan soldiers regularly skirmished with the rebels and from time to time announced the killing, capture, or defection of various senior UNITA officers and even the seizure of some of Jonas Savimbi's personal goods, including a hunting rifle given to him by former South African president P. W. Botha. By mid-February it was reported that Savimbi was traveling with a column of men weakened by malnutrition across the arid wastes of the "Hungry Country."

As Savimbi's situation worsened, his followers saw his behavior become increasingly erratic and self-destructive, veering from morose musings on his mistakes to periods of dangerous inaction. Inexplicably, he had insisted on moving into Moxico, despite the fact that his supplies were so low some of his men had starved to death. His senior military advisors pleaded with him to abandon the area, where he was likely to be tracked down and trapped. But he ignored them. He insisted on remaining in the *terras do fim do mundo*, the lands at the end of the earth, where UNITA had been founded and where he had launched his first attacks over thirty years before. Later, his actions would look to his followers like those of a man who had decided to die.

On February 22, 2002, sixty-seven-year-old Jonas Malheiro Savimbi slipped through the dense forest near the Luio River in eastern Moxico, accompanied by several of his wives and a column of bodyguards. They paused to rest; that was when the government troops chasing them closed in.

It had taken an immense and brutal two-year-long effort on the part of the Angolan armed forces to locate and surround Savimbi in the harsh landscape of the "Hungry Country." Until that day, despite all their efforts, they had never been able to pin down O *Mais Velho*. One account said the troops had been led to "the Eldest One" by a defector; another claimed they had tracked a satellite phone call he made to Lisbon from his forest hideout. What was known was that earlier that day the army had shot two of his most senior officers, Brigadier Mbula and Brigadier "Big Joe," whose troops had been diverting military attention away from their leader, leaving Savimbi without radio contact. He put his units on alert, but government commandos caught them by surprise on the muddy riverbank.

Savimbi had long ago vowed that he would never be taken from the Angolan bush alive. He fought to escape and was cut down in a hail of bullets at around 3:00 P.M. He died like a soldier, "with a gun in his hand," said Brigadier Simão Carlitos Wala, the young commander who led the government attack in which some two dozen of Savimbi's "presidential bodyguards" were also killed before the remainder fled. Savimbi's body, riddled with shots, was displayed later that afternoon, sprawled out on a low rough table under a leafy tree in the nearby village of Lucusse. The fascinated crowd of soldiers and villagers who came to look and photograph his corpse took in the unmistakable broad, bearded face and the puffy, closed lids of the eyes that had transfixed his followers, the disheveled, blood-soaked olive fatigues and shoeless feet, the bright green-and-white striped undershorts showing above the split-open pants, the corpulent belly circled by red and green tribal stings and the flies that were already crawling over him. Reporters counted and recounted fifteen bullet wounds from head to toe. The number was solemnly repeated in government releases, as if to convince the many doubtful Angolans that Jonas Malheiro Savimbi, the much-feared founder of the thirty-six-year-old *União Nacional para a Independência Total de Angola*, the National Union for the Total Independence of Angola, was really and truly dead.

At first there was talk of putting his body on view in the capital, but the government showed instead a convincing and gory videotape of his body on state television. The next day he was buried under a tree in the graveyard on the edge of the town of Luena, but not until the lid of the coffin was reopened at the insistence of onlookers so they could be sure it was really him. Celebrations broke out in Luanda, but it was a rather subdued display of honking cars and scattered singing; disbelief still lingered in the minds of many and others were already wondering if Africa's longest-running war, the hideous, almost thirty-year conflict that had devoured their country, left a million people killed or wounded, and turned a third of the population into refugees, would end now that the man who had done more than anyone else to prolong it had died.

That possibility was much in the air when Savimbi's archenemy, President José Eduardo dos Santos of Angola, sat across the polished conference table from President George W. Bush, the vice president, the secretary of state, and other U.S. officials in the Cabinet Room at the White House, four days after Savimbi was killed. The previously scheduled meeting had been planned to air regional issues with dos Santos and the presidents of Mozambique and Botswana. The agenda included stability and development in southern Africa, the conflict in the Great Lakes region, and the AIDS pandemic, but the meeting gained a sharp, new focus over the intervening weekend. Bush urged dos Santos "to move quickly toward achieving a cease-fire."

Twelve years ago it had been a beaming, nattily attired "Dr." Jonas Savimbi who had met with Bush's father in the Oval Office, confident of Washington's continued support. Since then the man who was regarded as a "key to Africa" and ruled the lion's share of Angolan territory, sending UNITA representatives to Washington and major capitals throughout Europe, had become nothing more than a terrorist, his movement reduced to a personality cult, his last days spent as a hunted man. By the time Savimbi met his fate in that desolate bush, events had stripped away his professed causes—fighting the Portuguese, the Cubans, the Soviets, and the one-party state—leaving him revealed as nothing but a savage warlord.

Did Savimbi ever have a legitimate vision for his country, or had his expressed aims always been a cynical, shifting cover to disguise his lust for power? He seems certain to be remembered as a ruthless tyrant, a brilliant and seductive psychopath who squandered his evident gifts for leadership. Yet what he long represented to many Angolans—the embodiment of the aspirations of the rural poor (never mind how much he betrayed them) in contrast to the ambitions of the Creole elite of the capital and the coast—has to be incorporated in any lasting peace.

A day after Savimbi's death a UNITA spokesman in Portugal said his movement was "deeply shaken" by the news, but vowed "this will never mean a military surrender." As if to underscore that, UNITA rebels attacked a truck carrying soldiers, police, and civilians on a remote road near the city of Malange on February 26, as dos Santos was on his way to Washington, killing nine people and wounding fifteen others—the violent spasm of an organization that had just been beheaded.

At the White House "minisummit," President Bush stressed that his policy "was to put Africa as a priority," but offered no specific commitments. Dos Santos, recognizing where American interests lay, noted that Angola already supplied 5 percent of U.S. oil imports. In a bid for a warmer bilateral relationship, he emphasized that his country would "want to work with the U.S. to contribute to its energy security." In exchange, Luanda would doubtless expect muted criticism over its conduct of the war or how it spent its oil revenues. Dos Santos initially ruled out a unilateral cease-fire—why should he reach out to an organization that was not only his mortal enemy but if allowed to regroup with its political wing might win the next presidential election? He would want a handpicked MPLA successor in office to ensure that no uncomfortable questions were asked about the billions that have disappeared into the pockets of the Luanda elite, including his own.

But after a week's stay in Brazil, ostensibly to discuss bilateral relations with President Fernando Cardoso but also to undergo medical tests, dos Santos had a change of heart. Government forces were ordered to cease offensive actions as of midnight on March 13—the thirty-sixth anniversary to the day of the founding of UNITA—in the expectation that the truce might create the conditions for a negotiated cease-fire. UNITA indicated it viewed the action as encouraging, and hungry rebels began preparing to leave the bush. Two days later, talks between the two sides were underway in Luena. On April 4, 2002, a formal cease-fire was signed in Luanda.

Now that Jonas Malheiro Savimbi no longer cast his long shadow over Angola, the country looked like it might have a future after all.

WHEN EXHAUSTED ANGOLA begins to recover from decades of war, many things that once seemed far beyond reach will be possible. Wouter van Hoven tells me that after hostilities cease, he plans to return to the giant sable lands and conduct a thorough air and ground survey to determine their numbers. Richard Estes will want to come, of course, and so will I. The best time to go would be toward the end of the brutal dry season, after the last of the annual grass fires, when the land turns leafy green more than a month before the arrival of the rains. The giant sables luxuriate then in the lush beauty of the *miombo* spring, feeding and resting among the bright pink forest flowers and mating to give birth to calves eight months later at the end of the coming rains. How the trees and plants are able to draw enough water from the blackened and cracked soil to put forth new leaves is a biological puzzle, but I find something deeply reassuring about a natural renewal that springs from a scorched earth long before there is any sign that it is possible.

NOTES

All reported dialogue is taken from my tapes, notes I made at the time, or in a few cases, soon afterwards. In some instances where it would not affect the chronology of the narrative I have conflated two or more interviews. For historical and political aspects of the story, I relied on a number of secondary sources to supplement the archives I researched and the interviews I conducted; the texts I found most useful are cited below. Passages are identified by the page on which they appear and their opening or key words.

1: TRACKS IN SHADOW

The historical outline here leans heavily on Gerald J. Bender's *Angola Under the Portuguese: The Myth and the Reality* (Berkeley: University of California Press, 1978), James Duffy's *Portugal in Africa* (Baltimore: Penguin, 1963), Thomas Pakenham's *The Scramble for Africa: White Man's Conquest of the Dark Continent from 1876 to 1912* (New York: Avon Books, 1992), and David Birmingham's *The Portuguese Conquest of Angola* (London: Oxford Institute of Race Relations, 1965), as well as John Reader's *Africa: A Biography of the Continent* (New York: A. A. Knopf, 1997). The accounts of explorers are taken largely from their own writings. Note: there are numerous variant spellings of Angolan place names; e.g., the Cuanza River also appears as the Quanza, Coanza, or Kwanza. To maintain consistency, I have employed common Portuguese usage, except to convey period flavor.

8 *"Varian found a new species"* Charles P. Curtis, Jr., and Richard C. Curtis, *Hunting in Africa East and West* (Boston: Houghton Mifflin Company, 1925), p. 214. All subsequent quotes from Curtis are from this volume.
9 *Chinese vessels had established contacts* Reader, pp. 328–9.
9 *As a result, fifteenth-century maps* Colin McEvedy's *The Penguin Atlas of African History* (New York: Penguin, revised edition, 1995) graphically underscores how rapidly the continent's cartography changed from terra incognita to colonies to countries.

10 *"In the year 6681 of the world"* Quoted in Reader, p. 344.

10 *The next year, 1483* This date is disputed; Inge Tvedten, *Angola: Stuggle for Peace and Reconstruction* (Boulder: Westview Press, 1997), note 10, p. 34.

10 *We know it now as the Congo* In colonial times the territory was known as the Congo Free State and subsequently the Belgian Congo. It became Zaire after independence; in 1997, the country was renamed the Democratic Republic of Congo. For clarity I refer to both the river and the country that straddles most of its vast basin as the Congo. There is, of course, the smaller Congo Republic (the former French Congo) on the western side of the river, usually referred to as Congo (Brazzaville).

11 *Starting in the first century* C.E. Tvedten, p. 11. Tvedten says this population might have been expected to reach 45 million by the 1990s. Currently, it is only 12.7 million, showing the "extreme impact of the slave trade and other aspects of colonial . . . policy," p. 12.

11 *"what heart could be so hard"* Quoted in Reader, p. 335.

12 *"bestial sloth"* Quoted in Bender, p. 13.

12 *Luanda became Africa's greatest slave port* See Duffy, pp. 54 and 61.

12 *Because four million slaves passed through the ports* Tvedten, p. 18.

13 *So great, Sir, is the corruption* Emphasis in the original. Mbemba Nzinga's letters are reprinted in Basil Davidson's *The African Past: Chronicles from Antiquity to Modern Times* (1964; New York: Grosset & Dunlap, 1967), pp. 191–4. See also Tvedten, p. 18, and Bender, p. 15.

13 *Afonso's "greatest flaw was a naive refusal"* Duffy, p. 40.

13 *with brief pauses marking the odd successful resistance* Queen Nzinga, who led the Ndongo from 1582 until her death in 1663, managed to stem Portuguese expansion, at least during her lifetime. She forged alliances with Dutch slave traders, and amassed enough wealth and power to conclude a favorable treaty with the Portuguese. Legend has it that when the Portuguese governor failed to offer her a seat at their meeting, she ordered the men in her retinue to form a human chair for her to sit on. Tvedten, p. 20, and note 16, p. 34.

14 *a practice of colonizing with* Bender, p. 60.

14 *According to an 1846 survey* Remarkably, these numbers still made Angola the second largest settler colony in Africa at the time. See Bender, p. 46.

14 *"Living in that country is a continual battle"* Quoted in Bender, p. 65.

15 *"To assume that the readiness of Portuguese . . . to mate"* Bender, p. 35

17 *"I never moved without drawing materials"* Cornwallis Harris, *The Wild Sports of Southern Africa* (1838; London, Henry G. Bohn, 5th ed., 1852), p. 284. All subsequent quotes from Harris are from this volume.

18 *"traders and freebooters and priests"* Duffy, p. 103.

19 *Yet what they did was amazing enough* Anne Hugon's *The Exploration of Africa: From Cairo to the Cape*, (1991; New York: Harry N. Abrams, trans. 1993) gives a concise, colorful summary of these exploits.

19 *The missionary impulse brought* Livingstone's account is contained in his *Missionary Travel and Researches in South Africa* (1857; New York: Harper & Brothers, 1858). All subsequent quotes from Livingstone are from this volume.

21 *More importantly, if, despite Lisbon's strict decrees* Duffy, p. 102.

22 *But in so doing Cameron became* Pakenham, p. 29.

22 *"I had to sell my shirts"* Verney Lovett Cameron, *Across Africa* (London: Daldy, Isbister & Co., 1877), p. 191. All subsequent quotes from Cameron are from this volume.

23 *Two years later, in 1877* Duffy, p. 107

23 *"for the sole purpose of labouring"* Maj. Serpa Pinto, *How I Crossed Africa: From the Atlantic to the Indian Ocean, through Unknown Countries; Discovery of the Great Zambesi Affluents, &c.* trans. Alfred Elwes (Philadelphia: J. B. Lippincott & Co., 1881), p. xix. All subsequent quotes from Serpa Pinto are from this volume.

24 *Although what the major discovered often confirmed his prejudices* "I speedily remarked that the feminine type among the Quimbandes approaches somewhat to the Caucasian, and I saw some women who would have been called pretty if they had not been black." p. 228.

25 *There were other explorers* In Capello and Ivens's *De Benguella ás Terras de Iácca* (Lisbon: Imprensa Nacional, 1881), *Hippotragus niger*, with its *"enormes pontas recurvadas,"* is cited as indigenous; further mention of the "harrisbuck" appears in their *De Angola á Contra-Costa* (Lisbon: Imprensa Nacional, 1886).

26 *But there was one nineteenth-century adventurer* Selous's biographer, J. G. Millais, spells Selous's middle name "Courtenay," in his *Life of Frederick Courtenay Selous, D.S.O.* (London: Longmans, Green and Co., 1919), but this appears anomalous. The portrait of Selous given here draws primarily on Selous's own works and Millais's book, as well as Bartle Bull's *Safari: A Chronicle of Adventure* (New York: Viking, 1988). Some additional details were gleaned from *Africa's Greatest Hunter: The Lost Writings of Frederick C. Selous*, ed. James A. Casada (Long Beach, Ca.: Safari Press, Inc., 1998).

26 *"A celebrated antelope-hunter"* The two met in Pretoria, where Serpa Pinto shared his notes on the antelope he had never seen before, the sitatunga. The Zambezi sitatunga, *Limnotragus spekei selous*, is named after Selous.

26 *"one of the handsomest animals in the world"* Quoted in Millais, p. 73.

26 *Decades before, when they pushed north* Pakenham, p. 491. The Matabele are also known as the Ndbele.

27 *"I said I had come to hunt elephants"* Quoted in Millais, p. 73.

27 *Shortly thereafter Selous met cigar* "Hottentot" is a Boer word, now considered, like "Kaffir," offensive. "Cigar" may have been Khoisian, or of mixed blood.

27 *This fearsome cannon left its mark* Millais, p. 158.

27 *For the next decade he hunted* A forty-pound tusk was worth £20 in the 1880s. Bull, p. 107.

27 *Selous wrote of seeing an entire river valley* *African Nature Notes and Reminis-*

cences by F. C. Selous, (London: Macmillan, 1908), p. 134. But by 1903, Selous was suggesting the need for the creation of game reserves. See Casada , p. 270n.

28 *he would be hired to procure specimens*   After his death, his widow donated Selous's collection of big-game specimens to the Natural History Museum. See Casada, p. 263.

28 *That particular collection, "La Specola"*   The Natural History Museum of Florence is thought to be the oldest zoological museum in the world.

28 *"I measured this phenomenal horn"*   Quoted in Russell Barnett Aitken, "Target: Giant Sable," *The Explorer's Journal* (fall 1955), p. 20.

28 *The horn is still there*   The horn is catalogued MZUF831. According to Dr. Paolo Agnelli, mammals collection manager, the length of the external curve is 151 cm (59.44 in), pers. comm. Varian, among others, usually referred to it as a 61-inch horn; Millais claimed it was 60 inches; shrinkage over the years doubtless accounts for the discrepancies.

29 *"They use their horns with marvelous quickness"*   Quoted, with some abbreviations, from *The Game Animals of Africa*, by R. Lydekker, 2nd edition, revised by J. G. Dollman (London: Rowland Ward, 1926), p. 286.

29 *According to Millais, Selous "always thought"*   See Millais, p. 94, and Selous's comments on sables, p. 454 of his *Travel and Adventure in South-East Africa* (1893; reprint, London: Century Publishing Co. Ltd, 1984).

29 *Selous left Bamangwato*   Selous wrote of this adventure in *Travel and Adventure in South-East Africa*, pp. 196–243.

31 *Instead, he went on to guide a gold-prospecting expedition*   Casada, p. xix.

32 *"You have said that it is me that is killing you"*   Quoted in Pakenham, pp. 494–5.

32 *Another revolt in 1896*   Pakenham, p. 495. Robert Baden-Powell, founder of the World Scout Movement, also fought in Matabeleland in 1896.

32 *"why they shouldn't try"*   Quoted in Pakenham, p. 500

33 *That year Rhodes spoke of Selous*   Millais, p. 196.

33 *a Portuguese quadroon he once saw*   Bull, p. 111.

33 *He was made captain of the 25th Royal Fusiliers*   Nicknamed "The Old and the Bold," the group included British and American millionaries, bartenders, hunters, a circus clown, a servant from Buckingham Palace, a professional strongman, stockbrokers, a lighthouse keeper, and an ex-general from Honduras. See Casada, p. xxiv.

33 *"He led a singularly adventurous and fascinating life"*   quoted in Millais, p. 375.

34 *His time in Africa coincided*   Selous's racial attitudes were complex. "There is no impassable gulf between a highly civilized race and an utterly savage one, as some people would have us believe," he wrote in 1893. Casada, pp. 75–6. Later, he expressed regret for his earlier slighting of the Bushmen. See Bull, p. 115.

34 *The giant sable antelope was recognized*   If Selous had heard of it, it's likely he would have reacted to it, and neither Millais nor Varian mention any such thing. In addition, as Selous's definitive article "African Antelope Heads and Horns" was

published first in 1908, the passing mention in its current reprinting in Casada of the subspecies *variani* (not so named until 1916) must have been a later interpola-tion (see Casada, p. 116). However, as a frequent contributor to *The Field*, Selous might have possibly seen Varian's first articles or, less likely, read of the subspecies declaration in 1916.

2: VARIAN'S GIANT

H. F. Varian's memoirs, *Some African Milestones* (Wheatley & Oxford: George Ronald, 1953), provide the essential biographical information. His articles and contributions to *The Field* and elsewhere, and his unpublished letters to Oldfield Thomas in the archives of the Natural History Museum (London), fill in the gaps.

35 *It was there, off a dim corridor*   June 17, 1998.
36 *"a glorious sunset over the mountains"*   Varian, *Milestones*, p. 14. All quotations from Varian come from this volume, unless otherwise noted.
37 *By 1912, it was a continent carved up*   See McEvedy, pp. 104–17.
38 *Portugal's hopes of expanding*   See Pakenham, pp. 387 and 506.
38 *"Who is that young man?"*   Quoted in Varian, p. 45
38 *Varian found himself in the country of the Mashukulumbwe*   Contradicting Selous, Varian states that the tip of the Mashukulumbwe headdress is made from a "finely-scraped piece of lechwe horn."
39 *Both Livingstone and Cameron had reported tales*   Pakenham, pp. 399–400.
39 *"Before the traders came"*   Quoted in *Angola: Promises and Lies,*   by Karl Maier (London: Serif, 1996), p. 43.
41 *"For the Portuguese this was a classic native war"*   Duffy, p. 118.
42 *but . . . no one ever returned*   Missionary Charles Swan in his *The Slavery of Today* (London: 1909), claimed that 70,000 to 100,000 Angolans had been shipped to the "Cocoa Islands" before 1908 and that not one had been repatriated. See Duffy, p. 136.
42 *"At last she reached the top"*   Henry W. Nevinson, *A Modern Slavery*, 1906, as quoted in Duffy, p. 135. Was Portugal's brand of colonialism during this period any worse for the inhabitants of its African possessions than the colonial rule of its neighbors was on their subject peoples? The international outcry over the atroci-ties in the Congo—the baskets of severed hands and all the rest—is covered in Pakenham and further detailed in *King Leopold's Ghost: A Story of Greed, Terror, and Heroism* by Adam Hochschild (Boston: Houghton Mifflin Co., 1998). Both books recount other colonial outrages on the borders of Angola—in the French Congo, where a French officer had been convicted for setting off a stick of dyna-mite in an African prisoner's rectum in celebration of Bastille Day, 1903; see

Pakenham, p. 637 and Hochschild, p. 280–1; and in South-West Africa, where German general Lothar von Trotha issued an extermination order against the Hereo people in 1904, giving them two choices: be shot on sight or driven into the Nambian Desert to die of thirst; Hochschild, p. 282, and Pakenham, p. 611.

43 *Some . . . two thousand Indians from Natal* According to contemporary reports, the Indian laborers suffered in the unhealthy conditions; many died within three months of their arrival in Angola and the survivors sent back to Natal were put into equally harsh quarantine camps.

44 *The rainbow trajectory of the breech-loading weapon* The Martini-Henry rifle, which fired a .577/450 cartridge, saw use as an infantry arm throughout the British Empire in the Victorian era. It was heavy, and prone to fouling, but effective at close range.

45 *Years before . . . in the Pungwe River district* During the same period man-eating lions terrorized the Indian laborers on the Uganda railway through Kenya, effectively stopping work until the engineer on that line, Lt. Col. J. H. Patteron, finally shot them. He later wrote a book about his experience, *The Maneaters of Tsavo*, with a foreword by Selous (London: Macmillan, 1907).

46 *One puzzling object unearthed* It was excavated by a Belgian prospector-geologist and donated to the museum in 1929. Later carbon-14 dating shows it to be more than a thousand years old. See Marie-Louise Bastin, "Chokwe Arts: Wealth of Symbolism and Aesthetic Expression," in *Chokwe! Art and Iniation Among Chokwe and Related Peoples*, ed. Manuel Jordán (Munich: Prestel-Verlag, 1998), p. 13.

47 *In 1904 Captain Cuninghame* Cuninghame's "A Pioneer Journey in Angola" appeared in *The Geographical Journal* 24 (London, 1904).

47 *in fact, they were cannibals* Pakenham offers several unappetizing instances of the practice during colonial times; see pp. 439 and 446–7.

47 *"Sable antelope have been shot on the Quanza"* Varian, "The West Coast Duiker," *The Field* 113 (March 20, 1909), p. 510. Presumably, Essington Brown is the Englishman who went by the name of "Long Brown" and worked as Varian's general assistant. See Varian, *Milestones*, p. 170.

47 *an acid reply* Mannlicher, "Big Game in Angola" *The Field* 113 (April 24, 1909), p. 706.

48 *Forty years later, he still smarted* Varian, "The Giant Sable of Angola," *African Wildlife* 7, no. 4 (December 1953), pp. 273–4.

48 *"Personally I only saw a photograph"* Varian, "Big Game in Angola" *The Field* 114 (October 9, 1909), pp. 617–8.

48 *Eight months later* Varian, "Record Horns of Sable Antelope," *The Field* 116 (July 9, 1910), p. 97.

48 *Mannlicher was still lying in wait* Mannlicher, "Record Horns of Sable Antelope," *The Field* 116 (July 16, 1910), p. 154.

49 *He questioned the natives closely* Varian, *Country Magazine* manuscript, p. 3, coll. Quentin Keynes. The Portuguese had established "Songo," their first outpost in the region, in 1904.

49 *Soon after he wrote to* The Field   Varian, "Sable Antelope from the Quanza River," *The Field* 118 (July 8, 1911), p. 112. The eager reader was F. N. Horne, "Sable Antelope from Quanza River," *The Field* 118 (July 15, 1911), p. 176. Varian, forgetting his own measurements, later remembered the Lane specimen as a 56-inch head. See his letter to *The Field* (February 26, 1916), pp. 327–8.

50 *one of the world's greatest libraries of taxonomy*   Today, the museum has some 359,000 catalogued specimens, including 8,000 type specimens.

51 *After the first Boer War, a number had made the hard trek*   Varian, "Angola, Portuguese West Africa," in *Big Game Shooting in Africa*, ed. Major H. C. Maydon (London: Seeley, Service & Co., 1932), p. 372. The Boers might have been joined in the Angolan highlands by a Jewish colony, had anything come of the negotiations between Portugal and the Jewish Territorial Organization of London. Settlement there was proposed as a measure to prevent German encroachment from South-West Africa. In June 1912, the Portuguese Chamber of Deputies passed a bill authorizing concessions to Jewish settlers. But no agreement was reached before the outbreak of the First World War, and thereafter the plan was dropped. See John Marcum, *The Angolan Revolution, Vol I, The Anatomy of an Explosion, 1950–1962* (Cambridge, Ma.: M.I.T. Press, 1978), pp. 3–4.

52 *After traveling through the district with Varian*   Varian, "The Sable Antelope of Angola," *The Field* (February 26, 1916), pp. 327–8, puts the date ambiguously. The trip is mostly likely to have taken place in 1913, as Statham, Curtis, and Vernay all mention 1913 as the year Varian first visited the giant sable territory. They all knew Varian personally, and presumably got their information from him. ‚

52 *In early 1914* The Field *ran a small item*   E. J. Boake, "Horns of Sable Antelope," *The Field* 123 (February 21, 1914), p. 381, and D. D. Lyell, "Horns of Sable Antelope," *The Field* 123 (March 7, 1914), p. 520.

52 *One offered the tantalizing remark*   R. L. Lydekker (author of *The Game Animals of Africa*), "Sable Antelope Horns," *The Field* 123 (March 14, 1914), p. 534.

52 *Even Mannlicher weighed in*   Mannlicher, "Large Horns of Sable Antelope," *The Field* 123 (March 21, 1914), p. 593.

53 *"I have a small box of skins"*   Varian to Oldfield Thomas, January 18, 1916. Natural History Museum archives, DF 232.

53 *A few days later Varian received "an almost excited letter"*   Varian, "The Giant Sable Antelope of Angola," *African Wildlife* no. 4 (December 1953), p. 273.

53 *"I was extremely pleased to get your letter"*   Varian to Thomas, February 8, 1916, NHM archives, DF 232.

54 *"This magnificent animal"*   Oldfield Thomas, *Abstract of the Proceedings of the Zoological Society of London*, no. 151 (February 8, 1916). A complete account of Thomas's analysis was published in March 1916 in *Annals and Magazine of Natural History*, ser. 8, vol. xvii.

54 *the International Code of Zoological Nomenclature*   See the discussion in Kurt

Johnson and Steve Coates, *Nabokov's Blues: The Scientific Odyssey of a Literary Genius* (Cambridge, Ma.: Zoland Books, 1999), p. 94.

55 *a notice by R. I. Pocock*   R. I. Pocock, "The Sable Antelope of Angola," *The Field* 127 (February 19, 1916), p. 315.

55 *At the War Office*   Varian is often vague about chronology and occasionally contradicts himself. In *Milestones*, p. 182, he states he was then thirty-eight, which would make the year 1914; but he must have muddled the date when he wrote his memoirs decades later.

55 *"I would have liked to have come to see you"*   Varian to Thomas, February 25, 1916. NHM archives, DF 232.

55 *Varian's letter of acknowledgment to* The Field   H. F. Varian, "The Sable Antelope of Angola," *The Field* 127 (February 26, 1916), pp. 327–8.

56 *Mannlicher's letter in the same issue*   Mannlicher (untitled), *The Field* 127 (February 26, 1916), p. 328.

56 *Robert Williams had applied to the army*   At first neutral, Portugal joined the Allies in 1916.

57 *Blaine arranged with the museum to do just that*   See Blaine, "Notes on the Zebras and some Antelopes of Angola," *Proceedings of the Zoological Society of London*, no. 23 (June 1922). Although the article states the expedition began in 1918, Statham and Varian claim 1919. Blaine also gave 1919 as the date his trip began in a letter to Quentin Keynes, September 25, 1954, coll. Quentin Keynes, and the copy of his article he had sent to Keynes has the date corrected to 1919 by hand in three places.

58 *But it would have been difficult . . . to dislike Blaine*   Blaine was generous to Varian; when he came to write of his Angola trip, he praised the engineer "for the unremitting care he took to insure the success of our enterprise." He also thought it fitting that the giant sable be named after Varian; not surprisingly Varian considered Blaine a friend.

58 *Blaine wrote lovingly of the majestic giant sable*   Blaine, "Notes on the Zebras and some Antelopes of Angola," pp. 319–23.

58 *Varian decided to hunt for a giant sable bull himself*   See Varian, "Angola, Portuguese West Africa," Maydon, pp. 385–7. It is apparently the only hunt for "his" antelope Varian ever wrote about; whether it is the only one he ever undertook is unclear. In *Milestones*, p. 230, he states he was allowed to collect an additional specimen for the "Chicago Museum"—presumably the Field Museum—but the specimen on display there was collected by Alan Chapman. In his memoirs one photo of "Varian's 'Giant'" is mistakenly captioned "Specimen collected by request for the Field Museum, Chicago. " In fact it is the mounted specimen collected by Prentiss Gray for the Academy of Natural Sciences of Philadelphia.

61 *Varian himself . . . would be able to give this superb specimen*   Varian's fully mounted specimen, BM(NH) 1920.6.15.1, has been mothballed for decades. Joseph Fénykövi underwrote an expedition to Angola to collect a giant sable for the Natural History

Museum now on display in a diorama partly funded by trustees of the late Rowland Ward. See Fénykövi, "In Search of Giant Sable," *The Field* (April 15, 1954). It is a shabby tale, as far as the hunting goes—Fénykövi wounds one and fails to finish off the other, choosing instead to photograph its death.

3: "THE FINEST HORNS IN THE WORLD"

Col. J. C. B. Statham's *Through Angola, A Coming Colony* (Edinburgh: Wm. Blackwood & Sons, 1922) and the Curtises' *Hunting in Africa East and West* tell the story of those two quests. The records of Arthur Vernay's 1925 expedition are held in the archives of the American Museum of Natural History (Vernay correspondence folder III); Vernay's article "Angola as a Game Country," *Natural History*, vol. 27, no. 6, Nov–Dec. 1927, gives additional details. Prentiss Gray's recently published 1929 journals, *African Game-Lands: A Graphic Itinerary*, ed. Theodore J. Holsten, Jr., and Susan C. Reneau (Missoula, Mo.: The Boone & Crockett Club, 1995), supplements the materials on the 1929–30 Gray Expeditions in the archives of the Academy of Natural Sciences of Philadelphia. The unpublished letters of Varian, Blaine, Vernay, Yebes, and others in the collection of Quentin Keynes, as well as his own articles, films, and photographs of his 1954 expedition, add to the story of this period. Unless otherwise noted, "Curtis" in the text refers to Richard C. Curtis.

62 *"I told him that I was returning"* Varian, "The Giant Sable Antelope of Angola," p. 282.

62 *"in quest of the giant sable"* Statham, pp. 3–4. All subsequent quotations from Statham are taken from this volume.

63 *the capital "full of American oil engineers"* H. Channing Beebe, an American petroleum geologist, spent 1917–21 in western Angola with his wife mapping potential oil fields to support the Allied cause. Before his death in his mid-nineties he wrote *Cannibals and Big Game* (Long Beach, Ca.: Safari Press, 2001), a colorful account of his experiences.

66 *But among closely related peoples of the region, antelope horn* Manuel Jordán, pers. comm.

66 *The Ndembu of northwestern Zambia* See Victor Turner's *The Forest of Symbols: Aspects of Ndembu Ritual* (Ithaca and London: Cornell University Press, 1967), pp. 280–1. See also Turner's *Blazing the Trail: Waymarks in the Exploration of Symbols*, ed. Edith Turner (Tucson & London: The University of Arizona Press, 1992), pp. 6–9.

67 *"witches, sorcerers, ghosts, were-lions"* Turner, *The Forest of Symbols*, p. 281.

67 *"The hunter has been unlucky and killed no animals for a long time"* Quoted in Turner, *Blazing the Trail*, p. 9.

70 *"After he had committed this slaughter"* Varian, *African Wildlife*, p. 282.

71 *A vigorous administrator*   De Matos was high commissioner from 1921 to 1924, which would plausibly put this meeting in 1921. He pursued an open-door policy to foreign capital and cleared thousands of miles of roads—women were included among the forced laborers—and ran up huge debts. See Duffy, pp. 124, 133, and 143.

71 *Varian used the opportunity to "explain to him about the rare animal"*   Varian, "The Giant Sable Antelope of Angola," *African Wildlife,* no. 4 (December 1953), p. 275.

72 *Slavery in Angola never really came to an end*   African slavery was tenacious, and not just in Angola. It lasted until 1910 in Ethiopia and up to 1918 in German East Africa. Slave caravans crossed Mozambique up to 1912, and trans-Saharan slave caravans continued up to 1929. At the end of the twentieth century slavery had yet to be eradicated on the continent; it was still hanging on in Mauritania and the Sudan. See William Finnegan's "A Slave in New York," *The New Yorker,* January 24, 2000.

72 *"whites continuing to exploit the services of the Negroes"*   Quoted in Bender, p. 139.

72 *"The state, not only as a sovereign of semi-barbaric populations"*   Quoted in Duffy, p. 132. Emphasis in the original.

73 *"one heard in the late hour"*   Quoted in Robert L. Rotberg, *A Political History of Tropical Africa* (New York: Harcourt, Brace & World, Inc., 1965), p. 303.

73 *"Our anti-social policy . . . to civilize the black"*   Quoted in Bender, pp. 140–1.

80 *This sable flower was named* Lactuca variani   Varian, in his "The Giant Sable Antelope of Angola," pp. 280–1, quotes from the September 1925 issue of the magazine of the Gray Herbarium of Harvard University: "In accord with a suggestion of Mr. C. P. Curtis this species has been named for Captain H. F. Varian, chief engineer of the Benguela Railroad, to whose hospitality and effective aid the success of the Angola hunting and collecting trip is largely attributed."

81 *Arthur Stannard Vernay was no ordinary hunter*   See his obituary in *The New York Times,* October 16, 1960.

81 *the golden age of museum collecting*   See *The World of Natural History* by John Richard Saunders (New York: Sheridan House, 1952).

82 *"preserve and portray Africa for posterity"*   Daniel E. Pomeroy, museum trustee and chairman of the African Hall Committee, as quoted in Saunders, p. 153.

82 *A year later, its president . . . wrote*   See Henry Fairfield Osborn, "The Vanishing Wild Life of Africa," *Natural History* 27, no. 6 (November–December 1927), pp. 515–24.

82 *urged "the immediate acquisition of a complete group of giant sable"*   Vernay, "Angola as a Game Country," p. 590.

83 *"It has been my experience in shooting"*   Vernay, "Big Game Shooting with an Object," *The Spur,* November 15, 1923, p. 29.

83 *"Many months were required to perfect our arrangements"*   Vernay, "Angola as a Game Country," p. 590.

83 *"the principal objective of this expedition . . . is to obtain a complete group of the Sable"*   Vernay to Lang Dec. 30, 1924, AMNH archives.

84 *Vernay thought Lang was cutting things too fine*   Vernay to Lang, January 8, 1925, AMNH archives.

84 *"Also, Mr. Varian"*   Vernay to Lang, February 16, 1925, AMNH archives.

84 *He made it clear . . . that "it would be impossible to to send an expedition"*   Lang to Sherwood, March 5, 1925, AMNH archives.

84 *and asked Lang if he had remembered to number the boxes*   Vernay to Lang, March 7 and March 9, 1925, AMNH archives.

85 *he and Boulton had collected "several hundred mammals"*   Lang to Ball, May 29, 1925; Lang to Sherwood, May 30, 1925; AMNH archives.

86 *they finally arrived in Huambo "enthroned in a mealies wagon"*   Lang to Duthie, June 12, 1925, AMNH archives.

86 *"Mr. Vernay thoroughly enjoys"*   Lang to Sherwood, July 28, 1925, AMNH archives.

88 *Lang wrote his final report*   Lang to Sherwood, August 31, 1925, AMNH archives.

89 *"We are not—just some madmen"*   Vernay to Anthony, December 13, 1925, AMNH archives.

90 *to examine the study specimens*   November 4, 1998.

90 *Prentiss N. Gray was appointed by Herbert Hoover*   Theodore Holsten's introduction to *African Game-Lands*, p. vii. To hunters, Gray is best remembered as the editor of the Boone and Crockett Club's *Records of North American Big Game* (1932).

90 *"every sportsman who has hunted these animals"*   T. Alexander Barnes, *Angolan Sketches* (London: Methuen & Co. Ltd., 1928), p. 192.

91 *Gray wrote to . . . Dr. Henry Tucker*   Gray to Tucker, July 17, 1928, ANS archives, coll. 113, IV #23.

91 *Tucker immediately wrote to Dr. Witmer Stone*   Tucker to Stone, July 18, 1928, ANS archives, coll. 113, IV #23.

91 *His letter to Gray a week later*   Stone to Gray, July 25, 1928, ANS archives, coll. 113, IV #23.

92 *Percival took them into the Serengeti . . . Gray wrote*   Gray, p. 47. Gray kept elaborate journals starting at eighteen, partly to share his travels and outdoor adventures with his sisters and the rest of his family. Four of these typed and leather-bound journals from 1929 were reprinted in *African Game-Lands*. Unless otherwise noted, all quotes from Gray are from this source.

92 *four new subspecies . . . a kingfisher . . . named in honor of Gray*   W. Wedgwood Bowen, "East African Birds Collected during the Gray African Expedition," *Academy of Natural Sciences of Philadelphia Proceeedings*, vol. 83 (1931), p. 11.

92 *"I still have my mind set on the Giant Sable"*   Gray to Cadwalader, July 3, 1929, ANS archives, coll. 113, IV #23.

97 *It was only a mild consolation that Bowen had discovered*   One of these new fish species was named after him: *Dinotopteroides prentissgrayi*.

98 *another expedition . . . led by Harold T. Green*   These specimens were apparently obtained on the same license, which Gray had not filled. See Gray, p. ix, and letter from Museum of Comparative Zoology at Harvard to Charles Cadwalader, June

13, 1933, ANS archives, coll. 509E, IV #23. Two more specimens were obtained for the Angolan government.

98 *Gray wrote to Charles Cadwalader . . . to suggest dispatching*   Gray to Cadwalader, April 27, 1933, ANS archives, coll. 509F, IV #23. The academy's diorama opened May 28, 1933.

98 *The offer of the "king"*   Edward Mallinckrodt, Jr., of St. Louis donated the money to have James L. Clark mount it. It was put on display in 1933. MCZ pamphlet, 2nd ed. (n.d. but after 1962), p. 30.

99 *"With many species" . . . report on the Gray African Expeditions*   Quoted in the foreword to Gray, p. vii.

99 *"the quite false idea that to professors"*   "Dr. Salazar," *The Times* (London), October 25, 1955, Portugal Supplement, p. ii. Also George Wright, *The Destruction of a Nation: United States' Policy Toward Angola Since 1945* (London: Pluto Press, 1997), pp. 1–2.

99 A *bachelor of austere tastes*   They may not have been all that austere; he is said to have kept a mistress while a seminary student. His doctorate may also have been questionable; David Birmingham, pers. comm.

100 *After nearly five hundred years of misrule*   Tvedten, p. 17.

100 *The vagrancy clause had been dropped*   Bender, pp. 141–2.

100 *a half-million Africans fled to neighboring countries*   Tvedten, p. 25.

100 *"like pieces of equipment"*   Quoted in Bender, p. 142.

101 "Only the dead are really exempt"   Quoted in Bender, p. 143. Emphasis in original.

101 *But under the forced labor system, an employer*   Bender, p. 144.

101 *By 1954 their total earnings had risen to $29.50*   Bender, note, p. 142. Bender points out that the government actually asked Diamang to double the salaries of Africans. This increase would have cost the company $410,000 in additional wages, which the company declared it could not afford—yet it paid its stockholder dividends amounting to ten times that sum.

101 *The company provided food and housing and supported three clinics*   See F. C. C. Egerton's *Angola Without Prejudice* (Lisbon: Agency-General for the Overseas Territories, 1955), pp. 6–7. This pamphlet, published by the Portuguese government, is an attack on Basil Davidson's *The African Awakening* (London: Macmillan 1955), specifically his reporting on native labor practices in Angola. Egerton quotes Portugese figures of 142,574 contract workers in 1953 and 99,771 in 1954; these figures are lower than those reported by Davidson, who claimed no fewer than 379,000 contract workers in 1954. Bender explains that since "contracts" for these workers were generally oral, there was no way to distinguish between *contratados* and *voluntéarios*. Bender, p. 114n.

101 *the Africans were controlled by laws that required identification cards*   Tvedten, p. 27.

102 the Reserva do Luando   Proclaimed a nature reserve April 16, 1938.

103 *"The giant sable antelope began to fascinate"*   Count Yebes, "A Big-Game Hunt-

ing Record?" *Country Life* (February 10, 1950), pp. 379–80. His descriptions of his hunt are taken from this article.

104 *prologue by José Ortega y Gasset* *Meditations on Hunting*, trans. Howard B. Wescott (New York: Charles Scribner's Sons, 1972, 1985).

104 *Dr. Abel Pratas* Pratas's actual title was chief of veterinary services. He oversaw wildlife in the colony.

105 *the world-record giant sable* The 1971 Rowland Ward *Records of Big Game* listed it as sixty-four and seven-eighths inches, and in the possession of the Madrid Museum.

106 *"high-school dropout"* Keynes, pers. comm. See Keynes's "The Labyrinthine Paths of Collecting Burton," in *In Search of Sir Richard Burton: Papers from a Huntington Library Symposium*, ed. Alan H. Jutzi (San Marino, Ca.: Huntington Library, 1993), pp. 107–31.

106 *"My father finally accepted what I was doing"* "A Darwin Descendent Works to Preserve Dying Species," Interview by Jim Detjen in the *Philadelphia Inquirer*, date missing (c1980s). Copy in author's files.

106 *That article, published in 1951* "Africa's Uncaged Elephants" by Quentin Keynes appeared in the March issue, Vol. XCIX, no. 3, pp. 371–82.

106 *"all sorts of books—books about elephants"* Keynes, "Labyrinthine Paths," p. 109.

107 *Sir Richard Burton; he has an outstanding collection* Correspondence between Burton and Speke and other material from Keynes's collection, edited by Donald Young, was published as *The Search for the Source of the Nile* (London: Bernard Quaritch Ltd., 1999).

107 *a hollowed-out baobab tree* Keynes links this unusual tree to a reference to a similar hollowed-out tree in Livingstone's journal entry of September 16, 1858.

107 *"And the giant sable is almost number one"* pers. comm.

107 *Only about 1 percent of Angola's African children* Tvedten, p. 28.

107 *development plans included nothing for education* See *The First Dance of Freedom: Black Africa in the Postwar Era* by Martin Meredith (New York: Harper & Row, 1984), p. 33.

108 *the improbability of any quagga* "Sobre a Improbabilidade da Sobbrevivência da Quagga no Sul de Angola," *Anais dos Serviços de Veterinária e Indústria Animal*, 1942.

108 *only fifty-three miles of asphalt roads* Bender, p. 177

108 *Late on the first day afield* August 13, 1954. Keynes's field notes. Coll. Quentin Keynes, copy in author's files.

108 *A lone bull that appeared in the distance* Keynes, letter to "Russ" Aitken, September 6, 1954. Coll. Quentin Keynes.

108 *They saw the herd on two occasions* Keynes's accounts of his experience are contained in his correspondence, in his brief field notes, in a BBC talk November 17, 1954, and in articles published in *The Times* (London), October 26, 1954, *The Illus-*

trated London News, November 6, 1954, and *Look,* April 19, 1955, and differ slightly. This account follows the more extensive one he gave in Aitken's "Target: Giant Sable," augmented by further details he shared with me on several occasions.

109 *"But it was my turn to be astonished"* Keynes, BBC talk, typescript coll. Quentin Keynes.

109 *"It is a trip that I have always wanted to do"* Varian to Keynes, Aug. 27, 1954. Coll. Quentin Keynes.

110 *he'd forgotten to load his motion picture camera* Keynes, pers. comm.

110 *a letter from Scotland from Gilbert Blaine* Blaine to Keynes, September 25, 1954. Coll. Quentin Keynes.

110 *Blaine replied that he understood* Blaine to Keynes, October 20, 1954. Coll. Quentin Keynes.

110 *Keynes had taken seventy-five feet of film* Keynes was credited with taking the first motion pictures of the animal, although Dr. Andreas Laszlo, an American physician, made a trip to Angola in 1953 and wrote a book, *Doctors, Drums and Dances* (Garden City, NY: Hanover House, 1955), in which he described a trip to the Luando Reserve to film giant sable close up. The accuracy of his account is thrown into question by his mention of "snow-white manes on top of and beneath the necks of the bulls," a wildly inaccurate description of the animal. If the film was made, it must have been damaged or lost, as nothing, apparently, ever came of it.

111 The Times *(London) ran a story on Keynes's trip* October 26, 1954. Keynes wrote a letter to the editor which appeared three days later clarifying da Silva's role and the assistance of the Portuguese. The *Illustrated London News* story ran November 6, 1954; *Look*'s story, under the inaccurate headline "First Photos of Africa's Rarest Animal," appeared April 19, 1955.

111 *Varian was delighted* Varian to Keynes, November 1, 1954. Coll. Quentin Keynes.

111 *"Are you going on any safaris"* Varian to Keynes, January 8, 1955. Coll. Quentin Keynes. But at least Varian had the opportunity to see Keynes's film when Keynes showed it at the Portuguese ambassador's in London in 1956.

111 *"the stabilization of the continent"* Varian, *Milestones,* p. 214.

111 *"Of course, I remember meeting you"* . . . *Vernay wrote* Vernay to Keynes, April 7, 1955. Coll. Quentin Keynes. Vernay is confused; he seems to think that Varian took the pictures in Statham's book, that Prentiss Gray was not from New York, and that he had no luck obtaining giant sable.

4: ENTER THE BIOLOGIST

Most of the biographical information on Richard and Runi Estes came primarily from interviews conducted in Peterborough, New Hampshire Sept. 19–20, 1998, supplemented by further interviews Jan. 29–30, 2000 and my later travels with Estes in Africa. Runi Estes's

1969 diary and the couple's 1969–70 field journals and subsequent papers, as well as Richard Estes's articles and books, supplied the rest.

113 *Percival . . . had never seen an actual lion kill*   Gray, p. 65. Percival came out to Africa in 1905.

113 *almost nothing was known about what the giant sable did*   Richard D. Estes and Runhild K. Estes, "The Biology and Conservation of the Giant Sable Antelope, Hippotragus Niger Variani Thomas, 1916," in *Proceedings of the Academy of Natural Sciences of Philadelphia*, vol. 126, no 7, pp. 73–104, December 31, 1974; p. 74. Previous researchers (Frade, Sieiro, and Cabral) had only spent periods of up to two months in the Luando Reserve.

116 *The Esteses began their sable research*   The Field Museum in Chicago has an exhibit of a field researcher's tent based on their various camps during this period.

117 *Cangandala National Park*   Also spelled Kangandala, this 231-square-mile area of *miombo* bushveld was declared a national park June 25, 1970 to protect the giant sable found there in 1963.

117 *He noted in their field journal*   Estes and Estes, Field Journals, 1969–70; entries for September 20–2, 1969.

117 *dropped off a hunk of reedbuck*   One of the warden's perks was permission to shoot smaller game for the pot.

118 *penile sheaths "as an added masculine garnish"*   Richard Despard Estes, *The Behavior Guide to African Mammals* (Berkeley: University of California Press, 1991), p. 116. See also pp. 11 and 123. Sexual dimorphism in bovids became one of Estes's major research interests. See his "Evolution of Conspicuous Coloration in the Bovidae: Female Mimicry of Male Secondary Characters as Catalyst," chap. 16, in *Antelopes, Deer, and Relatives: Fossil Record, Behavioral Ecology, Systematics, and Conservation*, ed. by George B. Schaller and Elizabeth S. Vrba (New Haven: Yale University Press, 2000), pp. 234–46.

120 *"The moonlight glanced off his great scimitar-shaped horns"*   See Richard D. Estes, "Sable by Moonlight," *Animal Kingdom*, August–September 1983, pp. 10–6.

121 *"knowledge of the home range is passed on"*   Estes, *Behavior Guide*, p. 124.

121 *such solitary bulls leave little evidence*   Estes and Estes, "Biology and Conservation," p. 85.

123 *like a "fencing master toying with a pupil"*   R. D. Estes, *Behavior Guide*, p. 126.

123 *no herd animals wanted to be punished with a charge*   R. D. Estes, *Behavior Guide*, p. 125.

124 *"One female giant sable was hotly pursued"*   Estes, *Behavior Guide*, pp. 126–7. The male was Red Top; Estes, pers. comm.

125 *the question remains open*   Estes, "Sable by Moonlight," p. 16 [box]. Thomas, "A New Sable Antelope," p. 5: "Judging by the greater length of the skull, it would, no doubt, prove that *H. n. variani* not only carried longer horns, but was larger in all dimensions than the true Sable."

125 *Portuguese claims . . . unfounded* They even observed sables feeding in flooded areas. Richard D. Estes and Runhild K. Estes, "National Geographic Society Hippotragine Antelope Study," Preliminary Report, April, 1970, Unpub., p. 12.

127 *in 1955, the Portuguese had raised the status of Luando* January 20, 1955.

128 *shooting the* palanca negra *was still possible* Brian Huntley, pers. comm.

128 *"It is unlikely," he later wrote* R. D. Estes, "Giant Sable Antelope," World Wildlife Fund nature brochure, n.d. (after 1982), p. 5.

128 *There was evidence that humans and mammals were competing* Estes and Estes, "Biology and Conservation," pp. 100–1.

129 *"Lack of evidence is no proof"* Estes and Estes, "Biology and Conservation," p. 84.

130 *a number of striking photographs of the animal* Silva reproduced them in *A Palanca Real* (Lisbon: Junta de Investigações do Ultramar, 1972).

130 *there had been a number of indications of serious unrest* See Duffy, pp. 213–7, Fieguerdo, p. 128, and Wright pp. 11–12, 32.

131 *as many sovereign states as colonies* McEvedy, p. 122.

132 *Settlers reacted by forming vigilante groups* See Bender, p. 158, and Duffy, p. 221. For Portuguese reaction to the uprising, see Bernardo Teixeira, *The Fabric of Terror* (New York: The Devin-Adair Co., 1965) and Ronald Waring, *The War in Angola — 1961* (Lisbon: Silvas [printer], n.d. [1962?]).

132 *There were some 2,000 white troops* See Waring, p. 7, and Bender, p. 158. There were also 5,000 black troops at the time of the uprisings, none of whom were officers.

132 *the severed head of an Angolan* See the introduction to *Sacred Hope* by Agostinho Neto, translated by Marga Holness (Dar es Salaam: Tanzania Publishing House, 1974), p. xxxiii. According to Holness, Neto was arrested for showing this photograph, which had already appeared in several papers.

132 *The official death toll soon exceeded* Bender, p. 158.

132 *more numbing numbers to come* Duffy, p. 221. Tvedten estimates up to half a million Africans fled to the Congo, p. 31.

133 *but never to mistakes in principle* "Doctor Salazar," *The Times* (London), October 25, 1955.

133 *"The work of centuries"* Quoted in Antonio de Figueiredo, *Portugal and Its Empire: The Truth* (London: Victor Gollancz Ltd., 1961), p. 136.

133 *Robert Ruark wrote* Ruark, introduction to Teixeira, p. viii. Ruark claimed it was even worse than what the Belgians had ever done in the Congo.

133 *"The world must realize that the Portuguese territories are slave states"* Quoted in Duffy, p. 222.

134 *"like giving a child of ten"* Quoted in Merideth, p. 12.

134 *it would take a thousand years* William Roger Louis, *Imperialism at Bay, 1941–1945* (Oxford University Press, 1977), pp. 185 and 237.

135 *Colonialism had always been a "highly visual phenomenon"* Johnson, *Modern*

Times: The World from the Twenties to the Eighties (New York: Harper & Row, 1983), p. 160.

135 *Portuguese teachers would show*   Figueiredo, p. 121.

135 *The number of high school graduates in the entire country*   Figueiredo, p. 135, claims that only twenty Angolans had ever graduated from universities as of 1961.

135 *In 1956 about 1 percent of African children*   Fred Bridgland, *Jonas Savimbi: A Key to Africa* (New York: Paragon House Publishers, 1986), p. 25.

135 *It was a matter of policy . . . Portugal . . . preferred employers*   Bender, pp. 151–2, 177n.

136 *As Gerald Bender wrote*   Bender pp. 157–8. See also pp. 160–2; 165 and 165n; 175–6.

138 *the little plaque over the door*   The National Geographic Society, which had supported Estes's doctoral research, provided support for the sable research as well.

138 *Runi made the last two entries*   Estes and Estes, Field Journals, Sept. 14–5, 1970.

5: Caught in the War Zone

There is substantial literature on Angola's war for independence and the civil war that followed. Piero Gleijeses' definitive *Conflicting Missions: Havana, Washington, and Africa, 1959–1976* (Chapel Hill: University of North Carolina Press, 2002), based on exhaustive archival research, sheds new light on the period covered in John Marcum's authoritative two-volume history, *The Angolan Revolution* (Cambridge, Ma: M.I.T. Press, 1978), George Wright's *The Destruction of a Nation: United States' Policy Toward Angola Since 1945* (London: Pluto Press, 1997), and Elaine Windrich's *The Cold War Guerrilla: Jonas Savimbi, the U.S. Media and the Angolan War* (New York: Greenwood Press, 1992) trace aspects of the conflict through the 1990s. I have also drawn on the accounts of direct observers and participants—Fred Bridgland's *Jonas Savimbi: A Key to Africa* (1986; New York: Paragon House Publishers, 1997) and *The War for Africa: Twelve Months that Transformed a Continent* (Gibraltar: Ashanti Publishing Limited, 1990), John Stockwell's *In Search of Enemies: A CIA Story* (New York: W. W. Norton & Co., 1978), Henry Kissinger's *Years of Renewal* (New York: Simon & Schuster, 2000), Ryszard Kapuscinski's *Another Day of Life* (New York: Harcourt Brace Jovanovich, 1987), Jan Breytenbach's *Forged in Battle* (Cape Town: Saayman & Weber (Pty) Ltd., 1986), *They Live by the Sword* (Alberton, South Africa: Lemur Books, 1990), *Eden's Exiles: One Soldier's Fight for Paradise* (Cape Town: Quelleries Publishers, 1997), and Paul Hare's *Angola's Last Best Chance for Peace: An Insider's Account of the Peace Process* (Washington, D. C.: U.S. Institute of Peace Press, 1998). Other key texts are cited below. Note: to avoid excessive acronyms, I refer to the armies of UNITA and the MPLA (later, the government), rather than FALA and FAPLA (later FAA).

141 *MPLA, FNLA, UNITA*   There was also a separate movement, FLEC, which sought the independence of the Cabinda enclave.

141 *Dr. Agostinho Neto* Marcum, vol 1, pp. 37–9.

141 *"Western Civilization"* from *Sacred Hope* by Agostinho Neto (Dar Es Salaam: Tanzania Publishing House, 1974), translated by Marga Holness, pp. 18–9.

142 *Dr. Neto was arrested in 1960* His June 9th arrest warrant gave as grounds his "subversive activities against the external security of the state" (the warrant is reproduced in Neto, *Sacred Hope*, p. xv).

143 *Patrice Lumumba* Wright, p. 7. Lumumba was elected prime minister of the Congo (Leopoldville) in June 1960, and according to Stockwell was beaten to death on January 17, 1961 by Congolese henchmen with CIA complicity, p. 237. In October 2000, the BBC reported on newly released documents that showed that Lumumba's death was directly ordered by President Eisenhower and engineered by the Belgians. See Gleijeses, *Conflicting Missions*, pp. 61–2.

143 *"This time the slaves did not cower"* from an interview by Pierre de Vos with Roberto in *Le Monde*, July 1961, quoted in "Afterword: The context of the Angola Revolt," by James Burnham in Teixera, p. 174.

143 *Jonas Malheiro Savimbi* Marcum, vol. 1, pp. 244–5.

143–44 *Savimbi . . . was suspicious of mestiços* Bridgland, *Key*, pp. 45–7.

145 *he would style himself "Dr. Savimbi"* According to the biographical outline posted on the former UNITA website, Savimbi obtained a license in political and juridical science, but no details were given.

145 *Savimbi's own movement, UNITA, was launched* Bridgland, *Key*, pp. 66–9. Savimbi was not there; he entered Angola on October 26, p. 70. The details of many of these events are missing or murky; many documents were destroyed, or buried by the combatants, and deliberate disinformation was widely disseminated. Various texts sometimes contradict each other. For example, Bridgland states that in 1964 Neto offered Savimbi the post of secretary of foreign affairs in the MPLA and that Savimbi declined (*Key*, p. 64). Wright, however, claims that Savimbi considered joining the MPLA if Neto gave him the post, but the MPLA refused (Wright, p. 11).

146 *Neto made it [MPLA] appear to espouse Soviet ideals* See "Moscow and the Angolan Crisis, 1974–1976: A New Pattern of Intervention" by Odd Arne Westad, 1996–7 (posted at the Cold War International History Project of the Woodrow Wilson International Center for Scholars (<http://cwihp.si.edu/default.htm>).

146 *"we should even take aid . . . from the Devil himself"* Quoted in Basil Davidson's *In the Eye of the Storm: Angola's People* (1972; London: Penguin, 1999), p. 290.

146 *National Security Council put Roberto on the CIA payroll* See Gleijeses, *Conflicting Missions*, pp. 279–80.

147 *China's foreign minister promised Roberto "large-scale military aid"* Wright, pp. 9 and 47.

147 *According to one account, a half-dozen Portuguese were killed* Bridgland, *Key*, pp. 72–3.

147–48 *a secret deal to collaborate militarily*   See *Operation Timber: Pages from the Savimbi Dossier*, ed. with an introduction by William Minter (Trenton, N. J.: Africa World Press, 1988), and Gleijeses, *Conflicting Missions*, pp. 239–41.

148 *"Portugal cannot gamble away the values"*   Bridgland, *Key*, pp. 82–3, quoting from Caetano's "Address on Overseas Provinces," November 28, 1968.

148 *a confidential report showed that at that time*   Bender, p. 175.

149 *Portuguese military documents from that period attributed*   Minter, pp. 11–2.

149 *The few adventurous journalists*   Steve Valentine, Fritz Sitte, and Leon Dash all visited Savimbi in the bush during the period 1969 to '73. See Minter, p. 10, and detailed descriptions in Bridgland, *Key*, and Windrich.

149 *English, French, Portuguese, Umbundu*   Umbundu is the language of the Ovimbundu people.

149–50 *the stationmaster's son posed for photos*   Bridgland, *Key*, pp. 94 and 99.

150 *China reacted . . . by sending advisors*   Stockwell, pp. 67 and 257.

151 *upped its payments to Holden Roberto to $10,000*   Gleijeses, *Conflicting Missions*, pp. 280–2.

151 *Alvor Accords*   Both FLEC, the Cabindan liberation movement, and the MPLA dissident group, led by Daniel Chipenda, were left out the accords. Tvedten, p. 36.

151 *Portugal was now eager to wash its hands of it*   Hare, p. 4.

151 *Neto . . . handed them a letter*   Letter from Neto to Cuban leadership, Dar-es-Salaam, January 26, 1975, in Gleijeses, *Conflicting Missions*, p. 247.

151 *United States . . . intervened in Angola only after Cuban military advisors*   See Kissinger's claim, p. 806. But documents made available in 2002 paint a different picture. As historian Piero Gleijeses pointed out, "When the U.S. decided to launch the covert intervention, in June and July [1975], not only were there no Cubans in Angola, but the U.S. government and the CIA were not even thinking about any Cuban presence in Angola." From "Old Files, a New Story of U.S. Role in Angolan War," by Howard French, *The New York Times*, March 31, 2002. The documents also reveal significant U.S. collaboration with South Africa during this period, contradicting official denials. See Gleijeses' analysis in his *Conflicting Missions: Havana, Washington, and Africa 1959–1976*.

151 *authorized the CIA to send $300,000 to Holden Roberto*   Stockwell, p. 67; Kissinger, p. 795; Gleijeses, p. 283.

151 *United States was unwilling to sit on its hands*   See Stockwell, pp. 43 and 68n; Kissinger, p. 339.

152 *the United States established normal diplomatic relations*   Kissinger, p. 629.

152 *What was at stake. . . . was prestige*   Gleijeses, *Conflicting Missions*, pp. 353–5.

152 *Kissinger credited Kenneth Kaunda*   Kissinger, pp. 791 and 796.

152 *"a man of humility and good qualities"*   Quoted in Kissinger, p. 797.

152 *"My assessment was"*   Quoted from a conversation with a dissenting Foreign

Service officer on October 16, 1975. Kissinger, pp. 792–3. He adds, "I continue to believe this analysis was, in its essence, correct."

152 *"Kissinger did his best to smash the one movement"* Gleijeses, *Conflicting Missions*, p. 359.

153 *Bureau of African Affairs took the position* The new assistant secretary for Africa, Nathaniel Davis, wrote: "We do not believe that U.S. interests are strong enough to warrant a high level of U.S. involvement or a significant commitment of U.S. resources, particularly in providing arms." May 24, 1975, as quoted in Kissinger, p. 804. Months later, Davis would resign in protest over U.S. intervention.

153 *"the only means" available* Kissinger, p. 792.

153 *announced, formal intervention* Kissinger, p. 802. See also Marcum, vol 2, p. 259; Bridgland, *Key*, p. 120.

153 *Although over $31 million was finally spent* Kissinger, pp. 808 and 826.

153 *the FNLA . . . attacking the MPLA* Wright, p. 60.

154 *In a letter to Raúl Castro* Letter from Raúl Díaz Argüelles to the minister of the armed forces Raúl Castro, August 11, 1975, in Gleijeses, *Conflicting Missions*, pp. 254–5.

154 *Castro began considering military intervention* Gleijeses, *Conflicting Missions*, pp. 254–56, 259–60.

155 *"one must not confuse the intelligence business"* Quoted from Church Committee testimony in Stockwell, p. 235.

155 *"I might have served my nation better"* Stockwell, p. 135.

156 *"the Angolan long shot," Jonas Savimbi* Stockwell, pp. 138–41. Stockwell left for UNITA territory on August 20, 1975. At this time, UNITA was the least well-equipped guerrilla movement, often relying on captured clothing and weapons. By 1974, UNITA commanders had adopted Portuguese-style rank insignia. See Peter Abbott and Manuel R. Rodrigues, *Modern African Wars 2: Angola and Moçambique 1961–74* (London: Osprey Publishing, 1998), pp. 43–4.

157 *"clear objectives and clean conscience"* Stockwell, p. 150.

157 *Savimbi's political leanings* Stockwell, p. 154.

157 *a threat to its stablity and regional power* Tvedten, p. 337.

157 *South Africa has dispatched special forces to Angola* Gleijeses, *Conflicting Missions*, pp. 275–76, 293–99.

158 *The MPLA . . . marshaled their forces* Gleijeses, *Conflicting Missions*, pp. 265–6, 269, 300–8.

158 *Luanda . . . was now racked with rumors* Kapuscinski's reportage from the capital in *Another Day of Life* remains the most vivid account of this period. See also David Lamb, *The Africans* (New York: Random House, 1982), pp. 170–1.

159 *unharvested coffee rotted* Mark Pendergrast, *Uncommon Grounds* (New York: Basic Books, 1999), p. 318.

159 *FNLA planes dropped leaflets* Kapuscinski, p. 102.

160 *the statue of de Matos . . . had been pulled down* Bridgland, p. 130. On his reforms, see Bender, p. 141n: "In 1921 Norton de Matos passed a decree which forbade the furnishing of forced labourers to private employers, but this was largely ignored and he was bitterly attacked for his insensitivity to the needs of Portuguese farmers."

160 *Moscow would not be outdone by Havana* See Westad.

161 *But his political fortunes were about to plummet* Bridgland, pp. 137–41.

161 *Stockwell would later comment* Stockwell, p. 202. He calls Fred Bridgland "Ken Bridgefield."

162 *Senate Foreign Relations Committee endorsed an amendment* Wright, pp. 65–7; Stockwell, pp. 229–31.

162 *"The Chinese will say"* Quoted in Wright, p. 69.

162 *"I feel no need to to involve the United States"* Congressman Joseph Addaba, as quoted in Wright, p. 74. See Wright's chapter "Henry Kissinger and the 1975 Angolan War," pp. 57–77.

162 *John Stockwell would resign* In June of 1976, the CIA wrote citations and commendations for over a hundred people involved in the Angola program.

162 *Back in August, Stockwell had argued* Stockwell, p. 158. Kissinger quotes this passage and adds that it was "precisely my view," Kissinger, p. 814. However, Kissinger stops well short of sharing Stockwell's additional concern over the morality of escalating a bloody civil war by halfhearted intervention; see Stockwell, p. 270.

163 *"prepared to fight on behalf of the free world alone"* Quoted in Bridgland, *Key*, p. 168.

163 *a 250-mile trip on the Benguela Railway* Bridgland, *Key*, pp. 164–5.

163 *Savimbi, unsure of U.S. intentions, flew to Kinshasa* Stockwell, pp. 193 and 234; Bridgland, *Key*, p. 168.

164 *The agency began recruiting mercenaries* Stockwell, pp. 217, 222–3, 226; Bridgland, *Key*, p. 179; Gleijeses, *Conflicting Missions*, pp. 334–7.

164 *Savimbi wrote a letter of farewell* Quoted in Bridgland, *Key*, pp. 197–8.

165 *Zambian freight would once more be welcome on the Benguela Railway* It was vital for Angola as well. At its preindependence peak in 1974 the railway carried some three million tons of freight, earning $43 million in revenue. Matloff, p. 32.

166 *"If the blacks are going to be given Angola"* This quote, and the information in this passage, is taken from Brian Huntley's "Angola: a Situation Report," *African Wildlife* 30, no. 1, February 1976.

167 *MPLA was following standard Soviet practice* Amnesty International reported that the MPLA held some three hundred political prisoners in 1976 and was carrying out executions. See Bridgland, p. 221.

167 *The Cubans . . . were careful to reassure Moscow* See Westad; Gleijeses, *Conflicting Missions*, pp. 373–80.

167 *"Things are going well in Angola"*   Transcript of the April 3, 1977 meeting at the House of the SED Central Committee in East Berlin between Castro and Honecker posted at the Cold War International History Project website.

168 *the United States . . . quickly reverted to anticommunist form*   Carter even complained that the Clark Amendment kept him from aiding Savimbi. See Piero Gleijeses' "Truth or Credibility: Castro, Carter, and the Invasions of Shata," *The International History Review*, vol. 18, no. 1, February 1996, p. 87.

168 *In May 1978, the CIA told the Senate Foreign Relations Committee*   CIA director Stansfield Turner, as quoted in Wright, p. 83.

168 *Gerald Bender repeated*   Both quoted in Wright, p. 85.

168 *The apartheid government . . . saw its regional security threatened*   Wright, p. 91. See also Bridgland, *Key*, p. 270.

168 *(SADF) began launching raids into Angola from Namibia*   Wright, p. 90. In the same year the UN Contact Group came up with a plan for achieving Namibian independence, but South Africa's objections stalled its implementation. See Hare, p. 5.

169 *"the best armed refugees I have ever come across"*   Breytenbach, *Eden's Exiles*, p. 106.

169 *South Africa's efforts to destabilize Angola were met*   According to Wright, Cuban troop strength went to 19,000 in 1979; 21,000 in 1980; and 23,000 in 1981; p. 91.

169 *Dash . . . wrote a series for the paper*   These were collected in the *Munger Africana Library Notes*, issue 40/41, December 1977, published by the California Institute of Technology, as "Savimbi's 1977 Campaign Against the Cubans and the MPLA— Observed for 7 1/2 Months, and Covering 2,100 Miles inside Angola," by Leon De Costa Dash, Jr.

169 *it was UNITA policy to execute*   Dash, pp. 53 and 56. See also Windrich, p. 4–5.

170 *"an enigma"*   Dash, pp. 107 and 113.

170 *"Meet Jonas Savimbi"*   November 8, 1979, quoted in Windrich, pp. 8–9.

171 *the so-called* Golpe Nitista   The 1977 coup is little discussed. See Bridgland, *Key*, pp. 263–7; Judith Matloff, *Fragments of a Forgotten War* (London: Penguin, 1997), pp. 62–3; Maier, p. 36; Gleijeses, *Conflicting Missions*, p. 372.

171 *dos Santos . . . A bricklayer's son*   Jon Lee Anderson, "Oil and Blood," *The New Yorker*, Aug 14, 2000, p. 51.

172 *"Gulf . . . would benefit"*   Quoted in Wright, p. 95.

172 *allowed to start talks with the MPLA*   Wright, p. 76. At the same time, Boeing was allowed to deliver two 737s to TAAG, the national airline.

172 *a policy of "constructive engagement"*   Wright, pp. 99–100, 109; Tvedten, p. 38.

174 *George Schaller . . . wrote to him*   Schaller to Estes, October 23, 1980.

174 *In mid-1982, Estes flew to Luanda*   This account of Estes's 1982 visit to Angola is taken from his "Sable By Moonlight" as well as my interviews.

177 *Jamba, his thatched-hut bush capital*   See Sousa Jamba's novel *Patriots* (New York: Viking, 1990) for a depiction of life in UNITA territory and Zambian exile.

178 *"To save UNITA's skin"*   Breytenbach, *Sword*, p. 230.

179 "*excellent propaganda coup for Savimbi*" Breytenbach, *Sword*, p. 236.

179 *John Stockwell's warning* From a letter to *The New York Times*, November 22, 1979, as quoted in Windrich, p. 10.

179 "*a legitimate political force*" Department of State Bulletin 82 (March 1982), as quoted in Windrich, p. 18. See Wright, pp. 109–10.

179 *a virtual Angolan Rambo* Smith Hempstone, "Angola: Where the West Can Still Win," *Reader's Digest*, February 1981, as quoted in Windrich.

179 *hiring a public relations firm to burnish his image* Windrich, p. 45. The principals in the firm also managed the Reagan/Bush campaigns.

180 "*The War Against Soviet Colonialism*" In the Heritage Foundation's *Policy Review*, winter 1986.

181 *battled UNITA along the Benguela Railway* Wright, p. 127.

181 *Cuba was "prepared to stay"* quoted in Wright, p. 128.

182 "*the giant sable must now be considered more endangered*" Estes to Anderson, December 1, 1987.

182 "*As Dr. Estes has stated*" Anderson to S. A. Nature Foundation, December 23, 1987.

183 *He wrote to Chester Crocker* Estes to Crocker, June 24, 1988.

183 *the highest-ranking Soviet officer ever posted* Bridgland, *War*, p. 17; Wright, p. 132.

183 *crushing some UNITA fighters* Breytenbach, *Sword*, pp. 245–6; Bridgland, *War*, pp. 136–62.

184 *By some accounts, some eight thousand UNITA* Bridgland, *War*, p. 224. See also Chester Crocker, *High Noon in Southern Africa* (New York: W. W. Norton, 1992), pp. 360–1.

184 *Savimbi professed to be "surprised"* Two days later General Malan revealed that President P. W. Botha and Ministers Pik Botha, F. W. de Klerk, and Barend du Plessis had visited Angola to congratulate South African troops on their victory. Windrich, p. 69.

184 *UN Security Council unanimously condemned* As quoted in Wright, p. 130.

184 *UNITA would be poised to take control of the Benguela Railway* Tvedten, p. 39.

185 *Fidel Castro came to the rescue* Bridgland, *War*, p. 229.

185 *The South African government feared that mounting white casualties* Bridgland, *War*, p. 223.

186 *the staggering human cost of a war* See Wright, pp. 128–9.

187 *the largest haul of illegal ivory ever seized* De Wet Potgieter, *Contraband: South Africa and the International Trade in Ivory and Rhino Horn* (Cape Town: Queilleries Publishers, 1995), pp. 41–2 and 44. Potgieter uncovers environmental plundering during the last years of the apartheid government. His survey of sordid criminality has it all: smugglers' meetings, briefcases of money, one-armed Chinese traders, drive-by shootings, rhino horns wrapped in women's underwear, etc. Unfortunately, there is a paucity of documentation. See also Windrich, p. 121.

187 *inviting the press to view elephants roaming wild* The Free Angola Information

Service in Washington, D.C., arranged for observers to stay in Jamba to view and photograph the local elephant herds with the understanding that they would report on their findings to groups such as the African Wildlife Foundation and Safari Club International.

187 *"I am all for a just war"* Jan Breytenbach, "Slaughter in Paradise: SADF and Ivory Smuggling," *Electronic Mail & Guardian,* Johannesburg, South Africa, December 18, 1997; Breytenbach, *Eden's Exiles,* p. 257.

187 *testimony accusing South Africa of supporting the slaughter* Van Note represented Monitor (the Conservation, Environmental and Animal Welfare Consortium) at the Merchant Marine and Fisheries Committee on July 14, 1988. See Potgieter, pp. 26–7.

188 *probe was nothing more than a whitewash* Potgieter, pp. 28–9. Breytenbach's earlier inquiries had cost him the post he had long coveted after his retirement, that of park warden of the western Caprivi. See Breytenbach, *Eden's Exiles,* p. 252. In 1994, under a new government, the minister of environmental affairs ordered an independent investigation of the alleged smuggling. The Kumblen Commission issued a report in January of 1996 which concluded that there had been large-scale destruction of wildlife in Angola and the Caprivi, and that the SADF had covertly participated in the sale of ivory and rhino horn to help fund military operations in neighboring countries, although it found no compelling evidence that the SADF had been involved in these activities after 1986.

188 *"a huge piece of worthless, mobile meat"* Breytenbach, *Eden's Exiles,* p. 248.

188 *"Savimbi had hardly settled down"* Quoted in Potgieter, pp. 48–9.

189 *A follow-up story based on his revelations ran in mid-November* The special report by De Wet Potgieter ran in the *Sunday Times* (Pretoria), November 19, 1989.

189 *UNITA was in fact trading ivory* Windrich, p. 83.

190 *The United States continued to push for negotiations . . . "without preconditions"* Wright, pp. 142–9.

190 *Portugal . . . eagerly embraced its role* Matloff, p. 43.

191 *Savimbi returned to Luanda* Matloff, pp. 245–6.

191 *Many thought Savimbi would win—he was sure of it* Maier, p. 72.

191 *"generally free and fair"* Hare, p. 9.

191 *Savimbi . . . fled the capital* Pers. comm. with the officer, Pretoria, September 22, 2000. Maier, Matloff, and Miles Bredin—*Blood on the Tracks* (1994; London: Picador, 1995)—give gripping firsthand accounts of the 1992 elections and the violence that followed.

192 *The government had . . . .to scramble to rearm* In July 1993, Portugal, Russia, and the United States allowed the Angolan government to "officially" acquire arms. Matloff, p. 217.

192 *he came to be regarded much like the makishi* See Manuel Jordán's 1996 University of Iowa Ph.D. dissertation, "Tossing Life in a Basket: Art and Divination Among Chokwe, Lunda, Luvale and Related Peoples of Northwestern Zambia," pp. 86–7, 90, and 110–5.

193 *"In the last couple of years"* Estes to Labuschagne, May 30, 1991.

193 *Labuschagne had proposed a giant sable captive breeding program* The project was outlined in "The Giant Sable Antelope: 'A Cri du Coeur for Survival'" n.d. (c1990), Public Services Department, National Zoological Gardens of SA (Pretoria). The Pretoria Zoo's plan was far more workable than an Australian scheme that had been proposed in 1990.

193 *how much trophy hunting was still going on* Bredin surmises from talking to a Portuguese professional hunter that "Hippotragus niger variani is no more;" pp. 153–4.

193 *He wrote Estes* Anderson to Estes October 7, 1991.

195 *"The black sable is a rare species and it is a UNITA symbol"* Quoted in Bridgland, *Key*, p. 285.

196 *the Lusaka Protocol was . . . finally signed* Hare's book covers the complex negotiations in detail.

196 *I had a chance to meet with Col. Fred Oelschig* October 16, 1999.

197 *a brief account of those days* These excerpts appear in "Postcript: UNITA," an appendix in Bridgland's *The War for Africa*.

197 *What he'd written to me* Oelschig to Walker, July 11 and 19, 1999, and July 19, 1999. Oelschig also stated that he never saw a live elephant in areas under MPLA control.

6: A Conflict of Crusaders

Much of the material here derives from interviews and travels in South Africa in 1998 and related correspondence.

201 *a letter that came to Richard Estes* Javier Alvarez to Estes, November 11, 1996.

203 *Savimbi . . . stayed in the UNITA stronghold* If Savimbi had made the transition from military to political leader at this point, he might have ended up as Angola's leader. See Tony Hodges's *Angola: From Afro-Stalinism to Petro-Diamond Capitalism* (Bloomington, Ind.: Indiana University Press, 2001), p. 172.

203 *an Italian firm started rebuilding the Benguela Railway* "Italians Rebuild Rail Line in Barter Deal," Barnaby Philips, *Business Day*, May 27, 1997; "Benguela Railway: Major Revamp in Pipeline," *Financial Mail, SA*, January 23, 1998. See also "Victim of War May Chug Again," Andrew Maykuth, *The Philadelphia Inquirer*, October 16, 1997. The Italian firm, Tor di Valle, planned to spend $500 million on the project in exchange for the right to harvest eucalyptus plantations along the line.

204 *"I have always said"* As quoted in "Angola Sceptical of Outside Offers to Save the Sable," *Inter Press Service*, November 4, 1997.

204 *"If there are enough animals"* Anderson fax to Rod East, July 24, 1997.

206 *The press invariably referred to this firm* Khareen Pech and David Beresford,

"Africa's New-Look Dogs of War," *Electronic Mail & Guardian*, Johannesburg, January 27, 1997; Angela Johnson, "Broker of War and Death," *Electronic Mail & Guardian*, Johannesburg, February 28, 1997; Ken Gooding, "Diamond Dogs of War," *Financial Times*, September 15, 1997; Khareen Pech, "Executive Outcomes—A Corporate Conquest," in *Peace, Profit or Plunder: The Privatisation of Security in War-Torn African Societies*, ed. by Jakkie Cilliers and Peggy Mason (Pretoria: Institute for Security Studies, 1999). See also Chris Gordon, "Mercenary Link to Angola Mine Attack," *Electronic Mail & Guardian*, Johannesburg, November 13, 1998.

207   *Huntley told Anderson that van Hoven intended to bring giant sable*   Anderson to East, August 2, 1997.

207   *Years before, the Esteses had warned*   Estes and Estes, "Biology and Conservation," p. 85. Translocating animals was not a recent idea; in the colonial government, the Seviços de Verterinária had expressed strong interest in moving animals to other parks.

207   *Anderson was flabbergasted*   Anderson to East, August 2, 1997.

208   *"I don't know much about it . . . This is not for us!!"*   Anderson to East and Estes, September 4, 1997.

208   *the level of tension in Angola*   See Hare, p. 145.

210   *the "king" cheetah*   See Maj. A. L. Cooper, "Notes on 'Acinonyx Rex' (Cooper's Cheetah)," in Maydon, pp. 335–6, and the discussion in James Mellon, *African Hunter* (New York: Harcourt Brace Jovanovich, 1975), pp. 445–6.

210   *mitochondrial DNA*   mtDNA is the genetic material of the tiny energy-producing organelles inside every cell; because only females pass on mitochondrial DNA via eggs, such transmission is matrilineal. Mitochondrial DNA is particularly suited to taxonomic and systematics studies

212   *My first stop was Terry Robinson's*   May 21, 1998.

215   *He suggested I come over*   May 23, 1998.

221   *"full support" for the "laudable initiative"*   Dos Santos to José Luís Guerra Marques and van Hoven, August 1, 1996.

222   *they wanted to see a detailed . . . proposal*   Gerhard Damm to van Hoven, April 2, 1998.

222   *Van Hoven's reply*   Van Hoven to Damm, May 4, 1998.

222   *was rejected by the chapter as too vague*   Damm to Andre de Georges, May 15, 1998.

222   *E-mail from Brian Huntley to Richard Estes*   Huntley to Estes, E-mail June 2, 1998.

223   *Anderson's growing doubts*   Anderson to Estes E-mail June 2, 1998.

223   *a letter to his old friend . . . de Almeida*   Huntley to de Almeida, fax June 16, 1998.

223   *His response*   Marques to de Almeida; the translated letter is dated June 16, 1998, i.e., a reply the same day; perhaps one of these dates is in error.

225   *a plane carrying Alioune Blondin Beye*   Beye was a former foreign minister of Mali before becoming a UN troubleshooter. See Hare, p. 145.

225   *General de Matos had been touring his frontline units*   "Angola—at the Precipice," Occasional Paper no. 32, Institute for Security Studies, Pretoria, July 1998.

225–26   *a celebratory dinner in Luanda*   July 22, 1998. Shell Angola donated $400,000 to the Kissama Foundation. This followed a reported $1 million donation by Sonangol, the state oil company. *The Kissama News*, vol. 1, no. 1, August 1998.

226 *Anderson . . . managed to arrange a meeting*   July 18, 1998; Anderson to Estes, E-mail June 20, 1998.

226 *According to Anderson, the deputy minister*   Anderson to Estes and Walker, E-mail September 21, 1998.

227 *I had the taxi drop me off*   December 3, 1998.

228 *In 1972 he had outlined a plan*   "A Plan for the Future of the Giant Sable of Angola," Rept. No. 11, Serviços de Veterninária, Luanda, November 1972, unpublished.

235 *"death of a zebra" that Robert Ruark once described*   Robert Ruark, *Uhuru, A Novel of Africa Today* (New York: McGraw-Hill, 1962), p. 206.

237 *Estes and I decided to drive up to White River*   December 7, 1998.

238 *who founded the park in 1898*   Kruger is the second oldest national park in the world.

239 *Disease . . . wasn't the only thing that prompted the shooting*   Peter Godwin's "Game Theory," *Departures*, July/Aug 1998 is a readable summary of the problems of controlling elephant numbers.

241 *Estes and I had a tour of Sable Ranch*   December 11, 1998.

247 *de Almeida . . . had just enough time to meet with us*   December 9, 1998.

248 *He pulled out a copy*   Published as *Lei de Bases do Ambiente e Convenções* (Luanda: Ministério das Pescas e Ambiente, 1999).

7: The Hunter's Bargain

I attended the twenty-seventh annual Safari Club International Hunter's Convention, Jan. 20–3, 1999, in Reno, Nevada, and conducted interviews there and in nearby Sparks; some information comes from previous and follow-up interviews.

255 *"there is no need to exercise much patience"*   T. Roosevelt, *Outdoor Pastimes of an American Hunter* (New York: Charles Scribner's Sons, 1925), p. 375.

255 *Peter Singer . . . concurs*   P. Singer, *Animal Liberation* (New York: Avon Books, 1975), p. 243.

257 *Kim Basinger would donate a set of her lacy bra and panties*   *Las Vegas Life*, April 2000. The actress's underwear raised $5,500.

260 *without a special permit he wouldn't be able to import the trophy*   Some endangered and threatened species may be brought in as hunting trophies under special permit if the Fish & Wildlife Service determines that the licensed hunting was part of a conservation management program based on biological data.

260 *Rod East . . . was convinced*   East to Estes, E-mail May 11, 1999, quoted in *Gnusletter* 18, no. 1. To be sure, not every member of ASG was convinced sport hunting was

a valid conservation tool; the draft position on the issue in vol. 19, no. 2 generated split reactions in the next issue. Also, see Estes's comment in vol. 20, no 2.

260 *In one of van Hoven's studies* "Madimbo Corridor: Habitat Preference of Elephant and Buffalo, Ecotourism Potential and Community Involvement," Centre for Wildlife Management, University of Pretoria, 1997, p. 51.

261 *"penitent butchers"* See Raymond Bonner, *At the Hand of Man: Peril and Hope for Africa's Wildlife* (New York: Vintage, 1993), pp. 40–1. Bonner details the contradictions in many conservation policies, in particular the ivory ban. See also Jonathan S. Adams and Thomas O. McShane, *The Myth of Wild Africa: Conservation Without Illusion* (New York: W. W. Norton, 1992).

262 *the kind of mammalian necropolis necessary* As excessive as it might seem, this "slay and display" behavior hardly compares with the monstrous indulgences of the past, when the elector of Saxony slew some 80,000 deer and boar during the Thirty Years' War; Roosevelt, *Outdoor Pastimes*, p. 375. See Matt Cartmill's *A View to Death in the Morning: Hunting and Nature Through History* (Cambridge, MA: Harvard University Press, 1993) for an overview of "the whole system of symbolic meanings that have distinguished hunting from mere butchery."

263 *One member, who was subsequently prosecuted* See Ted Kerasote, *Bloodties: Nature, Culture, and the Hunt* (New York: Random House, 1993), pp. 169–71.

263 *And then there's outright fakery* Jack O'Connor described this deception in his posthumous *The Last Book: Confessions of a Gun Editor*, ed. Jim Rikhoff (Clinton, NJ: Amwell Press, 1984), p. 145, but refrained from revealing the hunter's name.

264 *a ten-minute taxi ride from Reno* My portrait of Lee conflates two interviews with him at his office in Sparks, Nevada, on January 25 and July 30, 1999; some details were added from Lee's unpublished "Preliminary Bio December 15, 1998," his *China Safari* (New York: Sporting World Library, 1988) and "Altai High," *Sporting Classics*, Sept/Oct 1996, Dennis Adler's "A Man of Adventure," *Robb Report*, May 1996, and various Hunting World catalogs.

264 *the chance to hunt Marco Polo sheep* Marco Polo sheep, or *Orvis ammon Poli*, are among the world's largest wild sheep and a coveted trophy. A passage in Rudyard Kipling's "The Feet of the Young Men," 1897, sums up the attraction:

> *Do you know the long day's patience, belly-down on the frozen drift,*
> *While the head of heads is feeding out of range . . .*

265 *"I was told not to publicize the fact"* It was the reason Lee listed his trophy as "collection"—as if he'd bought them or picked them up—in Rowland Ward's.

8: WAITING FOR ANGOLA

I conducted interviews in Washington, D.C., in March and August 1999, and in South Africa in October of the same year.

269 *Clashes between both sides had escalated by then* Paul Hare, "Comments from the Executive Director," *The Angola Report* 8, no. 1, April 1999.

269 *UNITA was as well armed as it ever was* Lynne Duke, "Angola's Peace Withers Again Under Fire," *The Washington Post*, December 15, 1998; "Dozens Killed in Angola Attack," *The New York Times*, December 25, 1998.

270 *Ukrainian-made T-55 tanks* "UNITA arsenal unveiled," *Angola Peace Monitor* 5, no. 5, January 1999. The T-55 went out of production in Eastern Europe in 1981.

270 *UNITA's token fulfillment of the demobilization* Richard Cornwell and Jakkie Potgieter, "Angola—Endgame or Stalemate?" Occasional Paper no. 30, Institute for Security Studies, Pretoria, April 1998.

270 *"for the sake . . . of its own survival"* Quoted from *Le Figaro*, May 1996, in "A Rough Trade: The Role of Companies and Governments in the Angolan Conflicts," Global Witness report, 1998.

270 *UN Security Council . . . pronounced itself "actively seized of the matter"* Statement by the president of the UN Security Council concerning Angola, December 23, 1998.

270 *regime increasingly accused of skimming off substantial amounts* By some estimates, up to half the oil wealth may be siphoned off, but hard evidence is lacking. See Richard Cornwell and Jakkie Potgieter, "Angola—At the Precipice," Occasional Paper no. 32, OASIS Programme, Institute for Security Studies, Pretoria, July 1998.

270 *a chilling human rights record* "Angola," U.S. Department of State 1999 Country Reports on Human Rights Practices; Donald G. McNeil, Jr., "As Angola Erupts, Youths Fear Being Forced to Fight," *The New York Times*, January 20, 1999.

270 *branded a "war criminal"* January 27, 1999, in a unanimous resolution.

271 *evidence of his savage crimes mounted* See Marga Holness, "Wanted for Murder: Jonas Savimbi," published for the Mozambique Angola Committee, London, May 1999.

271 *"his own Messianic propaganda about himself"* Bridgland, *War*, p. 373; Bridgland made his later accusations at Chatham House, London. See *Angola Peace Monitor* 5, no. 5, January 1999, and Holness, "Wanted." Leon Dash, the journalist who had chronicled UNITA in the 1970s, denounced Savimbi as a ruthless dictator in 1990; see Windrich, p. 5.

271 *Tito Chingunji . . . was murdered* Chingunji was murdered along with several more of his relatives in 1991. See Matloff, pp. 246–9.

271 *Commandos grabbed her and threw her into the flames* The public burning took place September 7, 1983 in Jamba. The event was witnessed by ex–UNITA member Tony Fernandez, now Angola's ambassador to the U. K. See Holness, "Wanted." An ex–South African military officer I interviewed confirmed he had witnessed two of these public "witch burnings" in UNITA territory in the 1980s.

271 *A communiqué on the occasion of* "Commemoration of the 32nd anniversary of the revolution on 25.12.98," the Standing Committee, posted on UNITA's website (<http://www.kwacha.com>) in early January 1999.

272 *Paul Hare . . . blamed Savimbi* I interviewed Hare August 18, 1999. Hare also gave me a draft of his paper "Angola: What Next?"

273 *I reached Chester Crocker*   Phone interview with Crocker August 16, 1999. The quotation is from the op-ed "Death Is the Winner in Africa's Wars," *The New York Times,* August 6, 1999.

273 *Richard Estes, who wrote to them*   Estes to Dodgsons, January 8, 1999; April 19, 1999. See also *Gnusletter* 18, no. 1, p. 6.

274 *"The war has certainly hotted up"*   Van Hoven to Walker, E-mail February 5, 1999.

275 *I had a breakfast meeting with . . . Valentim*   August 18, 1999.

276 *Bridgland described him* Bridgland, *Key,*   pp. 131, 190, 366, and 373. See also Marcum, vol. 1, p. 306 note.

276 *Hare remembered him*   Hare, p. 28.

276 *joined the national unity government*   In fact, Manuvakola signed the Lusaka Protocol on behalf of UNITA.

276 *an enthusiastic booster of tourism*   See Rachel L. Swarns, "For an Adrenaline Rush, Try an Angola Vacation," *The New York Times,* February 25, 2000.

276 *UNITA had announced on its website*   "Com a administração do vasto território de Malange, a UNITA controla igualimente um dos mais importantes parques: o de Kangandala, onde se encontra a espécoe rara da fauna, a Palanca Preta Gigante." Comunicado Nr. 37/CPM/99, August 9, 1999 on kwacha.com.

277 *"But the government took all these causes away"*   Several months later Valentim's assessment was echoed by another former senior UNITA official, Gen. Jacinto Bandua, who headed the rebel movement's logistics department and surrendered to government forces in Andulo on November 10, 1999. In an interview on Radio Nacional de Angola November 17, he stated that " UNITA was founded during the anticolonial struggle. I think the goals for which UNITA was created have been achieved. One would need to have new conditions, a new source of inspiration [words indistinct] to wage another guerrilla war."

277 *"Savimbi even got special status"*   On October 27, 1999, the national assembly voted to remove his special status.

278 *Jardim agreed to meet with me*   August 18, 1999. An example of the depth of feeling Angolans have for their national animal can be found in "A Palanca Preta Gigante" by Sebastião Coelho: "*Não creio em milagres, mas tenho a secreta esperança de que ainda seja possivel salvar a palanca-real,*" which roughly translates to "I do not believe in miracles, but I secretly hope that it is possible to save the royal sable." On <http://www2.ebonet.net/kandimba/cronica9.htm>.

279 *"Jesus! I've never read such garbage"*   Estes to Walker and Huntley, E-mail August 22 1999, with typo corrected.

280 *Van Hoven . . . explaining in a follow-up conversation*   September 7, 1999.

280 *Estes and I received an E-mail from Huntley*   Huntley to Estes and Walker, E-mail September 7, 1999.

280 *he sent an acid, antagonistic letter*   Huntley to van Hoven, Estes et al. September 13, 1999, with several typos corrected.

281 *"Better put on your oven mitts"*   Estes to Walker, E-mail September 14, 1999.

281 *Van Hoven's reply . . . was surprisingly even-tempered*   Van Hoven to Huntley, Estes, and Walker, E-mail September 16, 1999.

282 *he wrote Huntley*   Estes to Huntley, E-mail September 18, 1999.

282 *Huntley replied calmly to van Hoven's letter*   Huntley to Van Hoven, Estes, Walker et al., E-mail September 20, 1999.

283 *a few days earlier to talk . . . Robinson*   October 15, 1999.

285 *We talked mostly about the Tuli elephants*   Widely reported; see *Gnusletter* 19, no. 2; *Electronic Mail & Guardian*, Johannesburg, November 13, 1998.

286 *We drove . . . to Hoedspruit*   October 25–26, 1999.

288 *hip dysplasia in German shepherds*   This example was suggested to me by Joelle Wentzel.

289 *a kind of loud knuckle-cracking*   See Estes, *Behavior Guide*, p. 190.

290 *Malange . . . had been swollen by rural Angolans*   Reuters, August 6, 1999.

290 *"annihilate the enemies"*   ANGOP (the Angolan press agency), August 27, 1999.

290 *In early September*   Reuters, September 10; BBC, September 13, 1999. In late September, President Clinton issued an executive order to continue U.S. sanctions against UNITA.

290 *Gen. Luis Faceira told journalists*   BBC, September 28, 1999.

290 *the U.S. State Department's warning*   "Angola—Consular Information Sheet," September 14, 1999.

291 *I met Van Hoven at his office*   October 17, 1999.

292 *the Johannesburg-to-Luanda flight*   October 18, 1999.

292 *Tannins not only taste bitter*   Van Hoven's work was reported in "Antelope Activate the Acacia's Alarm System," by Sylvia Hughes in *New Scientist*, September 29, 1990. See also "Thorns of Plenty," by Vicki Croke, *International Wildlife*, November-December 1999, which also discusses Richard Estes's research on the issue; <www.nwf.org/intlwild/1998/acacia.html>.

9: LUANDA & QUIÇAMA

I visited Angola's capital and Quiçama National Park in October 1999, and July/August 2000, with stopovers in South Africa.

300 *I switched cars to talk with Peter Osborne*   October 18, 1999, with some details added from a follow-up interview October 20, 1999 and subsequent meetings.

301 *Angola produces some eight hundred thousand barrels of oil a day*   See *Angola's War Economy: The Role of Oil and Diamonds*, ed. by Jakkie Cilliers and Christian Dietrich (Pretoria: Institute for Security Studies, 2000).

305 *Kruger has golf courses*   Kruger has a nine-hole course near Skukuza in an unfenced area of the park.

309 *it was more like a career than a crisis to these old pros*   At that point, Antonio Faceira had been in uniform for thirty-three of his fifty-two years, first as a colonial soldier, later as a freedom fighter, and finally as an army officer.

312 *Papa Kitoko's Traditional Medical Centre*   See Maier, pp. 211–2.

313 *the old photograph I had of it*   The specimens may have been collected by Dr. Abel Pratas.

313 *I lingered in the cool halls to . . . look at the splendid masks*   Some of the highlights are reproduced in *Angola e a Expressão da sua Cultura Material* by Ana Maria de Oliveira (Rio de Janeiro: Odebrecht, 1991).

315 *the number of needy people in Angola had increased to 3.2 million*   ANGOP, September 27, 1999.

315 *ESSO announced the discovery of a new oil field*   ANGOP, September 6, 1999; "Angola Civil War Leaves Grim Legacy," CNN, September 25, 1999.

315 *Considering the way the father of the country had been treated*   See Mercedes Sayagues, "Father of Angola Rots in a Grey Mausoleum," *Electronic Mail & Guardian*, Johannesburg, October 10, 1997. Still, Neto's face remains on the currency, there's a bust of him here and there, and of course, his powerful poetry endures.

316 *When I stopped in to see van Hoven*   October 27, 1999.

318 *national parks in Africa should be run by private enterprise*   African Eye News Service reported on News24.com, February 6, 2000, that some fity-four state-owned nature reserves in the Northern Province of South Africa may have to be commercialized after seven of them ran staggering deficits within three years due to bad management.

320 *"we know where Savimbi is"*   Remarks on Angolan television November 15, 1999, reported in *Angola Peace Monitor* 6, no. 3, November 30, 1999.

321 *Government forces reported* "New Landmine Allegations," IRINnews.org (UN Integrated Regional Information Networks), Johannesburg report, November 17, 1999.

321 *Peter Hain*   Speech to the Action for Southern Africa (ACTSA) Annual Conference, London, November 20, 1999.

321 *Richard Holbrooke*   "US Envoy Wants Action Against Unita, " BBC, December 4, 1999.

321 *The fighting continued to be savage*   "In Wake of Angolan Offensive, Destroyed Homes and Burned Bodies, " AP, December 19, 1999; Lara Pawson, "Angolan War Spills into Namibia," BBC, December 20, 1999; "UNITA Is Finished, Says Angolan Army," BBC, December 17, 1999.

322 *But those numbers hardly compared*   IRIN, December 21, 1999; "South African Aid for Angola," BBC, December 29, 1999; "Angola Fighting Draws Pleas for Humanitarian Aid," Reuters, December 29, 1999; "Angolan Refugees Flee into Zambia," BBC, December 10, 1999.

322 *Savimbi's days seemed numbered* "UNITA General Defects," IRIN, November 19, 1999; "Angolan Rebel Goes into Hiding," AP, December 5, 1999; "UNITA Is Finished, Says Angolan Army," BBC, December 17, 1999.

322 *On December 25, Angolan state radio announced* "Angolan Army Takes Key UNITA Rebel Base—State Radio," Reuters, December 25, 1999; Lara Pawson, "Angola Claims Rebel Base," BBC, December 25, 1999.

322 *On New Year's Eve* reported by ANGOP.

323 *dos Santos's remarks* "Angola's dos Santos Sees Hope for UNITA," BBC/Reuters, December 31, 1999.

323 *I reached Wouter van Hoven* January 4, 2000.

323 *"May 2000 be a banner year"* Estes to van Hoven, E-mail January 13, 2000.

323 *General de Matos was now talking* "Angola: FAA to End the War, Says Army Chief of Staff," ANGOP, January 13, 1999.

323 *a new compulsory draft* Announced by Defense Minister General Kundi Payhama, and reported by ANGOP, January 11, 1999.

324 *the rumors balanced each other out* "Savimbi Might Commit Suicide: Ex-Aide," ANGOP, February 28, 2000; "Angola's UNITA in Military Shake-up," Reuters, January 21, 2000; "ANGOLA: UNITA to Launch Guerrilla Campaign," IRIN, January 26, 2000.

324 *I talked to van Hoven by phone* February 26, 2000.

325 *"I'm really looking forward to the Angola trip"* Estes to Van Hoven, E-mail March 24, 1999.

325 *grounds for his nervousness* "Unita Accused of Crucifying Children," BBC, March 23, 2000 (the accusation, from Jaime Paulo, spokesman for the Angolan Christian Churches Council, could not be independently confirmed); Lara Pawson, "Analysis: The Savimbi Factor," BBC, April 19, 2000.

325 *de Matos had thought that the end of the war was in sight* Lara Pawson, "'End of War in Sight'—Angolan General," BBC, November 16, 1999.

325 *"I like confusion"* Quoted in Dash, p. 55.

326 *In this news dispatch it was described* "National Army Captures New Areas in Central Highlands," ANGOP, June 15, 2000.

326 *at a White House news conference* "Science Times," *The New York Times*, June 27, 2000.

326 *it had taken longer to set up his lab than he anticipated* Robinson to Walker, E-mails November 11 and December 6, 1999.

326 *"the giants remain the first order of priority"* Robinson to Walker, E-mail February 1, 2000.

326 *By April he wrote to tell me* Robinson to Walker E-mail April 5, 2000.

326 *By mid-June he had to admit failure* Robinson to Walker, E-mails June 20 and 21, 2000.

328 *It was a startlingly cold Monday morning* July 17, 2000.

330 *air attacks against the crippled city of Huambo*   See Matloff, p. 194. The siege, which began January 9, 1993, lasted fifty-five days.

330 *"only the total defeat of Savimbi"*   From *Le Monde*, February 16, 1995, as quoted in *Angola Unravels: The Rise and Fall of the Lusaka Peace Process* (New York: Human Rights Watch, 1999), p. 17.

338 *the ladies of Luanda*   Luanda was founded in 1575; by 1687 there were more than twenty churches and convents.

339 *Flagrant, open corruption*   Inefficiency, waste, greed, and appropriation of public funds are hardly Angolan—or African—specialties. Still, see Lynne Duke, "Angola's Chaos Liberates Forces of Corruption: Officials Line Up at Source of Nation's Oil, Gem Wealth," *The Washington Post*, January 1, 1999. Hodges states, "There is very little documented information about higher-level corruption, although there is a more or less universal presumption among Angolans that it is deeply entrenched in a system of public administration characterized by arbitrariness and lack of transparency," p. 72. One reason for the lack of documentation is that virtually no corruption cases have ever been brought to court in Angola.

340 *A substantial part of of it is apparently dispensed at will*   Hodges, pp. 51–7.

341 *ideal for kickback arrangements*   Hodges points out that "the Angolan government has no operative rules and procedures for [military] procurement," p. 72.

341 *Rewarding the loyalty of top generals with diamond concessions*   See Hodges, p. 161. Investment in Angola doesn't require an Angolan partner if it is substantial enough; oil companies are an obvious example. But one might well want an Angolan partner for other reasons. Hodges examined one mining contract which required the foreign partner to assume all the risks of mining while sharing the profits 50/50 with the Angolan concessionaires, who are in effect "sleeping partners"; p. 162.

341 *as one analyst put it*   See Christian Dietrich, "Power struggles in the diamond fields," in Cilliers and Dietrich, pp. 173–94. Deitrich also argues that the growing international outcry against traffic in "blood diamonds" that are funding some of Africa's dirtiest wars has allowed dos Santos and the Futungo elite to impose tighter controls over the domestic diamond industry—but for the purpose of restructuring it to suit their needs.

341 *profiting from protecting their own diamond holdings*   Companies such as Tricorn, which operates in conjunction with ITM Mining in the northeast of Angola, is connected to General de Matos, the chief of the Defense Force, according to "A Rough Trade: The Role of Companies and Governments in the Angolan Conflicts," Global Witness report, 1998. Lumanhe, another security firm, reportedly has Gen. Luis Faceira among its stockholders, and operates in partnership with ITM. Teleservices, one of Angola's largest private security companies, which has a management agreement with Gray Security Services, is reportedly owned by Gens. Luis Faceira, João de Matos, and França Ndalu. I was told this was common knowl-

edge by several credible sources. See Cilliars and Dietrich, p. 157, and n. 48, p. 169, and p. 178.

342 *dos Santos had even tried to buy off Savimbi* In 1996–97. See Hare, pp. 124–6 and Hodges pp. 161–2.

343 *the three of us met briefly with Brian Huntley* August 2, 2000.

344 *the ASG meeting with van Hoven* Skukuza, August 9, 2000.

345 *Jeremy Anderson would send van Hoven a list* Anderson faxed van Hoven on behalf of the ASG August 14, 2000; Livingstone's eland, roan, waterbuck, dwarf (forest) buffalo, and warthog were recommended, springbok and kudu were not.

10: FLIGHT OF ANTELOPES

I returned to South Africa and Angola in September/October 2000.

346 *the press report that appeared in September 2000* SAPA (South African Press Association), September 11, 2000.

347 *I called van Hoven* August 17, 2000.

347 *He had an offer of around thirty elephants* The North West Parks and Tourism Board donated several family groups to Angola.

347 *a late August phone conversation* August 28, 2000.

348 *fuming about a . . . report* Paul Salopek, "Angola Betting Precious Fund on Rehab of Wildlife Parks," *Chicago Tribune*, August 6, 2000.

348 *Van Hoven was on his cell phone* September 7, 2000.

349 *he'd written Brian Huntley* Estes to Huntley, E-mail September 10, 2000.

356 *but he had pulled it off* In recognition of his efforts, van Hoven was awarded the Joseph R. Daly Award for Excellence in Communication for Wild Nature at the Wild Foundation Awards held at the United Nations in New York in November 2000.

358 *"The Cuanza overflowing"* From "the green of the palm trees of my youth," written in Caxias Prison, February 26, 1955, in Neto, p. 54, translated by Marga Holness.

363 *one or another of its various websites* Kwacha UNITA Press (<kwacha.com>) and <afard-unita.asso.fr>, a French website, have not been updated since the fall of Andulo in October 1999, but <kwacha.org> was still active at the time of writing.

364 *I flew to Cape Town and found Terry Robinson* September 30, 2000.

364 *Robinson explained that they had to withdraw the offer* Zambian sables continued to be of interest to some. *The Star* (South Africa) reported November 16, 2000, that twenty mostly Tswana-speaking South Africans and a Zambian businessman were charged in Lusaka with possession of equipment to capture up to a hundred sable antelope from Zambia's Kafue National Park.

364 *he shot the second biggest elephant on record* The combined weight of the tusks is 372 pounds.

365 *"Tent up, odd jobs, tiff"* February 13, 1922 journal entry from Diary no. 61, Book no. 3, typescript, Powell-Cotton Museum archives.

367 *The news out of Angola* "Angolan Town 'Starves,'" BBC, September 5, 2000.

367 *"Young soldiers are hungry"* IRIN, September 6, 2000, quoting a report in Portugal's daily newspaper *Publico* the previous day.

367 *one of the most corrupt countries* BBC, September 13, 2000.

367 *if the new press law proposed* IRIN report on press freedom, September 11, 2000. However, there are other factors that suppress news; 60 percent of the adult population is illiterate, according to the government's own press agency, ANGOP, September 6, 2000.

368 *UNITA claimed he was in "good health"* As quoted in "Angolan Army Pursues Rebel Leaders in Major Offensive," AP, October 26, 2000.

368 *But Savimbi took the time to stop and execute* ANGOP, October 5, 2000.

368 *downing a Russian-built Antonov-26* There were a number of reports: Lara Pawson, "Row over Angola Air Crash," BBC, November 3, 2000; IRIN report, November 3, 2000.

368 *The twenty-fifth anniversary* "Angola Celebrates 25 Years of Independence," BBC, November 11, 2000; "25 Years: Situation Still Tough, President Admits," ANGOP, November 11, 2000; "Bomb Blamed on UNITA," IRIN, November 13, 2000; "UNITA Rejects Angolan Amnesty Offer," BBC, November 14, 2000; "Army Chief of Staff Calls for Surveillance," ANGOP, November 19, 2000.

369 *conditions in Cuito* "Cockroaches Invade Angolan Town," BBC, November 22, 2000.

369 *some five hundred children a day* According to Sergio Guimaraes, UNICEF representative to Angola, ANGOP reported December 7, 2000.

369 *Some twelve thousand refugees* "Zambia-Angola: Refugee Influx Continues," IRIN, November 7, 2000.

369 *a stomach-turning report* "Angola: Pretense of Normality" A report by Médecins Sans Frontières, Luanda, November 9, 2000. The report concludes: "Contrary to Angolan authorities' claim that the situation is simply a consequence of the war, MSF considers that it is the result of deliberate choices: for the parties to the conflict, the choice to expose the population to violence and use them in war strategy; for the government, the choice to relocate people back to their original areas and disinvest in health structures; for UNITA, the choice to refuse humanitarian access to zones under their control; for the international community, the choice to ratify this policy for the benefit of its own economic interests; for the United Nations, the choice to adapt their aid programs to fit the policy of 'relocalization' and not the needs of the population, and in doing so to renounce the principle of neutral and indiscriminate access to populations." The Norwegian Refugee Council/ Global IDP Project issued a "Profile of Internal Displacement: Angola," January 18, 2001, describing the plight of 3.8 million displaced Angolans in depressing detail (www.idproject.org).

370 *Even the Russians had come back* "Russia to Provide Military Aid to Angola's Fight Against Rebels," Reuters, December 6, 2000. Angolan diamonds are exported through a partnership set up earlier in 2000 between the government and a group of investors led by Israeli businessman Lev Leviev, who has the exclusive rights to buy all of Angola's diamonds and has a stake in two major Angolan mines.

370 *Luanda would no longer be able to so easily hide* See the summary "The IMF's Staff Monitoring Program for Angola: The Human Rights Implications," in Human Rights Watch 2000 World Report.

370 *now presented himself as a progressive leader* Hodges details some choice bits of presidential behavior, pp. 51–7.

371 *dos Santos was spending much of his time behind the stone walls* From 1992 to 1999, dos Santos never set foot in Angola's provinces. Hodges, p. 53.

371 *The president spoke* As reported by ANGOP, December 17, 2000.

372 *bronze statue of a giant sable bull* The statue, by Jean Clagget of Colorado, was commissioned by Magalen O. Bryant.

372 *He had something else to report, too* Van Hoven to Bryant, Estes, and Walker, E-mail December 21, 2000.

372 *Estes . . . wrote a cautious reply* Estes to van Hoven, Bryant, and Walker, E-mail December 21, 2000.

372 *But when the sighting was reported* "Giant Sable Spotted in Angola," AP (Lisbon), February 7, 2001.

375 *scandal involving Jean-Christophe Mitterrand* Global Witness described what emerged in the legal proceedings in France as a "gruesome tale of money laundering and state robbery at the expense of the long-suffering Angolan people"; IRIN report January 29, 2001. "Angolagate," as it came to be called, centered on the illegal sales of half a billion dollars' worth of weapons to Angola in the mid-1990s and caught up a number of prominent French officials. Angolan ambassador to France Elisio de Figueiredo fled to Tokyo after he was accused of receiving $18 million in commissions from Pierre Falcone, the arms dealer imprisoned by the French authorities. Falcone was reported to have said payments were made to Gen. João de Matos as well. "Angolan Ambassador to France Flees to Japan over Arms Scandal," IRIN, June 20, 2001.

376 *the noose . . . was tightening* ANGOP, February 8–10, 2001.

376 *Government news was, as always, upbeat* ANGOP, December 29, 00; "Angola: Savimbi Wanted—Dead or Alive," IRIN report, February 6, 2001.

376 *virtually running a state within a state* See J. Potgieter, "Taking Aid from the Devil Himself," pp. 255–73, in Cilliers and Dietrich.

376 *"I love this forest"* Bridgland, *Key*, p. 236, quoting Dash.

377 *he informed me in an E-mail* Van Hoven to Walker, March 1, 2001.

377 *dos Santos had relieved Gen. Luis Faceira* ANGOP, March 3, 2001.

377 *I spoke with van Hoven* March 3, 2001.

378 *my South African UNITA contact . . . sent me a reply* March 12, 2001.

378 *government troops recaptured Quibaxe* "Angola: Town's Population 'Missing,'" IRIN, March 7, 2001. But the army had done something unpleasantly similar in 1998, forcibly depopulating the entire town of Caculama in Malange Province, conscripting truckloads of young men and sending the remainder to Malange city, in order to turn Caculama into a military base. See "Internal Displacement in Southern Africa: Focus Angola," by Anna Richardson (Writenet Country Papers).

378 *Sixty-six died of starvation* "Angola: Civil War Refugees Die of Hunger in Camacupa," IRIN, April 19, 2001.

379 *he told the Voice of America radio service* Quoted in "Unita Leader Calls for Talks in Angola," Reuters, March 23, 2001. See also the Voice of America report by Alex Belida, March 23, 2001.

379 *war a . . . cover for continued military spending and the corruption it allows* The government managed to secure $1 billion in bank loans, a move that human rights groups and the IMF argued would allow Luanda to evade transparency in in the management of the country's oil revenues. See "Angola: Bank Loan Angers the IMF–EIU," IRIN, May 1, 2001.

379 *local village chiefs complaining of massacres* Max Hamata, "NDF Claims Major Victory Against Unita," *The Namibian* (Windhoek), May 17, 2001.

379 *kidnapping sixty children from an orphanage* "UNITA Attacks Town Near Luanda," BBC, May 6, 2001; "Angola: UN Calls for Release of Caxito Hostages," IRIN, May 8, 2001; Justin Pearce, "Child Kidnappings Seen as a Show of Strength by UNITA," *Electronic Mail & Guardian*, May 14, 2001.

380 *A week after the kidnapping, Savimbi wrote a letter* His Excellency Dr. Jonas Savimbi, president of UNITA, to the representatives of the Catholic Church, May 13, 2001.

380 *reports of bayoneting babies* See *Angola Peace Monitor*, no. 9, vol. VII, June 2001, which summarized claims of children and babies being speared by suspected UNITA rebels in northern Namibia.

380 *he wrote, "we are going full steam ahead"* May 13, 2001, with typos corrected.

380 *"dart one or two"* Van Hoven to Mike Fischer and Walker, E-mail April 13, 2001.

380 *Estes was pleased* Estes to van Hoven and Walker, E-mail May 14, 2001.

381 *UN aircraft carrying food aid was hit* Justin Pearce, "WFP Plane Hit in Angola," BBC, June 8, 2001.

381 *Without continuing airlifts* "Angola: Food Distribution Begins in Camacupa," IRIN, June 5, 2001; "Facing the Reality of War," IRIN, June 6, 2001; "UN warns of Angolan catastrophe," BBC, June 20, 2001.

381 *UNITA had not neglected Malange* "8 Dead in Angola Gun Attack," Reuters, June 4, 2001; "Angola: Landmine Kills 22," IRIN, June 11, 2001.

381 *The next day, van Hoven wrote* Van Hoven to Walker, E-mail June 12, 2001, with some typos corrected.

382 *the restoration of aid flights* "Angola Aid Flights Resume," BBC, June 21, 2001.

382 *Something else happened that day* "Thousands Gather in Zambia for Solar Eclipse," AP, June 21, 2001; "Solar Eclipse Begins in Africa," BBC, June 21, 2001.

383 *In Huambo Province there was even talk* "Huambo: Authorities Concerned About Solar Eclipse Speculations, " ANGOP, June 20, 2001.

11: EXPEDITION TO MALANGE

I made two trips to South Africa and Angola in September and November/December 2001.

384 *van Hoven E-mailed Estes and me from Luanda* July 5, 2001.

384 *Estes . . . E-mailed Van Hoven* July 7, 2001.

384 *I called van Hoven, who was in his backyard* July, 7, 2001.

385 *van Hoven E-mailed us the results of a meeting* July 23, 2001.

385 *Estes . . . found the giant sable news heartening* July 25, 2001.

386 *which was why there was little cause for celebration* "Cabinet Approves Benguela Railway Exploration Deal," ANGOP, January 25, 2001.

386 *UNITA had targeted the limping Luanda-Malange line* "Angola Train Toll Rises," Justin Pearce, BBC, August 12, 2001; "100 Feared Dead in Angola Train Ambush," Casimiro Siona, AP, August 12, 2001; "Rebels Claim Angolan Train Attack," BBC, August 13, 2001.

387 *an attack on an electrical substation* "Unita Hits Luanda Power Supply," Justin Pearce, BBC, September 25, 2001.

390 *we were looking at Boavista* "Angolan Police Clear 'Unsafe' Suburb," Justin Pearce, BBC, July 8, 2001; "Government Wants Help for Ex-Boavista Residents," IRIN, July 24, 2001; "Protesters Battle Shunting of a Shantytown in Angola," Danna Harman, *The Christian Science Monitor*, August 21, 2001.

391 *Perhaps there could be a negotiated settlement* Herman Cohen, assistant secretary of state for African affairs in the G. H. W. Bush administration, thought UNITA would just "fizzle out." Interview with John Rosenberg in "Imagining Angola," Special International Report, *The Washington Times*, April 27, 2001, p. A14.

391 *the president announced . . . that he would not run* "Angola's President to Stand Down," BBC, Aug. 23, 2001; "Angolan President Says He Won't Be Candidate," Reuters, August 23, 2001. Observers speculated that after twenty-two years in power, he would prefer to control the terms of his leaving than to be toppled.

391 *Savimbi countered with an unlikely "peace plan"* "Angolan Rebels Submit 'Peace Plan,'" Justin Pearce, BBC, August 24, 2001; "Angola's UNITA Makes Peace Proposals," Reuters, August 23, 2001.

396 *In 1993 starving war refugees here were so desperate* Maier, p. 146.

396 *a savage offensive* "Focus on Mexico Conflict," IRIN, December 10, 2001.

398 *as if to do battle with the mechanical monster* This passage draws on the capture methods and sable behavior variously described in *Proceedings of a Symposium on the Sable Antelope as a Game Ranch Animal,* reedited B. L. Penzhorn, (Onderstepoort, South Africa: South African Veterinary Association Wildlife Group, September 24–25, 1992, reprinted 1997). R. E. J. Burroughs stated, "Chemical capture of sable" by darting "can be done from a helicopter (although sable tend to 'fight' the helicopter). . . . Care should be exercised, however, to avoid being injured by the horns of partially immobilised sable" in "Mechanical and Chemical Capture of Sable Antelope," p. 133. Johan Kriek states, "Sable can be very aggressive. They are never intimidated by man" in "Translocation and Boma Management of Sable Antelope," p. 43.

401 *and revisit the Unicorn Tapestries* The Cloisters is the branch of the Metropolitan Museum devoted to the art and architecture of medieval Europe. See Adolfo Salvatore Cavallo, *The Unicorn Tapestries* (New York: Metropolitan Museum of Art/Harry Abrams, 1998).

402 *will be saved, guarded, and eventually fenced* Two recent examples of the accelerating process: The *Daily Nation* (Nairobi) reported that the Kenya Wildlife Service is considering ringing the Aberdare mountain range with a 320-kilometer fence to prevent illegal logging and protect the wildlife within its borders (allafrica.com (February 19, 2001); the UN Environment Programme (UNEP) declared that efforts to save the world's most important forests should be concentrated on fifteen nations while there is still time to protect them. Alex Kirby, "UN Call to Save Key Forests," BBC, August 20, 2001.

403 *I heard from Bettine van Vuuren* February 11, 2002.

404 *On February 22, 2002, sixty-seven-year-old Jonas Malheiro Savimbi . . . slipped through the dense forest* Savimbi's death was widely reported and commented on. See "Text of Angolan Army Statement on Death of Savimbi," allAfrica.com, February 22, 2002; "Text: Savimbi Death Announcement," BBC, February 23, 2002; "TV Networks Show Corpse Said to Be of Savimbi," Justin Pearce, BBC, February 23, 2002; "O Fim de Savimbi," *Jornal de Angola* on-line, February 24, 2002; the *Angola Peace Monitor* 8, no. 6, February 26, 2002.

406 *Eduardo dos Santos . . . sat across . . . from President Bush* "Bush Urges Angola Ceasefire," BBC, February 27, 2002; "President Meets with African Leaders," Office of the Press Secretary, February 27, 2002.

407 *to ensure no uncomfortable questions were asked* Nearly a third of Angola's oil revenues, approximately $1.5 billion, "went missing" in 2001, "five times the amount the UN barely scraped together" to feed the internally displaced, according to Global Witness director Simon Taylor (see its 2002 report "All the President's Men"). Efforts to increase financial transparency in the Angolan oil industry have not been welcomed by the government. See "'Ethical' BP Linked to Angola Claims," Terry Macalister, *The Guardian,* February 27, 2002. See also "Angola Briefing Under the Arria Formula to the UN Security Council," Human Rights Watch, March 5,

2002. According ANGOP, dos Santos "expressed belief that Angola may be of those countries where corruption levels are the lowest." ("Dos Santos Blast at IMF Policing," ANGOP, February 28, 2002).

407 *dos Santos had a change of heart* "Angolan Armed Forces and UNITA Sign Cease-Fire," ANGOP, March 30, 2002; "Angola Moves Closer to Peace," BBC, March 31, 2002.

407 *on April 4, 2002, a formal cease-fire was signed* "Angolans Rejoice at Peace Accord," BBC, April 5, 2002.

Acknowledgments

This book could not have been written without the help and generosity of a great many individuals. Those who appear in the narrative trusted me to tell their part in the story, and I am particularly indebted to them.

Dr. Richard D. Estes opened his files and correspondence to me, giving me not only access to his and others' research, but an insider's view of the long and complicated efforts to ensure the survival of the giant sable. Runi Estes shared her recollections of their joint research in Angola and her detailed diary from 1969 to 1970. The Esteses opened their home in New Hampshire to me and tolerated endless inquiries over the years.

Professor Wouter van Hoven of the Centre for Wildlife Management, University of Pretoria, made it possible for me to see firsthand the realities of wildlife conservation in Angola on four trips there and to journey into the giant sable lands; without his cooperation and assistance, this book would have been far more limited in scope. He and Suzanne van Hoven were my generous hosts in Pretoria on many occasions.

In the United States, Quentin Keynes shared his recollections of H. F. Varian and gave me access to his photographs and film footage of his 1954 expedition, his collection of early publications on the giant sable, and his correspondence with Varian, Blaine, Vernay, Yebes, and others. Clare Flemming and Darrin Lunde in the Department of Mammalogy at the American Museum of Natural History in New York, and Ted Daeschler, Robert McCracken Peck, Carol Spawn, and Earle E. Spamer at the Academy of Natural Sciences of Philadelphia gave me access to expedition archives and giant sable specimens. Bill Stanley and Chap Kusimba of the Field Museum in Chicago answered my inquiries, as did Janet E. Baldwin at the Explorers Club in New York, Scott Sutton at the Camp

Fire Club of America, and Richard M. Parsons and Stuart A. Marks at Safari Club International. Anne and Bill Dodgson of SCI's Utah chapter let me interview them at length. Robert M. Lee of Sparks, Nevada, shared his experiences in Angola with me.

Dr. Manuel Jordán responded in detail to my questions on the Songo and Lwimbi peoples and suggested several useful texts. Dr. James M. Dolan, Jr., director of collections at the San Diego Zoo, and Steven Kingwood and the late Arlene T. Kumamoto of the zoo's Center for Reproduction of Endangered Species made my visit there particularly informative. In Washington, D. C., Virginia Armat Hurt and Robert Hurt were my generous hosts on several occasions. Magalen O. Bryant, chairman, National Fish and Wildlife Foundation, and Ken Stansell, deputy assistant director for international affairs at the U.S. Fish and Wildlife Service, kindly shared their views on giant sable conservation. Christian Dietrich answered questions on conflict diamonds, and Williams Jenks allowed me to keep several texts, including his early edition of William Cornwallis Harris, for an unconscionable length of time without complaint. The staff at the New Milford Public Library, Connecticut, obtained a number of scarce volumes for me. On several trips to South Africa and Angola my travel was assisted in various ways by Rory Callahan, André Shearer, Patrice Tanaka & Co., Development Counsellors International, South African Airways, TAAG Angolan Airways, and Evaristo José, second secretary (press), embassy of the Republic of Angola.

In Great Britain, Dr. Paula Jenkins and Richard Harbord of the Natural History Museum's Zoology Department showed me Varian's specimens, and Christopher Mills, Neil Chambers, and Pamela Hunter searched the museum's archives for Varian's correspondence. Excerpts from those letters appear by permission of the Trustees of the Natural History Museum. At *The Field*, Christina Grindon found Varian's and others' contributions on the giant sable for me; excerpts from them are reproduced with kind permission from *The Field*. In addition, I was able to verify some information on Agostinho Neto with his translator, Marga Holness. Peter Grubb answered my taxonomic questions, and David McNeill, assistant map curator, Royal Geographical Society, and Malcolm Harman, assistant curator of natural history at the Powell-Cotton Museum, supplied valuable archival material.

Dr. Paolo Agnelli, mammals collection manager of the zoological museum "La Specola," of the University of Florence, told me what was known about its 1873 sable horn. Rod East, cochairman of the Antelope Specialists Group of the IUCN, sent me background material on antelopes and answered my questions from New Zealand.

In South Africa, Professor Brian J. Huntley, chief executive of the National Botanical Institute, met with me several times, answered my many follow-up questions, and shared important documents on Angola and previous conservation efforts there. Dr. Jeremy Anderson, with whom I had been in contact since 1994, was always happy to discuss giant sable conservation. Dr. Terrence Robinson of the Department of Zoology at the University of Stellenbosch let me interview him at length during various visits on his continuing research on the genetic status of the giant sable. The Hon. Roger Ballard-Tremeer, former South African ambassador to Angola, was always available to give me his insight on Angolan politics. Andre de Georges of SCI Africa, Eric Stockenströhm of Congo Safaris, Ian Whyte and Petri C. Viljoen, senior scientists at Kruger National Park, and Dr. Paul Bartels of Wildlife Darting Services gave me additional insights into African wildlife conservation.

Jakkie Potgieter and Hannelie de Beer of Safer Africa shared their analyses of the Angolan conflict and Col. Fred Oelschig recalled his experiences in Angola for me. Joelle Wentzel at the University of Pretoria clarified several questions on wildlife genetics. Ollie Coltman organized my visit to Sable Ranch, and Dr. Kobus du Toit and Chris Mostert showed me their endangered species game-breeding operation. I enjoyed Jaco Ackermann's hospitality in Pretoria, and Willem and Mercia Steenkampf and Marietjie van der Walt were particularly helpful during my stays there, as was Lyndon Estes in Mpumalanga, Gary Shearer in Cape Town, and Thelma Harris and André Morganthal in Stellenbosch. Achim Steiner and Simon Anstey, then of the IUCN's regional office for southern Africa in Harare, Zimbabwe, answered my early inquiries. David Allen, Phillip Hattingh, and Pierre van Heerden of Oracle Television Productions in Pretoria helped me in numerous ways on our expedition to Malange and in the weeks following our trip.

In Angola, I had the cooperation and assistance of a number of individuals associated with the Kissama Foundation, including Gen. Luis

Faceira, Gen. Antonio Faceira, Gen. C. A. Hendrik Vaal da Silva, Gen. João de Matos and Fillipe de Freitas. Jorge Alicerces Valentim, minister of hotels and tourism, Maria de Fátima Jardim, minister of fisheries and environment, and João Serodio de Almeida, senior lecturer, Agostinho Neto University, gave me informative interviews. Corrie Mynhardt, director (Angola), Gray Security Services, Ltd., assisted with immigration, and Cristiana Pereira and Cari MacLeod helped with translation. Peter L. Osborne, director, Shell (Angola), was a generous and informative host on several visits.

Many other people helped me along the way, some of whom preferred to remain anonymous. In addition, I made every effort to contact the holders of copyrighted material, but I was not always successful. I owe them all.

Several people were kind enough to read parts of the manuscript, often on short notice. David Birmingham, professor of modern history at the University of Kent at Canterbury, pointed out several fumbled facts. Piero Gleijeses, professor of American foreign policy at the School of Advanced International Studies at Johns Hopkins University, reviewed my account of the Angolan conflict and alerted me to various errors and misinterpretations of events. Terry Robinson, Bettine van Vuuren, and Conrad Matthee at the University of Stellenbosch clarified my layman's explanation of DNA extraction. Paul J. Hare, formerly the U.S. special representative for the Angolan peace process and now executive director of the United States-Angola Chamber of Commerce, gave me an overview of Angola's political situation and pointed me toward a more balanced view of recent events there. But whatever errors and shortcomings remain are my responsibility.

Cass Canfield, Jr., gave me encouragement when this book was little more than an idea. My agent, Kimberly Witherspoon, saw the book I hoped to write, and took my proposal to Morgan Entrekin, Grove/Atlantic's publisher. His patience and continuing enthusiasm for the book despite two deadline extensions gave me the time and support I needed. Brendan Cahill's thoughtful and judicious editing kept me firmly on the track of the giant sable, and Mary Flower led me through the thickets of permissions.

454

ACKNOWLEDGMENTS

Without the help of friends and family during the last difficult stages of writing this book, I might not have ever completed it. John Train, Bridget Potter, James Douglas Barron, John R. Battista, and Justine McCabe gave encouragement, advice, and critical support when it was needed most. My mother, Beatrice Walker, my brother, William Walker, and my sister, Barbara Walker, were there when I needed them, as always.

But my greatest debts are to those closest to me. My wife, Elin McCoy, has always been my first and best reader, and her belief that I had something to say has long sustained me, through this book and so much else. My son, Gavin McCoy Walker, managed to track down the texts I needed, no matter how obscure they were, and had enough faith in me and my book to put aside his misgivings over my traveling in Angola.

CREDITS

Giant sable track: John Frederick Walker sketch
Frederick Selous: African Museum, Johannesburg
A new subspecies: Proceedings of the Zoological Society of London
Keynes and Varian: Quentin Keynes
Anita Curtis: Richard C. Curtis
Arthur Vernay: John Frederick Walker/American Museum of Natural History
Giant sable diorama: John Frederick Walker/American Museum of Natural History
Specimen skull: John Frederick Walker sketch
Angolan stamp: coll. John Frederick Walker
Giant sable bulls: Quentin Keynes
Cuanza ferry: coll. Estes
Runi Estes: Richard D. Estes
Giant sable herds: Richard D. Estes
Patriarch: Richard D. Estes
UNITA soldiers: UNITA file
Jonas Savimbi: UNITA file
Van Hoven at Quiçama: John Frederick Walker
Quiçama fence: John Frederick Walker
Cargo plane: John Frederick Walker
Angolans watch: John Frederick Walker
Students and guards: John Frederick Walker
Dos Santos and van Hoven: John Frederick Walker
Richard D. Estes: John Frederick Walker
General Faceira: John Frederick Walker

General Hendrik and game guards: John Frederick Walker
Colonel Marinheiro: John Frederick Walker
Miombo forest: John Frederick Walker
Van Hoven: John Frederick Walker
Giant sable dung: John Frederick Walker
Endpaper Maps: Eureka Cartography, Berkeley, California

INDEX

459

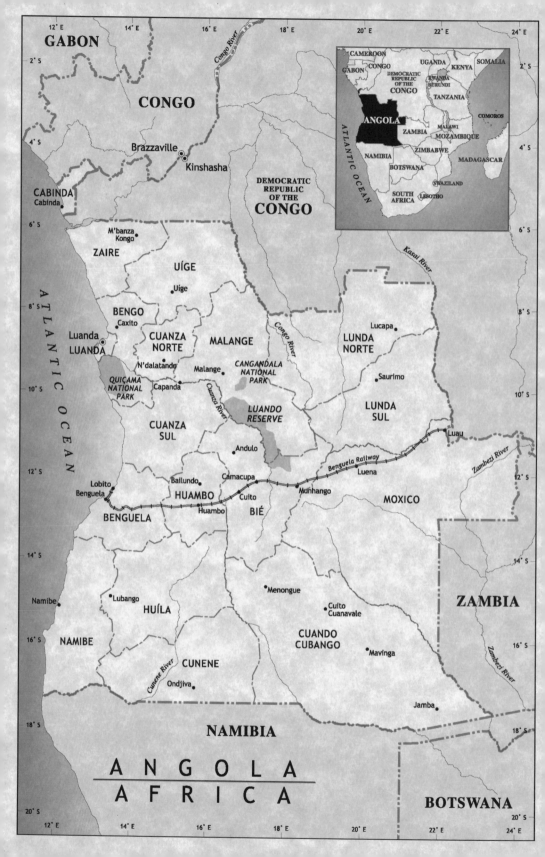